"Finally, the singular, comprehensive manuscript for bank investing I wish I'd had at the beginning of my career. Suhail and Weison clearly chronicle the evolution and current challenges of the industry for the amateur enthusiast, while simultaneously supplying the technical depth, practical execution, and operational guidance for institutional investors, sell-side analysts, and executive management teams."

—Tyler Stafford, CFA, *CEO and Co-Founder, Panacea Financial; Former Sell-Side Bank Analyst*

"Bank Investing: A Practitioner's Field Guide *explains and details all of the critical variables investors need to analyze in order to make the right decisions in bank stock investing. Chandy and Ding lay out both the macro and micro factors needed to accurately determine the fair value of a bank stock. This book will quickly become the go-to book for both neophyte and experienced bank stocks investors."*

—Gerard S. Cassidy, *Managing Director, Head of Bank Equity Strategy, and Large Cap Bank Analyst, RBC Capital Markets and creator of the Texas Ratio*

"Suhail and Weison have written a truly comprehensive guide to investing in banks. Their approach provides a comprehensive framework for analyzing the most critical and often most challenging topics, including a bank's interest rate sensitivity, credit exposure, and liquidity and capital position, and provides valuable case studies and insights from professional investors in this space. This book is a must-read for every bank investor, from the novice to the most seasoned."

—Eric Wasserstrom, *Equity Analyst; Former Hedge Fund Portfolio Manager*

"Suhail and Weison have collaborated on a must-read that will prove invaluable to all constituents of the bank and broader financial services sector. The commentary is insightful, educational, entertaining, and informative, helping the reader to understand the history of the sector, its fundamental underpinnings, and the transformation and convergence with fintech that is currently underway."

—Joe Fenech, *CIO, GenOpp Capital Management; former sell-side bank analyst*

Bank Investing

Bank Investing

A Practitioner's Field Guide

SUHAIL CHANDY
WEISON DING

WILEY

Published by John Wiley & Sons, Inc., Hoboken, New Jersey.
Published simultaneously in Canada.

For general information on our other products and services or for technical support, please contact our Customer Care Department within the United States at (800) 762-2974, outside the United States at (317) 572-3993, or fax (317) 572-4002.

Wiley publishes in a variety of print and electronic formats and by print-on-demand. Some material included with standard print versions of this book may not be included in e-books or in print-on-demand. If this book refers to media such as a CD or DVD that is not included in the version you purchased, you may download this material at http://booksupport.wiley.com. For more information about Wiley products, visit www.wiley.com.

Library of Congress Cataloging-in-Publication Data is available:

ISBN 9781119728047 (hardback)
ISBN 9781119729846 (ePDF)
ISBN 9781119729808 (ePUB)

Cover design: Wiley

SKY10024200_012221

In loving memory of my father, Jacob Chandy

– Suhail

For my mother and father

– Weison

Contents

Acknowledgments

Sincere thanks to the following individuals for their help and guidance at various stages: Chris Black, Eric Wasserstrom, Joe Fenech, Gerard Cassidy, Ashley Williams, Tula Weis, Vitaliy Katsenelson, Wes Gray, Stephanie Krewson-Kelly, Matt Flake, Dale Gibbons, Vernon W. Hill II, Chris Holmes, Denny Hudson, Abbott Cooper, Fred Cummings, Pete Duffy, Chris Fortune, Martin Friedman, Rich Hocker, Jeffrey Sherman, Ian Lyngen, and Loren Fleckenstein.

Last, but not the least, our thanks to the entire team at Wiley, especially Bill Falloon and Purvi Patel.

Disclaimer

The views and opinions presented in this publication are for informational purposes only as of the date of production/writing and may change without notice at any time based on numerous factors such as market conditions or legal and regulatory developments.

This publication is not intended to be an offer or solicitation of any investment advice or security in any jurisdiction. Any specific mentions of a publicly traded company are for illustrative purposes only. It is not intended to be relied upon as a forecast, research, or investment advice and is not a recommendation, offer, or solicitation to buy or sell any securities or investment strategy.

The authors make no representations or warranties, express or implied, about the accuracy or suitability for any use of the information, and expressly disclaim responsibility for any loss or damage, direct or indirect, caused by use of or reliance on information offered in this publication. All information has been obtained from sources believed to be reliable, and not necessarily all-inclusive, and its accuracy is not guaranteed. The views and opinions expressed in this publication are solely those of the authors and do not necessarily reflect the view of any entity and employers with which they have been, are now, or will be affiliated.

About the Authors

Suhail Chandy covers the Fintech, Financials, and Real Estate sectors and manages the Fintech Catalyst strategy at Penn Capital. He is a CFA charterholder and has an MBA from Yale University.

Weison Ding covers institutional investors from the equity trading desk of Piper Sandler, with a specialty in the Financials sector. He graduated from The George Washington University.

1 Introduction

"The judicious operations of banking enable him to convert this dead stock into active and productive stock; into materials to work upon, into tools to work with, and into provision and subsistence to work for; into stock which produces something both to himself and to his country."

– *The Wealth of Nations Book II: Of the Nature, Accumulation, and Employment of Stock*, Adam Smith

WHY A BOOK ON BANK INVESTING?

We believe that bank investing can be a fruitful pursuit. As authors of a book on the topic we have a vested interest, but we ask the reader to consider the following:

1. The most successful investor of our times, Warren Buffett, has had a sizeable investment in banks over time (close to a third of his portfolio weight used to be in banks). This is based on the minority investments in publicly listed entities, and we do not include Berkshire's operating subsidiaries.
2. Banks allow you to make macroeconomic bets since they are highly levered to business cycles.
3. Bank investing allows you to scale your knowledge, as they have relatively homogenized business models.
4. At the same time, banks are diverse enough to drive meaningful dispersion in price performance. This divergence of performance can be taken advantage of by an astute and prepared security analyst.
5. Banks are great vehicles to make specific investment plays on geographic regions, demographic trends (suburban to urban migration, aging), industries (agriculture, tech, energy), news flow (trade/tariffs, weather), real estate subsectors (NYC office, bay area apartments), and investing themes such as ESG, cryptocurrency, and venture capital.
6. The largest asset on a bank's balance sheet is its loan book. This is not directly analyzable; one cannot walk up to a bank and ask permission

to view the loan book. There are limited instances when a small bank is getting re-capitalized that its loan book may be made available in a selective sample manner, but those are very limited instances.

This information asymmetry makes it tougher but also in some instances rewards the diligent and dogged analyst. This relative opacity makes banks very different from an allied sector such as REITs. The real estate assets of a REIT are tangible and can be toured and independently assessed. There is a large CRE market where real estate assets trade, and one can use that to value the assets of REITs. We highly recommend an excellent book on the topic of REITs by our good friend Stephanie Krewson-Kelly and her co-author R. Brad Thomas. That book is *The Intelligent REIT Investor: How to Build Wealth with Real Estate Investment.*

7. Fintech disruption is real, but to understand this phenomenon one needs to understand the sector being disrupted. It is not a coincidence that some of the biggest fintech names have applied for and obtained a bank charter. That is a validation that a charter can provide benefits exceeding the regulatory cost. Finally, we believe that fintech disruption is creating an investing opportunity to play the digital divide between banks that embrace technology successfully and those that get left behind. Banks have to start viewing themselves as fintechs with the ability to accept deposits.

FINTECH ONSLAUGHT

The fintech onslaught is just getting started. There is no denying that fintech is disrupting the banking business. The challengers and "potential" challengers range in size from minnows being dreamt up in dorm rooms to giants such as Amazon. A study by the consulting firm Bain and Company in 2018 postulated that Amazon's banking services, if launched, could grow to more than 70 million US consumer relationships over a five-year period. See the link below: https://www.bain.com/insights/bankings-amazon-moment/

This would be the same size as Wells Fargo, founded in 1852, which is the fourth largest bank in the country. We are not privy to the plans of Amazon, but we are not surprised by the hypothetical growth trajectory of a potential challenger who has significant heft and has consumed entire industries. While not surprising, it is unsettling that someone takes 168 years to become the fourth largest bank and then find themselves rivaled by a digital upstart who took five years to get to the same size.

The relentless fintech onslaught has seen skyrocketing valuation, a burgeoning number of players, increasing interest in the concept, and a barrage of news flow all reinforcing each other.

EXHIBIT 1.1 Interest over Time for Search Term *Fintech*

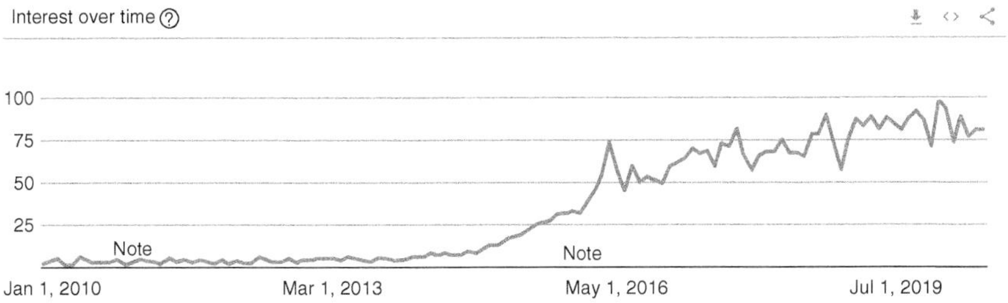

Interest over time

100
75
50
25
Note
Note
Jan 1, 2010 Mar 1, 2013 May 1, 2016 Jul 1, 2019

Source: Google Trends

Fintech unicorns, of which there are 58, have an aggregate valuation of $213.5B according to CB Insights. Nearly every transaction one would traditionally do with a bank can now be done through a fintech using a mobile app on your smartphone. The fintechs include SoFi, Earnest (owned by Navient), Chime, Varo, Money Lion, Stash, Square, Kabbage, OnDeck, Affirm, Klarna, Greensky, Afterpay, and a long list of vendors covering résidential mortgage loans, student loans, online checking and savings, SMB loans, point-of-sale financing, and more. The list is endless, and there is a virtual tapestry of fintech logos that cover a variety of areas.

Interest in fintech has grown immensely as can be seen in Exhibit 1.1, a chart of Google trends on the search term *fintech* over the last 10 years.

AN OPPORTUNITY TO LEVEL THE PLAYING FIELD

While innovation is exciting, it is important to not get caught up in the fintech narrative and lose sight that ultimately banking at its core is about accepting deposits, making loans profitably, acquiring customers efficiently, and engaging with customers meaningfully to increase the cross-sell of products. It is also important to remember that several new age fintech lenders have not been fully cycle tested.

Branchless banks are not a new concept. Telebank, a division of Tele-Banc Financial of Arlington, VA, was founded in 1990 and operated with a branchless strategy initially using the telephone network. Security First Network Bank (SFNB), founded in 1995, was a pure internet bank.

While branchless banking is at least 30 years old, the new age of the challenger banks is fueled by powerful smartphones, a mobile app ecosystem, and a bunch of critical technologies and APIs that allow the orchestration of bank transactions and activities in a seamless manner.

Banks, especially regional and community banks, have a lot to worry about given this relentless onslaught from nimble start-ups and the level of tech spending at the large banks. The largest seven banks in the country are collectively spending upwards of $45B on technology. Smaller banks will not be able to match that level of spending. However, in this David versus Goliath struggle, all is not lost for David.

It is accurate and intuitive that smaller banks simply do not have the resources (both talent and budget) to compete with the large banks. However, if they partner with the right technology vendors, for efficient digital acquisition of customers, frictionless services provided via mobile and online, and reassuring levels of cyber security, David will more than match Goliath.

In order to compete successfully banks, large and small, have to reimagine themselves as a fintech with a bank charter.

While they can't match the large banks in spending billions on technology a year, there is no one stopping small banks from architecting a vision for their digital journey and propelling this journey by embracing the right set of technologies. As anecdotes we can think of numerous examples of smaller banks across the country that have embraced technology appropriately and have seen great success with the ramp of customers using mobile and significantly better customer service scores.

The challenge to embarking on a successful digital journey is in part cultural and in some ways limited by imagination. A license to accept deposits and submit oneself to regulatory supervision does not imply that banks need to handcuff themselves to the past. It is time for small banks to unshackle themselves and embrace their digital future.

While the digital future is exciting, we have to accept that the bank model is a double-edged sword when it comes to regulation: on the one hand it affords protection and the ability to accept deposits, but on the other hand the burden can be onerous for small banks. Thus, on the one hand, we have seen fintechs that have shown interest in seeking bank charters, which validates the view that the bank model is a source of strength albeit one that needs to be reinvigorated with new technology. On the other hand, there are fintechs that do not wish to seek a bank charter in part due to their view that the regulatory burden is not worth their while; where required, these fintechs partner with banks white labeling the product. The increasing regulatory burden is one reason we believe that the number of de-novo applications has been well below pre-Global Financial Crisis (GFC) levels (Exhibit 1.2).

EXHIBIT 1.2 De Novo Bank Applications

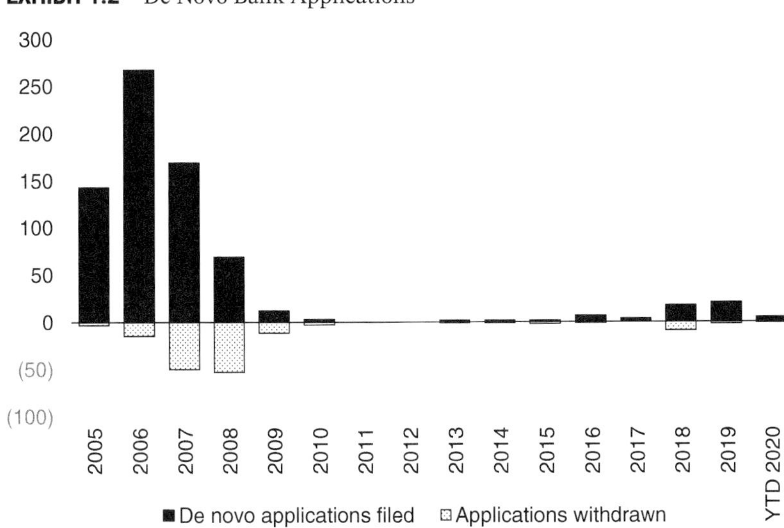

Source: S&P Global Market Intelligence
Note: as of 6/9/2019

We are very encouraged by the steps taken by FDIC Chair Jelena McWilliams to encourage new bank formation. Here are comments she made in the 2018 FDIC Annual Report.

> *"One of my top priorities as FDIC Chairman is to encourage more de novo formation, and we are hard at work to make this a reality . . .*
>
> *De novo banks are a key source of new capital, talent, ideas, and ways to serve customers, and the FDIC will do its part to support this segment of the industry."*
>
> *"The FDIC also took robust steps this year to reduce the regulatory burden on community banks, without sacrificing safety and soundness or consumer protections. We eliminated over one-half of the more than 800 pieces of supervisory guidance outstanding. We also launched a pilot program to use technology to reduce the number of on-site days needed to conduct an examination, and took other steps to reduce the costs of examinations to our regulated institutions."*
>
> *– Message from the Chairman, FDIC 2018 Annual Report*

FINTECH TRAILBLAZERS

We will be interviewing a few management teams of banks that have both successfully adopted technology as well as a fintech CEO who is a key supplier to the fintech arms race between banks.

PAST IS PROLOGUE: THE ULTIMATE FINANCIAL INNOVATION

It is a given that banks today are a deeply integrated cornerstone in modern economies. And when we say "banks," what we really mean is the fractional reserve banking system. That is, the pooling together of deposits and the subsequent lending out of most of those deposits. Without this system, vast sums of wealth would be stuck "dead" in vaults, generating zero economic value and massively increasing friction within the economy. Indeed, a world without banks is a hard one to imagine, but modern banking was not always around.

The story goes that European goldsmiths in the seventeenth century served as "depositories" for precious metals, charging customers a small fee to store their wealth within their vaults. The goldsmiths would issue redeemable receipts, which would represent their physical holdings. At the time, fees were a necessity. Security, bookkeeping, and other expenses to maintain a vault were all costly. Even so, customers were willing to pay this fee, as the alternative of protecting your own wealth was even more expensive and frankly, risky.

Soon these goldsmiths realized the vast majority of wealth within the walls of their vaults was collecting dust, and so they began to lend out and earn interest on a portion of these deposits. A portion of money was kept as "reserves" to service potential withdrawals. These loaned-out monies would be spent or invested, making their way through the economy and eventually ending up as another deposit in another vault, ready to be lent out again, creating a virtuous multiplier. Thus, fractional reserve banking was born.

Though it seems straightforward, at the time this must have been a groundbreaking innovation. Imagine being a depository customer at one of these goldsmiths, and suddenly being offered interest to have them protect and bookkeep your wealth!

Further developments, such as the permanent issuance of banknotes, central banking, and the eventual decoupling of a currency to an underlying commodity (i.e., the transition from the gold standard to fiat), soon followed. But the fundamental nuts and bolts of gathering and lending deposits remain in place today.

THE HERE AND NOW

Today, the pooling of deposits to create credit is foundational to the efficient allocation of resources from those that have (depositors) to those that need (borrowers), and is an important mechanism for the application of monetary policy.

In the United States, banks have accumulated over $13 trillion in deposits, and thanks to the fractional-reserve banking system, a huge chunk of these deposits has been productively lent out into every corner of the economy.

Banks are certainly not the only financial intermediary in town though. The Federal Reserve's Z.1 Tables show us that although banks have a plurality of the total loan market, banks only hold about a third of the $27 trillion in total loans that exist in the economy (Exhibit 1.3). Banks contend with Government Sponsored Entities (like Fannie Mae and Freddie Mac) and other private institutions like asset-backed securities issuers and finance companies. Out of all of these, credit unions are perhaps the most similar in form and function.

Banks also have a meaningful physical presence and are ubiquitously woven into the built environment around us through extensive ATM and branch networks. Despite the seeming pervasiveness of banks, America as a whole remains underbanked. The Federal Deposit Insurance Corporation (FDIC) recently reported that 19% of households in the United States (a whopping 24 million households) were "underbanked," while an additional 8.5 million households were unbanked altogether (2017 FDIC National Survey of Unbanked and Underbanked Households). We recommend *The*

EXHIBIT 1.3 Loans Held Across All Sectors

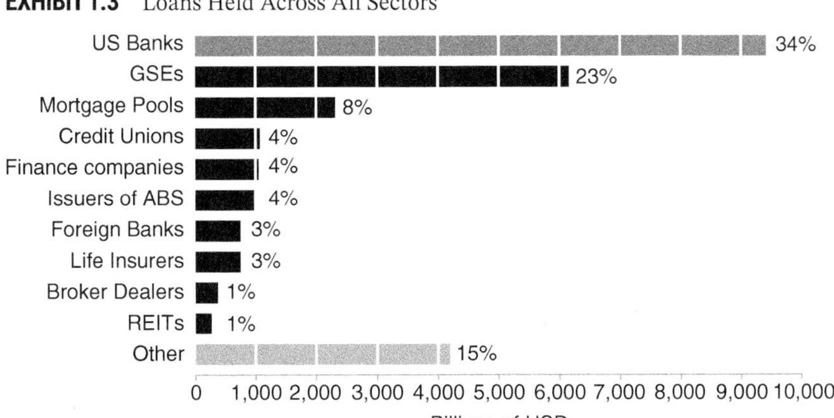

Source: Federal Reserve

Unbanking of America by Lisa Servon for more on this topic. That said, the remaining population is overbanked to a degree. According to the World Bank, commercial bank branches per 100,000 adults sit in the thirties for the United States, as compared to mid-twenties for other high-income countries. In a city like Dallas, there are 74 different banks with 370 branches between them competing for customers. Only three of these banks have a deposit market share greater than 5%.

The map in Exhibit 1.4 shows all US bank branches (except Hawaii and Alaska) as well as state level population density, illustrating the non-uniform distribution of branches.

The banking industry has been going through a remarkably steady period of consolidation, even despite economic cycles. The total number of FDIC-insured depositories peaked in 1985 at 18,000, and now sits below 6,000 (Exhibit 1.5).

Shifting to a public securities market perspective, banks make up a meaningful proportion of aggregate market value. For instance, if we look at the S&P 500, financials are about 10% of the index. Within financials, banks are the largest *subsector* at $3.0 trillion, and incredibly, have a market value equal to that of some *entire* industries in the S&P 500 such as energy and industrials:

https://eresearch.fidelity.com/eresearch/markets_sectors/sectors/sectors_in_market.jhtml

Community Banks are a type of bank that focuses on banking local communities, deriving the majority of their income from spread income, that is arbitraging the spread between interest paid on gathered deposits and interest earned on loans. Community banks are deeply embedded within their local communities, and as a result they have an integral understanding of the communities they operate within. This local expertise is irreplaceable when it comes to efficient reallocation of capital. Whereas the J.P. Morgans of the world have the size and scale to bank multinational corporations, community banks have the ability to devote their resources in a bespoke way for their local communities.

The term *community banks* has never had a strict definition, though often times an asset cap is used as a proxy. Most put this asset cap in the $10 billion range, which we find reasonable. However, we will resist committing to a hard number, as inflation and the regulatory environment make this somewhat of a moving target.

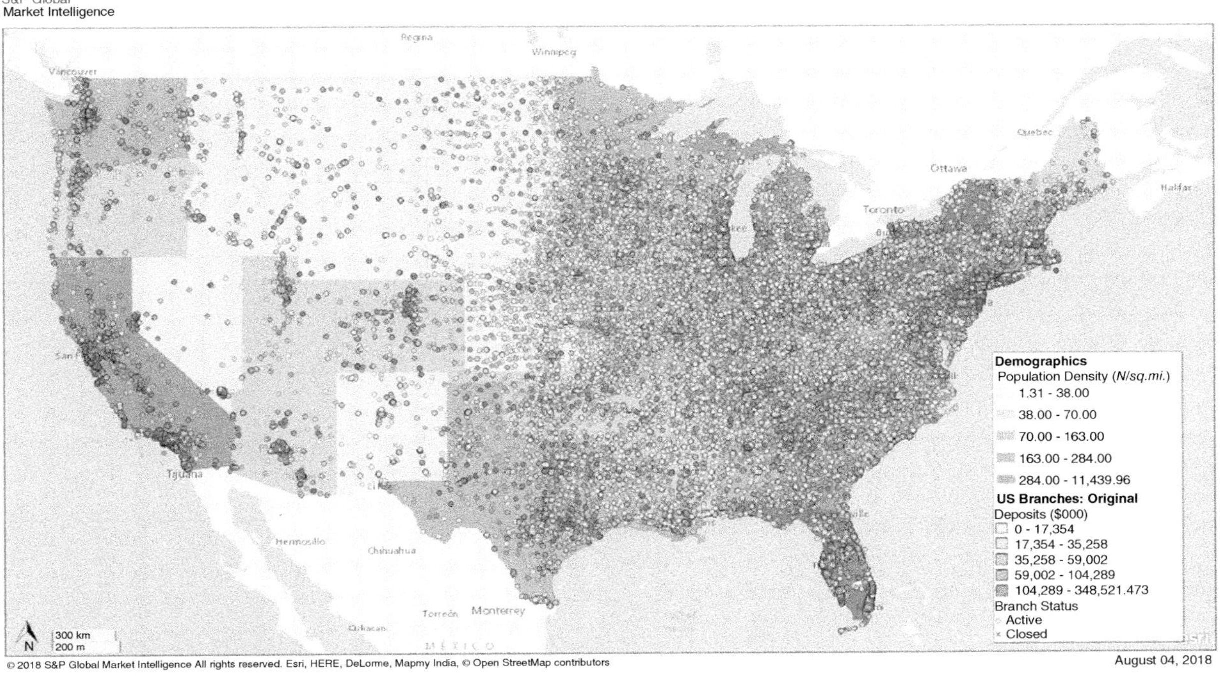

EXHIBIT 1.4 Distribution of Bank Branches and Population
Source: S&P Global Market Intelligence

EXHIBIT 1.5 Number of Banks

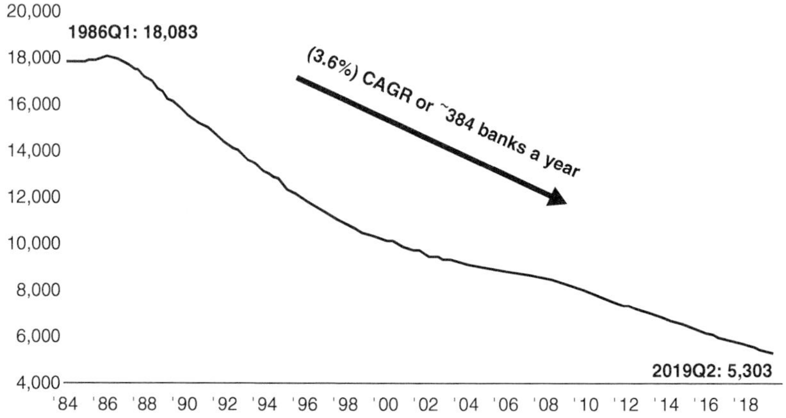

1986Q1: 18,083
(3.6%) CAGR or ~384 banks a year
2019Q2: 5,303
20,000 18,000 16,000 14,000 12,000 10,000 8,000 6,000 4,000
'84 '86 '88 '90 '92 '94 '96 '98 '00 '02 '04 '06 '08 '10 '12 '14 '16 '18

Source: FDIC

WHY INVEST IN COMMUNITY BANKS?

For starters, there are a lot of them to choose from. Nearly 800 publicly traded banks have assets below $10 billion, giving any potential investor a huge pool of investable securities. Further, once you've familiarized yourself with the peculiarities of the industry, your knowledge will be mostly applicable to this rather homogeneous business model.

That's not to say that returns *within* the bank space are homogenized though. There is enough specialization within the industry, whether it be geographically or in lending and deposit gathering strategies, that performance can vary wildly between banks. For instance, a business bank based in Texas would benefit more from rising oil prices and a rising Fed Funds rate, than a mortgage bank based in the Northeast.

Consolidation is also a secular tailwind that benefits bank investors as well. For instance, in 2017 there were a total of 305 deals announced, and 80 of the targets were publicly traded, implying nearly 1 in 10 publicly traded banks were taken out in just one year.

In this book, you will get insights from interviews conducted with real industry leaders, from those that operate banks, and those that invest in bank stocks and in the credit markets. Further, we will provide the requisite information that any investor would want to know, including the idiosyncrasies in financial statement analysis, capital and credit, the regulatory environment, and valuation. Ultimately, we hope to leave you with all the tools necessary to be successful in investing in bank stocks.

This book gives you the essential tool kit to become a successful bank investor. It packages practical lessons, theoretical knowledge, and historical context, all into one compelling and entertaining book. This is a basic 101 on investing in banks, as there is a lot of material that has been left on the cutting room floor. We are sure to have made some errors as well. We invite readers to send all comments to bankinvesting101@gmail.com.

2

Financial Statement Analysis

Banks don't make bad loans in bad times; they make bad loans in good times.
– William J. McDonough, President and CEO of the NY Fed 1993–2003

Analyzing the financial statements of a bank requires a somewhat specialized framework. Unlike, say, a consumer, technology, or industrial company, banks are fundamentally balance sheet driven, with the income statement mostly a consequent output of interest earned on loans held on the balance sheet funded by interest paying deposits.

Despite requiring the development of some specialized knowledge, the endeavor is well worth it, as the fragmented and homogenized nature of banking means the skills you develop will be leveragable to a large universe of investable securities.

Though banks are predominantly balance sheet driven, banks still generate a decent chunk of revenues from fees (about 20% of net revenues for banks less than $10B in assets), while noninterest expenses can meaningfully impact profitability.

Cash flow statements are largely ignored for these cash flush financial intermediaries, doubly so as banks have unique access to the federal funds market and FHLB (Federal Home Loan Bank) advances among other pools of liquidity. Additionally, liquidity at these depositories is already tightly monitored by banking regulators. Further, as financial intermediaries, the application of US GAAP leads to some unintuitive results, such as deposit inflows being categorized as financing activities, underwriting loans being categorized as investing outflows.

Banks use a special set of financial ratios to describe the profitability, credit quality, capital, and liquidity of an institution. Understanding and interpreting these ratios will give us a better ability in making informed investing decisions, and we will go over the most important ones in this and the following chapters on capital and credit.

We must also pay particular attention to asset quality, or the overall credit risk of the loan and securities portfolio. This is one of the most critical areas in assessing the health of a bank, as bank failures often are triggered by credit problems. We touch upon this topic both here in this chapter, and in Chapter 4, which is devoted to credit.

Finally, decomposing the loan portfolio and deposit base provides insights to the drivers of value for a bank, as well as gives clues to a bank's sensitivities to interest rates and other macroeconomic variables.

In the following section, we will be referencing real-world financial statements of a previously publicly traded depository, FNB Bancorp (FNBG), a $1.3B asset community bank based in San Francisco, which was acquired for a healthy 15% premium back in December of 2017.

THE BALANCE SHEET

The balance sheet is a terrific place to start. As mentioned in the introduction, a bank's balance sheet is a collection of financial assets, specifically interest earning assets, funded by a collection of interest-bearing liabilities, cushioned with a sliver of equity to protect depositors. Thus, the balance sheet is the primary driver for earnings, and projecting items on the balance sheet are the starting point when modeling forward expectations. We will be focused on the more idiosyncratic aspects of a typical bank's balance sheet (Exhibit 2.1).

The Accounting Equation

Starting with the fundamental accounting equation, that assets are equal to liabilities plus equities, we see that in our example bank, FNB Bancorp, assets are mostly funded by liabilities. This is normal. Banks unilaterally have significantly higher leverage ratios than in other industries. Case in point, the debt-to-equity ratio of the S&P 500 is close to 1.5× while our example, FNBG, has a 10× debt-to-equity ratio. This is simply due to the classification of deposits, the main funding source of banks, as liabilities. Fittingly, due to the low spreads and subsequent ROAs of banks, leverage is the only way for a bank to generate ROEs that are comparable with other industries.

An important aside: In bank land, leverage ratios (in the traditional sense where equity or EBITDA is in the denominator) are rarely referenced. As we shall see in Chapter 3 on capital, we like to follow the lead set by regulators, and use capital ratios, which are defined as some measure of equity in the numerator divided by some measure of assets in the denominator.

Assets

Total Assets are an important metric given the highly regulated nature of banks. Total assets at the top-tier Bank Holding Company (BHC) level will be

EXHIBIT 2.1 Consolidated Balance Sheet

FNB BANCORP AND SUBSIDIARY

Consolidated Balance Sheets

December 31, 2017 and 2016

Assets		
(Dollar amounts in thousands)	2017	2016
Cash and due from banks	$ 18,353	$ 15,758
Interest-bearing time deposits with financial Institutions	130	205
Securities available-for-sale, at fair value	355,857	360,105
Other equity securities	7,567	7,206
Loans, net of deferred loan fees and allowance for loan losses of $10,171 and $10,167 on December 31, 2017 and December 31, 2016	829,766	782,485
Bank premises, equipment, and leasehold improvements, net	9,322	9,837
Bank-owned life insurance	16,637	16,247
Accrued interest receivable	5,317	4,942
Other real estate owned, net	3,300	1,427
Goodwill	4,580	4,580
Prepaid expenses	825	856
Other assets	13,584	15,746
Total assets	$ 1,265,238	$ 1,219,394
Liabilities and Stockholders' Equity		
Deposits		
Demand, noninterest-bearing	$ 313,435	$ 296,273
Demand, Interest-bearing	130,988	121,086
Savings and money market	467,788	487,763
Time	138,084	114,384
Total deposits	1,050,295	1,019,506
Federal Home Loan Bank advances	75,000	71,000
Note payable	3,750	4,350
Accrued expenses and other liabilities	16,913	14,224
Total liabilities	1,145,958	1,109,080
Commitments and Contingencies (Note 12)		
Stockholders' equity		
Common stock, no par value, authorized 10,000,000 shares; issued and outstanding 7,442,279 shares at December 31, 2017 and 7,280,122 shares at December 31, 2016	85,565	84,283
Retained earnings	34,654	27,577
Accumulated other comprehensive loss, net of tax	(939)	(1,546)
Total stockholders' equity	119,280	110,314
Total liabilities and stockholders' equity	$ 1,265,238	$ 1,219,394

Source: FNBG 2017 10-K

EXHIBIT 2.2 Major Asset Thresholds

Asset Threshold	Impact
>$3 Billion	▪ Banks under this threshold qualify for an 18-month examination cycle (vs. normal 12-month cycle).
>$5 Billion	▪ Banks under this threshold are allowed to file short-form call reports for the first and third quarters.
>$10 Billion	▪ **Durbin Amendment drastically reduces debit interchange fees that a bank can charge.** ▪ **Volcker Rule comes into effect, banning prop trading.** ▪ **Can no longer use the simplified Community Bank Leverage Ratio.**
>$100 Billion	▪ Certain Dodd-Frank enhanced prudential standards come into effect. ▪ Dodd-Frank stress tests on a 2-year cycle.
>$250 Billion	▪ **Dodd-Frank stress tests on a 1-year cycle.** ▪ **Designation as a Systemically Important Financial Institution (SIFI).** ▪ **Banks are required to apply enhanced prudential standards, including 165(d) resolution plans "living wills."**
>$700 Billion	▪ Designation as a "Category II" which includes advanced approaches capital requirement.

one of the inputs used by bank regulators (Fed, FDIC, and OCC) to determine what set of regulations an institution will be beholden to. The most important asset thresholds are shown in Exhibit 2.2.

As a result, you will rarely see banks cross those thresholds organically. Crossing these thresholds by just a whisker will just saddle you with higher costs. Banks will thus choose to stall organic growth, jump over said thresholds via acquisitions, or sell.

Asset size and valuation multiples have also shown historical correlation, allowing us to anticipate multiple expansion or contraction by forecasting asset growth (Exhibit 2.3).

Loans make up the largest chunk of assets on the balance sheet, usually over 50% of total assets, and are the most important revenue driver on a bank's balance sheet. This item represents outstanding loans and leases held on the balance sheet that the bank expects to receive interest and principal payments from. These loans can be either originated or purchased. Loans are generally reported by the principal amount outstanding if they are held for investment (Exhibit 2.4).

EXHIBIT 2.3 US Publicly Traded Banks by Asset Size

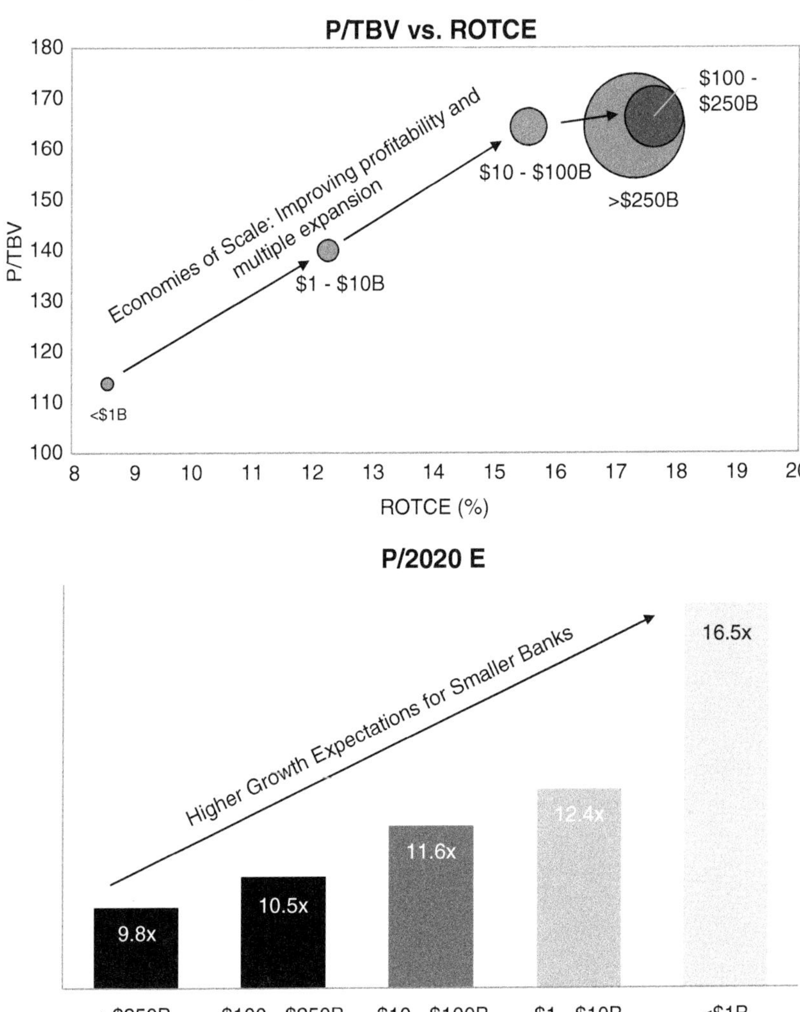

Source: S&P Global Market Intelligence

For FNB Bancorp, loan balances are condensed into one line item on the balance sheet: *Loans, net of deferred loan fees, and allowance for loan losses* (Exhibit 2.5).

EXHIBIT 2.4 Net Loans to Total Assets

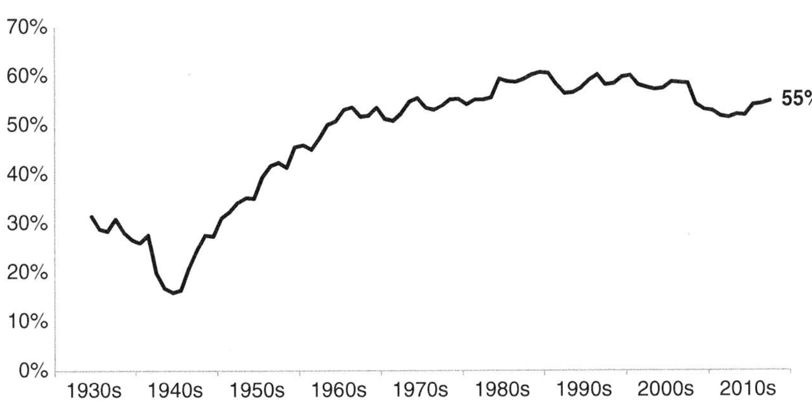

Source: FDIC

Net Loan Growth

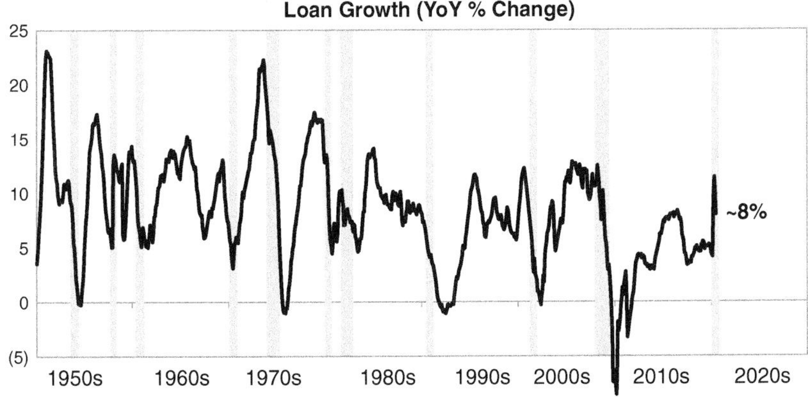

Source: Federal Reserve, St. Louis Fed

EXHIBIT 2.5 FNBG Loan Balances

	2017	2016
Loans, net of deferred loan fees and allowance for loan losses of $10,171 and $10,167 on December 31,2017 and December 31, 2016	829,766	782,485

Source: FNBG 2017 10-K

As you can see from FNBG's balance sheet, the balance sheet itself does not provide a lot of granularity on the loan book, with net loans distilled down to a single item. We must dive deeper into the footnotes to learn about the loan composition, structure, maturity schedule, and yields. Additionally, the classification of assets by their credit status (whether it is special mention, nonaccrual, nonperforming, etc.) is found in the footnotes. We expand on this later in this chapter in sections covering loan composition and asset quality.

Loan growth is one of the primary growth metrics investors will use to assess the growth of a bank. Bank investors are lucky in this respect, as it is a more stable metric than revenue growth, which can exhibit significant seasonality. Loan growth is usually cited on a linked-quarter annualized basis, though year-over-year is often used as well. Depositories that are growing loans at a faster clip will tend to trade at a higher premium, all things being equal. However, growth that is too fast versus the industry might be suspect. As to what constitutes "fast" or "slow" growth, apart from comparing growth at peer banks, we also like to look at the Federal Reserve's weekly H.8 data, which shows aggregate loan growth for the entire US banking industry (Exhibit 2.4, 2nd panel).

Loan Loss Reserves or *Allowance for Loan and Lease Losses (ALLL)* are a contra-asset account to cover estimated losses on loans due to defaults and non-payments. Think of it as the bank equivalent of an allowance for doubtful accounts. Some banks will report them as their own line item on the consolidated balance sheet, while others do not. Reserves are usually quoted as a percentage of loans.

Banks will maintain specific reserves against certain credits as well as a general reserve for the entire loan portfolio. Loan loss reserves are increased through *provision expenses* that run through the income statement, and are decreased by net charge-offs (which are actual gross write-downs of the book value of loans when collectability of principal is deemed unlikely, less any recoveries).

Whether or not a bank has adequate reserves is the million-dollar question. Reserves are cyclical, and thus getting a historical perspective is helpful and will allow us to assess if the bank's reserves line up with our expectations for the broader economy. Reserves usually do not dip below 1% of total loans. Once we determine where we are in the credit cycle, we can then go on to assess whether a particular bank's reserves are adequate for the risk profile of their loan book. Riskier loans (with generally higher yields) will require higher reserves. If a bank has too little reserves, there is risk they will have an outsized provision in the future. Conversely, an over-reserved bank could potentially boost earnings by releasing reserves in future periods. Finally, reserves between banks can sometimes be incomparable due to M&A (Exhibit 2.6).

EXHIBIT 2.6 Reserves

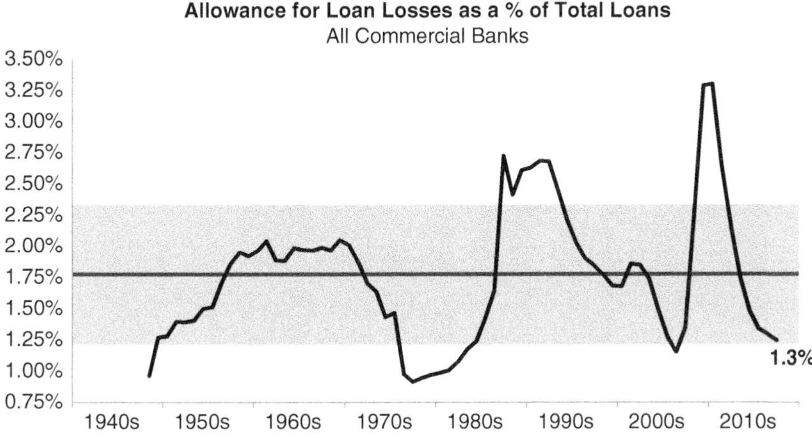

Source: FDIC

Current Expected Credit Losses (CECL) is a new accounting standard (FASB ASU 2016-13) that will meaningfully change how loan loss reserving is implemented. Under CECL, banks will need to establish a reserve equal to the expected losses over the *entire* life of a loan. This has the potential to meaningfully change the amount of reserves a bank must maintain, especially for certain long-dated loans such as mortgages. We cover this in greater detail in Chapter 4.

Deferred Loan Fees are fees that are collected by the bank when underwriting a loan. These fees are considered unearned and are capitalized on the balance sheet to be later amortized over the life of the loan.

Securities are the other major category of interest earning assets on a bank balance sheet. In most community banks, securities average around 25% of the asset base. Buying and selling marketable securities is not the primary business model for banks. As a result, securities held by banks tend to be high quality with minimal credit risk and good liquidity, allowing banks to quickly convert securities into cash and redeploy into more lucrative loan opportunities and service other liquidity needs. This premium placed on liquidity and credit quality means that the securities portfolio will have a lower average yield than the loan portfolio. The securities portfolio is also adjusted to manage interest rate risk and match the duration of certain liabilities. Popular security types include agency backed MBS, treasury securities, and nontaxable municipal securities.

Exhibit 2.7 shows us details on FNBG's $356MM securities portfolio, including the average yield (2.54%) and maturity (6.76 years) of the total

EXHIBIT 2.7 Securities Book

TABLE 10

(Dollar amounts in thousands)	Due In 1 Year Or Less	Yield	After 1 Year Through 5 Years	Yield	After 5 Years Through 10 Years	Yield	Due After 10 Years	Yield	Fair Value	Maturity In Years	Average Yield
US Treasury securities	$ —	—%	$ 1,975	1.88%	$ —	—%	$ —	—%	$ 1,975	2.92	1.83%
Obligations of US Government Agencies	6,000	1.10%	35,822	1.74%	—	1.77%	—	—	41,823	3.12	1.59%
Mortgage-backed securities	—	—	44,580	2.48%	31,732	2.61%	43,481	2.78%	119,792	11.03	2.35%
Asset-backed securities	—	—	—	—	1,628	2.43%	2,058	3.95%	3,686	9.71	3.32%
Obligations of states and political subdivisions	4,636	2.54%	81,470	2.33%	54,503	2.62%	10,493	3.73%	151,103	5.11	2.45%
Corporate debt	2,011	1.70%	26,272	2.64%	8,136	5.14%	1,060	5.84%	37,478	4.32	3.95%
Total	$ 12,647	1.72%	$ 190,119	2.29%	$ 95,999	2.83%	$ 57,092	3.06%	$ 355,857	6.76	2.54%

Source: FNBG 2017 10-K

EXHIBIT 2.8 Loans and Securities to Assets

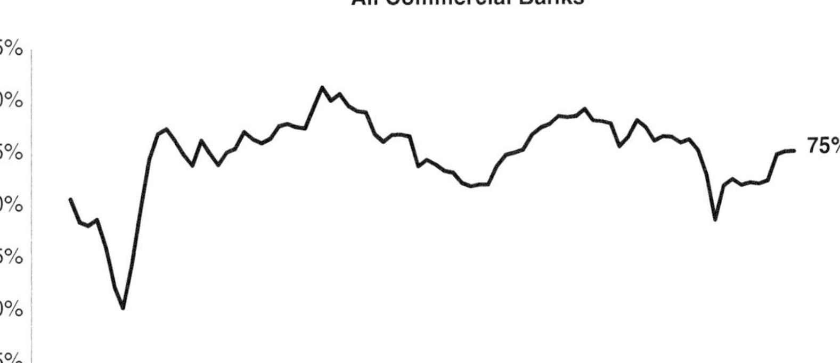

Source: FDIC

securities portfolio. The largest exposures are to municipal debt ($151MM) and mortgage-backed securities ($120MM).

An important nuance is to recognize whether the securities are held to maturity (HTM), available for sale (AFS), or held for trading (HFT), as it has implications as to if and where unrealized and realized gains will be recorded. Most community banks hold the majority of securities in AFS, a smaller amount in HTM, and practically zero in HFT.

Finally, *Interest Earning Assets* are simply a subtotal of securities and loans. They are the revenue generating financial assets that are held on the balance sheet and collectively make up north of 70% of a typical bank's balance sheet (Exhibit 2.8).

The notes to the financial statements will provide an insightful table similar to Exhibit 2.9, which shows *average* balances for interest earning assets, interest income generated from said assets, and their calculated yields.

Our example bank, FNBG, compares favorably to the industry, with ~90% of assets comprised of interest earning assets. Looking deeper at our *mix* of interest earning assets, we see that higher yielding loans make up about 69% of the interest earning asset base, which is about in-line with the industry aggregate.

Other real estate owned (OREO) represents physical real estate and other assets that are owned by the bank due to repossession of collateral on a defaulted loan secured by an underlying asset. Generally, the value is initially recorded at the lesser of the carrying amount of the loan or fair value of the property. Valuations are periodically performed, and any subsequent

EXHIBIT 2.9 Average Yields and Rates Paid

TABLE 1				Net Interest Income and Average Balances		
	2017			2016		
(Dollar amounts in thousands)	Average Balance	Interest Income Expense	Average Yield Cost	Average Balance	Interest Income Expense	Average Yield Cost
INTEREST EARNING ASSETS						
Loans, gross[(1)(2)]	$ 823,333	$ 41,956	5.10%	$ 746,829	$ 38,313	5.13%
Taxable securities	224,600	5,209	2.32%	209,257	4,213	2.01%
Nontaxable securities[(3)]	133,467	3,653	2.74%	135,412	3,916	2.89%
Interest on deposits—other financial institutions	10,681	126	1.18%	7,694	44	0.57%
Total interest earning assets	1,192,081	50,944	4.27%	1,099,192	46,486	4.23%
Cash and due from banks	15,168	92,889		15,041		
Premises and equipment	9,500			10,086		
Other assets	41,087			39,135		
Total noninterest earning assets	65,755			64,262		
TOTAL ASSETS	$ 1,257,836			$ 1,163,454		

Source: FNBG 2017 10-K

revisions in the estimate of fair value are reported as an adjustment to the carrying value of the real estate. The ultimate goal is to dispose of OREO, which can prove to be a costly and lengthy process.

Cash and Due from Banks are fairly self-explanatory. A bank will require a certain amount of cash to deal with regular business expenses and deposit withdrawals. The nuance for depositories is that banks are required by regulators to maintain minimum balances of cash "in the vault" or deposited at their local reserve bank. The amount of required reserves is based upon a percentage of certain deposits at a bank. This cash cushion, known as the reserve requirement, is also one of the core monetary tools used by central banks around the world (though the US Federal Reserve has a strong preference for other tools). Cash in the vault yields nothing, while balances held at the Reserve Banks yield what is called the IORR (Interest on Required Reserves) and IOER (Interest on Excess Reserves), more on this later in this book, and are low in comparison to yields on the securities and loan portfolios. In March of 2020, the Federal Reserve reduced the reserve requirement to zero percent effectively eliminating the reserve requirement.

Fed Funds Sold is cash lent out in the Federal Funds market on an overnight basis in order to meet their reserve requirements. The amount of interest earned is *de minimis,* as it is essentially a risk-free overnight investment. Fed Funds sold are occasionally broken out as a separate line item on the balance sheet if the amounts are significant.

Goodwill and Other Intangible Assets is typically recognized on the balance sheet following acquisitions and in short represent the difference between the price paid and the *identifiable* tangible and intangible net assets. Though the accounting treatment for goodwill is not unique for banks, the fact that bank valuation relies much more heavily on asset-based approaches means that goodwill and intangibles deserve a little extra attention.

Bank-Owned Life Insurance is life insurance policies owned by the bank to insure the lives of certain employees. Either the bank or the employee can be the beneficiary. For the latter, BOLI can provide a tax efficient means of providing employee benefits. Generally, BOLI is not a major focus for investors, and is not seen as a franchise enhancing or detracting item.

Liabilities

Deposits represent the largest chunk of liabilities, and are the funds placed by individuals and businesses (collectively known as depositors) into a bank for safekeeping (Exhibit 2.10). One cannot overemphasize the importance that a bank's deposit base has on a bank's business model and franchise value. Thanks to the fractional reserve banking system, deposits are the primary funding source for loans at a bank, and due to their low cost, give banks a

EXHIBIT 2.10 Liabilities

Liabilities and Stockholders' Equity		
	2017	**2016**
Deposits		
Demand, noninterest-bearing	$ 313,435	$ 296,273
Demand, interest-bearing	130,988	121,086
Savings and money market	467,788	487,763
Time	138,084	114,384
Total deposits	1,050,295	1,019,506
Federal Home Loan Bank advances	75,000	71,000
Notes payable	3,750	4,350
Accrued expenses and other liabilities	16,913	14,224
Total liabilities	1,145,958	1,109,080

Source: FNBG 2017 10-K

significant competitive advantage in their overall cost of capital over other lenders. Similar to loan growth, deposit growth is used as a measuring stick for overall growth. Not all deposits are equal, and certain types of deposits are valued more highly than others. We will go into further detail on deposit composition later in the chapter; however, a quick proxy for the quality of a bank deposit base is the cost of deposits (expressed as a percentage of interest paid on deposits divided by average deposits). Our example bank, FNBG, has a cost of deposits of 27 bps in 2017, which compares favorably to the 2017 industry average of 36 bps.

Federal Home Loan Bank advances (FHLB advances) represent borrowings under a collateralized line of credit with the regional FHLB. The FHLB are government-sponsored banks that provide credit to its member institutions in order to support lending activity, specifically for home and community loans. Advances from the FHLB may be short-term or long-term in nature. Typically, the cost associated with FHLB advances will be above a bank's cost of deposits, but below other forms of debt financing.

Equity

Chapter 3 covers much of the ins and outs of equity. Equity generally makes up only a sliver of the total capital structure of a bank, usually less than 10%. There are many abstract ways to think about equity, but perhaps the most insightful way to think about equity within the context of a bank is it is the loss absorbing buffer that protects the depositors in the event of losses sustained in the loan portfolio. Too much equity would result in subpar ROEs, while too little would expose the bank to too much risk and crimp growth prospects (Exhibit 2.11).

EXHIBIT 2.11 Equity

	2017	2016
Stockholders' equity		
Common stock, no par value, authorized 10,000,000 shares; issued and outstanding 7,442,279 shares at December 31, 2017 and 7,280,122 shares at December 31, 2016	85,565	84,283
Retained earnings	34,654	27,577
Accumulated other comprehensive loss, net of tax	(939)	(1,546)
Total stockholders' equity	119,280	110,314
Total liabilities and stockholders' equity	$ 1,265,238	$ 1,219,394

Source: FNBG 2017 10-K

THE INCOME STATEMENT

Net Interest Income (NII) represents the interest earned on interest earning assets less interest paid on interest bearing liabilities. It is the most important earnings driver for a bank. Bank investors tend to focus directly on NII as opposed to its constituents, *interest income* and *interest expense*. However, it is important to be cognizant that a sequential increase or decrease in NII can be caused by a change in *either* interest income *or* interest expense. In Exhibit 2.12, NII makes up over 90% of total net revenues; this is pretty typical for a community bank.

Provision for Loan Losses (LLP) is the expense item that contributes to the allowance for loan losses. The amount of provisioning expense is a complex calculation requiring many judgment calls by management, based on changes on the expected credit quality of the existing portfolio and to cover newly underwritten loans. Note that it is possible, though unusual, for the provision to be a negative, as it was for FNBG in 2017. It is most appropriate to exclude negative provisions when assessing core operating trends. Finally, it is helpful to look at the LLP in the context of other metrics, such as *net loan growth*, *net charge-offs*, and the already existing size of the *loan loss reserve*. We will cover the ins and outs of asset quality in the upcoming sections.

Noninterest income, also known as *fee income*, is revenue that is derived from sources other than interest earned on assets. These tend to be secondary revenue streams for a community bank. Common examples of noninterest income include service charges on deposits, realized gains and losses on securities, trading gains and losses, mortgage banking fees, and trust or asset management fees. Fee revenues, such as deposit service charges and asset management fees, can help insulate a bank's business model from moves in interest rates. However, that is not to say fee income is completely uncorrelated to interest rates. For instance, mortgage banking fees are a function of

EXHIBIT 2.12 Income Statement

FNB BANCORP AND SUBSIDIARY		
Consolidated Statements of Earnings		
Years ended December 31, 2017, 2016, and 2015		
(Dollar amounts and average shares are in thousands, except earnings per share amounts)		
	2017	**2016**
Interest income:		
Interest and fees on loans	$ 41,956	$ 38,313
Interest and dividends on taxable securities	5,209	4,213
Interest on tax-exempt securities	2,927	2,943
Interest on deposits with other financial institutions	126	44
Total interest income	50,218	45,513
Interest expense:		
Interest on deposits	2,807	2,780
Interest on FHLB advances	850	67
Interest on note payable	214	222
Total interest expense	3,871	3,069
Net interest income	46,347	42,444
(Recovery of) provision for loan losses	(360)	150
Net interest income after provision for (recovery of) loan losses	46,707	42,294
Noninterest income:		
Service charges	2,264	2,461
Net gain on sale of available-for-sale securities	210	438
Earnings on bank-owned life insurance	390	402
Other income	996	1,294
Total noninterest income	3,860	4,595
Noninterest expense:		
Salaries and employee benefits	19,366	19,474
Occupancy expense	2,747	2,528
Equipment expense	1,646	1,765
Professional fees	1,482	1,363
FDIC assessment	400	600
Telephone, postage, supplies	1,267	1,199
Advertising expense	451	524
Data processing expense	571	657
Low income housing experts	472	284

Source: FNBG 2017 10-K

EXHIBIT 2.12 *(Continued)*

FNB BANCORP AND SUBSIDIARY		
Consolidated Statements of Earnings		
Years ended December 31, 2017, 2016, and 2015		
(Dollar amounts and average shares are in thousands, except earnings per share amounts)		
	2017	**2016**
Surety insurance	349	347
Director expense	288	288
Other real estate owned expense (recovery)	80	(5)
Other expense	1,430	1,668
Total noninterest expense	30,549	30,692
Earnings before provision for income taxes	20,018	16,197
Provision for income taxes	9,307	5,696
Net earnings	$ 10,711	$ 10,501
Earnings per share available to common stockholders:		
Basic	$ 1.46	$ 1.45
Diluted	$ 1.41	$ 1.42
Weighted average shares outstanding:		
Basic	7,361	7,233
Diluted	7,607	7,417

mortgage underwriting volumes, which tends to be inversely correlated to longer term interest rates. In this example, mortgage banking fees act almost as a natural hedge to the typical asset sensitive balance sheet.

Noninterest expenses represent all other expenses not related to interest paid on liabilities. Personnel, occupancy, and equipment costs are some of the larger items typically found.

Pre-provision Net Revenues (PPNR) represents NII and noninterest income less noninterest expenses, but *excludes* loan loss provision expenses. Investors will use this metric as a way to look at underlying "run rate" earnings power, with credit noise stripped away. It is helpful as a directional reference, especially when compared on a QoQ or YoY basis.

RATIOS

Return on Assets (ROA) is calculated the regular way, net income over average assets (Exhibit 2.14). ROAs in bank land historically hovered in the low

EXHIBIT 2.13 Quarterly Pre-Tax ROA

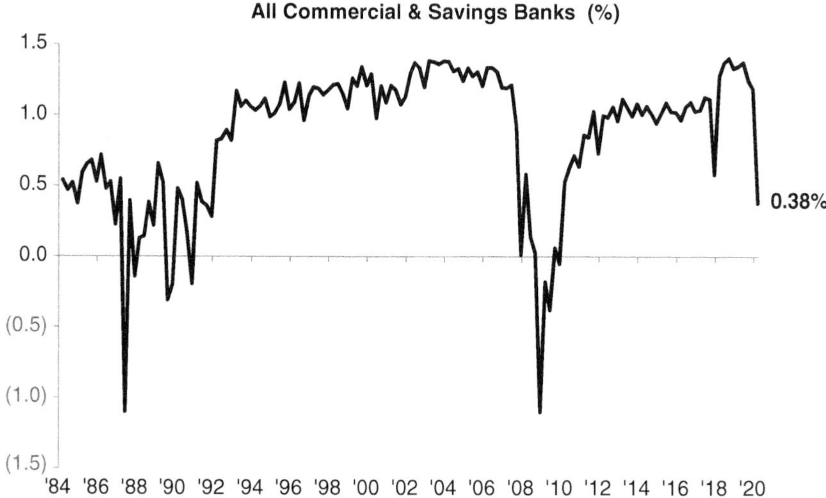

Source: FDIC

EXHIBIT 2.14 ROA Composition

	FNBG		Banks $1–3B in Assets	
	$000s	**% of Avg Assets**	**$000s**	**% of Avg Assets**
Interest Income	50,218	**3.99%**	22,501,695	3.87%
Interest Cost	(3,871)	**(0.31%)**	(2,518,790)	(0.43%)
Loan Loss Provision	360	**0.03%**	(901,622)	(0.15%)
Fee Income	3,860	0.31%	8,129,979	**1.40%**
Non-Interest Expenses	(30,549)	**(2.43%)**	(17,732,963)	(3.05%)
Tax Provision	(9,307)	(0.74%)	(3,084,420)	**(0.53%)**
Net Income/ ROA	**10,711**	**0.85%**	**6,393,879**	**1.10%**
Average Assets	1,257,836		582,081,276	

Source: FNBG 10K, S&P Global Market Intelligence

single digit range (Exhibit 2.13). Mathematically, this is expected given that NIMs, which are effectively the "interest-earning" ROA, hover in this same range. As discussed earlier, banks makeup for their "lackluster" ROAs through leverage.

One helpful way to break down ROA is to divide each major line item by average assets. This type of ratio analysis allows us to better understand the

EXHIBIT 2.15 Average ROE and ROA by Asset Size

Asset Size	Count	ROA	Leverage	ROE
>$250B	8	0.90	× 8.8	= 7.85
$50 - $250B	14	1.08	× 9.0	= 9.76
$10 - $50B	60	0.97	× 8.3	= 8.03
$1 - $10B	284	0.86	× 9.4	= 8.08
<$1B	481	0.65	× 9.8	= 6.42
All	**847**	**0.76**	× **9.5**	= **7.18**

Source: S&P Global Market Intelligence, 2017

drivers of profitability. In our example bank, FNBG, we can see that ROA is below peer levels due predominately to below average fee income and, to a lesser extent, higher than average taxes.

Return on Equity (ROE) is similarly calculated in the typical way, net income divided by average equity. DuPont analysis shows us that ROE can be simply broken down as ROA multiplied by financial leverage. However, further DuPont analysis – breaking down ROA into net profit margin and asset turnover – does not yield any economic insights for a bank. Bank investors are blessed by the fact that regulators have strict rules for leverage and capital ratios. The regulatory framework gives us approximate goalposts for us to estimate what a fully levered balance sheet should look like, making it easier for us to recognize whether an exceptional ROE is from unsustainably high leverage, or from a truly exceptional business model. Conversely, a lagging ROE could simply be a function of an under-levered balance sheet. Exhibit 2.15 shows us average ROA and leverage, and consequently ROE, for banks in different asset size buckets.

Our example bank, FNBG, logged a 2017 ROA and ROE of 0.85% and 8.9%, respectively. With $1.2B in assets, the company generated an in-line ROA, but due to its lower capital ratios/higher leverage, FNBG was able to earn a higher ROE.

Return on Tangible Common Equity (ROTCE) is a more refined way to look at returns to common equity holders. It adjusts both net income and common equity:

$$ROTCE = \frac{Net\ Income + (1 - t)(intangible\ amortization)}{Common\ Equity - Intangible\ Assets}$$

ROTCE is a more accurate metric of the real return on tangible capital. ROEs can get bogged down by the artifacts of acquisition accounting and unfairly penalize those companies with lots of goodwill on their balance sheets. This reduces comparability between companies. ROTCE strips away these issues.

A frequently used valuation framework that you will see later in Chapter 5 is ROTCE vs. P/TBV to screen for potentially undervalued or overvalued stocks.

Earnings Per Share (EPS) is simply net income available to common shareholders divided by average share count. Estimated "core" EPS is more of an art than a science, but some of the more common adjustments include backing out unusual reserve developments (such as negative provisions) and accretion income on acquired loans.

$$\text{Asset Growth} \rightarrow \text{EPS Growth}$$

As bank investors and management teams speak frequently on asset growth, being able to assess the approximate impact that a given asset growth will have on EPS is useful. A quick and dirty back-of-the-envelope calculation that is frequently used is simply to use change in assets and ROA as inputs:

$$\Delta EPS = \frac{\$\,\Delta\,NI}{sharecount} = \frac{\$\,\Delta\ in\ assets \times ROA}{sharecount}$$

For example, if a bank is targeting to grow assets by \$250MM, and has historically generated a 1.1% ROA, with a static share count of 3MM shares, the pro-forma EPS impact would be:

$$\frac{\$250MM \times 1.1\%}{3MM} = \$0.91\ increase\ in\ EPS$$

$$\text{NIM Growth} \rightarrow \text{EPS Growth}$$

Additionally, it is helpful to assess how changes in the NIM impact EPS. Some simple algebra yields the following:

$$\Delta EPS = \frac{(\Delta NIM \times Average\ Earning\ Assets)(1 - T)}{sharecount}$$

Continuing our example, if a bank with \$1.2B in average earning assets expects a 5 bps increase in its NIM, and assuming a 35% tax rate, the EPS impact would be:

$$\frac{(0.05\% \times \$1{,}200MM)(1 - 0.35)}{3MM} = \$0.13\ increase\ in\ EPS$$

Net Interest Margin (NIM) represents Net Interest Income (NII) divided by Average Earning Assets (AEAs). This profitability metric is one of the most important figures looked at by bank management teams and investors:

$$NIM = \frac{Net\ Interest\ Income}{Average\ Earning\ Assets} = \frac{Interest\ Income - Interest\ Expense}{Average\ Earning\ Assets}$$

EXHIBIT 2.16 A Brief History of NIM

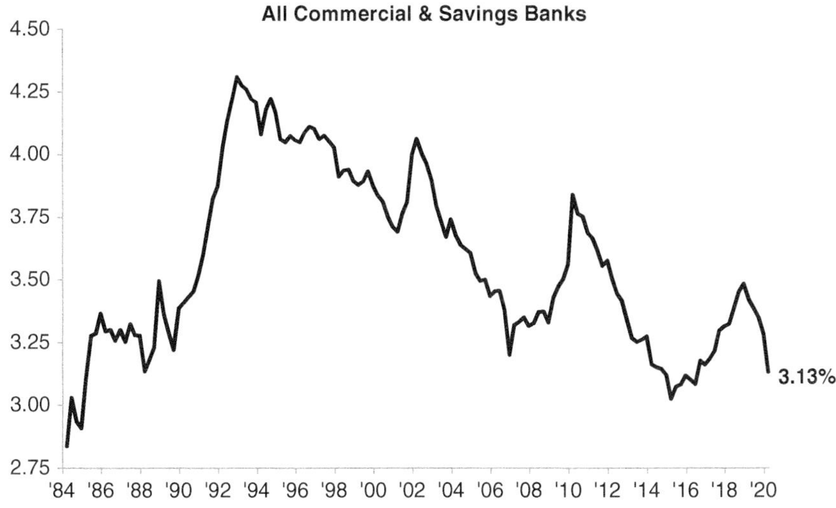

Source: FDIC

Though it is technically a profitability metric calculated from NII and AEAs, NIM is often used as an input in quick models to project NII. This is especially true as bank management teams will often provide NIM guidance, giving us an easy input to use for modeling purposes. NIMs are often thought of as the "spread" that a bank earns, which is technically untrue. Instead, it is similar to an *ROA*, as it a measure of income (interest income) over assets (interest earning assets). NIMs are annualized figures, so if you are looking at quarterly results, don't forget to annualize the NII 2.16.

EXHIBIT 2.17 2017 Net Interest Margin for All US Banks

Percentile	NIM
95th Percentile	4.54
90th Percentile	4.28
75th Percentile	3.91
50th Percentile	3.58
25th Percentile	3.24
Median	**3.58**

Source: S&P Global Market Intelligence

EXHIBIT 2.18 All US Banks: Higher Yields = Higher Risk

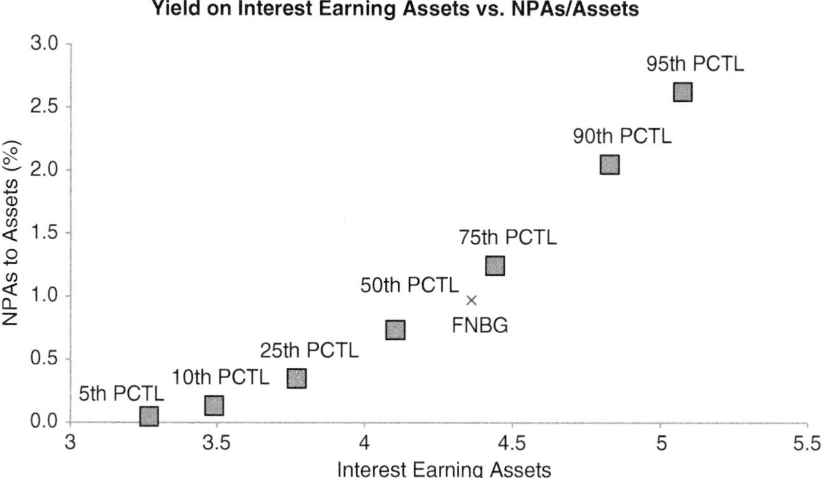

Source: S&P Global Market Intelligence

Our example bank, FNBG, had a 2017 NIM of 3.95%, good enough to be in the 77th percentile.

Yield on Interest Earning Assets represents total interest earned divided by average earning assets, on an annualized basis. In a vacuum, a higher yield on interest earning assets is of course better. However, markets are efficient, which means a higher return entails a higher degree of risk. We can see that this is broadly true within our universe of publicly traded US banks, a higher yield on assets is associated with a higher level of non-performing assets (our proxy for risk) (Exhibit 2.18).

FNBG's risk and return profile seems to be consistent with the broader industry. FNBG had a 2017 yield on interest earning assets of 4.27%, good enough to be in the 64th percentile, with NPAs/Assets of 88 bps, which puts them at the 60th percentile.

Cost of Interest-bearing Liabilities represents interest paid on liabilities divided by total interest-bearing liabilities. Interest bearing liabilities only include interest-bearing instruments such as CDs, interest-bearing deposit accounts, debt, and FHLB borrowings. This metric does *not* represent the total cost of funding for a bank, as it excludes noninterest-bearing liabilities from the denominator. As a result, this metric is less helpful than one would initially think. A bank like FNBG has nearly $300MM in noninterest-bearing demand deposits, nearly a third of its $1.0B deposit base.

EXHIBIT 2.19 All US Publicly Traded Banks: A Lower Cost of Funds Drives Higher ROA

	Cost of Funds (%)	ROA (%)
95th Percentile	0.18	0.94
90th Percentile	0.25	0.87
75th Percentile	0.38	0.85
50th Percentile	0.55	0.85
25th Percentile	0.75	0.80

Source: S&P Global Market Intelligence

Cost of Funds represents a more complete look at the cost of liabilities that provide capital for a bank (Exhibit 2.19). It is calculated by dividing interest paid on liabilities by *total* liabilities, which includes all interest-bearing and noninterest-bearing liabilities. Noninterest-bearing liabilities mainly consist of noninterest-bearing deposits – an important value driver for a bank, which we go through further in our deposit composition section. As non-interest bearing deposits bear no interest, a quick reconciliation between cost of funds and cost of interest bearing liabilities is possible through the following calculation:

$$\text{Cost of Funds} = \%\ \text{of interest bearing liabilities to total liabilities} \\ \times \text{Cost of Interest bearing liabilities}$$

Cost of Deposits refers specifically to the interest paid on deposits divided by average deposit balances. Gathering low-cost deposits is one of the fundamental ways banks compete with each other. Because depositors don't necessarily view the monies deposited at a bank as an investment, the market for deposits is not necessarily efficient. Said another way, depositors are not depositing money looking for the highest risk adjusted return, they take into consideration things such as deposit services, the ATM/branch network, and digital or mobile applications. Thus, banks have an opportunity to create sustainable systematic advantages over their peers by focusing on deposit gathering.

Deposit Beta is an important concept relating to the sensitivity of deposit costs as compared to an underlying interest rate (usually the Federal Funds rate). Deposit betas are calculated as the change in deposit costs divided by the change in interest rates over the same period. Logically then, in a rising rate environment, a lower deposit beta is better as interest costs won't rise as quickly. However, calculating deposit beta can only be done in retrospect, and by then, the information will already be reflected in a bank's stock.

EXHIBIT 2.20 Cost of Deposits vs. Fed Funds

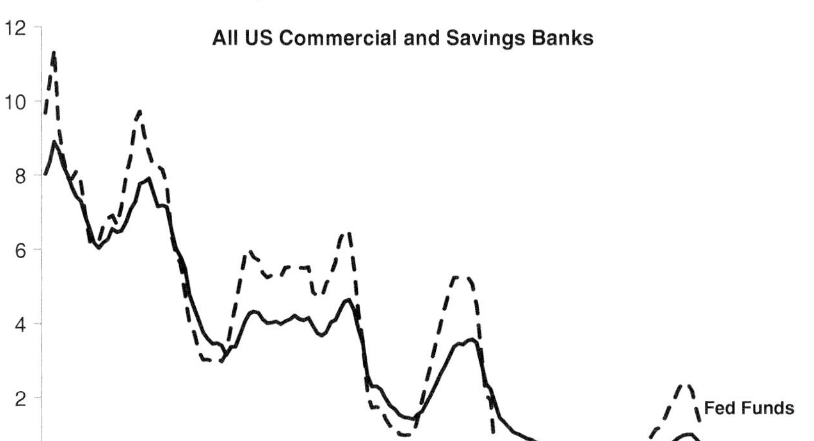

Source: FDIC and St. Louis FRED

Thus, estimates must be made based on things such as company guidance, the local competitive market, growth aspirations, judgments on the quality of the deposit franchise, and past history (Exhibit 2.20).

Loans to Deposits (L/D) is a straightforward calculation that simply shows loans divided by deposits. The industry average is around 70%. This simple metric has important implications. A relatively low loan to deposit ratio implies that the bank has a large amount of "underutilized" funds, sitting in relatively low-yielding cash and securities. A bank thus has the opportunity to remix their balance sheet and increase interest income. This is an especially powerful dynamic in an environment where interest rates are generally moving higher, allowing the bank to deploy funds into loans with ever increasing yields. Conversely, a high loan to deposit ratio implies that the bank's balance sheet is "loaned up," with little room for easy improvements. This is not necessarily a bad thing. First, returns are most likely higher than compared to a bank with a lower loan/deposit ratio. Second, in a falling rate environment, having funds tied up into longer duration higher-yielding loans will mitigate the effects of falling interest rates. Finally, and perhaps unintuitively, the L/D ratio can be well in excess of 100%. Some banks, particularly those that write a large proportion of mortgage loans, end up funding a decent percentage of their loans through FHLB borrowings.

Securities to Assets shows the proportion of securities to total assets. Similar to the loan to deposit ratio, it is a measure that shows balance sheet

EXHIBIT 2.21 Efficiency Ratio by Asset Size

Assets	Count	Efficiency Ratio (%)
<$1B	500	73.1
$1B – $10B	292	60.8
$10B – $50B	63	56.7
$50B – $250B	14	59.9
>$250B	8	59.4
All	**877**	**67.3**

Source: S&P Global Market Intelligence

remixing potential. The industry average has been trending down and is now in the mid-teens.

Efficiency Ratio (E/R) in bank land is calculated as non-interest expenses divided by net revenues (NII plus noninterest income). The industry average at a healthy bank is in the 50s to 60s, though some exceptional banks have efficiency ratios in the 40s. An important element of analyzing the efficiency ratio is recognizing that an efficiency ratio can be improved by *either* decreasing non-interest expenses through cost saving initiatives, *or* through improving net revenues. Sometimes it is easy to focus narrowly on just the numerator, but understand that a bank with for example, a higher NIM, could support a higher expense base, and thus could be reporting an impressive efficiency ratio, and yet have further room to improve its cost structure.

Exhibit 2.21 suggests that there is a "sweet spot" when it comes to size and efficiency, somewhere in the $10B to $50B in asset range. Our bank, FNBG, had a better than average efficiency ratio of 54%.

Noninterest Expense to Average Assets. This is also a measure of efficiency. The industry average has been trending down and sits in the ~2.6% range. This ratio is helpful when used in conjunction with the efficiency ratio in understanding the cost structure of a bank. For instance, a bank with a subpar ROA and a high efficiency ratio coupled with a low noninterest expense to average asset ratio could suggest that the cost structure is not the problem, and that instead the bank is not generating enough spread income. In our example, FNBG, net operating expenses measured 1.85% of average assets.

Deposits per Branch divides total deposits by total branches, which yields the average deposits per branch. This metric gives clues to the bank's deposit gathering strategy and the non-interest expenses associated with deposits. The national median sits around $40MM per branch.

Noninterest Income to Revenues represents the percentage of net revenues that are derived from non-interest income related sources. There are minor variations to the calculation (e.g., using operating revenues or using net revenues in the denominator), but the general idea is the same. The industry average is in the 20s to 30s. Investors tend to interpret a higher noninterest income percentage to being less sensitive to interest rates. This is partially true, though as we noted earlier in the section on noninterest income, certain fee revenues exhibit sensitivity to rates.

Equity to Assets represents total equity divided by total assets. It is mathematically the inverse of the leverage ratio, and thus can be used to reconcile ROA with ROE. The industry average is around 11%. Note that this ratio includes intangibles such as goodwill.

Tangible Equity to Tangible Assets represents total equity less intangible assets divided by total assets less intangible assets. The industry average is around 9%.

Tangible Common Equity to Tangible Assets, also referred to as the TCE ratio, represents common equity less intangible assets divided by total assets less intangible assets. The TCE ratio is the "cleanest" way for us to look at the leverage of an institution from the perspective of a common shareholder, and helps us reconcile ROA and ROTCE, which has important implications to valuation.

Asset Quality Metrics are used to monitor the credit quality of assets held on the balance sheet. Loans with payments past due, nonperforming credits, write-downs, and foreclosures are all part of the normal business of underwriting and holding risky financial assets. We will delve deeper into this very important topic in the next section.

Finally, the ratios that bank investors don't use are illustrative as well. Since interest expense is such a fundamental part of the business model, any ratio that excludes or isolates interest expense, such as EBITDA or the interest coverage ratio, has no relevance. Likewise, inventory based metrics (e.g., inventory turnover) and day cycles (e.g., cash conversion cycles) have no applicability.

ASSET QUALITY

Asset quality, also referred to as credit quality, represents the quantity and severity of existing and potential credit problems that exist on bank's balance sheet. From a theoretical framework, banks should *not* have *zero* credit losses. The market for loans is fairly efficient, thus for loans to earn more than the risk-free rate, a certain amount of risk must be taken.

Asset quality problems pose the largest existential risk for a bank, and have been the primary trigger for failure and bankruptcy in the past. Due to the highly levered nature of banks, and the relatively thin returns earned on assets, a seemingly small write-off (relative to assets) could have major financial implications. Let's use median bank industry metrics to illustrate an example. Let's say a hypothetical bank with a $2B book of loans is suffering from credit problems and requires a 2% write-off. This would equate to $40MM, or ~$30MM after-tax. Let's say the bank was otherwise generating an 85 bps ROA, with loans making up 60% of the asset base, implying total assets of $3.3B, and net income of $28MM. Thus a 2% write-off would push net income into a $2MM loss for the bank.

Unfortunately for us bank investors, it is sometimes very difficult to anticipate credit issues at a bank. Most of the times, we learn of credit issues through public disclosures and scramble to analyze how it affects a bank's intrinsic value (at least before everyone else in the market does). Further, bank management teams implement their own credit policies and have a certain degree of latitude in the classification of assets, making comparisons difficult.

Bank investors need to put on their macro hat to look into economic trends to anticipate impacts to certain geographies, industries, and asset types. For instance, a supply glut in certain commodities could affect local economies that rely heavily on said commodities and impact not just business loans, but eventually the housing market (mortgage) and consumers (credit card loans) as well. Finally, even when we correctly anticipate eventual credit issues, it may take a long time for them to manifest in the financials, while the magnitude is difficult to assess.

Before we get ahead of ourselves, see Exhibit 2.22 to go over some definitions and accounting mechanics.

As described earlier, the ALLL is a contra asset account that reflects estimated credit losses within a bank's asset portfolio. Said another way, it represents the amount of write-offs a bank estimates it will take. The word *estimate* should trigger some consternation, as the "appropriate"

EXHIBIT 2.22 Mechanics of the Allowance for Lease and Loan Loss Reserves (ALLL)

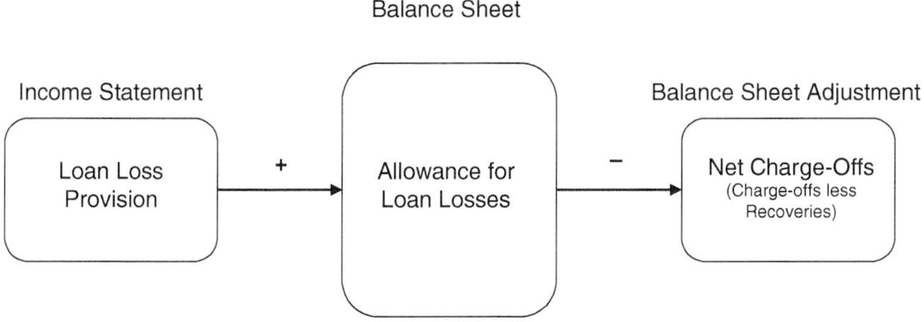

size of the ALLL is indeed an opaque calculation with many estimates up to the discretion of management. It is helpful to know that the industry average is for the ALLL to be about 1.1% of the gross loan portfolio, with a standard deviation of 0.5%. Any significant deviations should be looked into. The size of the ALLL is a function of the overall size of the loan portfolio, the estimated probability of default, and the estimated severity of losses in the event of default. Loan reviews are done both for specific loans and also incorporate a general reserve, which reflects an assessment of local economic conditions as well as historical loan losses. Every quarter, an expense on the income statement, the provision for loan losses, is credited to the ALLL. Conversely, actual charge-offs do not impact the P&L directly, but instead are debited from the ALLL. Charge-offs are generally taken after debt is delinquent after a certain period of time (90 days or 120 days being common thresholds).

Loan Classifications (Internal)

A loan classification system uses buckets to classify loans by their risk of nonpayment. Regulators require banks to have robust loan classification systems to categorize assets by credit quality. Public disclosures will not show the degree of granularity that a bank uses internally. In fact, banks have latitude from regulators in implementing a credit risk rating system that is most appropriate for them. That said, understanding the internal framework is helpful, and there are some common regulatory guidelines that give us insight into this process:

Loans not adversely classified:

1. Pass – performing as underwritten with no expectations of deterioration in the foreseeable future.
2. Special mention – potential weaknesses that deserve management's close attention. If left uncorrected, these potential weaknesses may result in deterioration of the repayment prospects for the asset or in the institution's credit position at some future date. Special Mention assets are not adversely classified and do not expose the institution to sufficient risk to warrant adverse classification.

Loans adversely classified:

3. Substandard – inadequately protected by the current sound worth and paying capacity of the obligor or of the collateral pledged, if any. Assets

so classified must have a well-defined weakness, or weaknesses, that jeopardize the liquidation of the debt. They are characterized by the distinct possibility that the bank will sustain some loss if the deficiencies are not corrected

4. Doubtful – all of the weaknesses inherent in those classified Substandard with the added characteristic that the weaknesses make collection or liquidation in full, on the basis of currently known facts, conditions, and values, highly questionable and improbable.
5. Loss – uncollectible and of such little value that their continuance as a bankable asset is not warranted. This classification does not mean that the loan has absolutely no recovery or salvage value but rather that it is not practical or desirable to defer writing off this basically worthless asset even though partial recovery may be effected in the future.

Source: Various regulatory circulars

Credit Quality (Public Disclosures)

There are common descriptions that banks use to describe the credit quality of loans and other risky assets. We will go over some definitions before delving into ratios that bank investors like to look at.

Nonperforming Assets (NPAs) consist of loans classified as non-accrual loans, OREO, and other nonperforming assets (such as securities). A loan will be classified as nonperforming after being a certain number of days past due (often times 90 days for commercial loans, 150 days for residential mortgages), or earlier if repayment of principal and interest is in doubt. When loans are placed on nonaccrual, accrued interest income is reversed with current year accruals charged to interest income and prior year amounts generally charged off as a credit loss. Note that it is possible that an NPA can move back to accrual status if the collectability is no longer in doubt (though this is relatively rare).

Nonperforming Loans (NPLs) consist solely of adversely classified loans, that is, the sum total of loans classified as substandard, doubtful, and loss. NPLs will typically make up the bulk of NPA balances.

Troubled Debt Restructuring (TDRs) are modified loans where a concession was provided to a borrower experiencing financial difficulties. Classification of TDRs can be tricky. Technically, TDRs can be classified as either accruing or nonaccruing loans. Nonaccruing TDRs are included in NALs, and thus NPAs, whereas accruing TDRs can be technically excluded, as expectations are for contractual principal and interest due under the restructured terms will be collected. However, for the sake of conservatism, we tend to lump TDRs into NPAs.

Other Real Estate Owned (OREO) is broken out as a line item on the balance sheet and is thus defined in our prior section on the balance sheet. For a loan secured by a real asset, OREO is the last stop on the balance sheet before a nonperformer is completely off the books. When collateral is foreclosed upon and repossessed, the loan is written off and the fair value of the collateral is brought onto the balance sheet as held-for-sale.

Loan to Value (LTV) is a term used for collateralized loans that represents the value of the loan divided by the value of the underlying collateral. Low LTVs are more conservative for two reasons: (1) The borrower is more likely to be motivated to stay current as they have more of their own equity tied to the collateral; and (2) the severity of loss may be lessened if the repossessed asset has a fair value that can cover the unpaid principal balance of defaulted loan.

NPAs/Assets shows assets classified as nonperforming as a percentage of total assets. The industry average has been declining steadily post the financial crisis of 2008 and sits at around 54 bps. This is one of the most common metrics used when describing a bank's asset quality (Exhibit 2.23).

NPAs + 90 Days Past Due/Assets is a more conservative metric that includes loans that are at least 90 days past due. Remember, a loan that is 90 days past due could still be classified as accruing interest, and won't be included in NPAs. As this metric relies on stricter definitions, it is inherently less subjective, making it a helpful metric to use when making cross-sectional comparisons. Mathematically it's clear that this ratio will always be larger

EXHIBIT 2.23 NPAs to Assets

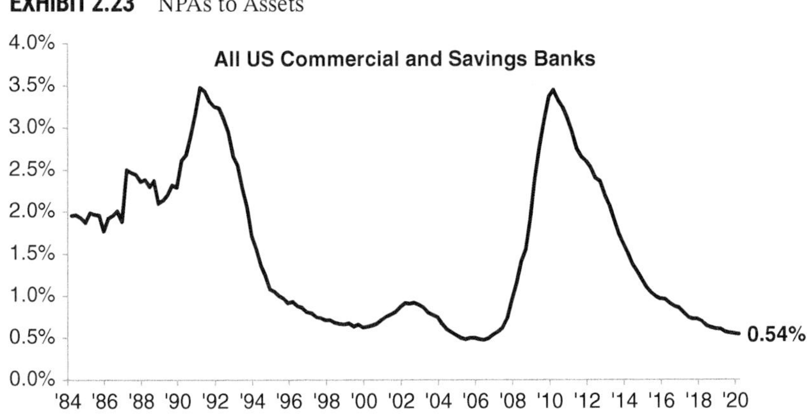

Source: FDIC

EXHIBIT 2.24 ALLL to Total Loans

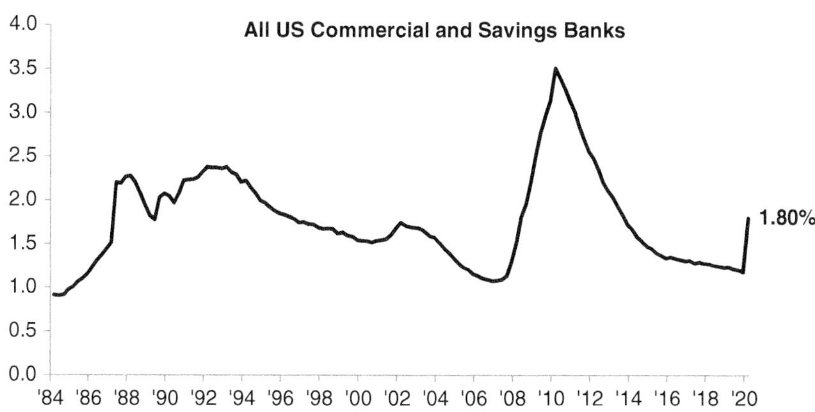

Source: FDIC

than just NPAs/Assets. An increase in the *differential* between these two ratios, however, could be a lead indicator for credit quality issues.

NPLs/Loans looks at the proportion of nonperforming loans to total loans. The NPL/Loans ratio will be higher than the entire NPAs/Assets ratio. The industry average has likewise declined steadily and is now in the 1.40% range.

Loan Loss Reserves Loans is a helpful way to judge the size of the loan loss reserve of a bank (Exhibit 2.24). For reference, the industry average is in the 1.25% range, and has trended down from the crisis peak of ~3.65%. Remember, loan loss reserves represent management *expectations* on future losses, and not actual losses taken. A relatively larger LLR can provide a tailwind (albeit a temporary one) to earnings, as management normalizes the size of their LLR (as we saw post financial crisis). Conversely, an unusually light LLR could be a problem in forward periods as its replenishment will drag on expenses.

Loan Loss Reserves/NPAs is a critical metric when assessing the adequacy of the reserve (Exhibit 2.25). Since write-offs usually come from assets already classified as nonperforming, this coverage ratio will help in determining if the bank has already set aside enough reserves to cover expected losses.

NCOs/Loans gives perspective to the size of charge-offs taken by expressing it as a percentage of loans (Exhibit 2.26). For reference, the industry average is in the 50 bps range, falling from a crisis peak of around 3% in 2010. The metric is usually reported at an annualized rate. Also note that NCOs drain the reserve, so this ratio in conjunction with the LLR/Loans ratio can give us a sense at how well reserved a bank is. For instance, if we see that NCOs

EXHIBIT 2.25 ALLL to Non-Current Loans and Leases

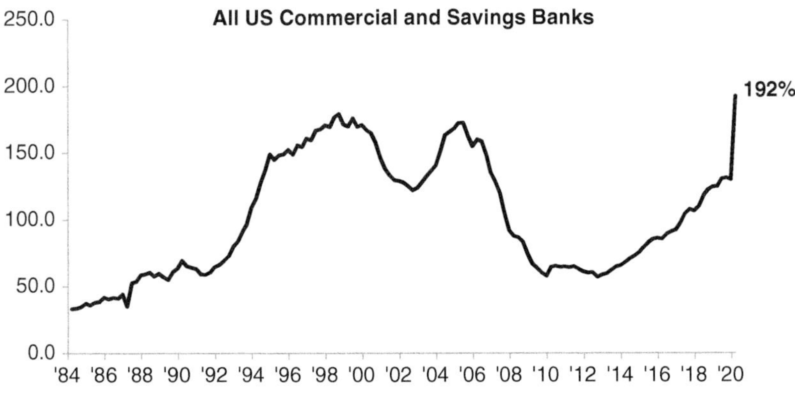

Source: FDIC

EXHIBIT 2.26 NCOs to Loans

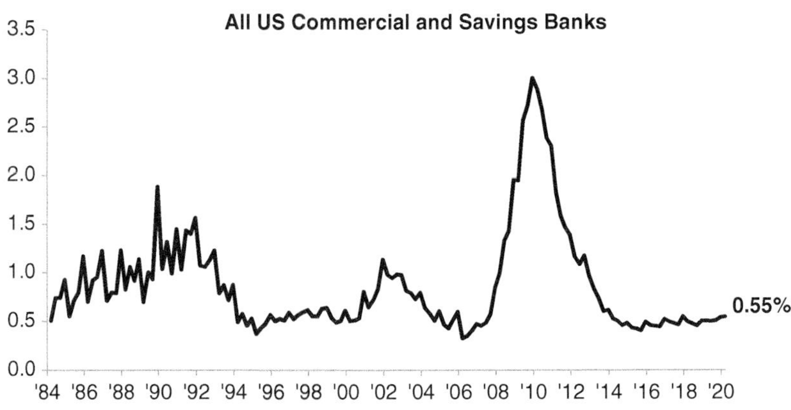

Source: FDIC

have been running at 20 bps of loans (annualized), and the loan loss reserve is 120 bps of loans, the reserve as-is would be able to absorb about six years of charge-offs before being completely depleted.

LLP/NCOs is a clever metric that shows us the directional change in the size of the reserve. Recall that loan loss provisions replenish the reserve, while NCOs drain the reserve. Thus, an LLP/NCO ratio of <1 indicates a decline in the size of the reserve, and generally represents improving sentiment for credit. In 2008, this ratio hit its peak at 176%; it subsequently bottomed out in 2013 at 57% and currently sits right around 100%.

LOANS AND DEPOSITS

Drilling down into the composition of the loan book and deposit base is one of the most critical aspects of understanding a bank. As we've reiterated before, a bank's core business is to take in deposits and to make loans, thus understanding what *type* of loans are being underwritten and held, and what *type* of deposits are gathered will help us ascertain a fair value of a bank franchise.

LOAN COMPOSITION

Banks undertake an incredibly diverse spectrum of lending, from unsecured short-term loans extended to businesses for working capital to 30-year mortgages for prospective homeowners. Likewise, the structure, term, and sensitivities to underlying economic trends will vary widely. Though banks have latitude with how they categorize and report their loan balances in public disclosures, regulatory guidelines are much more strict. As a result, most banks will report similar loan categories in their Qs and Ks.

Exhibit 2.27 represents the aggregate loan composition for all FDIC insured depositories. In total, it represents over $9.7 trillion in aggregate loans as of 1Q2018. As you can see, the largest lending categories are residential mortgage, commercial and industrial, and nonfarm nonresidential real estate. Though this aggregate pie chart gives a good idea of the entire banking landscape, it is important to note that the *average* bank certainly won't have a loan book as well-diversified as this. In fact, most would aspire to have a portfolio as well-balanced as this one. Most community banks are specialized, whether it be in commercial lending products (CRE, C&I) or in consumer lending products (1-4 family, HELOC).

Exhibit 2.28 shows the yield and credit quality metrics by loan types for the entire industry.

1–4 Family Residential Mortgage, also called *single-family residential (SFR) loans*, represent mortgages extended for the purchase of single-family residences, or the refinancing of such loans. These loans are collateralized by the underlying residential property. Mortgage within the US tends to be longer-dated: 10-year or 30-year terms with fixed rate, though Adjustable Rate Mortgages (ARMs) are a popular instrument as well. ARM structures can vary; general characteristics include a fixed-rate period, a benchmark interest rate, a cap on how frequently the rate can change, how much the interest rate

EXHIBIT 2.27 Loan Composition for All FDIC Insured Depository Institutions

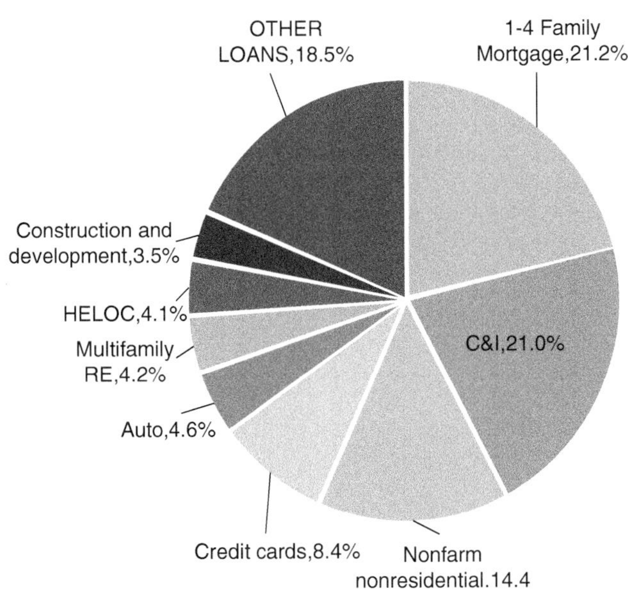

Source: FDIC

can change yearly, and how much the rate can cumulatively change over the entire term. For example, a 7/1 ARM is fixed for the first seven years before being adjustable once every year for the remaining term of the loan.

Stepping back for a moment, the mortgage market in the US is by-and-large a commoditized one, and as a result it is highly competitive. Mortgage-backed securities (MBS), packaged and guaranteed by Government Sponsored Entities (GSEs) like Fannie Mae and Freddie Mac, have helped in this homogenization. Institutions can sell "conforming" loans that conform to the standards set forth by the GSEs to be later securitized and resold into the market as low risk MBS. The conforming metrics change over time and by state but include the size of the loan, the borrower's loan-to-value, credit score, debt-to-income, and other documentation requirements. The commoditization of this product is purposeful, as the Federal government has strongly promoted home ownership. The result is that SFR is very competitive and it is difficult to earn high risk-adjusted returns on this product.

We can see evidence of the long-dated nature of mortgages in FNBG's loan maturity schedule (Exhibit 2.29), over 80% of mortgage matures after five years, compared to ~71% for the entire loan portfolio. The fixed rate nature

EXHIBIT 2.28 Interest Yield and Credit Metrics by Regulatory Loan Type

Loans Yields & Credit Quality	Avg Balance ($000)	Income ($000)	Yield (%)	30-89 Days Past Due Balance	30-89 Days Past Due % of Loan Type	30-89 Days Past Due % of 30-89 PD	90+ Days Past Due Balance	90+ Days Past Due % of Loan Type	90+ Days Past Due % of 90+ PD	Nonaccrual Balance	Nonaccrual % of Loan Type	Nonaccrual % of NonAccr	Tot Past Due & Nonaccr Balance	Tot Past Due & Nonaccr % of Loan Type	Tot Past Due & Nonaccr % of PD & NonAccr
1–4 family RE loans	2,214,159,251	22,612,357	4.09	22,085,551	1.00	38.11	27,328,397	1.23	67.15	28,704,556	1.29	47.60	78,118,504	3.52	49.14
other RE loans	2,036,940,818	23,123,460	4.54	275.052	0.40	0.47	32,933	0.05	0.08	275,064	0.40	0.46	583,049	0.84	0.37
Commercial & Industrial Loans	1,755,443,558	19,144,686	4.36	971,161	0.38	1.68	129,975	0.05	0.32	1,086,563	0.43	1.80	2,187,699	0.86	1.38
Credit Card Loans	701,909,860	23,385,166	13.33	1,246,213	0.39	2.15	162,908	0.05	0.40	1,361,627	0.42	2.26	2,770,748	0.86	1.74
Consumer Loans	740,826,919	9,484,141	5.12	451,643	0.13	0.78	37,679	0.01	0.09	435,014	0.13	0.72	924,336	0.28	0.58
Agricultural Loans	71,208,950	761,635	4.28	2,152,910	0.43	3.71	398,193	0.08	0.98	4,443,315	0.88	7.37	6,994,418	1.38	4.40
Leases	124,672,417	1,254,795	4.03	2,057,896	0.26	3.55	307,701	0.04	0.76	2,853,655	0.36	4.73	5,219,252	0.65	3.28
All Other Loans	906,499,941	7,623,943	3.36	3,149,339	0.30	5.43	321,788	0.03	0.79	1,872,793	0.18	3.11	5,343,920	0.52	3.36
Total Loans & Leases	**8,999,459,664**	**112,006,305**	**4.98**	**697,803**	**0.70**	**1.20**	**223,087**	**0.22**	**0.55**	**1,379,152**	**1.39**	**2.29**	**2,300,042**	**2.32**	**1.45**

Source: FDIC, S&P Global Market Intelligence

EXHIBIT 2.29 FNBG Loan Composition

TABLE 9

(Dollar amounts in thousands)	Maturing Within 1 Year	Maturing After 1 But Within 5 Years	Maturing After 5 Years	Total
Commercial real estate	$ 25,702	$ 76,323	$354,967	$456,992
Real estate construction	27,279	4,740	3,187	35,206
Real estate multi family	3,130	18,892	83,116	105,138
Real estate 1–4 family	11,007	22,777	139,692	173,476
Commercial & industrial	33,604	17,958	4,165	55,727
Consumer	1,294	391	12,372	14,057
Sub total	102,016	141,081	597,499	840,596
Net deferred loan fees	(104)	(323)	(232)	(659)
Total	$101,912	$140,758	$597,267	$839,937
With predetermines fixed interest rates	$ 15,459	$ 55,977	$195,757	$267,193
With floating interest rates	86,453	84,781	401,510	572,744
Total	$101,912	$ 140,758	$597,267	$839,937

Source: FNBG 2017 10-K

of mortgages means the asset class tends not to benefit from rising rates (at least not immediately). Additionally, the long-dated nature of most mortgages means their pricing is usually biased towards the longer end of the yield curve. Thus in an environment where short rates are increasing but long rates are not moving much, mortgage-heavy banks tend to suffer as their funding costs increase but their loan yields do not improve.

Commercial & Industrial (C&I) loans are simply loans extended to business and corporations. C&I comes in many flavors: They can be secured (other than by real estate) or unsecured, single-payment or installment, and fixed or floating. Generally, C&I loans are extended to small businesses, as larger entities have the ability to tap the capital markets directly for more favorable pricing. Generally, C&I loans tend to be shorter term in nature, with many of them floating-rate and tied to LIBOR or Prime. As a result, a rising interest rate environment benefits C&I loans more so than other types of loans, and bank investors will naturally flock to those banks that specialize in that type of lending.

As we mentioned, C&I is not a homogenous category. Some more popular ways of slicing up business loans include:

- *Working Capital/Seasonal Loans* – As the name suggests, these are shorter term loans extended to companies to fulfill seasonal or short-term cyclical capital needs. These can be secured or unsecured, though usually they are secured by accounts receivable or inventory.
- *Term Loans* – These loans are typically used to finance the acquisition of long-term capital assets, such as property, plant, and equipment. Term loans are longer-term in nature and can match the depreciable or useful life of the asset being financed. Again, these loans tend to be secured.
- *Asset Based Financing* refers to loans (both working capital and term) that are secured by collateral.
- *SBA Loans* are small business loans guaranteed by the Small Business Administration (SBA), a government agency that provides support to entrepreneurs and small businesses. SBA loans have to conform to the standards set forth by the SBA to qualify for a partial guarantee (usually 75–85% of the loan balance). SBA Loan programs include: 7(a)-, which is the most popular type of SBA lending and provides working capital needs for up to $5MM; 504-, which finances the purchasing of owner-occupied CRE; CAPLines for lines of credit; Export Loans for export financing; Microloans for working capital needs up to $50K; and Disaster Loans for companies that have been impacted by a declared natural disaster.

Commercial Real Estate (CRE) loans are essentially mortgage loans secured by a lien on a commercial property. Broad categories of commercial properties include office, retail, industrial, hospitality, and residential (as in residential buildings used to generate profits through rental or sale). In terms of interest rate sensitivity, much of the CRE financing provided by banks is on a floating-rate basis, while the term is usually shorter than in residential mortgage but longer than in C&I. *Loan-to-Values* for commercial real estate loans has regulatory limits that ranges from 65% (undeveloped land) up to 90% (owner-occupied).

Non-owner Occupied CRE is commercial property that is occupied by tenants *other* than the owner. This is the most classic type of CRE. The bank will focus more on analyzing the expected cash flows at the property level during its underwriting process.

Owner-occupied CRE is a commercial property where the owner is also the primary occupant (other than residential). Since the income at the property level is very much dependent on the cash flows of the owner, owner-occupied CRE loans can interpreted as a commercial loan that is collateralized by property. Thus, the underwriter will look more closely at the credit worthiness and projected cash flows of the owner-occupier, as opposed to being more focused on property level metrics.

We can see that our example bank, FNBG, is primarily a CRE lender as over 50% of loans are categorized as CRE.

DEPOSIT COMPOSITION

Deposits are arguably the marquee feature of a bank, giving them a substantial funding advantage over other types of lenders and representing a significant differentiating factor between banks. A good deposit franchise will be low cost, with low sensitivity to rising interest rates, and "sticky" with regards to flows. There are a few important deposit types that a bank has, each with its own unique features and sensitivities (Exhibit 2.30).

Transaction Accounts, as defined by the Federal Reserve, represent a bank account type that allows full and immediate access to funds with no delays or waiting periods. The positive side is that these types of accounts generally pay lower rates of interest. In fact, many deposit accounts pay zero interest. Transaction accounts are often the primary bank account for individuals and businesses, meaning there is a stickier and deeper relationship, which contributes to franchise value. The minor negative is that regulators require higher level of reserves for these deposits to ensure the liquidity of the depositor. However, the funding advantage more than makes up for the drag from the reserve requirement. According to the FDIC, transaction accounts make up about 18% of total domestic deposits.

Transaction accounts include *Demand Deposit* accounts and *Negotiable Order of Withdrawal (NOW)* accounts. *Demand Deposits* are payable on demand with no limit on the number of withdrawals or transfers that the account holder can make. These types of accounts are particularly sought after for commercial relationships. *NOW* accounts have pretty much the same characteristics except the bank reserves the right at any time to require at least seven days' prior written notice of an intended withdrawal. This type of deposit has become rarer in recent years.

Savings Accounts are interest-bearing deposits that provide a modest interest rate to depositors, but in turn, limit the number of "convenient" withdrawals or transactions that can be done per month to six. The bank also reserves the right to require seven days' advance written notice of an intended withdrawal (however this is rarely exercised).

Money Market Accounts and *Money Market Demand Accounts (MMDAs)* offer higher interest rates than savings and demand deposits, but generally require higher minimums and provide fewer transactions per month for the depositor. Before the mid-1980s, MMDAs had more distinctive characteristics from ordinary savings accounts; however, now they are more-or-less the same.

Time deposits are also known as certificates of deposits (CDs) or term deposits, and carry a fixed maturity date paying a specified interest rate. A CD

EXHIBIT 2.30 Deposit Composition

Table CB15													
Federal Deposit Insurance Corporation													
Deposits FDIC-Insured Commercial Banks US and Other Areas													
Balances at Year End, 1934–2017													
(Dollar amounts in thousands)													
Year	**Deposits / Domestic and Foreign**							**Domestic Office Deposits**					
						Memo						**Memo**	
	Individuals, Partnerships and Corporations	**US Government**	**States & Political Sub-divisions**	**All Other**	**Total Deposits, Domestic & Foreign**	**Interest Bearing**	**Non-Interest Bearing**	**Demand**	**Savings**	**Time**	**Total Domestic Deposits**	**Transaction**	**Non-Transaction**
2017	11,413,864,817	3,828,989	510,393,409	540,093,848	12,468,181,063	9,183,512,354	3,284,668,753	1,682,242,133	7,957,282,289	1,511,045,923	11,150,570,345	2,026,778,720	9,123,791,625

Source: FDIC

restricts access to funds until the maturity date, and as a result, pays a higher level of interest. Bank investors typically do not assign a lot of value to CDs. Depositors view them more like an investment vehicle, resulting in a very price competitive market for CDs. On the plus side, CDs can be raised relatively quickly; all it takes is a temporary promotion offering higher than market rates to attract deposits. Time deposits have *early withdrawal penalties,* which dissuade depositors from withdrawing money early. This is helpful in a low-rate environment, as a bank can "lock-in" low-cost funding. A bank and bank investors need to be wary of the maturity schedule for time deposits in order to assess liquidity and interest rate risk. Banks will also break out "jumbo" and "regular" CDs, with the delineation at $100,000.

Brokered deposits are defined by the FDIC as a deposit that is obtained (directly or indirectly) through the mediation or assistance of a deposit broker. Brokered deposits *can* be a suitable funding source, but as they do not require any direct relationship with a deposit customer, they are generally not assigned much value by bank investors. Additionally, a study by the FDIC in 2011 concluded that shares of brokered deposit funding used at failed institutions were significantly higher than at non-failed institutions during the past three bank crises. Interestingly, the study found that on average brokered deposits are an indicator of higher risk appetite, which drove higher growth and higher subsequent nonperforming loan ratios. See the link below for the study.

https://www.fdic.gov/regulations/reform/coredeposit-study.pdf

Banks will provide a similar table to Exhibit 2.31 that provides the average balances and rates for different deposit categories. Our example bank,

EXHIBIT 2.31 Average Rates by Deposit Type

TABLE 12

Average Deposits			
		2017	
(Dollar amounts in thousands)	**Average Balance**	**Average Rate**	**% of total Deposits**
Interest-bearing demand	$ 124,267	0.10%	12%
Money market	395,960	0.39%	38%
Savings	88,249	0.10%	9%
Time deposits $100,000 or more	89,594	0.91%	9%
Time deposits under $I00,000	34,377	0.66%	3%
Total interest bearing deposits	732,447	0.38%	71%
Demand deposits	300,670	—	29%
Total deposits	$1,033,117	0.27%	100%

Source: FNBG

FNBG, has a decent deposit franchise with only 27 bps in average cost, 29% in noninterest-bearing demand deposits, and only a relatively small 12% reliance on time deposits.

REGULATORY FILINGS

Public regulatory filings provide bank investors with additional financial data to use in their analysis. The two main benefits bank investors enjoy from regulatory filings are (1) advantageous timing compared to SEC filings and (2) the standardized nature of the forms and schedules, which make cross-sectional analysis more straightforward. However, we must be cognizant that regulatory filings do not necessarily reconcile with those made by public companies to the SEC. The two most helpful regulatory filings specific to banks that we will go over are the FFIEC Call Reports and the Federal Reserve Y-9s.

Call Reports, specifically forms FFIEC 031 and FFIEC 041, are required by every national bank, state member bank, insured state nonmember bank, and savings association. The Federal Financial Institutions Examination Council (FFIEC) is an interagency body that oversees the call reporting process required for all regulated depositories. Call reports are filed for the *bank level* entity, which means it might not match up one-for-one to bank holding company (BHC) level financials. Additionally, certain BHCs have multiple bank charters/subsidiaries, meaning multiple call reports for one entity.

Call reports are due 30 days after the end of the quarter. While in most cases the call reports come after the earnings release and before the filing of the 10-Q and 10-K, in some cases the call reports are available before the earnings release. Tracking this can sometimes give the investor an advantage.

FR Y-9s are financial reports that are required by the Federal Reserve for domestic *bank holding companies*. In 1985, the Y-9 reports were revised to parallel the call reports, thus the reporting fields are nearly identical to those in the call reports. FR Y-9's come in a variety of flavors.

- The FR Y-9Cs are required by domestic BHCs with total consolidated assets of $1 billion or more and all multibank holding companies with debt outstanding to the general public or engaged in certain nonbanking activities. These filings are done on a *consolidated* basis, making them the most useful filing for bank investors.
- The FR Y-9LPs are parent-company only financial statements for *large* BHCs.
- The FR Y-9SPs are parent-company only financial statements for *small* BHCs with below $1B in consolidated assets. These reports are only made on a semi-annual basis.

We recommend readers review an interesting academic study on the market reaction to bank regulatory reports:

Badertscher, B.A., Burks, J.J. & Easton, P.D. "The market reaction to bank regulatory reports." *Rev Account Stud* 23, 686–731 (2018).

https://doi.org/10.1007/s11142-018-9440-8

Exhibit 2.32 is a reconciliation between the matching schedules in the call report and Y-9s.

The income schedules are analogous to the income statement, showing financial performance metrics *over a period of time.* In addition, the schedule will have a detailed table on charge-offs and its effects on the loan loss reserve.

EXHIBIT 2.32 Call Report and Y-9s

	Call Report	**Y-9**
Income Statement	Schedule RI—Income Statement	Schedule HI—Consolidated Income Statement
	Schedule RI-A—Changes in Bank Equity Capital	Schedule HI-A—Changes in Equity Capital
	Schedule RI-B—Charge-offs and Recoveries on Loans and Leases and Changes in ALLL	Schedule HI-B—Charge-Offs and Recoveries on Loans and Leases and Changes in ALLL
	Schedule RI-C—Disaggregated Data on the Allowance for Loan and Lease Losses	Schedule HI-C—Disaggregated Data on the Allowance for Loan and Lease Losses
	Schedule RI-E—Explanations	
Balance Sheet	Schedule RC—Balance Sheet	Schedule HC—Consolidated Balance Sheet
	Schedule RCA—Cash and Balances Due from Depository Institutions	-
	Schedule RC-B—Securities	Schedule HC-B—Securities
	Schedule RC-C—Loans and Lease Financing Receivables	Schedule HC-C—Loans and Lease Financing Receivables
	Schedule RC-D—Trading Assets and Liabilities	Schedule HC-D—Trading Assets and Liabilities
	Schedule RC-E—Deposit Liabilities	Schedule HC-E—Deposit Liabilities

(Continued)

EXHIBIT 2.32 *(Continued)*

Call Report	Y-9
Schedule RC-F—Other Assets	Schedule HC-F— Other Assets
Schedule RC-G—Other Liabilities	Schedule HC-G—Other Liabilities
-	Schedule HC-H—Interest Sensitivity
	Schedule HC-I—Insurance-Related Underwriting Activities (Including Reinsurance)
Schedule RC-K—Quarterly Averages	Schedule HC-K—Quarterly Averages
Schedule RC-L—Derivatives and Off-Balance Sheet Items	Schedule HC-L—Derivatives and Off-Balance Sheet Items
Schedule RC-M—Memoranda	Schedule HC-M—Memoranda
Schedule RC-N—Past Due and Nonaccrual Loans, Leases, and Other Assets	Schedule HC-N—Past Due and Nonaccrual Loans, Leases, and Other Assets
Schedule RC-O—Other Data for Deposit Insurance and FICO Assessments	-
Schedule RC P—1-4 Family Residential Mortgage Banking Activities	Schedule HC-P—Closed-End 1-4 Family Residential Mortgage Banking Activities
Schedule RC-Q—Assets and Liabilities Measured at Fair Value on a Recurring Basis	Schedule HC-Q—Financial Assets and Liabilities Measured at Fair Value
Schedule RC-R—Regulatory Capital	Schedule HC-R—Regulatory Capital
Schedule RC-S—Servicing, Securitization, and Asset Sale Activities	Schedule HC-S—Servicing, Securitization, and Asset Sale Activities
Schedule RC-T—Fiduciary and Related Services	-
Schedule RC-V—Variable Interest Entities	Schedule HC-V—Variable Interest Entities

Meanwhile, the *report of condition* is related to all things balance sheet. That is, it provides information on the financial conditions of a bank at a *specific point in time.* Since banks are balance sheet driven entities, and regulators are concerned with the financial health of an entity, these schedules are

EXHIBIT 2.33 Who Files What

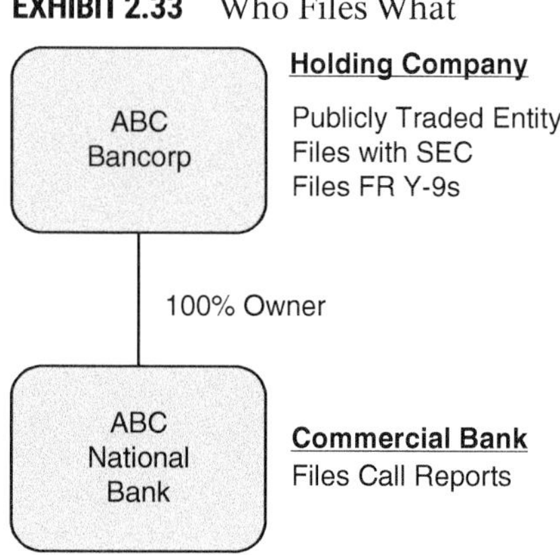

substantially longer and more comprehensive than the income schedules. Specifically, there is enhanced granularity when it comes to the nonperforming assets on the balance sheet.

As a refresher, Exhibit 2.33 is a diagram showing the most common type of organization structure, a simple one-bank holding company structure. The wholly owned commercial bank is the entity that files call reports, while the holding company files Y-9s.

Reconciliation Example

We will look at how the call report, Y-9, and 10-K financial tables match up for our example bank, FNBG, which is structured as a simple one-bank holding company (Exhibits 2.34, 2.35, 2.36 and 2.37).

We can see that the constituents of spread revenues, interest income, and interest expense items line up pretty closely. Total interest income is virtually identical between the call report, Y-9C, and 10-K. Meanwhile, total interest expense differs by $214,000 on the call report. This is because there is outstanding debt at the bank holding company level, thus the interest expense on that debt does not show up at the bank level call reports. Provision for loan losses match up, and is one of the more important insights one can glean from the call reports, as it rarely differs from the BHC.

On to the noninterest-related items: Fee revenues line up fairly directly. One note: Realized gains on AFS securities are *not* included in the noninterest income subtotal for the call report and Y-9, but *are* included in the 10K. Meanwhile, call report expenses are a bit lower than on the consolidated financials.

EXHIBIT 2.34 Income Statement – A

CALL REPORT

Schedule RI - Income Statement

Dollar amounts in thousands			
1. Interest income:			
a. Interest and fee income on loans:			
1. Loans secured by real estate:			
a. Loans secured by 1-4 family residential properties	RIAD4435	7,892	
b. All other loans secured by real estate	RIAD4436	30,551	
2. Commercial and industrial loans	RIAD4012	2,911	
3. Loans to individuals for household, family, and other personal expenditures:			
a. Credit cards	RIADB485	239	
b. Other (includes revolving credit plans other than credit cards, automobile loans, and other consumer loans)	RIADB486	363	
4. Not applicable			
5. All other loans[1]	RIAD4058	0	
6. Total interest and fee income on loans (sum of items 1.a.(1)(a) through 1.a.(5))	RIAD4010	41,956	
b. Income from lease financing receivables	RIAD4065	0	
c. Interest income on balances due from depository institutions[2]	RIAD4115	126	
d. Interest and dividend income on securities:			
1. U.S. Treasury securities and U.S. Government agency obligations (excluding mortgage-backed securities)	RIADB488	819	
2. Mortgage-backed securities	RIADB489	2,934	
3. All other securities (includes securities issued by states and political subdivisions in the U.S.)	RIAD4060	4,382	
e. Not applicable			
f. Interest income on federal funds sold and securities purchased under agreements to resell	RIAD4020	0	
g. Other interest income	RIAD4518	0	
h. Total interest income (sum of items 1.a.(6) through 1.g)	RIAD4107	50,217	A
2. Interest expense:			
a. Interest on deposits:			
1. Transaction accounts (interest-bearing demand deposits, NOW accounts, ATS accounts, and telephone and preauthorized transfer accounts)	RIAD4508	19	
2. Nontransaction accounts:			
a. Savings deposits (includes MMDAs)	RIAD0093	1,752	
b. Time deposits of $250,000 or less	RIADHK03	535	
c. Time deposits of more than $250,000	RIADHK04	501	
b. Expense of federal funds purchased and securities sold under agreements to repurchase	RIAD4180	0	
c. Interest on trading liabilities and other borrowed money	RIAD4185	850	
d. Interest on subordinated notes and debentures	RIAD4200	0	
e. Total interest expense (sum of items 2.a through 2.d)	RIAD4073	3,657	B
3. Net interest income (item 1.h minus 2.e)	RIAD4074	46,560	
4. Provision for loan and lease losses	RIAD4230	-360	C

EXHIBIT 2.34 *(Continued)*

Y-9

Schedule HI—Consolidated Income Statement

Dollar Amounts in Thousands	BHCK	Amount	
1. Interest income			
a. Interest and fee income on loans:			
(1) In domestic offices:			
(a) Loans secured by 1–4 family residential properties	4435	7,892	
(b) All other loans secured by real estate	4436	30,551	
(c) All other loans	F821	3,513	
(2) In foreign offices, Edge and Agreement subsidiaries, and IBFs	4059	0	
b. Income from lease financing receivables	4065	0	
c. Interest income on balances due from depository institutions[1]	4115	126	
d. Interest and dividend income on securities:			
(1) U.S. Treasury securities and U.S. government agency obligations (excluding mortgage-backed securities)	B488	819	
(2) Mortgage-backed securities	B489	2,934	
(3) All other securities	4060	4,382	
e. Interest income from trading assets	4069	0	
f. Interest income on federal funds sold and securities purchased under agreements to resell	4020	0	
g. Other interest income	4518	0	
h. Total interest income (sum of items 1.a through 1.g)	4107	50,217	A
2. Interest expense			
a. Interest on deposits:			
(1) In domestic offices:			
(a) Time deposits of $250,000 or less	HK03	535	
(b) Time deposits of more than $250,000	HK04	501	
(c) Other deposits	6761	1,771	
(2) In foreign offices, Edge and Agreement subsidiaries, and IBFs	4172	0	
b. Expense on federal funds purchased and securities sold under agreements to repurchase	4180	0	
c. Interest on trading liabilities and other borrowed money (excluding subordinated notes and debentures)	4185	850	
d. Interest on subordinated notes and debentures and on mandatory convertible securities	4397	0	
e. Other interest expense	4398	214	
f. Total interest expense (sum of items 2.a through 2.e)	4073	3,871	B
3. Net interest income (item 1.h minus item 2.f)	4074	46,346	
4. Provision for loan and lease losses (from Schedule HI-B, part II, item 5)	4230	-360	C

EXHIBIT 2.34 *(Continued)*

10-K

FNB BANCORP AND SUBSIDIARY
Consolidated Statements of Earnings
Years ended December 31, 2017, 2016 and 2015
(Dollar amounts and average shares are in thousands, except earnings per share amounts)

		2017	
Interest income:			
Interest and fees on loans	$	41,956	
Interest and dividends on taxable securities		5,209	
Interest on tax-exempt securities		2,927	
Interest on deposits with other financial institutions		126	
Total interest income		50,218	A
Interest expense:			
Interest on deposits		2,807	
Interest on FHLB advances		850	
Interest on note payable		214	
Total interest expense		3,871	B
Net interest income		46,347	
(Recovery of) provision for loan losses		(360)	C
Net interest income after provision for (recovery of) loan losses		46,707	
Noninterest income:			
Service charges		2,264	
Net gain on sale of available-for-sale securities		210	
Earnings on bank-owned life insurance		390	
Other income		996	
Total noninterest income		3,860	
Noninterest expense:			
Salaries and employee benefits		19,366	
Occupancy expense		2,747	
Equipment expense		1,646	
Professional fees		1,482	
FDIC assessment		400	
Telephone, postage, supplies		1,267	
Advertising expense		451	
Data processing expense		571	
Low income housing expense		472	
Surety insurance		349	
Director expense		288	
Other real estate owned expense (recovery)		80	
Other expense		1,430	
Total noninterest expense		30,549	
Earnings before provision for income taxes		20,018	
Provision for income taxes		9,307	
Net earnings	$	10,711	
Earnings per share available to common stockholders:			
Basic	$	1.46	
Diluted	$	1.41	
Weighted average shares outstanding:			
Basic		7,361	
Diluted		7,607	

EXHIBIT 2.35 Income Statement – B

CALL REPORT

Item	Code	Amount	
5. Noninterest income:			
a. Income from fiduciary activities [1]	RIAD4070	0	
b. Service charges on deposit accounts	RIAD4080	1,232	
c. Trading revenue[2]	RIADA220	0	
d. Not available			
1. Fees and commissions from securities brokerage	RIADC886	0	
2. Investment banking, advisory, and underwriting fees and commissions	RIADC888	0	
3. Fees and commissions from annuity sales	RIADC887	0	
4. Underwriting income from insurance and reinsurance activities	RIADC386	0	
5. Income from other insurance activities	RIADC387	0	
e. Venture capital revenue	RIADB491	0	
f. Net servicing fees	RIADB492	0	
g. Net securitization income	RIADB493	0	
h. Not applicable			
i. Net gains (losses) on sales of loans and leases	RIAD5416	94	
j. Net gains (losses) on sales of other real estate owned	RIAD5415	0	
k. Net gains (losses) on sales of other assets[3]	RIADB496	0	
l. Other noninterest income*	RIADB497	2,324	
m. Total noninterest income (sum of items 5.a through 5.l)	RIAD4079	3,650	D
6. Not available			
a. Realized gains (losses) on held-to-maturity securities	RIAD3521	0	
b. Realized gains (losses) on available-for-sale securities	RIAD3196	210	E
7. Noninterest expense:			
a. Salaries and employee benefits	RIAD4135	19,366	
b. Expenses of premises and fixed assets (net of rental income) (excluding salaries and employee benefits and mortgage interest)	RIAD4217	3,685	
c. Not available			
1. Goodwill impairment losses	RIADC216	0	
2. Amortization expense and impairment losses for other intangible assets	RIADC232	171	
d. Other noninterest expense*	RIAD4092	7,010	
e. Total noninterest expense (sum of items 7.a through 7.d)	RIAD4093	30,232	F
8. Income (loss) before applicable income taxes and discontinued operations (item 3 plus or minus items 4, 5.m, 6.a, 6.b, and 7.e)	RIAD4301	20,548	
9. Applicable income taxes (on item 8)	RIAD4302	9,307	
10. Income (loss) before discontinued operations (item 8 minus item 9)	RIAD4300	11,241	
11. Discontinued operations, net of applicable income taxes (Describe on Schedule RI-E - Explanations)*	RIADFT28	0	
12. Net income (loss) attributable to bank and noncontrolling (minority) interests (sum of items 10 and 11)	RIADG104	11,241	
13. LESS: Net income (loss) attributable to noncontrolling (minority) interests (if net income, report as a positive value; if net loss, report as a negative value)	RIADG103	0	
14. Net income (loss) attributable to bank (item 12 minus item 13)	RIAD4340	11,241	G

EXHIBIT 2.35 *(Continued)*

Y-9

Item	Code	Amount	
5. Noninterest income:			
a. Income from fiduciary activities	4070	0	
b. Service charges on deposit accounts in domestic offices	4483	1,232	
c. Trading revenue[2]	A220	0	
d. (1) Fees and commissions from securities brokerage	C886	0	
(2) Investment banking, advisory, and underwriting fees and commissions	C888	0	
(3) Fees and commissions from annuity sales	C887	0	
(4) Underwriting income from insurance and reinsurance activities	C386	0	
(5) Income from other insurance activities	C387	0	
e. Venture capital revenue	B491	0	
f. Net servicing fees	B492	0	
g. Net securitization income	B493	0	
h. Not applicable			
i. Net gains (losses) on sales of loans and lease	8560	94	
j. Net gains (losses) on sales of other real estate owned	8561	0	
k. Net gains (losses) on sales of other assets[3]	B496	0	
l. Other noninterest income[4]	B497	2,324	
m. Total noninterest income (sum of items 5.a through 5.l)	4079	3,650	D
6. a. Realized gains (losses) on held-to-maturity securities	3521	0	
b. Realized gains (losses) on available-for-sale securities	3196	210	E
7. Noninterest expense:			
a. Salaries and employee benefits	4135	19,366	
b. Expenses of premises and fixed assets (net of rental income) (excluding salaries and employee benefits and mortgage interest)	4217	3,685	
c. (1) Goodwill impairment losses	C216	0	
(2) Amortization expense and impairment losses for other intangible assets	C232	171	
d. Other noninterest expense[5]	4092	7,326	
e. Total noninterest expense (sum of items 7.a through 7.d)	4093	30,548	F
8. Income (loss) before applicable income taxes and discontinued operations (sum of items 3, 5.m, 6.a, and 6.b minus items 4 and 7.e)	4301	20,018	
9. Applicable income taxes (foreign and domestic)	4302	9,307	
10. Income (loss) before discontinued operations (item 8 minus item 9)	4300	10,711	
11. Discontinued operations, net of applicable income taxes[6]	FT28	0	
12. Net income (loss) attributable to holding company and noncontrolling (minority) interests (sum of items 10 and 11)	G104	10,711	
13. LESS: Net income (loss) attributable to noncontrolling (minority) interests (if net income, report as a positive value; if net loss, report as a negative value)	G103	0	
14. Net income (loss) attributable to holding company (item 12 minus item 13)	4340	10,711	G

EXHIBIT 2.35 *(Continued)*

10-K

FNB BANCORP AND SUBSIDIARY
Consolidated Statements of Earnings
Years ended December 31, 2017, 2016 and 2015
(Dollar amounts and average shares are in thousands, except earnings per share amounts)

		2017	
Interest income:			
Interest and fees on loans	$	41,956	
Interest and dividends on taxable securities		5,209	
Interest on tax-exempt securities		2,927	
Interest on deposits with other financial institutions		126	
Total interest income		50,218	
Interest expense:			
Interest on deposits		2,807	
Interest on FHLB advances		850	
Interest on note payable		214	
Total interest expense		3,871	
Net interest income		46,347	
(Recovery of) provision for loan losses		(360)	
Net interest income after provision for (recovery of) loan losses		46,707	
Noninterest income:			
Service charges		2,264	
Net gain on sale of available-for-sale securities		210	
Earnings on bank-owned life insurance		390	
Other income		996	
Total noninterest income		3,860	D+E
Noninterest expense:			
Salaries and employee benefits		19,366	
Occupancy expense		2,747	
Equipment expense		1,646	
Professional fees		1,482	
FDIC assessment		400	
Telephone, postage, supplies		1,267	
Advertising expense		451	
Data processing expense		571	
Low income housing expense		472	
Surety insurance		349	
Director expense		288	
Other real estate owned expense (recovery)		80	
Other expense		1,430	
Total noninterest expense		30,549	F
Earnings before provision for income taxes		20,018	
Provision for income taxes		9,307	
Net earnings	$	10,711	G
Earnings per share available to common stockholders:			
Basic	$	1.46	
Diluted	$	1.41	
Weighted average shares outstanding:			
Basic		7,361	
Diluted		7,607	

EXHIBIT 2.36 Balance Sheet – A

CALL REPORT

Schedule RC - Balance Sheet

All schedules are to be reported in thousands of dollars. Unless otherwise indicated, report the amount outstanding as of the last business day of the quarter.

Dollar amounts in thousands			
1. Cash and balances due from depository institutions (from Schedule RC-A):			
a. Noninterest-bearing balances and currency and coin[1]	RCON0081	14,086	A
b. Interest-bearing balances[2]	RCON0071	4,397	
2. Securities:			
a. Held-to-maturity securities (from Schedule RC-B, column A)	RCON1754	0	
b. Available-for-sale securities (from Schedule RC-B, column D)	RCON1773	355,857	B
3. Federal funds sold and securities purchased under agreements to resell:			
a. Federal funds sold	RCONB987	0	
b. Securities purchased under agreements to resell[3]	RCONB989	0	
4. Loans and lease financing receivables (from Schedule RC-C):			
a. Loans and leases held for sale	RCON5369	0	
b. Loans and leases held for investment	RCONB528	839,937	
c. LESS: Allowance for loan and lease losses	RCON3123	10,171	
d. Loans and leases held for investment, net of allowance (item 4.b minus 4.c)	RCONB529	829,766	C
5. Trading assets (from Schedule RC-D)	RCON3545	0	
6. Premises and fixed assets (including capitalized leases)	RCON2145	9,277	
7. Other real estate owned (from Schedule RC-M)	RCON2150	3,300	
8. Investments in unconsolidated subsidiaries and associated companies	RCON2130	0	
9. Direct and indirect investments in real estate ventures	RCON3656	1,358	
10. Intangible assets:			
a. Goodwill	RCON3163	4,580	D
b. Other intangible assets (from Schedule RC-M)	RCON0426	344	
11. Other assets (from Schedule RC-F)	RCON2160	42,510	
12. Total assets (sum of items 1 through 11)	RCON2170	1,265,475	E

EXHIBIT 2.36 *(Continued)*

Y-9

Schedule HC—Consolidated Balance Sheet

Dollar Amounts in Thousands			BHCK	Amount	
Assets					
1. Cash and balances due from depository institutions:					
a. Noninterest-bearing balances and currency and coin[1]			0081	14,086	A
b. Interest-bearing balances:[2]					A
(1) In U.S. offices			0395	4,397	A
(2) In foreign offices, Edge and Agreement subsidiaries, and IBFs			0397	0	
2. Securities:					
a. Held-to-maturity securities (from Schedule HC-B, column A)			1754	0	
b. Available-for-sale securities (from Schedule HC-B, column D)			1773	355,857	B
3. Federal funds sold and securities purchased under agreements to resell:					
a. Federal funds sold in domestic offices			BHDM B987	0	
b. Securities purchased under agreements to resell[3]			BHCK B989	0	
4. Loans and lease financing receivables:					
a. Loans and leases held for sale			5369	0	
b. Loans and leases, net of unearned income	B528	839,937			
c. LESS: Allowance for loan and lease losses	3123	10,171			
d. Loans and leases, net of unearned income and allowance for loan and lease losses (item 4.b minus 4.c)			B529	829,766	C
5. Trading assets (from Schedule HC-D)			3545	0	
6. Premises and fixed assets (including capitalized leases)			2145	9,277	
7. Other real estate owned (from Schedule HC-M)			2150	3,300	
8. Investments in unconsolidated subsidiaries and associated companies			2130	0	
9. Direct and indirect investments in real estate ventures			3656	1,358	
10. Intangible assets:					
a. Goodwill			3163	4,580	D
b. Other intangible assets (from Schedule HC-M)			0426	344	
11. Other assets (from Schedule HC-F)			2160	42,510	
12. Total assets (sum of items 1 through 11)			2170	1,265,475	E

EXHIBIT 2.36 *(Continued)*

10-K

FNB BANCORP AND SUBSIDIARY
Consolidated Balance Sheets
December 31, 2017 and 2016

Assets

(Dollar amounts in thousands)	2017	
Cash and due from banks	$ 18,353	A
Interest-bearing time deposits with financial institutions	130	
Securities available-for-sale, at fair value	355,857	B
Other equity securities	7,567	
Loans, net of deferred loan fees and allowance for loan losses of $10,171 and $10,167 on December 31, 2017 and December 31, 2016	829,766	C
Bank premises, equipment, and leasehold improvements, net	9,322	
Bank owned life insurance	16,637	
Accrued interest receivable	5,317	
Other real estate owned, net	3,300	
Goodwill	4,580	D
Prepaid expenses	825	
Other assets	13,584	
Total assets	$ 1,265,238	E

Liabilities and Stockholders' Equity

Deposits		
Demand, noninterest bearing	$ 313,435	
Demand, interest bearing	130,988	
Savings and money market	467,788	
Time	138,084	
Total deposits	1,050,295	
Federal Home Loan Bank advances	75,000	
Note payable	3,750	
Accrued expenses and other liabilities	16,913	
Total liabilities	1,145,958	
Commitments and Contingencies (Note 12)		
Stockholders' equity		
Common stock, no par value, authorized 10,000,000 shares; issued and outstanding 7,442,279 shares at December 31, 2017 and 7,280,122 shares at December 31, 2016	85,565	
Retained earnings	34,654	
Accumulated other comprehensive loss, net of tax	(939)	
Total stockholders' equity	119,280	
Total liabilities and stockholders' equity	$ 1,265,238	

EXHIBIT 2.37 Balance Sheet – B

CALL REPORT

Item	Code	Amount	
13. Deposits:			
a. In domestic offices (sum of totals of columns A and C from Schedule RC-E)	RCON2200	1,052,242	F
1. Noninterest-bearing[4]	RCON6631	315,382	
2. Interest-bearing	RCON6636	736,860	
b. Not applicable			
14. Federal funds purchased and securities sold under agreements to repurchase:			
a. Federal funds purchased[5]	RCONB993	0	
b. Securities sold under agreements to repurchase[6]	RCONB995	0	
15. Trading liabilities (from Schedule RC-D)	RCON3548	0	
16. Other borrowed money (includes mortgage indebtedness and obligations under capitalized leases) (from Schedule RC-M)	RCON3190	75,000	G
17. Not applicable			
18. Not applicable			
19. Subordinated notes and debentures[7]	RCON3200	0	
20. Other liabilities (from Schedule RC-G)	RCON2930	17,137	
21. Total liabilities (sum of items 13 through 20)	RCON2948	1,144,379	
22. Not applicable			
23. Perpetual preferred stock and related surplus	RCON3838	0	
24. Common stock	RCON3230	20,899	
25. Surplus (exclude all surplus related to preferred stock)	RCON3839	21,530	
26. Not available			
a. Retained earnings	RCON3632	79,606	
b. Accumulated other comprehensive income[1]	RCONB530	-939	
c. Other equity capital components[2]	RCONA130	0	
27. Not available			
a. Total bank equity capital (sum of items 23 through 26.c)	RCON3210	121,096	
b. Noncontrolling (minority) interests in consolidated subsidiaries	RCON3000	0	
28. Total equity capital (sum of items 27.a and 27.b)	RCONG105	121,096	H
29. Total liabilities and equity capital (sum of items 21 and 28)	RCON3300	1,265,475	I
1. Indicate in the box at the right the number of the statement below that best describes the most comprehensive level of auditing work performed for the bank by independent external auditors as of any date during 2016	RCON6724	NR	
2. Bank's fiscal year-end date (report the date in MMDD format)	RCON8678	NR	

EXHIBIT 2.37 *(Continued)*

Y-9

Item	Code	Amount	Mark
Liabilities			
13. Deposits:			
a. In domestic offices (from Schedule HC-E):			
(1) Noninterest-bearing[1]	6631	313,435	F
(2) Interest-bearing	6636	736,860	
b. In foreign offices, Edge and Agreement subsidiaries, and IBFs:	BHFN		
(1) Noninterest-bearing	6631	0	
(2) Interest-bearing	6636	0	
14. Federal funds purchased and securities sold under agreements to repurchase:	BHDM		
a. Federal funds purchased in domestic offices[2]	B993	0	
	BHCK		
b. Securities sold under agreements to repurchase[3]	B995	0	
15. Trading liabilities (from Schedule HC-D)	3548	0	
16. Other borrowed money (includes mortgage indebtedness and obligations under capitalized leases) (from Schedule HC-M)	3190	78,750	G
17. Not applicable.			
18. Not applicable.			
19. a. Subordinated notes and debentures[4]	4062	0	
b. Subordinated notes payable to unconsolidated trusts issuing trust preferred securities, and trust preferred securities issued by consolidated special purpose entities	C699	0	
20. Other liabilities (from Schedule HC-G)	2750	17,150	
21. Total liabilities (sum of items 13 through 20)	2948	1,146,195	
22. Not applicable.			
Equity Capital			
Holding Company Equity Capital			
23. Perpetual preferred stock and related surplus	3283	0	
24. Common stock (par value)	3230	85,564	
25. Surplus (exclude all surplus related to preferred stock)	3240	0	
26. a. Retained earnings	3247	34,655	
b. Accumulated other comprehensive income[5]	B530	-939	
c. Other equity capital components[6]	A130	0	
27. a. Total holding company equity capital (sum of items 23 through 26.c)	3210	119,280	
b. Noncontrolling (minority) interests in consolidated subsidiaries	3000	0	
28. Total equity capital (sum of items 27.a and 27.b)	G105	119,280	H
29. Total liabilities and equity capital (sum of items 21 and 28)	3300	1,265,475	I

EXHIBIT 2.37 *(Continued)*

10-K

FNB BANCORP AND SUBSIDIARY
Consolidated Balance Sheets
December 31, 2017 and 2016

Assets

(Dollar amounts in thousands)		2017	
Cash and due from banks	$	18,353	
Interest-bearing time deposits with financial institutions		130	
Securities available-for-sale, at fair value		355,857	
Other equity securities		7,567	
Loans, net of deferred loan fees and allowance for loan losses of $10,171 and $10,167 on December 31, 2017 and December 31, 2016		829,766	
Bank premises, equipment, and leasehold improvements, net		9,322	
Bank owned life insurance		16,637	
Accrued interest receivable		5,317	
Other real estate owned, net		3,300	
Goodwill		4,580	
Prepaid expenses		825	
Other assets		13,584	
Total assets	$	1,265,238	

Liabilities and Stockholders' Equity

		2017	
Deposits			
Demand, noninterest bearing	$	313,435	
Demand, interest bearing		130,988	
Savings and money market		467,788	
Time		138,084	
Total deposits		1,050,295	F
Federal Home Loan Bank advances		75,000	G
Note payable		3,750	
Accrued expenses and other liabilities		16,913	
Total liabilities		1,145,958	
Commitments and Contingencies (Note 12)			
Stockholders' equity			
Common stock, no par value, authorized 10,000,000 shares; issued and outstanding 7,442,279 shares at December 31, 2017 and 7,280,122 shares at December 31, 2016		85,565	
Retained earnings		34,654	
Accumulated other comprehensive loss, net of tax		(939)	
Total stockholders' equity		119,280	H
Total liabilities and stockholders' equity	$	1,265,238	I

This is usually the case as there will be some separate expenses that the holding company recognizes.

The net result of this exercise shows that we can use Y-9C filings as a very close proxy to the 10-K results. Further, we see that *revenues* match up relatively well, as one would expect as the bank-level entity *should* be the entity generating all the operating revenues. Unfortunately, the final number that we need to calculate EPS, weighted average shares outstanding, is not disclosed in either the call report or Y-9C.

In our example bank, FNBG, the important line items on the asset side of the balance sheet line up: cash and equivalents, securities, gross loans, and the loan loss reserve.

On the other side of the balance sheet, important items like deposits match up between the Y-9 and 10-K. Importantly, the call report misses the $3.75MM in notes payable, since it is debt held at the parent company level. Instead, proceeds from that note are downstreamed to the bank in the form of equity capital; hence, the higher equity capital in the bank level call report compared to the BHC level figures.

CHAPTER 3

Capital

"An essential message of the M & M Propositions as applied to banking, in sum is that you cannot hope to lever up a sow's ear into a silk purse. You may think you can during the good times; but you will give it all back and more when the bad times roll around."

– Merton H. Miller, *Journal of Banking and Finance,* 1995

CAPITAL FOR A BANK

Capital serves as a cushion that allows a bank to absorb losses. The assets of a bank, namely the loans made and securities held, carry risk. Specifically, the loans may not be repaid, and the securities may fall in value. Regulators therefore require that a certain portion of these assets be supported by capital to protect depositors. Regulators, given the desire to protect depositors, are likely to want higher capital levels. Equity investors would be more desirous of an optimal capital level which is high enough to support growth and assuage regulators and yet be low enough to allow for an adequate return on capital.

The protection that capital affords comes in different forms. Apart from common equity, preferred stock and subordinated debt are also counted as different types of capital.

Likewise, there are many different capital and leverage ratios that bank investors can use in their capital adequacy analysis. We are partial to using what is known as the *TCE Ratio* (Tangible Common Equity/Tangible Assets) as it is conservative, intuitive, and easily comparable between institutions. There is no obligation for repayment of equity and thus this permanent capital is therefore the last line of safety. Theoretically, from the perspective of a bank investor, the capital level should be the least amount allowed by regulation during normal times. During times of stress, having some excess capital will reduce the likelihood of a dilutive capital raise. Though not every bank is identical, if we were to draw a baseline TCE/TA, we would think around 9% TCE/TA would be the baseline for pre-COVID-19 credit conditions, and we would have viewed anything additional as excess capital. Chapter 5 on

EXHIBIT 3.1 TCE/TA Ratio by Asset Size

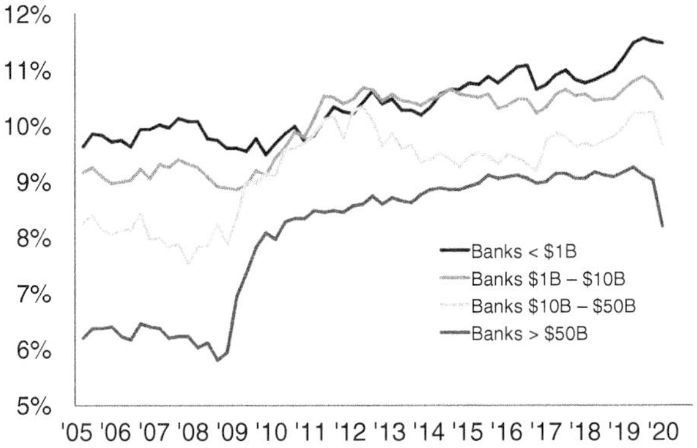

Source: S&P Global Market Intelligence

valuation goes over our thoughts on valuing excess capital. Exhibit 3.1 plots the TCE/TA Ratio for US banks over time, grouped by asset size. Observe that smaller banks generally have higher capital ratios as they tend to grow faster and have less diversification benefits.

CAPITAL LEVELS

After the global financial crisis, there has been a school of thought that believes that banks need to be fortified with higher capital. Having some slack with excess capital will definitely reduce fragility in the banking system. However, forcing banks to have higher levels of capital would by no means be a panacea to prevent the next financial crisis. It is our view that having improved risk monitoring and management processes and an active dialog between regulators, management teams, and investors is better than forcing banks to just have higher levels of equity capital. Forcing excess capital requirements without risk management could potentially lead to perverse reactions such as a bank transferring its assets off balance sheet (making analysis tougher and taking overall risk higher). It can also increase the cost of capital for banks, forcing them to increase pricing. This in turn could lead to reduced credit availability and lower GDP growth. Reduced credit availability from banks may drive borrowers to alternative lenders (shadow banks) who may not have the same capital constraints. All this would do is displace the epicenter of the next financial crisis from regulated financial institutions to shadow banks. During times of stress and contagion, risk will not remain contained in one sector; it will ripple through adjacent sectors. The market has a relative value framework and thus when spreads in one sector blow up, they typically do not blow up in isolation. We view the research in this area to be interesting, albeit inconclusive.

Recommended Reading

1. "Optimal Bank Capital" by David Miles, Jing Yang, and Gilberto Marcheggiano, published as a discussion paper by the Bank of England;
2. "Benefits and Costs of a Higher Bank Leverage Ratio" by James R. Barth and Stephen Matteo Miller, published as a working paper by the Mercatus Center at George Mason University; and
3. "Do the M&M Propositions Apply to Banks" by Merton H. Miller in the *Journal of Banking & Finance*.

CAPITAL STRUCTURE FOR A BANK

Franco Modigliani and Merton Miller are the authors of the eponymous Modigliani and Miller Propositions (M&M) on capital structure. The M&M propositions state:

1. The value of a firm is independent of the percentage of debt or equity in its capital structure. Thus, the value is determined by the left-hand side of the balance sheet (assets) and not by the proportion of debt and equity capital financing the assets.
2. The cost of equity capital increases with the proportion of debt in the capital structure.

These propositions assume conditions where there are no taxes, costs for financial distress, and agency costs, and where there is no information asymmetry.

Investors unfortunately live in the real world where these simplifying assumptions cannot be made. When we make adjustments to M&M for taxes, the value of the levered firm is higher than the unlevered firm due to the value of the tax shield of debt. As leverage increases, the cost of financial distress increases, and thus there is a tradeoff to get to an optimal capital structure. While M&M gives an excellent backdrop on how to think about capital structure, we regretfully live in a world where M&M does not completely hold for banks given friction costs, government regulation, deposit insurance, access to the Fed discount window, and of course their very unique source of leverage: deposits.

MEASURES OF CAPITAL

There are a few key approaches to measure capital. These include the approach taken by regulators, ratings agencies, and equity and fixed-income investors. We shall discuss next regulatory capital and some examples to illustrate how equity and fixed-income investors view capital. The approach taken by ratings agencies mirrors that of regulatory capital for the most part, except that agencies also gauge the equity content of debt and preferred stock. The ratings agencies include S&P, Moody's, Fitch, Kroll, and Egan-Jones. Kroll is especially active in the community bank space.

REGULATORY CAPITAL

While as investors we care mostly about TCE/TA, it is important to understand regulatory capital ratios as regulatory constraints can shape the behavior and growth prospects of a bank.

The regulatory capital rules under US Basel III is a 983-page document issued by the regulators. We shall highlight some salient aspects relevant for regional and community banks, review some elements of the regulatory capital stack, and explain the concept of risk weighting of assets later in this chapter. Here is a quick explanation of some elements highlighted in Exhibit 3.2.

AOCI – Accumulated Other Comprehensive Income (AOCI) consists of unrealized gains and losses on available for sale securities.

SBLF – Small Business Lending Fund is a $30B fund that invests in preferred stock in banks under $10B to encourage lending to small businesses.

TARP – TARP was the Troubled Asset Relief Program conducted by the US Treasury.

EXHIBIT 3.2 Regulatory Capital in Blocks

Total Capital		
Tier 1 Capital		**Tier 2 Capital**
Common Equity Tier 1 (CET1) ▪ Common Equity ▪ AOCI ▪ Qualifying Minority Interest Adjustments	**Additional Tier 1 (AT1)** ▪ Non-cumulative perpetual preferred ▪ SBLF ▪ TARP	**Tier 2** ▪ Allowance for Loan Losses (up to 1.25% of RWA) ▪ Other Preferred Stock ▪ Subordinated Debt

CAPITAL EROSION

As one would expect, capital erodes precipitously during times of crises. Exhibit 3.3 is sourced from *The Impact of the Recent Financial Crisis on the Capital Positions of Large U.S. Financial Institutions: An Empirical Analysis* by Scott Strah, Jennifer Hynes, and Sanders Shaffer (Federal Reserve Bank of Boston; July 16, 2013).

CAN CAPITAL RATIOS SERVE AS A PREDICTOR OF BANK FAILURES?

As investors, this a pertinent question. We looked at the Global Financial Crisis (GFC) to see whether a fall in capital ratios would serve as a predictor of failure. During the GFC and its aftermath, around 489 banks failed over the six-year period from 2008 to 2013. The costliest and biggest failures respectively were IndyMac and Washington Mutual (WaMu). IndyMac with $32B in assets failed in June 2008. This was the costliest failure in the history of the FDIC and cost $12B for the FDIC's insurance fund. WaMu with $307B in assets failed in September 2008. This was the largest failure in terms of assets in the history of the FDIC. We took a closer look at IndyMac as can be seen in Exhibits 3.4 and 3.5 from the stock charts and tables of metrics earnings deterioration, as shown in declining ROA, occurs before the precipitous fall in capital ratios.

The lesson we have drawn from the global financial crisis is that while capital ratios can serve as a predictors, they may not be early enough for investors. Earnings deterioration serves as an earlier indicator.

Apart from earnings deterioration, it would be helpful to pay heed to the Texas ratio detailed in Chapter 4 on credit, combined with a view on macro factors detailed in Chapter 9 on cycle.

We see that the stock prices of banks dip before earnings deterioration. Thus, it is important to understand if the stock price deterioration is a signal. This should not come as a surprise. Stock markets lead economic activity by around six months on average, and the S&P 500 is one of the 10 components of The Conference Board Leading Economic Index®.

EXHIBIT 3.3 Capital Erosion

		Capital Ratio Erosion (in Basis Points)	
Institution	**Crisis Period**	**Tier 1 Common Capital**	**Tangible Common Equity**
Washington Mutual, Inc.	2007:Q4 - 9/25/08	(1,202)	(1,032)
Countrywide Financial Corp.	2007:Q3 - 7/1/08	(769)	(547)
Merrill Lynch & Co., Inc.	6/30/07 - 12/31/08	(756)	(407)
National City Corp.	2007:Q4 - 12/31/08	(751)	(796)
Ally Financial Inc.	2007:Q3 - 2009:Q4	(636)	(621)
Lehman Brothers Holdings Inc.	3/1/08 - 9/15/08	(610)	(460)
Wachovia Corp.	2008:Q1 - 12/31/08	(590)	(521)
State Street Corp.	2007:Q4 - 2009:Q2	(527)	(283)
Citigroup Inc.	2007:Q4 - 2008:Q4	(380)	(150)
Bear Stearns Companies Inc.	9/1/07 - 5/30/08	(358)	(309)
Capital One Financial Corp.	2010:Q1	(327)	(106)
MetLife, Inc.	2008:Q1 - 2009:Q1	(315)	(205)
KeyCorp	2008:Q2 - 2010:Q1	(242)	(215)
Morgan Stanley	9/1/07 - 12/31/08	(145)	(24)
Regions Financial Corp.	2008:Q4 - 2011:Q1	(140)	(101)
American Express Co.	2010:Q1	(96)	(79)
Fifth Third Bancorp	2008:Q2 - 2008:Q4	(93)	(111)
Bank of New York Mellon Corp.	2008:Q1 - 2008:Q4	(90)	(101)
PNC Financial Services Group, Inc.	2008:Q1 - 2008:Q4	(87)	(85)
Wells Fargo & Co.	2008:Q3 - 2008:Q4	(81)	(44)
SunTrust Banks, Inc.	2008:Q2 - 2010:Q1	(69)	(89)
Bank of America Corp.	2010:Q4 - 2011:Q3	(66)	7
Goldman Sachs Group, Inc.	8/30/08 - 12/26/08	(36)	(25)
BB&T	2010:Q4	(10)	(9)
JPMorgan Chase & Co.	2008:Q3	(4)	0
U.S. Bancorp	—	—	—

Source: Federal Reserve Bank of Boston

EXHIBIT 3.4 IndyMac Stock Price and TCE Ratio

Source: S&P Global Market Intelligence

EXHIBIT 3.5 IndyMac Metrics and Stock Price

Date	Close	ROAA	TCE/RWA	TCE/TA	Report Date	Report Time	QoQ Return
12/31/08	0.15	**(38.2%)**	**(34.6%)**	**(19.7%)**			**(9.4%)**
9/30/08	0.16	**(30.7%)**	**(14.6%)**	**(8.5%)**			**(74.2%)**
6/30/08	0.62	**(7.6%)**	2.8%	1.6%			**(79.7%)**
5/12/08	3.06	**(2.1%)**	6.4%	3.7%	5/12/08	11:00	**(62.9%)**
2/12/08	8.24	**(6.0%)**	7.7%	4.6%	2/12/08	12:00	**(34.0%)**
11/6/07	12.49	**(2.3%)**	10.1%	6.0%	11/6/07	Bef-mkt	**(43.2%)**
7/31/07	22.00	0.7%	10.8%	6.6%	7/31/07		**(31.2%)**
4/26/07	31.98	0.8%	12.7%	7.4%	4/26/07		**(15.2%)**
1/25/07	37.71	1.1%	13.0%	7.4%	1/25/07	Bef-mkt	**(18.1%)**
11/2/06	46.07	1.4%	13.1%	7.6%	11/2/06	Bef-mkt	11.7%
7/27/06	41.26	1.9%	1.9%	1.9%	7/27/06	Bef-mkt	**(13.3%)**
4/25/06	47.61	1.5%	1.5%	1.5%	4/25/06	Bef-mkt	20.6%
1/26/06	39.49	1.6%	12.9%	7.9%	1/26/06	Bef-mkt	5.8%
10/31/05	37.33	1.8%	12.9%	7.7%	10/31/05	Bef-mkt	**(17.0%)**
7/28/05	44.96	1.9%	12.8%	7.3%	7/28/05		18.8%
4/27/05	37.86	1.7%	13.0%	7.5%	4/27/05		6.1%
1/27/05	35.70	1.6%	13.6%	7.7%	1/27/05	Bef-mkt	

Note: RWA is Risk Weighted Assets. The concept is explained later in the chapter
Source: S&P Global Market Intelligence

Recommended Reading

1. "Earliest Indicator of Bank Failure Is Deterioration in Earnings" by Yadav K. Gopalan, Federal Reserve Bank of St. Louis.
2. "Capital Ratios as Predictors of Bank Failure" by Arturo Estrella, Sangkyun Park, and Stavros Peristiani in *FRBNY Economic Policy Review*, July 2000.
3. "Predicting Bank Failures Using a Market-based Measure of Capital" by Keith Friend of the OCC and Mark Levonian of Promontory Financial Group.
4. "Are the New Basel III Capital Buffers Countercyclical? Exploring the Option of a Rule-Based Countercyclical Buffer" by Filippo Occhino of the Federal Reserve Bank of Cleveland.

MARKET VIEWS ON CAPITAL

What does the market implicitly assume when a bank trades below its tangible book? We take a look at this and a couple of illustrative examples, one a relatively recent example of a small community bank and the other of a notable investment bank during the global financial crisis.

BANK TRADING BELOW TANGIBLE BOOK

Let us assume bank A trades at a P/TBV of 0.8×. A hard-core value investor would want to go out and buy as many of these 80¢ dollars as they could, but before we do that, as good students of the market, we should assess as to why this is the case.

We have seen stocks of banks declining well ahead of earnings deterioration, capital ratio erosion, and failures. Hence, we need to understand as to what loss rate the market is imputing and compare this with prior peak loss periods.

Let us also say that this bank A trades at a P/E of 8.4×, 8.0×, and 7.6× for the one-, two-. and three-year forward periods and has a market cap of $4B and loans of $40B.

A P/TBV of 0.8× would imply a TCE of $5B and hence an implied loss of $1B (TCE less market cap). Assuming a tax rate of 22%, the implied pre-tax loss would be $1.3B.

Making a few more assumptions, the PPNR (Pre-provision Net Revenues) for years one, two, and three are $734MM, $771MM, and $809MM.

Thus, the cumulative PPNR of the next 3 years would be $2,314MM. The cumulative NCOs assumed by the market is $3,596MM ($2,314MM + $1,282MM), which is an implied cumulative loss rate of 9%.

In order to assess if this loss rate is likely, a starting point could be to compare it with the cumulative NCOs over the three-year peak period during the GFC. Not every crisis is going to mirror the GFC; hence this is just a starting point. This would also not be an exercise in isolation; it would need to be done in conjunction with an assessment of the quality of underwriting and consideration of where we are in the credit cycle (nobody knows with any degree of precision, but it needs to be thought through). Chapter 4 on credit and Chapter 9 on cycle cover more ground on these topics.

The two examples below, one a small community bank and the other a large global investment bank, will hopefully illustrate the critical importance of assessing capital.

FIRST NBC BANK HOLDING COMPANY

First NBC was a bank headquartered in Louisiana that was closed by the state regulator in April 2017, and the FDIC took receivership. The FDIC report reviewing the failure highlighted seven factors that contributed to the failure of the bank: 1. Dominant official not controlled by board, 2. Rapid growth, 3. Weak risk management practices, 4. Reliance on high cost volatile funding, 5. Concentrations to individuals (large loan relationships), 6. Significant involvement in accounts receivable exchange (emerging market), and 7. Level of investments in tax credits (dimension of complexity). While this postmortem analysis is an excellent read in its entirety, it would be important to highlight the capital position of the bank.

First NBC had significantly high net DTA (deferred tax assets). DTA was about two-thirds of tangible common which was 2× larger than any other publicly traded bank holding company. Under Basel III, DTA was not going to get counted as regulatory capital, and this would have forced the bank to raise dilutive equity capital. This situation with the capital position was well articulated in four public letters from Holdco Asset Management to First NBC between August and November of 2016. These letters are a recommended reading and are accessible at:

https://web.archive.org/web/20160909063920/http://holdcoam.com/wp-content/uploads/Letter_to_FNBC.pdf

https://web.archive.org/web/20160909095350/http://holdcoam.com/wp-content/uploads/Second_Letter_to_FNBC.pdf

https://web.archive.org/web/20200704184957/http://holdcoam.com/wp-content/uploads/Third_Letter_to_FNBC.pdf

http://web.archive.org/web/20200704185305/http://holdcoam.com/wp-content/uploads/fourth_letter_to_fnbc.pdf

LEHMAN BROTHERS

Lehman was a large and complex investment bank and an entity most readers will remember. Analyzing large investment banks with any level of precision and being correct can be difficult. David Einhorn of Greenlight Capital was able to achieve this with his famous successful short of Lehman. If we were to boil it down to its essence, Greenlight's argument was that if Lehman were to mark their assets appropriately, there would be more significant write-downs and they would have to raise more capital.

Please see the following for a longer review.

1. David Einhorn, Greenlight Capital, "Accounting Ingenuity" Remarks at Ira Sohn Conference, May 21, 2008; available at: https://web.archive.org/web/20190920224723/https://web.stanford.edu/~jbulow/Lehmandocs/docs/DEBTORS/LBHI_SEC07940_336846-336854.pdf
2. Email exchange between David Einhorn and Erin Callan, the then CFO of Lehman Brothers, May 19–20, 2008; available at: https://web.archive.org/web/20200704214527/https://web.stanford.edu/~jbulow/Lehmandocs/docs/DEBTORS/LBHI_SEC07940_098608-098612.pdf

REGULATORY COMPLEXITY

We are firm believers that increasing complexity of regulations does not make any institution safe. Perversely, these increase costs of compliance, divert management and investor attention, force unforeseen errors, and raise cost of doing business, which in turn is a GDP growth dampener.

All things being the same, we view European banking regulations as incrementally more complex than regulations in the U.S.

We believe the primary sources of confusion arise from interpretation of terms of legacy issued securities when viewed through the prism of new capital requirements regulations. These can be compounded by the changing of competent authorities from national level regulators to the European Banking Authority. We believe that allowing large banks to use their own internal models has limited benefits and can cause more inefficiencies and have the perverse effect of disadvantaging smaller banks.

Not surprisingly there have been a few situations in Europe where investors, regulators, and the security issuing bank could not seem to agree with respect to capital treatment.

The regulatory congruence between Europe and the US is not 100%. During the US rule-making process tweaks are made. We are not claiming that such disputes do not arise in the US and readily admit that our relative lack of proximity to Europe and a possible home bias could well be factors causing us to conclude that the US regulatory regime is less complex than the ones in Europe.

We highlight a few examples below and would note that we do not have an opinion on the matter (and if we did, we would probably not publish it in a book). We are merely drawing attention to these matters as emblematic of confusion from complex regulations as smart people on multiple sides appear to be drawing different conclusions on the same issue.

UNICREDIT – CASHES

Caius Capital in May of 2018 wrote to the European Banking Authority (EBA) regarding the capital treatment of the Convertible And Subordinated Hybrid Equity-Linked Securities (CASHES) of UniCredit (Italy's largest bank by assets). The EBA declined to investigate the matter, UniCredit subsequently sued Caius for €90MM, and the dispute was ultimately settled with the terms not being disclosed.

HSBC – DISCOS

A group of eight investors holding the discount perpetual floating rate securities (Discos) wrote to the EBA expressing several concerns over classification of these securities and their eligibility as Tier 2 capital and MREL (Minimum Requirement for Own Funds and Eligible Liabilities) debt.

OTHER DISPUTES

These other disputes have been mostly about recapitalizations and could very easily have arisen in the US.

Banca Monte dei Paschi di Siena – The annulment of Floating Rate Exchangable Bonds (FRESH) following restructuring.

Novo Banco – After the failure of Banco Espírito Santo in Portugal, the bank was split into the classic "good bank" (Novo Banco) and a "bad bank." The bondholders filed a lawsuit when the bonds were transferred to the bad bank. These note holders maintained a website to document their communications at www.novonotegroup.com

Banco Popular of Spain – Following the sale of the bank to Santander for 1 Euro, bondholders filed lawsuits in both Europe and New York.

REVISITING ELEMENTS OF THE REGULATORY CAPITAL STACK

Earlier on in this chapter in Exhibit 3.2, we had highlighted some elements of the capital stack. Here is a more detailed clarification on these elements.

AOCI

Accumulated Other Comprehensive Income (AOCI) consists of unrealized gains and losses on available for sale securities and is discussed in greater detail in Chapter 2 on financial statement analysis. The original proposal would have allowed AOCI to be included as capital. AOCI is inherently volatile and moves with market changes. However, community banks were given the option to elect to opt-in or opt-out from including AOCI. This election was made in the first regulatory report submitted in 2015 by the bank (Call Reports for 3/31/2015). If an M&A transaction is consummated between a bank that has opted-out and one that had opted-in, the surviving entity needs to make a fresh election in the first regulatory report filed after the close of the transaction.

QUALIFYING MINORITY INTEREST

Minority interest exists when the consolidated subsidiary of a bank holding company has issued regulatory capital that is not owned by the holding company. This difference shows up as a liability on the consolidated balance sheet. These minority interests are not all counted as capital. To be clear, the minority interest does allow the subsidiary to absorb losses incurred at the subsidiary but not at a consolidated level. There are hence limitations on how much of this minority interest can be counted as capital.

PREFERRED STOCK

Holders of Preferred Stock have no voting rights, unlike the holders of the common. They receive a fixed dividend which has a priority over common dividends. A perpetual preferred has no maturity and is quite like debt except that it is junior in priority of claims. A cumulative preferred would have to pay any missed dividends when payout of dividends resume, and thus is closer to a fixed-income instrument. The more equity-like noncumulative convertible perpetual preferreds are included in Additional Tier 1.

Cumulative preferreds and TruPS (Trust Preferred Securities) were phased out of Tier 1 and are included in Tier 2. TruPS have been issued since 1993 and were popular since the dividends were tax deductible for the issuer; these were originally counted as Tier 1 since 1996 but were phased out of Tier 1 with the Dodd-Frank Act. Smaller banks typically used to sell TruPS to CDOs due to issue size limitations.

SBLF

Small Business Lending Fund (SBLF) is a $30B fund that invests in preferred stock in banks under $10B to encourage lending to small businesses. The dividend rate is 5% and if the lending to small businesses increases by >10%, then the rate declines to 1%. If the lending to small businesses increases by <10%, then the dividend rates are between 2 and 4%. Conversely if the lending does not increase within 2 years of the investment by the UST, the dividend rate is hiked to 7%, and after 4.5 years it increases to 9%. US Treasury has invested about $3.8B under the SBLF program.

TARP

TARP was the Troubled Asset Relief Program conducted by the US Treasury (UST) to combat the Global Financial Crisis. One component of this was CPP (Capital Purchase Program) which infused $205B into QFIs (Qualifying

EXHIBIT 3.6 BAC Warrants Exercise Price Adjustments

Adjustments to A Warrants to Purchase BAC Common Stock[1]		
Record Date	**Warrant Share Number After Record Date**	**Exercise Price After Record Date**
Original Terms	1.00	$13.300
September 5, 2014	1.00	$13.267
December 5, 2014	1.00	$13.236
March 6, 2015	1.00	$13.203
June 5, 2015	1.00	$13.171
September 4, 2015	1.00	$13.137
December 4, 2015	1.00	$13.107
March 4, 2016	1.00	$13.067
June 3, 2016	1.00	$13.032
September 2, 2016	1.00	$12.980
December 2, 2016	1.00	$12.938
March 3, 2017	1.00	$12.904
June 2, 2017	1.00	$12.867
September 1, 2017	1.00	$12.807
December 1, 2017	1.00	$12.757
March 2, 2018	1.00	$12.713
June 1, 2018	1.00	$12.666
September 7, 2018	1.00	$12.609
December 7, 2018	1.00	$12.544

Source: Bank of America

Financial Institutions), which included banks and some non-banks such as insurers who reorganized themselves into BHCs (Bank Holding Companies) in order to participate. The CPP was a success and helped stabilize the financial system by protecting institutions and has earned a return for the US Treasury. Each QFI was allowed to issue senior perpetual preferreds between 1 and 3% of risk-weighted assets not exceeding $25B. The preferreds pay cumulative dividends at a 5% rate for the first five years, and this steps up to a rate of 9%. UST received attached warrants to purchase common at 15% of the investment subject to some reduction terms. The bank had the option to repurchase the warrants from UST when the preferreds were redeemed. When the banks repaid TARP, the UST either sold the warrants back to the bank or conducted auctions to sell the warrant positions. One unique feature in the TARP warrants that is generally not seen in other warrants is that the strike price is adjusted lower for quarterly dividends. In the extreme example of Bank of America Class A Warrants (BAC WS A), the strike price is adjusted for a quarterly cash dividend in excess of $0.01 per share (Exhibit 3.6). In other

EXHIBIT 3.7 WFC Warrants Exercise Price Adjustments

Adjustments to Warrants to Purchase Common Stock (1)		
Record Date	**Warrant Share Number After Record Date**	**Warrant Exercise Price After Record Date**
Original Terms	1.00	$34.010
May 9, 2014	1.00	$34.010
August 8, 2014	1.00	$33.995
November 7, 2014	1.00	$33.996
February 6, 2015	1.00	$33.984
May 8, 2015	1.00	$33.962
August 7, 2015	1.00	$33.942
November 6, 2015	1.00	$33.920
February 5, 2016	1.00	$33.896
May 6, 2016	1.00	$33.869
August 5, 2016	1.00	$33.840
November 4, 2016	1.00	$33.811
February 3, 2017	1.00	$33.787
May 5, 2017	1.00	$33.762
August 4, 2017	1.00	$33.731
November 3, 2017	1.00	$33.701
February 2, 2018	1.00	$33.675
May 4, 2018	1.00	$33.643
August 10, 2018	1.00(2)	$33.592

Source: Wells Fargo

instances, such as the Wells Fargo warrants, the strike price was adjusted lower if the quarterly cash dividend exceeded a set amount, $0.34 in the case of the Wells Fargo warrants (Exhibit 3.7). The TARP warrants made for good investments.

SUBORDINATED DEBT

Subordinated debt ("sub debt" for short) ranks beneath senior debt but above Preferred stock in the capital stack (Exhibit 3.8). Some of the issuance has been to refinance higher cost debt. We have seen banks issue sub debt to redeem SBLF before the dividend gets hiked. We also saw banks issue sub debt to redeem their TruPS when these got phased out of Tier 1 capital following Dodd-Frank. Depending on where their stock trades and what the cost of sub debt would be, banks can determine whether it is optimal to redeem securities with sub debt or do equity raises. Sub debt is often the more attractive option over doing a dilutive equity raise. The interest is deductible for tax and is counted as Tier 2 if it is unsecured and has a maturity of at least 5 years. All things being equal, investors prefer bank level sub debt over holding company (holdco) sub debt. If the parent has less equity capital than the subsidiary, this implies that double leverage exists.

EXHIBIT 3.8 Community and Regional Bank Subdebt Issuance

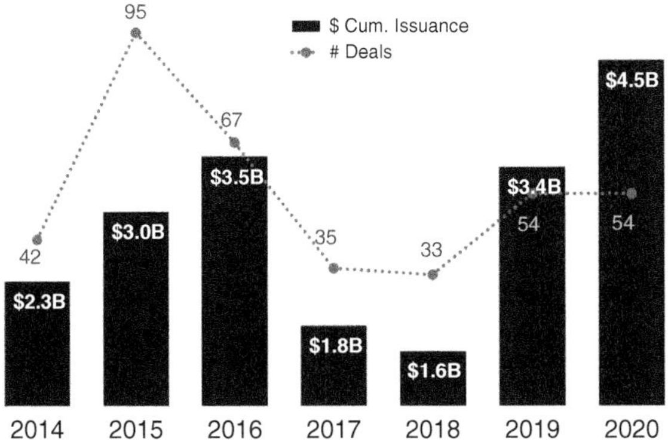

	2014	2015	2016	2017	2018	2019	2020
$ Cum. Issuance	$2.3B	$3.0B	$3.5B	$1.8B	$1.6B	$3.4B	$4.5B
# Deals	42	95	67	35	33	54	54

Source: S&P Global Market Intelligence

Note: Subordinated debt offerings for banks < $50B in assets

Double Leverage

When a bank holdco issues debt and downstreams the proceeds to the subsidiary as equity, this creates *double leverage,* as the holdco's equity capital is essentially levered twice (once at the holdco level, and then at the subsidiary bank level). If the ratio of the parent holdco's equity investment in subsidiaries to the consolidated equity is >100%, then the holdco has double leverage. Investors should pay closer attention if this ratio exceeds 120%. Levels below 120% should be analyzed if the debt service ratio is weak. Holders of the holdco debt are reliant on the bank upstreaming capital to the holdco. The bank holdco debt service is the total interest expense and amortization of the holdco note per year. This debt is serviced by the dividend payments from the equity investment into the subsidiary (Exhibits 3.9 and 3.10).

Double Leverage is best explained by using an example (Exhibit 3.11). We chose Ally Bank to demonstrate this for no great reason other than that we had looked at this recently. The easiest way to find this is to access the BHCPR (Bank Holding Company Performance Report) from the website of the FFIEC (Federal Financial Institutions Examination Council) for Ally Financial (the holdco).

EXHIBIT 3.9 Double Leverage: Hold Co Equity "Levered Twice"

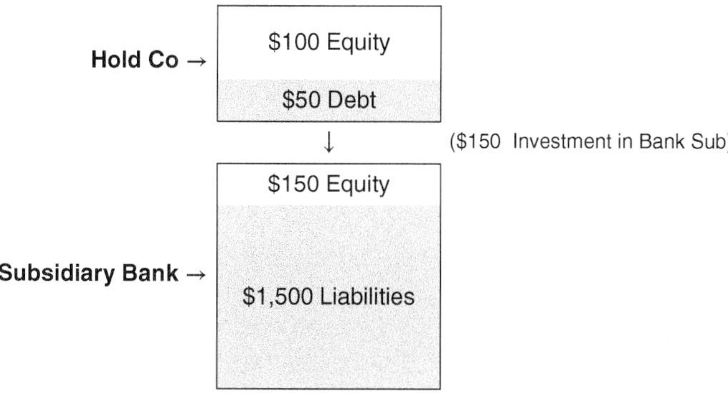

EXHIBIT 3.10 Hold Co Interest Serviced by Subsidiary Dividends

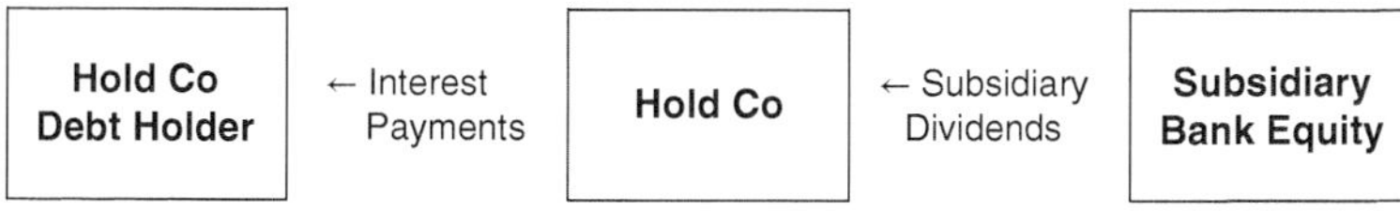

EXHIBIT 3.11 Double Leverage

Double Leverage	
Equity investment in subs/Equity capital	163.73
Total investment in subs/Equity capital	166.04

Source: Page 22 of the BHCPR for Ally Financial for Dec 2019

EXHIBIT 3.12 Double Leverage Calculation

Numerators		($000s)
	Equity Investment in Subsidiaries	23,603,000
	Total Investment in Subsidiaries	23,936,000
Denominators		**($000s)**
	Parent Total Equity	14,416,000
	GMAC Capital Trust I	2,667,000
	Parent Total Equity + TRUPs	17,083,000
Ratios		**(%)**
	Equity Investment in Subs/Equity Capital	163.7%
	Total Investment in Subs/Equity Capital	166.0%
	Equity Investment in Subs/Equity Capital + TRUPs	138.2%

For the more analytically curious, the approach would be to calculate this as shown in Exhibit 3.12.

We note that for Ally the Double Leverage is 163.7%, but one can adjust the equity capital to include the TRUPs, in which case the Double Leverage would be 138.2%. Typically, when determining whether to include TRUPs as equity capital, one must review the prospectus and see if it has a dividend stopper clause, and if dividends are cumulative or noncumulative. If dividends can be stopped and if they are noncumulative, then it can be treated as equity capital.

ADVANTAGE HOLDCO CREDITORS IN BANKRUPTCIES?

During normal times, all things being the same, bank level debt is "preferable" to holdco debt, in that its obligations are higher up in the cash flow waterfall. However, there are situations where holdco debt holders come out ahead. These formed some good capital structure arbitrage trades from the GFC, events where the holdco debt was accumulated for pennies on the dollar, and the holdco estate prevailed against the FDIC and in some cases even financed the litigation for the holding company bankruptcy estate against the FDIC.

WHAT DOES THE HOLDCO HAVE THAT COULD BE VALUABLE TO THE HOLDCO CREDITORS IN A BANKRUPTCY?

The value here would primarily be tax refunds from the IRS based on NOLs (Net Operating Losses) of the holdco. The TCJA (Tax Cuts and Jobs Act) effectively removed the carryback for NOLs created in 2018 and after. However, tax credits and capital losses can still be carried back.

Investors need to study the TSA (Tax Sharing Agreement) between the holdco and the bank as well as state law to understand if the refunds would belong to the FDIC (the receiver for the bank) or to the holdco creditors who form the bankruptcy estate of the holdco.

Tax law does not provide rules for the split of the refund. Typically, the FDIC claims the refund, arguing generally on the following lines:

- **(a)** That the holdco received the refund driven by the losses at the bank sub;
- **(b)** That the claim is based on the Bob Richards rule (a 50-year-old precedent that maintains that in the absence of a tax sharing agreement, a tax refund belongs to the group member responsible for the losses that led to it);
- **(c)** That the claim is based on the source-of-strength doctrine (that the bank holding company is a source of strength to the subsidiary).

HAVE THESE ARGUMENTS HELD UP IN COURT?

Circuit Court of Appeals

FDIC has lost a few cases in the Circuit Courts of Appeals including the following:

IndyMac – The 9th Circuit held that $55MM of tax refunds was the property of the holdco since there was no express language in the TSA. See *FDIC v. Siegel* (In re IndyMac Bancorp, Inc.).

Downey – The 3rd Circuit upheld the bankruptcy court judgment that $370MM in tax refunds would be part of the estate. See *Cantor v. FDIC* (In re Downey Fin. Corp.).

FDIC won in the following cases:

BankUnited – The 11th circuit held that $45MM in tax refunds belong to the FDIC as the receiver of the bank subsidiary since there was no debtor-creditor relationship between the holdco and the bank sub, and the holdco was holding the refund in escrow for the benefit of the bank. See *Zucker v. FDIC* (In re BankUnited Fin. Corp.)

NetBank – The 11th circuit held that $6.1MM in tax refunds belong to the FDIC since there was no debtor-creditor relationship between the holdco and the bank sub; the holdco was holding the refund as an agent of the bank. See *FDIC v. Zucker* (In re NetBank).

AmFin – AmFin's bank sub was placed into receivership in 2009. A 2008 tax return had $805MM in NOLs and the FDIC argued that $170MM of $194MM in refunds belong to the subsidiary. The 6th Circuit reversed and remanded the district court's decision to award the tax refund to the bankruptcy estate. See *FDIC v. AmFin Financial Corp.*

Supreme Court

The Supreme Court delivered a unanimous verdict in *Rodriguez v. FDIC* (In re United Western Bancorp) on February 25, 2020 that Federal courts should defer to state law to resolve the issue of whether the holdco or the bank has the right to the tax refunds. The court vacated the judgment of the 10th Circuit and remanded it. Previously the 10th Circuit had ruled for the FDIC that it was entitled to the $4MM in tax refund as the receiver for United Western Bank.

The SCOTUS order is accessible at:

http://web.archive.org/web/20200225152405/https://www.supremecourt.gov/opinions/19pdf/18-1269_h3dj.pdf

Since 2014, the bank regulators have required that the TSA be amended to ensure that the bank sub has the entitlement to any tax refunds. The regulators under Reg W now require that the TSA is amended to specifically acknowledge an agency relationship between the holdco and the sub with respect to any tax refunds and that there is no language to the contrary in the TSA (Exhibit 3.13).

EXHIBIT 3.13 Sample Language Required by Regulators

The [holding company] is an agent for the [IDI and its subsidiaries] (the "Institution") with respect to all matters related to consolidated tax returns and refund claims, and nothing in this agreement shall be construed to alter or modify this agency relationship. If the [holding company] receives a tax refund from a taxing authority, these funds are obtained as agent for the Institution. Any tax refund attributable to income earned, taxes paid, and losses incurred by the Institution is the property of and owned by the Institution, and shall be held in trust by the [holding company] for the benefit of the Institution. The [holding company] shall forward promptly the amounts held in trust to the Institution. Nothing in this agreement is intended to be or should be construed to provide the [holding company] with an ownership interest in a tax refund that is attributable to income earned, taxes paid, and losses incurred by the Institution. The [holding company] hereby agrees that this tax sharing agreement does not give it an ownership interest in a tax refund generated by the tax attributes of the Institution.

Source: https://www.federalregister.gov/documents/2014/06/19/2014-14325/addendum-to-the-interagency-policy-statement-on-income-tax-allocation-in-a-holding-company-structure

Recommended reading to get a broader perspective of the topics at issue:

1. *Zucker v. FDIC*
   "Aberration or Seminal Decision?: Examining the Impact of Zucker v. FDIC (In re BankUnited Financial Corp.) on Bankruptcy Law," 34 REV. BANKING & FIN. L. 369 (2014) by Lisa A. Bothwell
   https://web.archive.org/web/20200705052602/https://www.bu.edu/rbfl/files/2015/03/RBFL_34-1_Bothwell.pdf/
2. Source-of Strength Doctrine
   The Source-of-Strength Doctrine: Revered and Revisited - Part II, November/December 2012, *The Banking Law Journal* by Paul L. Lee
   https://www.debevoise.com/-/media/files/insights/publications/2012/11/the-sourceofstrength-doctrine-revered-and-revisi__/files/view-article/fileattachment/lee10192012.pdf

LIQUIDITY

Liquidity unsurprisingly is very important for banks. During times of stress, liquidity can get pricey. There are many ways to gauge the liquidity profile of banks. Banks above $50B in assets are subject to the LCR (Liquidity Coverage Ratio) and the NSFR (Net Stable Funding Ratio).

LIQUIDITY COVERAGE RATIO (LCR)

The LCR is the proportion of unencumbered high-quality liquid assets (HQLA) to the expected net cash outflows over a stressed 30-day period. That is to say, the ratio tells us if a bank has enough cash, treasuries, and other easily sellable securities to cover potential deposit runoffs expected during stressed conditions. Regulations dictate that this ratio must exceed 1.

$$Liquidity\ Coverage\ Ratio\ LCR = \frac{High\ Quality\ Liquid\ Assets\ HQLA}{30\ Day\ Net\ Cash\ Outflow}$$

The ratio is applicable to banks with greater than $50B in assets in the US. Typically, the runoff rates to calculate the denominator are: retail deposits $\leq 5\%$, financial institutions 100%, and public funds 40%.

NET STABLE FUNDING RATIO (NSFR)

NSFR assesses a bank's reliance on short-term funding.

$$Net\ Stable\ Funding\ Ratio = \frac{Available\ amount\ of\ stable\ funding}{Required\ amount\ of\ stable\ funding}$$

Basel III requires a bank to maintain an Available Stable Funding (ASF) to Required Stable Funding (RSF) ratio of at least 100%. The ASF is determined by giving funding a weighting based on maturity and reliability: 100% is assigned to funding that will be available beyond 12 months, 90–95% to deposits with greater than one-year maturity, and 0% to funding that is less reliable.

The RSF is determined by looking at the bank's liquidity and maturity profile of assets and its commitments exposure. Assets that are extremely liquid and unencumbered require none or low levels of stable funding, whereas assets that are less liquid and carry longer maturities will require stable funding.

Exhibit 3.14 lists assets by liquidity. The 10-K and 10-Q filings will have the maturity profiles of investment securities, loans, and deposits. We provide some samples in Exhibit 3.15. We have used the filings of Comerica, for no particular reason other than that we had reviewed it recently.

In gauging liquidity, it is important to assess the off-balance sheet exposure of the bank as well. In a period of elevated risk, assess how much of the lines of credit are extended to industries that are seeing stress and whether they are likely to draw on it. In early 2020, as we wrote this portion, the spread of COVID-19 was rampant and several states in the US had different levels of

EXHIBIT 3.14 Liquidity Continuum

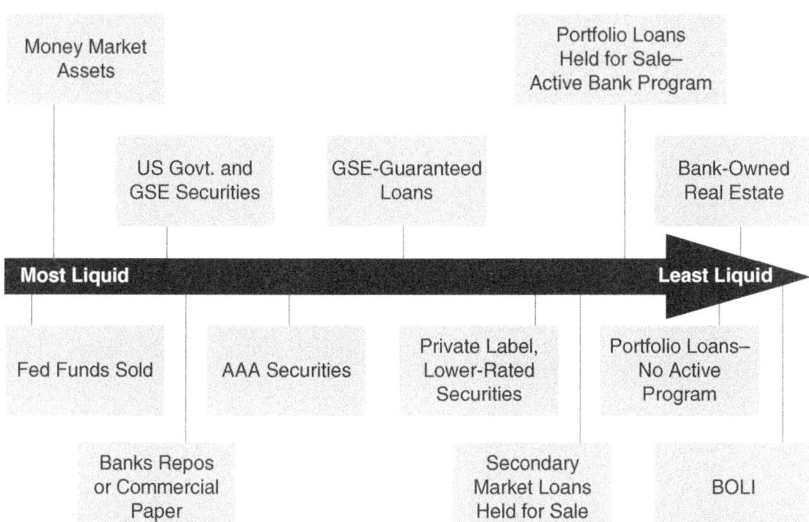

Source: OCC Comptroller's Handbook June 2012

social distancing introduced. Sectors such as restaurants, retail, lodging, airlines, theme parks, theatres, essentially any business that gets impacted by social distancing, are seeing stress, and it is important to understand through various sources as to how much of the commitments are made to these industries (Exhibit 3.16). Similarly, during periods of energy and commodity price disruption, one needs to assess the commitments made to the energy and metals and mining complex. The level of commitments made to sectors seeing stress needs to be compared with the level of cash and liquid securities held by the bank and then assume a % of utilization of the lines of credit to estimate a stressed LCR.

During normal times, the Loans to Deposit L/D ratio gives a quick check of the liquidity. Having a low number indicates that the bank is being risk averse or having a difficult time loaning up, but in general this is a good problem to have.

This gap is an opportunity for the bank's management to address or alternatively screen an attractive acquisition candidate for a bank with a higher L/D that is seeking deposit rich franchises. Conversely, having a high L/D may have implications for the future growth and funding needs of the bank. There are also geographic skews: Generally banks in the North East run high L/D while rural franchises can be low L/D.

The equity investor should assess if the bank is likely to suspend dividends to preserve liquidity. Bank dividend payouts have limitations and are

EXHIBIT 3.15 Maturity Profiles from Sample Filings

Investment Securities

(dollar amounts in millions)	Maturity (a)										Weighted Average Maturity
	Within 1 Year		1–5 Years		5–10 Years		After 10 Years		Total		
December 31, 2019	**Amount**	**Yield**	**Amount**	**Yield**	**Amount**	**Yield**	**Amount**	**Yield**	**Amount**	**Yield**	**Years**
US Treasury and other US government agency securities	$ 30	1.68%	$ 2,762	2.48%	$ —	—%	$ —	—%	$ 2,792	2.47%	2.2
Residential mortgage-backed securities (b)	—	—	132	3.62	1,013	2.26	8,461	2.42	9,606	2.42	22.3
Total investment securities	$ 30	1.68%	$ 2,894	2.53%	1,013	2.26%	$ 8,461	2.42%	$ 12,398	2.43%	17.9

(a) *Based on final contractual maturity.*

(b) *Issued and/or guaranteed by US government agencies or US government-sponsored enterprises.*

Loan Maturities and Interest Rate Sensitivity

(in millions)	Loans Maturing			
December 31, 2019	**Within One Year (a)**	**After One But Within Five Years**	**After Five Years**	**Total**
Commercial loans	$ 15,068	$ 15,423	$ 982	$ 31,473
Real estate construction loans	1,321	1,978	156	3,455
Commercial mortgage loans	1,856	4,922	2,781	9,559
International loans	343	583	83	1,009
Total	$ 18,588	$ 22,906	$ 4,002	$ 45,496
Sensitivity of loans to changes in interest rates:				
Predetermined (fixed) interest rules	$ 595	$ 2,147	$ 588	$ 3,330
Floating interest rates	17,993	20,759	3,414	42,166
Total	$ 18,588	$ 22,906	$ 4,002	$ 45,496

(a) *Includes demand loans, loans having no stated repayment schedule or maturity, and overdrafts.*

EXHIBIT 3.15 *(Continued)*

	Contractual Obligations				
		Minimum Payments Due by Period			
(in millions) **December 31, 2019**	**Total**	**Less than 1 Year**	**1–3 Years**	**4–5 Years**	**More than 5 Years**
Deposits without a stated maturity (a)	**$ 54,093**	**$ 54,093**			
Certificates of deposit and other deposits with a stated maturity (a)	**3,202**	**2,970**	**180**	**26**	**26**
Short-term borrowings (a)	**71**	**71**	—	—	—
Medium- and long-term debt (a)	**7,125**	**675**	—	**1,350**	**5,100**
Operating leases	**438**	**60**	**115**	**88**	**175**
Commitments to fund low income housing partnerships	**160**	**98**	**52**	**5**	**5**
Other long-term obligations (b)	**356**	**101**	**92**	**34**	**129**
Total contractual obligations	**$ 65,445**	**$ 58,068**	**$ 439**	**$ 1,503**	**$ 5,435**
Medium- and long-term debt (parent company only) (a)(c)	**$ 1,650**	**$ —**	**$ —**	**$ 850**	**$ 800**

(a) *Deposits and borrowings exclude accrued interest.*
(b) *Includes unrecognized tax benefits.*
(c) *Parent company only amounts are included in the medium- and long-term debt minimum payments above.*

EXHIBIT 3.16 Unfunded Commitments

(in millions)	*Commercial Commitments*				
	Expected Expiration Dates by Period				
December 31, 2019	**Total**	**Less than 1 Year**	**1–3 Years**	**4–5 Years**	**More than 5 Years**
Unused commitments to extend credit	**$ 26,861**	**$ 10,863**	**$ 8,648**	**$ 4,507**	**$ 2,843**
Standby letters of credit and financial guarantees	**3,320**	**2,837**	**319**	**103**	**61**
Commercial letters of credit	**18**	**17**	—	**1**	—
Total commercial commitments	**$ 30,199**	**$ 13,717**	**$ 8,967**	**$ 4,611**	**$ 2,904**

Source: Comerica 2019 10K

subject to Title 12 Section 208.5 of the code of Federal Regulations (12 CFR 208.5) (Exhibit 3.17). Suspension of dividends to common and preferred equity investors is, in and of itself, a positive to credit investors.

EXHIBIT 3.17 Title 12 CFR Section 208.5

§ 208.5 Dividends and other distributions.

(a) *Definitions. For the purposes of this section: (1) Capital surplus means the total of surplus as reportable in the bank's Reports of Condition and Income and surplus on perpetual preferred stock. (2) Permanent capital means the total of the bank's perpetual preferred stock and related surplus, common stock and surplus, and minority interest in consolidated subsidiaries, as reportable in the Reports of Condition and Income.*

(b) *Limitations. The limitations in this section on the payment of dividends and withdrawal of capital apply to all cash and property dividends or distributions on common or preferred stock. The limitations do not apply to dividends paid in the form of common stock.*

EXHIBIT 3.17 *(Continued)*

(c) *Earnings limitations on payment of dividends. (1) A member bank may not declare or pay a dividend if the total of all dividends declared during the calendar year, including the proposed dividend, exceeds the sum of the bank's net income (as reportable in its Reports of Condition and Income) during the current calendar year and the retained net income of the prior two calendar years, unless the dividend has been approved by the Board. (2) "Retained net income" in a calendar year is equal to the bank's net income (as reported in its Report of Condition and Income for such year), less any dividends declared during such year.*[3] *The bank's net income during the current year and its retained net income from the prior two calendar years is reduced by any net losses incurred in the current or prior two years and any required transfers to surplus or to a fund for the retirement of preferred stock.*[4]

(d) *Limitation on withdrawal of capital by dividend or otherwise. (1) A member bank may not declare or pay a dividend if the dividend would exceed the bank's undivided profits as reportable on its Reports of Condition and Income, unless the bank has received the prior approval of the Board and of at least two-thirds of the shareholders of each class of stock outstanding. (2) A member bank may not permit any portion of its permanent capital to be withdrawn unless the withdrawal has been approved by the Board and by at least two-thirds of the shareholders of each class of stock outstanding. (3) If a member bank has capital surplus in excess of that required by law, the excess amount may be transferred to the bank's undivided profits account and be available for the payment of dividends if: (i) The amount transferred came from the earnings of prior periods, excluding earnings transferred as a result of stock dividends; (ii) The bank's board of directors approves the transfer of funds; and (iii) The transfer has been approved by the Board.*

(e) *Payment of capital distributions. All member banks also are subject to the restrictions on payment of capital distributions contained in §208.45 of subpart D of this part implementing section 38 of the FDI Act (12 U.S.C. 1831o).*

(f) *Compliance. A member bank shall use the date a dividend is declared to determine compliance with this section.*

EXHIBIT 3.17 (*Continued*)

Footnotes
3: In the case of dividends in excess of net income for the year, a bank generally is not required to carry forward negative amounts resulting from such excess. Instead, the bank may attribute the excess to the prior two years, attributing the excess first to the earlier year and then to the immediately preceding year. If the excess is greater than the bank's previously undistributed net income for the preceding two years, prior Board approval of the dividend is required and a negative amount would be carried forward in future dividend calculations. However, in determining any such request for approval, the Board could consider any request for different treatment of such negative amount, including advance waivers for future periods. This applies only to earnings deficits that result from dividends declared in excess of net income for the year and does not apply to other types of current earnings deficits.
4: State member banks are required to comply with state law provisions concerning the maintenance of surplus funds in addition to common capital. Where the surplus of a State member bank is less than what applicable state law requires the bank to maintain relative to its capital stock account, the bank may be required to transfer amounts from its undivided profits account to surplus.

Source: https://www.law.cornell.edu/cfr/text/12/208.5

BAIL-IN RISK

The hierarchy for increasing bail-in risk is as follows:

Senior Debt → Subordinated Debt → Trust Preferreds and Cumulative Preferreds → Non-Cumulative Perpetual Preferreds → Non-Cumulative Convertible Perpetual Preferreds → Common Stock

RISK WEIGHTING

Risk weighting is an adjustment made to asset categories based on the perceived riskiness for each type of bank asset. We multiply the carrying value of various asset categories by a percentage (provided in Basel III), then aggregate to reach a total risk-weighted assets figure. Risk-weighted assets are used in the denominator for many important regulatory capital metrics; thus a lower risk weighting helps the various regulatory capital ratios. As an example, Treasury securities are deemed virtually riskless (0% risk weighting), while past-due loans are assigned high risk (150% risk weighting). Thus, a pool of \$10MM in Treasury securities and \$10MM in past-due loans would equate to (\$10MM×0%+\$10MM×150%) \$15MM in risk-weighted assets.

RISK WEIGHTINGS FOR MAJOR ASSET CATEGORIES

These details can be tedious and can be skipped by most readers. We have presented these as reference for the more curious readers (Exhibit 3.18). As always, no guarantees are made as to the accuracy of these ratios. The information provided in this book is not an official interpretation of any regulations passed by regulatory agencies or other rule-making bodies. The compilation is based on our understanding at the time of writing, and readers must consult the relevant regulatory rulebook. As of the time of writing this book the Financial Institution Letters and Supervisory Guidance were available at:

https://www.fdic.gov/regulations/capital/capital/fils.html

Zero Percent Risk-Weighted:

- Cash and gold bullion;
- Direct and unconditional claims on the US government, its central bank, or a US government agency;
- Exposures unconditionally guaranteed by the US government, its central bank, or a US government agency;
- Claims on certain supranational entities (such as the IMF) and certain multilateral development banking organizations.

20 Percent Risk-Weighted:

- Cash items in the process of collection;
- Exposures *conditionally* guaranteed by the US government, its central bank, or a US government agency;
- Claims on government sponsored entities (GSEs);
- Claims on US depository institutions and NCUA-insured credit unions;
- General obligation claims on, and claims guaranteed by, the full faith and credit of *state* and *local* governments (and any other public sector entity, as defined in the proposal) in the United States;
- Claims on and exposures guaranteed by foreign banks and public sector entities if the sovereign of incorporation of the foreign bank or public sector entity meets certain criteria (as described below).

EXHIBIT 3.18 Risk Weights 1–4 Family Residential Mortgages

Loan-to-value (LTV)	Category 1 resi mortgage	Category 2 resi mortgage
LTV ≤ 60%	35%	100%
LTV > 60% and ≤ 80%	50%	100%
LTV > 80% and ≤ 90%	75%	150%
LTV > 90%	100%	200%

50 Percent Risk-Weighted:

- "Statutory" multifamily mortgage loans meeting certain criteria;
- Presold residential construction loans meeting certain criteria;
- Revenue bonds issued by *state* and *local* governments in the United States.

100 Percent Risk-Weighted:

- Home equity;
- Auto;
- CRE (term);
- Multifamily;
- Consumer;
- C&I;
- Agricultural loans.

These are generally assigned a 100% risk weight unless >90 days past due.

Past-Due Exposures are assigned a 150% percent risk-weight to loans over 90 days past due with some exceptions.

High Volatility Acquisition, Development, or Construction Loans (HVADC) are assigned a 130% risk weighting. These are loans where >50% of the proceeds is directed towards Acquisition, Development, or Construction. These would have been assigned a 150% risk weight but was reduced to 130% under Economic Growth and Regulatory Paperwork Reduction Act (EGRPRA). AD&C loans for 1–4 residential, purchase, development of agricultural land, or community development projects are exempted. Previously, CRE projects meeting certain criteria were also exempt from the higher risk weighting. CRE projects that were exempt had LTVs under the supervisory maximum ratios and borrower contributed capital of at least 15% of the appraised value at completion (and this contribution was made before the loan was originated and remains in place until it goes to permanent financing). These are no longer exempt and will have a 130% risk weight.

ADJUSTMENTS

Mortgage Servicing Rights (MSRs). MSRs are created when the bank originating the mortgage loan sells the loan but retains the right to service the loan. These MSRs are limited to 25% of CET1, and MSRs exceeding this are deducted from regulatory capital and are assigned a 250% risk weight.

Deferred Tax Assets (DTAs). DTAs created by temporary differences are limited to 25% of CET1.

Investments in Unconsolidated Financial Institutions. Once again these are limited to 25% of CET1, and excess levels are deducted from regulatory capital. Equity investments under 10% of total capital are assigned a 100% risk weight; those above 10% are assigned a 300% risk weight if the securities are publicly traded and are assigned a 400% risk weight if the securities are unlisted. Debt investments that are not past due and under 25% of CET1 are assigned a 100% risk weight.

THRESHOLDS FOR CAPITAL CONSTRAINTS AND RATIOS

$$CET1\ RBC\ Ratio = \frac{Common\ Equity\ Tier\ 1\ Capital}{Total\ Risk\ Weighted\ Assets}$$

$$Tier\ 1\ Capital\ Ratio = \frac{Tier\ 1\ Capital}{Total\ Risk\ Weighted\ Assets}$$

$$Total\ Capital\ Ratio = \frac{Total\ Capital}{Total\ Risk\ Weighted\ Assets}$$

$$Leverage\ Ratio = \frac{Tier\ 1\ Capital}{Adjusted\ Average\ Consolidated\ Assets}$$

$$Total\ Loss\ Absorbing\ Capacity\ (TLAC) = CET1 + AT1 + Tier2 + Unsecured\ Debt$$

PCA PROMPT CORRECTIVE ACTION

A regulator may issue a PCA directive if a ratio falls below its specified threshold. See Exhibit 3.19 for threshold ratios.

EXHIBIT 3.19 Threshold Ratios for Prompt Corrective Action (PCA)

	Threshold Ratios				
PCA Capital Category	**Total RBC ratio**	**Tier 1 RBC ratio**	**CET1 RBC ratio**	**Tier 1 Leverage ratio**	**CBLR**
Well capitalized	10%	8%	6.5%	5%	> **9.0%**
Adequately capitalized	8%	6%	4.5%	4%	≥ **7.5%**
Undercapitalized	< 8%	< 6%	< 4.5%	< 4%	< **7.5%**
Significantly undercapitalized	< 6%	< 4%	< 3%	<3%	< **6.0%**
Critically undercapitalized	Tangible Equity/Total Assets ≤ 2%*				

Source: FDIC

ADEQUATELY CAPITALIZED RATIOS

Current rules require banks to maintain a minimum level in order to be considered Adequately Capitalized. These are 4.5%, 6%, 8%, and 4% for the CET 1, Tier 1 RBC, Total RBC, and the Leverage Ratio respectively.

In order to be considered Well Capitalized these ratios have to be 6.5%, 8%, 10%, and 5%, respectively. To avoid restrictions on capital distributions, banks also have to maintain a Capital Conservation Buffer of 2.5%. Adding this buffer to the minimum levels raises CET 1, Tier 1 RBC, and the Total RBC Ratio 7%, 8.5%, and 10.5%, respectively.

CAPITAL CONSERVATION BUFFER

Beginning 2016 banks were required to maintain a capital conservation buffer (Exhibit 3.20).

EXHIBIT 3.20 CET1 Conservation Buffer Schedule

Year	CET1 Capital Conservation Buffer
2016	0.625%
2017	1.25%
2018	1.875%
2019	2.50%

Source: FDIC

COMMUNITY BANK LEVERAGE RATIO (CBLR)

$$CBLR = \frac{Tangible\ Equity}{Total\ Consolidated\ Assets}$$

Community banks under $10B in assets can use the simplified Community Bank Leverage Ratio framework. This requires a bank to maintain a CBLR $\geq$ 9% and have MSRs and temporary difference DTAs each under 25% of CBLR tangible equity, with trading assets and liabilities under 5% of consolidated assets and off-balance sheet exposure under 25% of consolidated assets. These are considered qualifying community banks and are exempt from Basel III.

DODD-FRANK ACT STRESS TEST (DFAST)

DFAST is a quantitative evaluation of how bank capital ratios would be impacted under scenarios of stress tests. Under new rules banks with $10B–250B of assets are no longer required to perform company run stress tests. Banks with $100B–$250B in assets will see periodic testing. DFAST assumes that common dividends are maintained flat from the prior year and scheduled dividends, interest, or principal payments for any Tier 1 or Tier 2 capital instrument are paid and there are no repurchases of Tier 1 or Tier 2 capital instruments. For the 2019 DFAST cycle, 18 banks were tested and the scenarios included 28 variables. The severely adverse scenario for the 2019 cycle assumed a global recession with the unemployment rate in the US rising to 10%.

DFAST 2020: COVID-19 EDITION

2020 brought about a devastating exogenous shock to the global economy in the form of the COVID-19 pandemic, which led to unprecedented shutdowns in the economy. As the duration and severity of the pandemic, and thus the impact to the economy, was an unknown to even medical experts, financial regulators opted to adjust the DFAST and CCAR for banks in 2020 to reflect for this uncertainty.

Multiple Scenarios – Due to the uncertainty over the duration and severity of the virus impact, banks were asked to conduct stress tests on a number of probable scenarios: a sharp V-shaped rebound, a slower U-shaped recovery, and a W-shaped "double dip" recession (Exhibit 3.21). We would not pretend to have any insights into the path of the recovery, and we thought it prudent for the regulators to also tweak the stress tests to reflect the huge amount of uncertainty going into the next four to six quarters.

Capital Return – Additionally, the Federal Reserve conservatively opted to suspend large bank share repurchases for 3Q20, and cap dividends to a formula based on recent income. Specifically, dividend payments at large banks cannot exceed the trailing four-quarter average net income.

Stressed Capital Buffer (SCB) – In March 2020, The Federal Reserve implemented a simplification to its capital rules for large banks, known as the stressed capital buffer. As the name suggests, the SCB integrates the annual stress test results to determine a capital buffer appropriate for a company's risk profile. In this way, the amount of capital a large institution is required to hold is uniquely calculated based on its estimated risk profile.

EXHIBIT 3.21 Fed's COVID-19 Sensitivity Scenarios

Table 2. Select scenario variables in the severely adverse and alternative downside scenarios

Scenario	Peak unemployment rate	Peak-to-trough GDP change	Lowest 10-year Treasury rate
Severely adverse	10.0	−8.5	0.7
V-shaped scenario	19.5	−10.0	0.8
U-shaped scenario	15.6	−13.8	0.6
W-shaped scenario	16.0	−12.4	0.5

Source: Federal Reserve

COMPREHENSIVE CAPITAL ANALYSIS AND REVIEW (CCAR)

CCAR uses the quantitative framework of DFAST and includes planned dividend payments and stock repurchases. CCAR does a qualitative assessment of capital plans.

EVOLUTION OF CAPITAL RATIOS

The history of capital to asset ratios is interesting. The ratio of capital to assets fell remarkably since 1860 through about 1945. It held roughly flat before declining at a moderate pace from 1945 to 1980. From 1980 to 1985 it increased to 6% uniform capital guidelines. In 1974, the Governors of the Central Banks of the G10 member nations formed the Basel Committee. This started the first multilateral coordination of regulatory capital rules. Basel I of 1988 called for a minimum ratio of capital to risk weighted assets of 8% to be in place by 1992. Basel II of 2004 maintained the 8% requirement while making substantial revisions. It introduced three pillars: 1. Minimum capital requirements; 2. Supervisory review process; and 3. Market discipline and disclosure. Basel III was issued in December 2010 in response to the Global Financial Crisis. Community Banks in the US became subject to Basel III in 2015 with a phase-in through 2019. See Exhibit 3.22 for a timeline of the evolution of capital to assets ratio in the US since 1860.

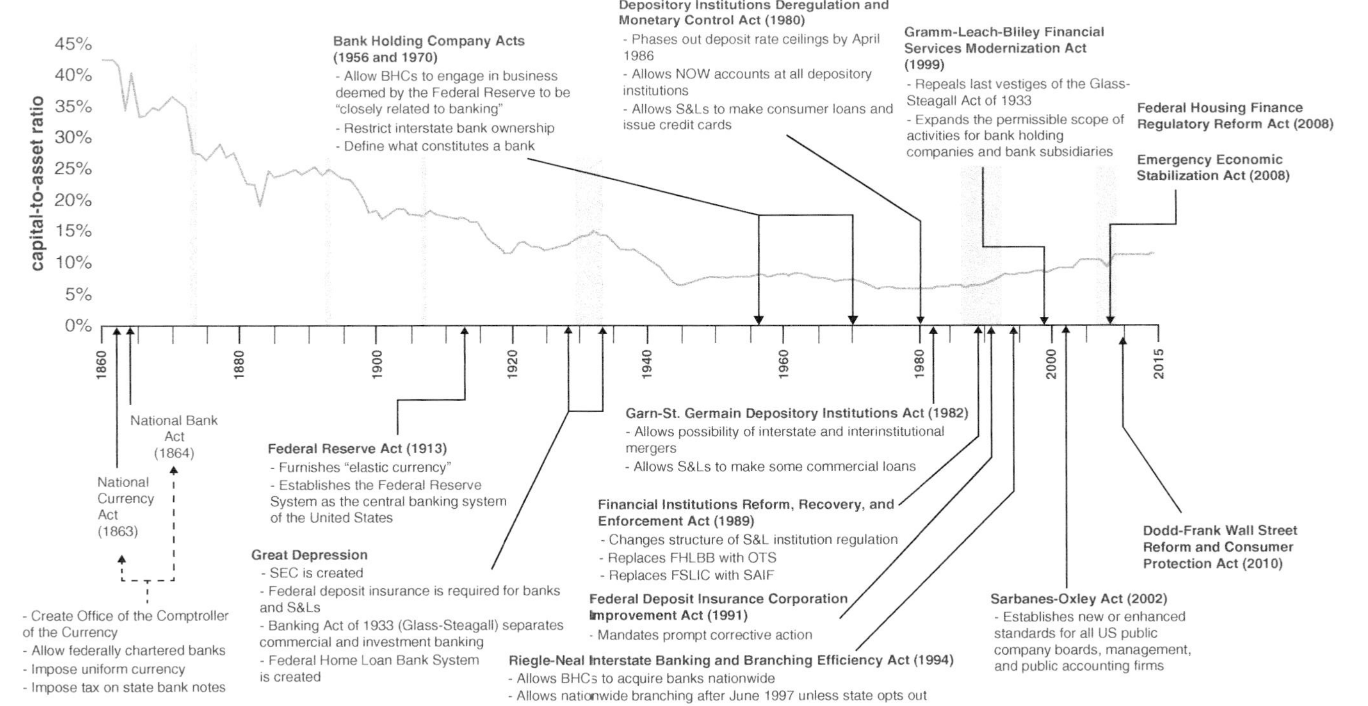

EXHIBIT 3.22 Timeline of Evolution of Capital to Asset Ratio

Notes: Shaded areas indicate crisis periods. BHC = bank holding company; FHLBB = Federal Home Loan Bank Board; FSLIC = Federal Savings and Loan Insurance Corporation; NOW = negotiable order of withdrawal; OTS = Office of Thrift Supervision; S&Ls = savings and loans; SAIF = Savings Association Insurance Fund; SEC = Securities and Exchange Commision.

Source: Benefits and Costs of a Higher Bank Leverage Ratio, James R. Barth and Stephen Matteo Miller, February 2017; Mercatus Working Paper.https://www.mercatus.org/system/files/barth-leverage-ratio-mercatus-working-paper-v1.pdf

4

Credit

"But Credit being nothing but the expectation of Money within some limited time, Money must be had or Credit will fail."

—John Locke 1632–1704

This chapter delves a little deeper on the topic of credit. We had previously discussed allowances for credit losses (also called loan loss reserves) in Chapter 2.

AREN'T HIGHER RESERVES BETTER?

Not really. Reserves need to be appropriate. While a low level of reserves may very well be inadequate and a high level of reserves may indicate conservatism, it is not always the case. Banks that have been acquisitive may have reserves that appear understated. This is because historically, the loan loss reserves of the acquired bank do not carry over, and the target's loans are brought onto the acquiror's balance sheet at fair value, inclusive of credit marks. Prospectively, this has changed under the new CECL accounting standards (colloquially pronounced "see-sul") which we dive into in Chapter 8.

There was a time when not many banks set up reserve accounts, and there was also a time when banks were told by regulators that their reserve levels were too high! (Exhibit 4.1) It would be instructive to take a short detour through history to see how we got here.

Prior to 1947, most banks deducted loan losses directly from earnings on the income statement and retained earnings from the balance sheet when the loan was charged off.

As can be seen in Exhibit 4.1, the percentage of banks with a reserve account went up significantly from 1948 onwards. Driving this increase was a

EXHIBIT 4.1 Percentage of Banks with a Reserve Account

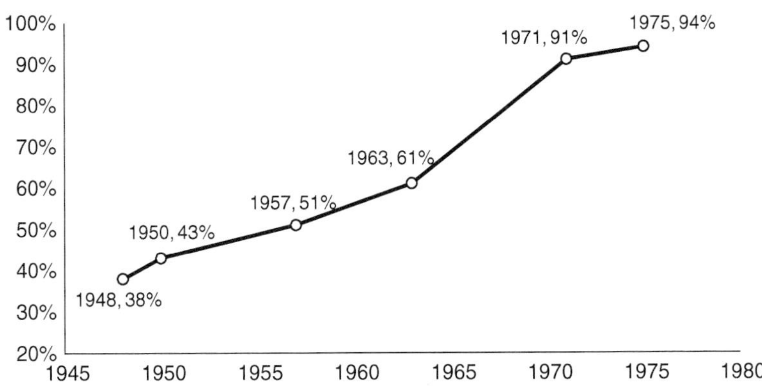

Source: Richmond Fed

regulatory change implemented December 1947 that permitted banks to calculate loan loss reserves in a manner different than other entities. Specifically, banks were allowed to hold reserves equal to three times the average annual loss rate over the prior 20-year period. This benefit gave banks a tax advantage as the provision is a tax-deductible expense. In 1969 the Tax Reform Act was passed, requiring banks to reduce reserves in a phased manner. The prescribed maximum reserves to loans above which deductions could not be made to pre-tax income were 1.8% from 1969 to 1975, 1.2% from 1975 to 1981, and 0.6% from 1982 to 1987.

Subsequently, in 1986, the Tax Reform Act was passed, and it allowed banks with assets under $500MM to continue under the 1969 act, while banks with over $500MM in assets were not allowed to make additional provisions above the current year's charge-offs. These tax regulations took away the tax incentive to maintain a reserve level at a certain percentage of loans. Additionally, accounting regulations were also issued that had an impact. In 1973, FASB issued FAS Statement 5 (FAS 5). FAS 5 laid the foundation for impairment to be recognized, based on it being probable and the amount of loss being reasonably estimable.

Note: FAS 5 was later amended by FAS 114 issued in 1993, which also amended FAS 15 for TDR (Trouble Debt Restructuring). We promise not to wade deep into accounting waters as we want to keep the matter as simple as possible. Readers who are keen to learn more should visit FASB.org and read FAS 5, FAS

15, FAS 114 (an amendment of FAS 5 and 15), ASU Accounting Standards Update 2016-13, and ASU 2018-19.

In the 1980s bank failures increased and regulators allowed banks to deviate from the fixed percentage of loans (the default practice following the tax reform act of 1969). Instead, banks were allowed to look at loss history, specific loan level analysis, and a comparison of peers to determine reserve levels.

In the late 1990s, accounting regulators were concerned about excessive reserves as a mechanism for cookie jar accounting and earnings management. Congress held hearings, and in November 1998 Suntrust announced they had agreed to decrease its reserves by $100mm and restate earnings for 1994, 1995, and 1996. These hearings and actions had the effect to somewhat reduce the level of reserves.

In 2020, the FASB accounting standard known as CECL came into effect, requiring banks to set aside loss reserves for the *entire* life of a loan, effectively increasing the reserve ratios in the industry (Exhibits 4.2 and 4.3).

Where does that leave us today? As we alluded to earlier, banks have a certain amount of latitude when it comes to determining the appropriate levels of loan loss reserves. As we can see in the following distribution, as of 2017 the average loan loss reserve sits at about 1.3% of gross loans, with a standard deviation of ±0.8% (Exhibit 4.4).

EXHIBIT 4.2 Reserves as a % of Noncurrent Loans & Leases (Also Known as the "Reserve Coverage Ratio")

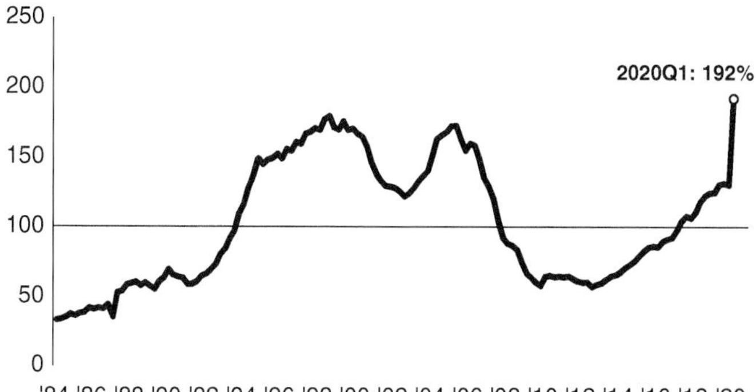

Source: FDIC

EXHIBIT 4.3 Loan Losses and Reserve to Loans

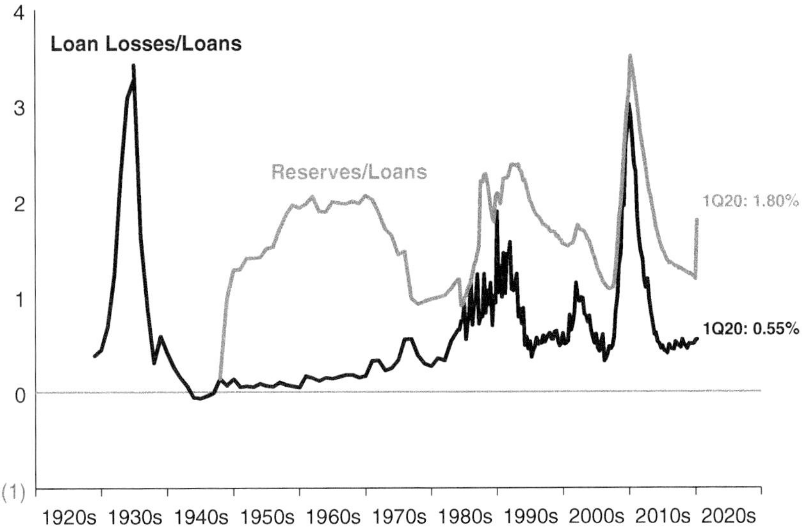

Source: St. Louis Fed, FDIC

EXHIBIT 4.4 All US Banks: Loan Loss Reserve to Loans

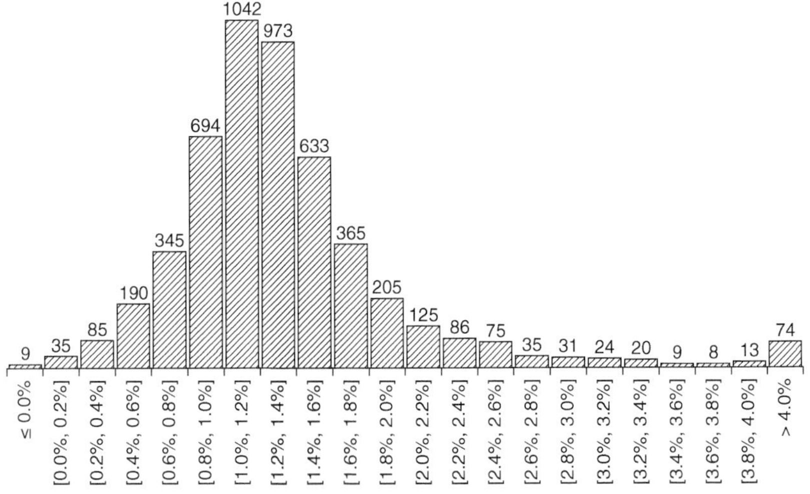

Source: FDIC

WHY IS CREDIT SO IMPORTANT?

The average bank is about 10 times levered. Thus, a 10% write-off to the asset base of a bank could hypothetically wipe out shareholder equity entirely. Given the high leverage, the underwriting and risk management functions are critical to the health and survival of the bank. When evaluating the credit quality of a bank's loan book, we look at the following.

CREDIT METRICS

Texas Ratio, Net Charge-Offs (NCOs) as a % of loans, Non-Performing Loans (NPLs) as a % of loans, Non-Performing Assets (NPAs) as a % of Assets, Reserve Coverage Ratio (LLR to noncurrent loans and leases), Reserves to Loans, Provisions to Loans, and Increase in OREO.

	Loans Past Due
+	*Non-Accruals*
+	*Troubled Debt Restructurings (TDRs)*
	Non-Performing Loans (NPLs)
+	*Other Real Estate Owned (OREO)*
	Non-Performing Assets (NPAs)

All these metrics have been covered in Chapter 2 with the exception of the Texas Ratio. If one is looking at historical reserve data, we would make one clarification. Under the incurred loss method (the accounting standards preceding CECL) a bank that has been acquisitive could have an artificially depressed reserve level. Consider a bank with $1B in gross loans and an ALLL of 1.5%; the net loans will be $985MM. Say this bank acquires another which has $500MM in gross loans and an ALLL of 3%. The reserves of the seller do not transfer, hence, these are cancelled. Say the acquirer takes a credit mark of 5%. The pro forma LLR as % of loans shows 1.01% which is below the original 1.5% of the acquirer and the 3% of the target; this is understated since there was a credit mark of 5% taken. See Exhibit 4.5, which depicts this example.

EXHIBIT 4.5 Understated Reserves for an Acquirer Under Historical Purchase Accounting

($000s)	Acquiror +	Target +	Adjustments =	Pro Forma
Gross Loans	1,000,000	500,000	(25,000) 5% Credit Mark 12,500 2.5% Interest Rate Mark	1,487,500
Loan Loss Reserve	15,000	15,000	(15,000) Cancel Target's LLR	15,000
Net Loans	985,000	485,000		1,472,500
LLR to Loans	***1.50%***	***3.00%***		***1.01%***

TEXAS RATIO

The Texas Ratio was developed by Gerard Cassidy of RBC during the 1980s recession to analyze banks in the Texas region. It is defined as *NPAs/(TCE + LLR)*. As this ratio gets closer to 100%, the likelihood of a bank's failure increases. The relationship is intuitive as the denominator represents the buffer for depositors against loan losses, the reserve denoting the specific allowance against losses, and the TCE denoting the equity capital, which is the last line of defense before the bank needs to get re-capitalized. This was first seen among Texas banks in the 1980s and has been borne out during various periods of financial crises. As of Q2:2018, there are about 25 banks with Texas ratio above 100%; this compares to about 500 banks at the peak of the global financial crisis. During the last banking crisis Georgia, Florida, and California had a higher percentage of banks with a Texas Ratio > 100%. Geographies matter when one does bank analysis (Exhibits 4.6 and 4.7).

Exhibit 4.8 is from a publication by Moody's Analytics, "Bank Failures Past and Present: Validating the RiskCalc" v3.1 U.S. Banks Model.

The panel on the left depicts the months prior to default of banks that closed during the period 1982–2004. The panel on the right displays average over quarter ending for bank closures during the period July 2004–2009.

The left panel in Exhibit 4.8 displays the historical time period (1982–2004), while the right panel displays recent events (July 2004–July 2009). As displayed in Exhibit 4.8, the Texas Ratio was much more pronounced during the prior historical period. During the S&L crisis, the median Texas Ratio one year prior to failure was 110%, while it was 37% for the latter period.

EXHIBIT 4.6 Texas Ratio and Bank Failures

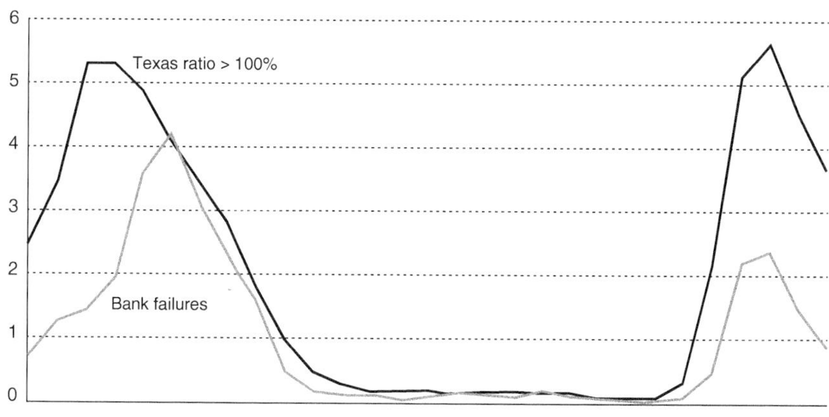

Source: Federal Reserve Bank of Dallas

EXHIBIT 4.7 Texas Ratio in the States of GA, FL, CA, and TX

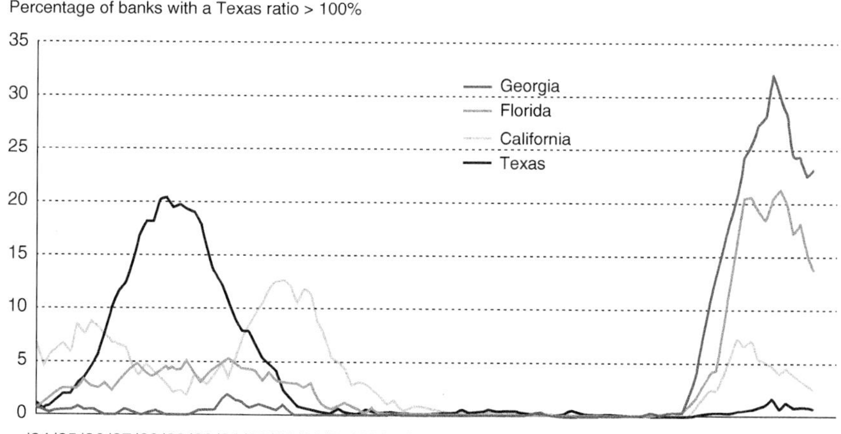

Source: Federal Reserve Bank of Dallas

EXHIBIT 4.8 Texas Ratio for Failing Banks Prior to Closure

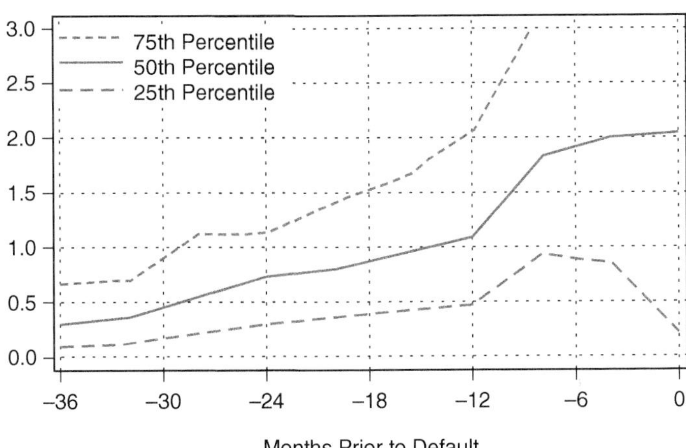

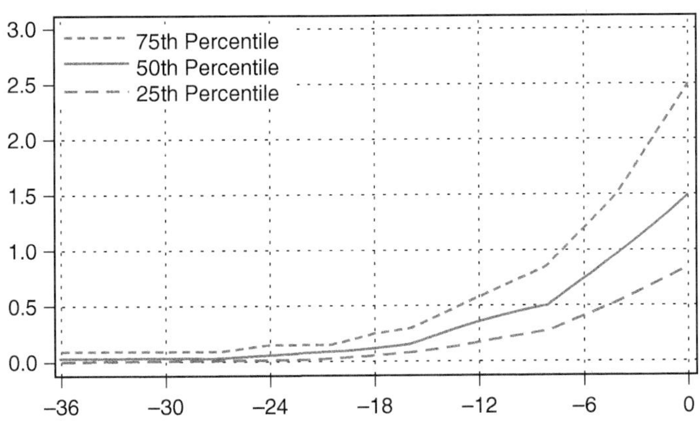

Source: Moody's Analytics (October 8, 2009)

CREDIT QUALITY INDICATORS

It is instructive to look at the *changes* in credit quality classifications over time, the language in the footnotes, as well as the age analysis in the 10-Q and 10-K filings to discern any emerging credit trends. Loans are classified by the potential for nonpayment as Pass, Special Mention, Substandard, Doubtful, and Loss (Exhibits 4.9, 4.10, and 4.11).

Not all banks will publish loan classifications to this degree of granularity; some only provide non-classified versus classified, while others may provide their own categories for credit quality indicators. In case you find public disclosures deficient, you may pull up the call reports, which use the standardized reporting metrics described earlier. However, it is possible that a bank does not disclose these in the call report either. Instead, you may only see "CONF," meaning confidential since regulators only require certain metrics by large and/or highly complex institutions to be disclosed.

While tracking the changes in quality classification can be edifying, predicting the future course of credit migration is not easy. One particularly counterintuitive example is commercial banking line-of-credits. One may see increases in classified assets driven by more advances made to a relationship that had already been moved to classified during a prior period. This can be perplexing: Why would a bank extend *more* credit to an at-risk customer? We distinctly remember two situations. In one situation we were told that the loan was still performing and since there was no violation of covenants, the bank was obliged to make advances as required in the loan agreement, and they were only able to cut off advances when there was a violation of terms. In the other situation, there was an offshore pipe that had burst, and the borrower was unable to make payments and needed an additional loan in order to repair the pipe. It would have clearly been better for the bank to cut off a relationship and not make any more advances at the first sign of deteriorating fundamentals and not have to wait for specific violations; however, in some cases, the loan agreements do not permit this.

EXHIBIT 4.9 Classification Categories

	CRITICIZED			
Pass	**Special Mention**	**CLASSIFIED**		
		Substandard	**Doubtful**	**Loss**
(1)	(2)	(3)	(4)	(5)

EXHIBIT 4.10 Credit Quality for FNB Bancorp 1Q 2018 vs. 4Q 2017

Credit Quality Indicators As of March 31, 2018

(Dollar amounts in thousands)

	Pass	Special mention	Sub-standard	Doubtful	Total loans
Originated					
Commercial real estate	$ 395,216	$ —	$ 2,082	$ 33	$ 397,331
Real estate construction	35,984	—	791	—	36,775
Real estate multi-family	92,949	—	2,348	—	95,297
Real estate – 1 to 4 family	165,029	—	134	—	165,163
Commercial & industrial	46,844	771	288	—	47,903
Consumer loans	17,993	—	—	—	17,993
Totals	$ 754,015	$ 771	$ 5,643	$ 33	$ 760,462
Purchased					
Not credit impaired					
Commercial real estate	$ 56,104	$ —	$ 565	$ —	$ 56,669
Real estate multi-family	10,483	—	—	—	10,483
Real estate – 1 to 4 family	10,493	—	—	—	10,493
Commercial & industrial	3,617	—	—	—	3,617
Total	$ 80,697	$ —	$ 565	$ —	$ 81,262
Purchased					
Credit impaired					
Commercial real estate					$ —
Total					$ —

Credit Quality Indicators As of December 31, 2017

(Dollar amounts in thousands)

	Pass	Special mention	Sub-standard	Doubtful	Total loans
Originated					
Commercial real estate	$ 397,311	$ —	$ 3,846	$ —	$ 401,157
Real estate construction	34,392	—	814	—	35,206
Real estate multi-family	91,642	—	—	—	91,642
Real estate – 1 to 4 family	159,881	—	544	—	160,425
Commercial & industrial	51,968	—	302	—	52,270
Consumer loans	14,057	—	—	—	14,057
Totals	$ 749,251	$ —	$ 5,506	$ —	$ 754,757
Purchased					
Not credit impaired					
Commercial real estate	$ 53,656	$ 873	$ 1,306	$ —	$ 55,835
Real estate multi-family	13,496	—	—	—	13,496
Real estate – 1 to 4 family	13,051	—	—	—	13,051
Commercial & industrial	3,457	—	—	—	3,457
Total	$ 83,660	$ 873	$ 1,306	$ —	$ 85,839
Purchased					

EXHIBIT 4.11 Age Analysis for FNB Bancorp 1Q 2018 vs. 4Q 2017

Age Analysis of Past Due Loans As of March 31, 2018

(Dollar amounts in thousands)

	30-59 Days Past Due	60-89 Days Past Due	Over 90 Days	Total Past Due	Current	Total Loans
Originated						
Commercial real estate	$ 1,150	$ 611	$—	$ 1,761	$ 395,570	$ 397,331
Real estate construction	—	—	—	—	36,775	36,775
Real estate multi family	—	—	2,348	2,348	92,949	95,297
Real estate – 1 to 4 family	1,971	443	135	2,549	162,614	165,163
Commercial & industrial	1,117	—	693	1,810	46,093	47,903
Consumer	102	—	—	102	17,891	17,993
Total	$ 4,340	$ 1,054	$ 3,176	$ 8,570	$ 751,892	$ 760,462
Purchased						
Not credit impaired						
Commercial real estate	$—	$—	$ 484	$ 484	$ 56,185	$ 56,669
Real estate multi-family	—	—	—	—	10,483	10,483
Real estate – 1 to 4 family	—	736	—	736	9,757	10,493
Commercial & industrial	—	—	—	—	3,617	3,617
Total	$ $	$ 736	$ 484	$ 1,220	$ 80,042	$ 81,262

Age Analysis of Past Due Loans As of December 31, 2017

(Dollar amounts in thousands)

	30-59 Days Past Due	60-89 Days Past Due	Over 90 Days	Total Past Due	Current	Total Loans
Originated						
Commercial real estate	$ 989	$ 597	$—	$ 1,586	$ 399,571	$ 401,157
Real estate construction	—	—	—	—	35,206	35,206
Real estate multi- family	—	2,348	—	2,348	89,294	91,642
Real estate – 1 to 4 family	1,603	1,082	464	3,149	157,276	160,425
Commercial & industrial	69	250	745	1,064	51,206	52,270
Consumer	52	—	—	52	14,005	14,057
Total	$ 2,713	$ 4,277	$ 1,209	$ 8,199	$ 746,558	$ 754,757
Purchased						
Not credit impaired						
Commercial real estate	$—	$ 85	$—	$ 85	$ 55,750	$ 55,835
Real estate multi-family	—	—	—	—	13,496	13,496
Real estate – 1 to 4 family	—	—	—	—	13,051	13,051
Commercial & industrial	—	—	—	—	3,457	3,457
Total	$—	$ 85	$—	$ 85	$ 85,754	$ 85,839

CREDIT QUALITY REGRESSION

This is only possible in a category where there are specific reserves and disclosure. Bank of Oklahoma (BOKF) ran an interesting regression of credit quality versus reserves in energy, quality being defined as the criticized, classified, and nonaccruals % of the energy loan book. The level of reserves needs to be commensurate with the level of quality. Interestingly, BOKF had one of the larger energy exposures during the 2014 energy price decline and came out not just unscathed but looking really good (Exhibit 4.12).

EXHIBIT 4.12 Credit Quality Regression

Energy credit quality regression

Energy Credit Quality vs. LLR%

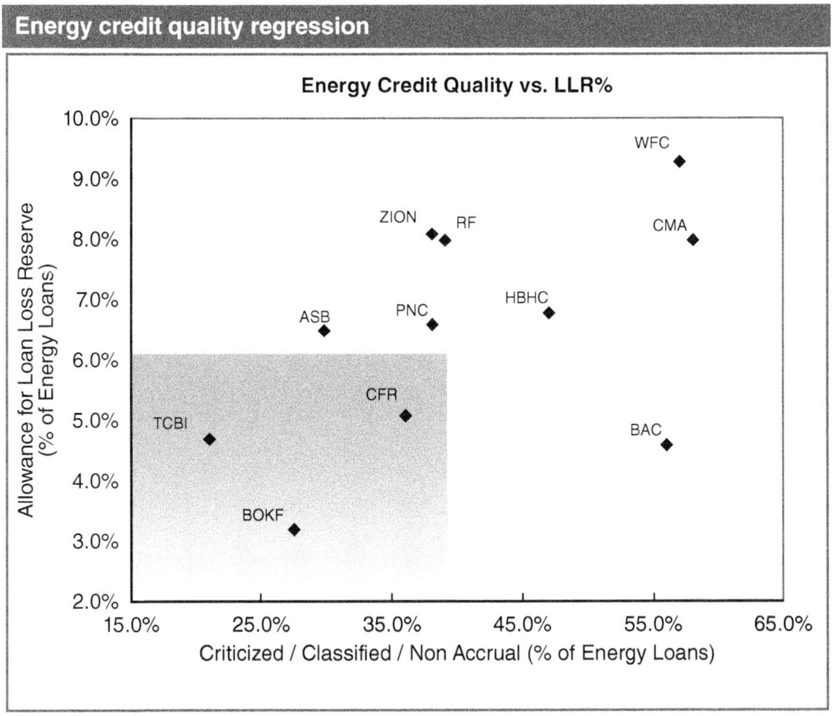

Source: BOKF 2016 filing

SHOCK SCENARIOS

Community banks with assets under $10B are not subject to stress testing requirements. These are generally difficult to obtain and will be close to impossible to calculate for the outside investor. However, a discussion with the management team can get you a sense of how they think about these items. Commercial Real Estate (CRE) loans can be north of 60% of a community bank's loans. The two measures that are key to CRE underwriting are advance rates (LTV, most commonly or LTC) and the Debt Service Coverage Ratio (DSCR). LTV refers to the Loan to Value ratio (also called the advance rate), while LTC is Loan to Cost.

For example, if the appraised value of a real estate asset is $10MM and the loan made by the bank is $8MM, the LTV is 80%. The credit analyst may feel that there is some margin of safety here, but if this asset is actually being purchased for $8MM, the LTC is 100%. LTC is the more conservative measure. If a bank is making loans on LTV, try to get a sense of the cap rate assumptions being made to impute value. If the cap rates used are significantly lower than comparable properties, the LTV might be understated.

$$\textit{Debt Service Coverage Ratio (DSCR)} = \frac{\textit{Annual Net Operating Income}}{\textit{Annual Debt Service}}$$

The DSCR is simply a ratio of income to expense. Thus, we would want this ratio to be >1 (aka, the available operating income can more than cover the debt expense). The debt service can vary based on the loan terms. For a fully amortizing loan, this would equal the principal and interest payment due.

The typical max LTV ratios are 75–80%, and typical minimum DSCR is 120–125%. If there is a CRE loan category where one expects to see some credit migration downward, one must ask management teams if they have tested for shock scenarios and seen how the LTV and DSCR ratios hold up. These shock scenarios may include widening cap rates, which lower property value and hence stresses LTV, or declining occupancy rate assumptions stressing DSCR.

GAUGING THE UNDERWRITING PROCESS

The underwriting process at the bank can be gauged by asking quantitative and qualitative questions related to the limits, policies, exceptions, and overall process underpinning the credit decisions. There are no right or wrong answers; one is trying to gauge the robustness of the underwriting process and getting an outsider view on the overall credit culture permeating the bank.

What Is the House Limit?

The house limit is the maximum loan exposure per relationship. This is generally going to be well below the legal lending limit. The legal lending limit is set at 15% of the unimpaired capital and surplus of the bank plus an additional 10% if this is fully secured by readily marketable collateral.

$$\begin{aligned} \textit{Legal Lending Limit} &= 15\% \times (\textit{Capital} + \textit{Surplus}) \\ &= 15\% \times (\textit{Tier } 1 + \textit{Tier } 2 + \textit{ALLL not in } T2) \end{aligned}$$

At our example bank, FNBG, the legal lending limits were $19,129,000 on an unsecured basis and $31,882,000 on a fully secured basis as per their 2017 10-K.

As a back-of-the-envelope shortcut, simply taking 15% of total stockholder equity *should* get you an estimate that's below the actual value, but within the wheelhouse. For instance, FNBG's stockholder equity of $119MM x 15% = ~$18MM

How Many Loans Exceed the House Limit?

What Are the Largest Relationships (Size and Category)?

Loan size matters, doubly so as banks are highly levered institutions. A loan that might not be a large percentage of the loan book could still be a large percentage of the equity capital, as illustrated in Exhibits 4.13 and 4.14. Intuitively, a larger size loan going bad is worse than a smaller size loan. Thus, generally we have a preference for a more granular loan book.

What Are the Approval Limits and the Hierarchy of Approvals?

Several banks have tiers for approvals, with the highest levels sometimes requiring decisions by a board level committee. But just because a committee decides whether credit is to be advanced or not and a longer process is taken does not make the decision process sounder or the credit any safer. There are other banks that have built systems to give a quicker answer to borrowers, and these could arguably be just as safe. We had one risk officer tell us how reliance on committees can be counterproductive since group think can quickly take over and there is no incentive for any one member to deviate from the consensus. Conversely, the banks that have built systems that

EXHIBIT 4.13 A $40MM Charge-off at a Hypothetical Bank

ABC Bank	($MMs)	ABC Bank after a $40MM charge	($000s)
Loans (Net of $200MM allowance)	2,000	Loans (Net of $200MM allowance)	1,960
Investments	850	Investments	850
Other	450	Other	490
Intangibles	100	Intangibles	100
Total Assets	**3,400**	**Total Assets**	**3,400**
Non-Int. Bearing Deposits	1,100	Non-Int. Bearing Deposits	1,100
Other Deposits	1,850	Other Deposits	1,850
Borrowings	40	Borrowings	40
Other	60	Other	100
Common Equity	350	Common Equity	310
Total Liabilities & Equity	**3,400**	**Total Liabilities & Equity**	**3,400**
Tangible Common Equity	250	Tangible Common Equity	210
Tangible Assets	3,300	Tangible Assets	3,300
TCE/TA	**7.58%**	**TCE/TA**	**6.36%**
Legal Lending Limit (Unsecured)	68		
Impaired Credit	60		
Charge Off	40		
as % of Credit	*67%*		
as % of Net Loans	*2%*		

EXHIBIT 4.14 Charge-off Size and Impact to TCE

	TCE/TA Sensitivity to Charge-Offs						
Charge Off ($MM)	**10**	**20**	**30**	**40**	**50**	**60**	**70**
TCE/TA	7.27%	6.97%	6.67%	6.36%	6.06%	5.76%	5.45%
Impact (bps)	(30)	(61)	(91)	(121)	(152)	(182)	(212)

respond faster may be lauded for their efforts, but we are yet to see a model that has been able to predict risk. Any model is only as good as the inputs, and during benign credit environments the inputs are unlikely to cause the model to give a result that goes against the grain.

Are there any collateral exceptions?

How many loans are made out of market?

Does the bank use loan brokers?

Are there early warning measures?

Some banks have built systems where they can ingest monthly financials and quickly highlight credits that need a closer look.

How Many Loans Are Made Under Regulation O?

Reg O is a Federal Reserve regulation governing the lending towards insiders. There is nothing wrong with making loans to insiders so long as these are disclosed appropriately and they are made with generally a similar pricing and structure as comparable loans made to non-insiders and similar to what these insiders could have obtained at other banks.

How Are Loan Officers Compensated?

Are there incentives based on performance over time or are the incentives primarily based on growth?

Names of relationship officers in specific sectors where the bank has a large book. Tracking the underwriting history of specific loan officers from institution to institution has helped us build confidence and also avoid certain situations. Talk to local bankers in the market.

PRICING AND STRUCTURE

Markets are generally efficient. A bank that is able to underwrite loans at higher-than-average yields might be taking on more risk. Indeed, we can see the tight correlation between loan yields and loans past due across a sample of all US banks (Exhibit 4.15). Has the bank seen a big increase in loan yields and are the loan yields higher than peer medians? Is this bank stretching for yield, getting adversely selected in the market, sacrificing structure and underwriting standards for pricing?

Questions to ask management on pricing & structure:

1. *What are the typical covenants used in the loan agreements?*
2. *Under what exceptions are the covenants waived?*
3. *Does the bank do second liens, mezzanine, leveraged loans, or subordinated debt?*
4. *Do the commitments have accordion features?*

EXHIBIT 4.15 Loan Yields vs. Loans Past Due

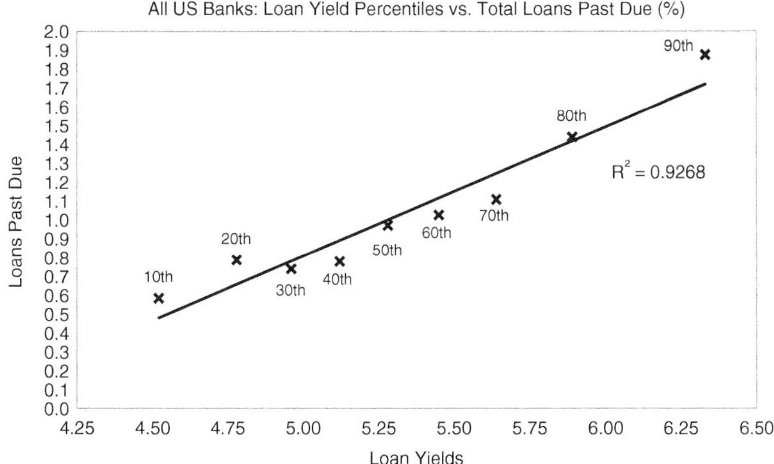

Source: S&P Global Market Intelligence

SHARED NATIONAL CREDITS (SNCs)

How Many Loans ($ Commitments, $ Outstanding, and Number of Loans) Are SNCs?

SNCs (pronounced "snicks") are syndicated bank loans that are shared by three or more banks with an aggregate loan commitment of greater than $100MM. This loan commitment threshold used to be $20MM since 1977 and was revised to $100MM effective 1/1/2018. See Exhibits 4.16, 4.17, and 4.18 for the impact of the SNC definition change.

How many loans ($ commitments, $ outstanding, and number of loans) are club deals? Club deals are loan arrangements that do not technically meet the SNC definition but share similar characteristics.

Which banks do they mostly participate with? This can be a signal for affinity and personal relationship but more importantly a signal of trust in the underwriting process.

Do You Do Your Own Underwriting in a Participation?

Who is typically the agent bank in the SNC deals? The agent is the administrative agent or lead bank that reports the SNC. This is good to know since if the agent banks are very large institutions, their decision to push a credit to

EXHIBIT 4.16 SNC Change

	SNC Using $20 Million	SNC Using $100 Million	Net Change	% Change
Commitments ($ Billions)	$4,310	$4,218	($92)	(2%)
Borrower Count	7,036	5,463	(1,573)	(22%)
Bank Count	197	115	(82)	(42%)

Source: FDIC

EXHIBIT 4.17 SNC Volume

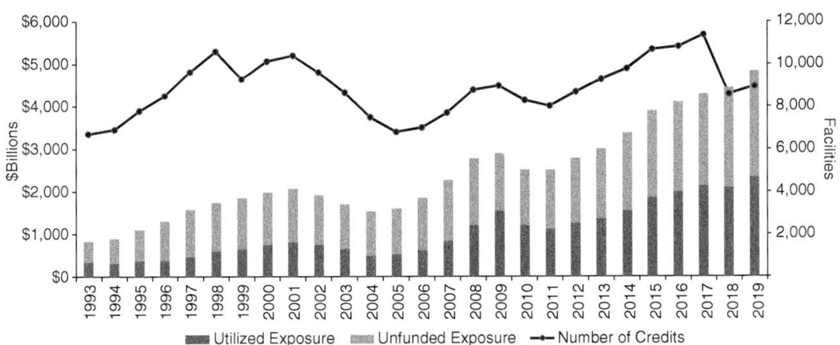

Note: The decline in the number of SNC facilities between 2017 and 2018 mainly reflects the minimum commitment increase from $20 million to $100 million.

Source: FDIC

EXHIBIT 4.18 SNC Special Mention and Classified

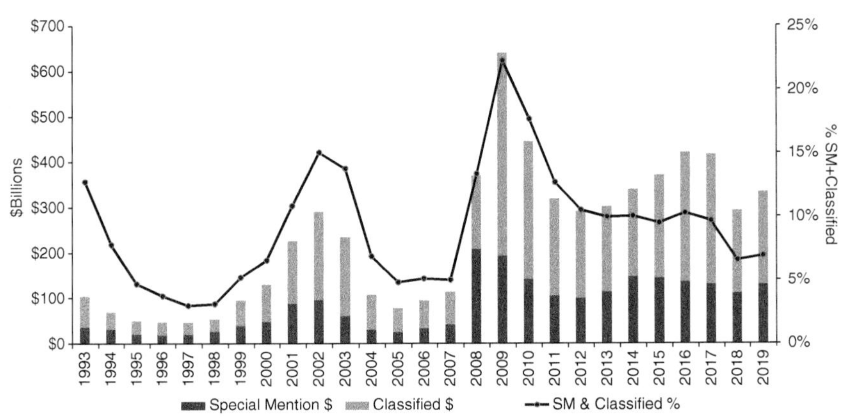

Source: FDIC

the workout team and take a charge can have significant consequences for a smaller bank on the deal. The credit may be small enough to not cause any impact to the large bank from an EPS and capital standpoint but may be big for the smaller bank. This is not to say that this consideration on its own should determine whether a credit gets adversely classified or not, but a larger bank can get more trigger-happy on a borderline credit that is small while it may be addressed more appropriately by spending more time to understand the situation and determine if a loan modification may benefit all parties.

Do they participate in syndicated term loan Bs? These loans have advantages since they are marketable, albeit they take much longer to settle. However, they can be potentially more volatile than a nontraded credit. Essentially, if a loan has a CUSIP number, it needs to be treated differently by investors.

Do They Make Leveraged Loans?

Leveraged loans meet some or all of the following four characteristics:

1. Total Debt / EBITDA > 4× or Total Senior Debt/EBITDA > 3×
   Note: This is total debt, not net of cash.
2. The use of proceeds includes LBO, M&A, or dividend payouts to equity holders
3. The borrower is recognized as a highly leveraged firm as determined by debt to equity and debt to assets.
4. The leverage ratios pro forma for the leveraged loan causes leverage ratios such as debt to assets, debt to EBITDA, and debt to FCF to exceed the peer group medians.

Do they make oil and gas loans? Oil and Gas credits have their own dynamic and need to be addressed differently.

HISTORY OF CREDIT

What were the cumulative NCOs over the cycle?

What were the peak NCOs?

Exhibit 4.19 provides a good frame of reference for assessing peak NCOs.

EXHIBIT 4.19 GFC Peak NCOs by Loan Type (2009 Q4)

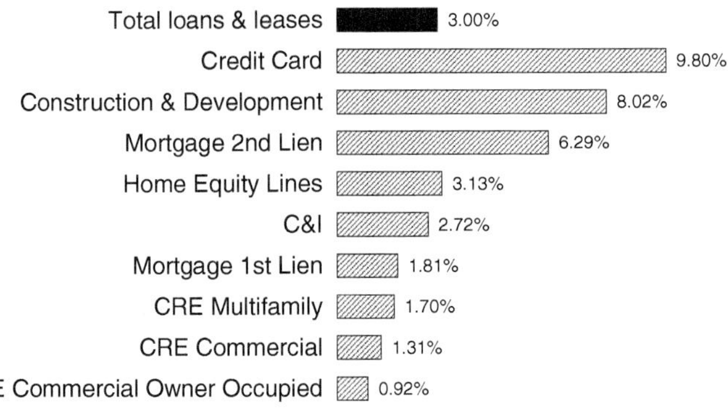

Source: FDIC

CONCENTRATION RISK

Credit concentrations are important to monitor since these exposures are likely to be positively correlated (Exhibit 4.20). Identify the large loan categories as a percentage of total loans. Identify concentration of the large

EXHIBIT 4.20 CRE as a % of Total Risk Based Capital

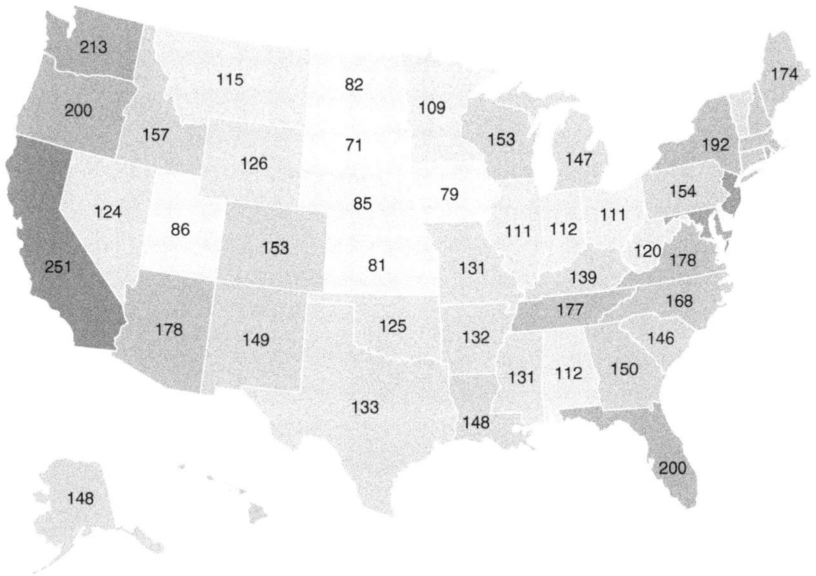

Source: S&P Global Market Intelligence

loan categories as percentage of risk-based capital. What has been the growth in the large loan categories over the last one-, two- and three-year periods? For CRE, most regulators and investors look at the following three:

1. CRE concentration as % of risk-based capital: CRE here includes investor CRE, Construction and Development (C&D), and Multifamily, but *does not* include owner-occupied CRE. The guideline is 300% but there are no hard-and-fast rules. Some banks can be >300% but have other risk mitigating factors.
2. Construction and Development (C&D) as a % of risk-based capital: The guideline is 100%.
3. Growth in CRE: The guideline is to not exceed 50% over the past three years.

HISTORY OF TEAM

Where were the CEO, CFO, and Chief Credit Officer during the Global Financial Crisis?

How did their loan book fare during that time?

What were the lessons learned during the Global Financial Crisis?

The list of topics on credit that we have presented is by no means exhaustive. To be sharp on credit, one has to be creative with the questions to elicit a response and ask questions without subjecting management to an inquisition.

CECL AND ACCOUNTING CHANGES

In 2016, FASB introduced the Current Expected Credit Loss (CECL) model (ASU 2016-13) as the new accounting standard to estimate allowances for credit losses. This will replace the current methodology based on FAS 5 and FAS 114. The change is to take effect from 1/1/2020 for SEC filers with a calendar fiscal year.

WHY CECL?

CECL seeks to temper the procyclicality of reserve accounting under the current "probable" and "incurred" methodology. As seen in Exhibit 4.21, which is a recreation from a FASB webcast for investors posted on YouTube, during the run up into the Great Financial Crisis, gross loans outstanding increased 44% but the absolute level of loan loss reserves (LLR) decreased

EXHIBIT 4.21 LLR and Loan Growth

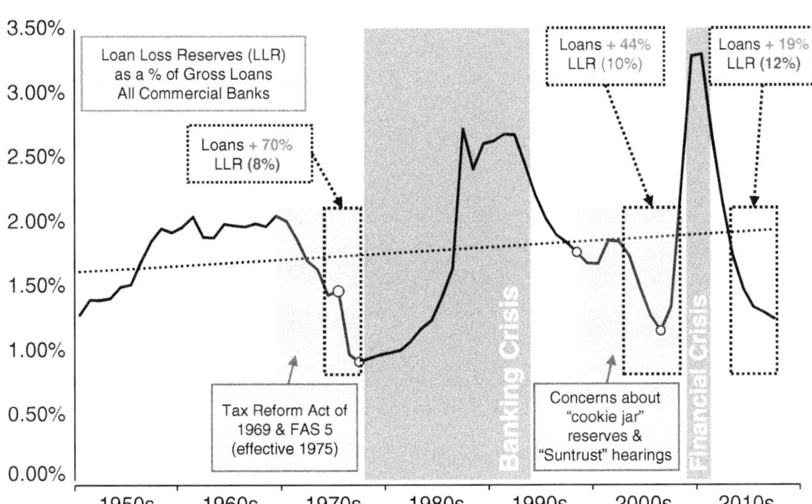

Source: FDIC, FASB (FASB Credit Losses Standard: Webcast for Investors)

10%. In 2007, loans grew 11% while reserves grew at a more rapid 29% pace, as banks were caught under-reserved. Going through the crisis, from 2007 to 2010, gross loans declined 51bps while reserves went up another 144% (Exhibit 4.22).

EXHIBIT 4.22 Reserves to Loans 2003–2012

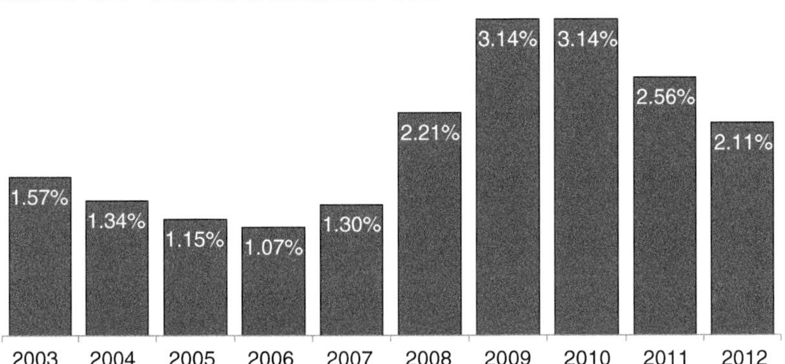

Source: FDIC

WHAT IS CHANGING?

The pre-2019 methodology is an incurred approach, meaning a loss is recognized when it is probable and the amount of loss can be reasonably estimated. General reserves are based on loss history and qualitative factors and applied across loan categories. Specific reserves are based on analysis at an individual loan level. With CECL, allowance for *lifetime losses* will be made on Day 1. Arguably, since an allowance is made on Day 1, variance over the life of the loan should be muted. We believe that allowance levels will increase for some and decrease for others depending on the mix of duration and extent of problem loans. Overall, we expect reserves to increase moderately across the banking system and, given that they are allowed three years for regulatory phase-in, unlikely to see issuance of capital.

WHAT WILL BE IMPACTED?

Loans

- Loans Held for Investment (HFI) – Changes with CECL
- Loans Held for Sale (HFS) – Lower of cost or market, no change under CECL

Securities

- Held to Maturity (HTM) – Changes with CECL
- Available for Sale (AFS) – Losses recorded through an allowance; difference between fair value and amortized cost basis
- Trading securities – no change under CECL

CECL VS. CURRENT "INCURRED LOSS" APPROACH – AN EXAMPLE

Let us walk through a simplified example. Assume:

1. A $100MM 5-year interest-only loan is underwritten.
2. The probability of default in Year 1 is 0.5%, and halves every year (i.e., Year 1 = 0.5%, Year 2 = 0.25%, etc.).
3. Loss given default is 30% of unpaid principal balance.

The current "incurred loss" methodology is actually based on two standards – FAS 5 and FAS 114.

1. **FAS 5** for general reserves allows banks to establish reserves if losses are probable (but performing) and the amount of loss can be reasonably estimated. These reserves are "pooled" by category.
2. **FAS 114** for specific reserves is concerned with evaluating impaired loans at the individual level and reserving accordingly.

In our example loan, the day 1 specific provision and hence allowance would be zero. Meanwhile, banks have some options with establishing general provision, but a common method is to look at historical loss rates from loans with similar characteristics and set aside a reserve based on probable charge-offs in the next twelve months. In this case, that would equate to 15 bps of the loan.

FAS 5 General Reserve:

$$\$100MM \times 0.5\% \times 30\% = \$150,000$$

Under the CECL approach, there is a single measurement to replace FAS 5 and FAS 114, which is the current expected losses over the *life* of the loan. One method to do this is using probabilities of default and loss given defaults. In this case, we'd calculate a 29 bps reserve.

CECL Reserve:

	Yr 1	**Yr 2**	**Yr 3**	**Yr 4**	**Yr 5**	**Cumulative**
P(Loss)	0.500%	0.250%	0.125%	0.063%	0.031%	
P(No Loss)	99.500% ×	99.750% ×	99.875% ×	99.938% ×	99.969% =	99.034%
				Cumulative P(Loss)		0.966%
				Loss Given Default		30%
				Exposure		$ 100,000,000
						$ 289,718
						0.29%

Let us say in Year 2, economic conditions deteriorate and the probability of default for the remaining life of the loan rises to 25% while loss given default remains at 30%. Under FAS 114, no specific reserve may be taken unless an actual impairment occurs. Likewise, if the bank uses historical loss rates to establish FAS 5 general reserves, they will have very limited latitude in adjusting general reserves (via qualitative adjustments). In contrast, reserves under CECL could rise to $7.5MM, requiring an additional $7.2MM provision to be taken.

WILL IT REDUCE PROCYCLICALITY?

We get the need to reduce procyclicality. The data seen in Exhibit 4.21 is stark. The increases in loan loss reserves and growth in loans have not only not kept up with each other but have even gone the opposite way. While CECL will reduce procyclicality since you take the reserves up front, we suspect procyclicality will return in other forms. A bank that is forced to take a large up-front credit reserve may, during recessionary times, just turn off underwriting new loans. This exacerbates a tighter credit environment further and worsens recessionary conditions.

OUR TAKE ON CECL

We are going to be limited in our take on CECL since regulators are expected to provide additional guidance once CECL is adopted.

We believe that CECL penalizes duration and loss content and thus certain loan categories will be impacted more, especially consumer loans. Within consumer loans we expect Student Loans, Personal, Card, and Auto to be impacted in decreasing order (Exhibit 4.23).

EXHIBIT 4.23 Duration and Loss Content Matrix

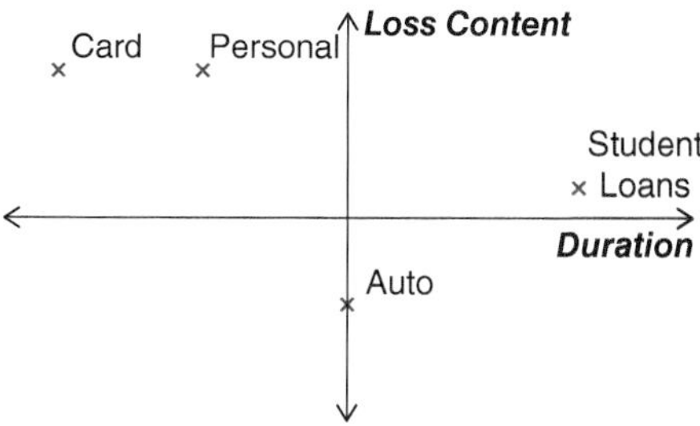

We expect ALLL for Consumer Finance books will likely go up 50–100% while other books likely go up 25–50%. The Day 1 impact likely reduces TCE by 10–15%. Since regulatory capital phase-in is allowed over three years, we suspect more banks will take a bigger Day 1 hit to capital and avoid EPS impact over the life of the loan. In our view banks are being given a fair amount of latitude in determination, and we believe that not all are decisions are going to be congruent. There will be those that are conservative, others less so, and still others who could try to game the process. Either way you either recognize credit losses at the beginning as with CECL, during the life of the loan, or at the end which is more or less the approach today.

5
Valuation

"Long ago, Ben Graham taught me that 'Price is what you pay; value is what you get.' Whether we're talking about socks or stocks, I like buying quality merchandise when it is marked down."

—Warren Buffett

VALUATION

Firms are valued more or else accurately at the time of birth (IPO) and at the time of death (liquidation); everything else in between is sentiment. This was a remark made by an investor to us some time back. We do not recall who it was; otherwise, we would gratefully attribute it to the individual.

We are not so sure if firms are valued accurately at the time of their birth, but that remark stirred us into thinking on what would be an appropriate valuation approach for entities, especially regulated entities, with cost of capital advantages such as banks.

What about M&A (probably a wedding event in the aforementioned investor's analogy)?

This chapter is going to look at traditional approaches to value a bank's common equity, and not the other pieces of the capital structure.

The theoretically justified approach for intrinsic valuation is to project the free cash flow to the firm and discount this using the weighted average cost of capital to obtain the total present firm value, then subtract the value of the debt to get the equity value. This approach is not applicable to banks since they use deposits for financing. Estimating the appropriate cost of capital for noninterest-bearing deposits would be an interesting academic exercise, but not something we would recommend for most investors as it is not going to be very practical. Arguably one can project the free cash flow to equity and discount that using the equity cost of capital to arrive at the equity value, but projecting free cash flow to equity holders is a perilous path fraught with false precisions, and one can easily make errors without gaining incremental insights.

There are a couple of other approaches such as Dividend Discount Model and Abnormal Earnings that need some introduction. Dividend discount model assumes that the value of the equity is the present value of future dividends. It also makes the simplifying assumption that dividends grow at a constant growth rate into perpetuity. Intuitively, the equity value should be higher since banks do not pay the entire potential free cash flow to equity holders as dividends. We illustrate the dividend discount model to trace a relationship between price and book value. Abnormal earnings, also called residual income, is an approach that can be used if the bank pays no dividends. Abnormal earnings is the difference between the earnings and the required return on book value: $(ROE - R_e) \times Book\ Value$. This is then discounted using the cost of equity R_e.

The five relative valuation approaches that we prefer are Price to Tangible Book Value (P/TBV), Price to Earnings (P/E), Price to Pre-provision Net Revenue (P/PPNR), Core Deposit Premium, and Precedent Transactions. We prefer P/TBV over P/BV (Price to Book Value), as the former is a more conservative measure since it excludes intangibles.

Enterprise Value to EBITDA (EV/EBITDA) is not used for banks since both EV and EBITDA for a bank is meaningless. Meanwhile, dividend yield comparison is too simplistic in our view and comparability is limited.

Valuation metrics are like a Swiss army knife, the use of each part is determined by where we are in the cycle.

We believe that investors rely on different ones based on where we are in the cycle. P/E and P/TBV are used across the cycle. P/PPNR is used when we are close to the trough of the cycle. Core deposit premium is more likely to be used during the recovery and closer to the peak of the cycle. During the trough of the cycle, investors will also consider burn-down analysis in conjunction with P/TBV. A burn-down analysis consists of stressing the balance sheet under severe loss scenarios where net charge-offs are significantly elevated. The scenario analysis of the burn-down of the loan book and consequent charges to equity will help clarify the amount of re-capitalization that the bank will need.

P/TBV

The net tangible asset value of a bank is a good starting point for valuation. One can impute discounts or premiums to baseline to reflect a variety of factors including core deposit base, moats in key lending niches, top decile ROE lines of business, presence in markets with good demographic trends supporting growth of population, jobs, income, and household formation—metrics that are either strong or beginning to inflect, loyalty of customers, fee revenue,

M&A scarcity value, projected earnings growth, underwriting criteria, quality of loan book, and most importantly, quality of the management team. Clearly several of these factors are subjective inputs over which most people will disagree. That disagreement is what makes a market. Over the long term, however, like a universal law, these qualitative factors will endow the high-quality banks with a higher than peer median P/TBV. Most practitioners have their own approaches to determining these factors. We believe that most of these factors can be at least semiquantified. Moats exist but are relatively rarer in regional and community banks. The banking industry is fairly commoditized with the exception of credit cards which enjoy network effects and payment processors that enjoy scale benefits. Customer loyalty can be gauged using measures such as net promoter score but are tougher to obtain for smaller businesses, hence more difficult to include into the valuation calculus.

We like two excellent books on the topic of customer loyalty:

1. *FANS! Not Customers* by Vernon W. Hill II, Chairman of Republic Bank and Founder of Commerce Bancorp of New Jersey and Metro Bank in the U.K.
2. *The Loyalty Effect* by Frederick F. Reichheld (also the creator of the Net Promoter Score).

Before we look at P/TBV, we shall look at the more basic P/BV price to book value. P/BV has a fundamental relationship with ROE (Return on Equity). The premium to book is a function of the spread between ROE and the cost of equity capital.

In order to draw the relationship, we shall start with using the Gordon Discount Model.

This makes a couple of simplifying assumptions: (1) The market price of a stock is the present value of future dividends received discounted by the cost of equity capital; and (2) The dividends grow annually at a constant rate.

$$P = \frac{D_1}{(1+R_e)} + \frac{D_2}{(1+R_e)^2} + \frac{D_3}{(1+R_e)^3} + \cdots \frac{D_n}{(1+R_e)^n}$$

Where P is price per share, D_n is the dividend received in year n, and R_e is the cost of equity capital.

Assuming a constant yearly growth of dividends g

$$P = \frac{D_1}{(1+R_e)} + \frac{D_1 \times (1+g)}{(1+R_e)^2} + \frac{D_1 \times (1+g)^2}{(1+R_e)^3} + \cdots \tag{5.1}$$

Multiplying either side by $\dfrac{(1+g)}{(1+R_e)}$

$$P \times \frac{(1+g)}{(1+R_e)} = \left[\frac{D_1}{(1+R_e)} + \frac{D_1 \times (1+g)}{(1+R_e)^2} + \frac{D_1 \times (1+g)^2}{(1+R_e)^3} + \ldots\right] \times \frac{(1+g)}{(1+R_e)}$$

$$P \times \frac{(1+g)}{(1+R_e)} = \frac{D_1 \times (1+g)}{(1+R_e)^2} + \frac{D_1 \times (1+g)^2}{(1+R_e)^3} + \frac{D_1 \times (1+g)^3}{(1+R_e)^4} + \cdots \quad (5.2)$$

Subtracting Equation 5.2 from Equation 5.1

$$\begin{aligned} P - P \times \frac{(1+g)}{(1+R_e)} &= \frac{D_1}{(1+R_e)} \\ P \times (1+R_e) - P \times (1+g) &= D_1 \\ P \times (R_e - g) &= D_1 \\ P &= \frac{D_1}{(R_e - g)} \end{aligned} \quad (5.3)$$

Next, we break down D_1. Where *RR* = *Retention Ratio* (portion of earnings retained and not paid out as dividends)

$$D_1 = (1 - RR) \times EPS_1$$

$$D_1 = (1 - RR) \times ROE \times BV$$

Plugging this expression back into Equation 5.3

$$P = \frac{(1 - RR) \times ROE \times BV}{(R_e - g)}$$

$$\frac{P}{BV} = \frac{(1 - RR) \times ROE}{(R_e - g)}$$

P/BV is thus a linear function of *ROE*

Substituting *ROTCE* for *ROE* and *TBV* for *BV* we can derive

$$\frac{P}{TBV} = \frac{(1 - RR) \times ROTCE}{(R_e - g)}$$

Therefore, *P/TBV* is thus a linear function of *ROTCE*.

We view P/TBV as a more conservative measure and hence prefer it over P/BV. TBV excludes goodwill created during M&A (excess of purchase price over fair value) and intangible assets (core deposits, bank charters, trademarks, intellectual property, leases and other contracts). Some of this may be meaningful, but it would be a subjective exercise and makes comparison a little more difficult.

While we have mathematically demonstrated that P/TBV is a linear function of ROTCE, we see empirically that banks that earn an outsized ROTCE have P/TBV that have an exponential relationship with ROTCE. Intuitively, this makes sense; banks that are earning well above their cost of capital and can sustainably do this, because of their business model, management quality, and strategy, have in some sense achieved escape velocity from the gravitational pull that other banks may face.

We ran both a linear and an exponential regression and calculated the respective R^2 on the data set in Exhibit 5.1, which represents over 600 publicly traded community and regional banks.

Linear: $y = 7.1x + 52.4$; ROTCE explains 58% of P/TBV variance.
Exponential: $y = 73.6e^{0.050x}$; ROTCE explains 60% of P/TBV variance.

What is equally crucial is to remember that having a rich public currency in the form of a high P/TBV comes with a responsibility. Using this currency wisely to do deals is important. Nearly all deals will be accretive financially when the acquirer has a sufficiently high P/TBV. However, if the

EXHIBIT 5.1 Regression of ROTCE vs. P/TBV for Regional Banks

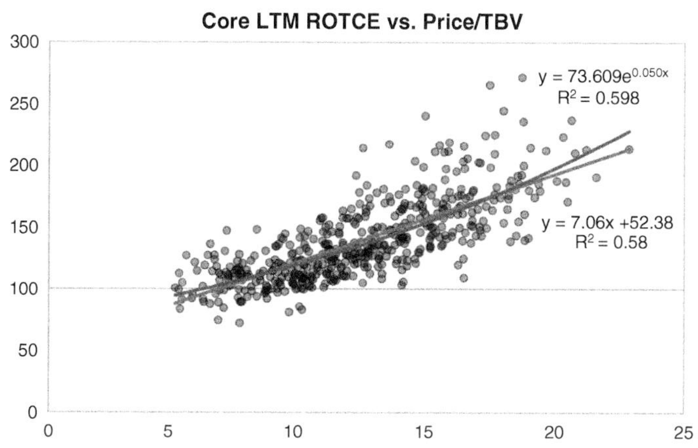

Source: S&P Market Intelligence (09/08/2019)

acquirer fritters this currency away, the market can easily take away what the market has given.

IMPLIED OR JUSTIFIED P/TBV AND P/BV

Is the book multiple that a bank, or indeed the whole group, trades at a "fair" multiple? We can use implied, or justified, P/TBV and P/BV to assess.

The constant growth rate g has been a simplifying assumption.

We can connect this growth rate with ROE and ROTCE by making some simplifying assumptions that RR and ROE are constant across all time periods as well. Thus, the growth in dividends would be the same as the growth in EPS.

EPS_n refers to EPS earned during year n. BV_n refers to the Book Value at the end of year n.

$$g = \frac{(EPS_n - EPS_{n-1})}{EPS_{n-1}}; EPS_n = ROE \times BV_{n-1}$$

$$g = \frac{(ROE \times BV_{n-1} - ROE \times BV_{n-2})}{ROE \times BV_{n-2}}$$

$$g = \frac{(BV_{n-1} - BV_{n-2})}{BV_{n-2}}$$

$$BV_{n-1} = BV_{n-2} + EPS_{n-1} \times RR$$

$$g = \frac{(BV_{n-2} + EPS_{n-1} \times RR) - BV_{n-2}}{BV_{n-2}}$$

$$g = \frac{EPS_{n-1} \times RR}{BV_{n-2}}$$

$$\frac{EPS_{n-1}}{BV_{n-2}} = ROE$$

$$g = ROE \times RR$$

Going back to the linear function we had derived

$$\frac{P}{BV} = \frac{(1 - RR) \times ROE}{(R_e - g)}$$

$$\frac{P}{BV} = \frac{(ROE - g)}{(R_e - g)}$$

This is the implied, or justified, book value.

Substituting ROTCE for ROE and TBV for BV we can derive

$$\frac{P}{TBV} = \frac{(ROTCE - g)}{(R_e - g)}$$

This is the implied, or justified, tangible book value. What does this equation tell us? If ROTCE is below the cost of equity capital, the stock should trade at a discount to tangible book value. As ROTCE increases, so should the multiple on tangible book value. Likewise, as growth increases, so should the P/TBV multiple.

Conversely, one can use the current P/TBV, ROTCE and g to calculate the implied Re or the implied cost of equity.

EXCESS CAPITAL CONSIDERATIONS

Not all banks are levered to the same degree. In this aspect, we are actually lucky to have capital adequacy regulations, which provide helpful guideposts for determining how much capital a bank *should* have. Establish a baseline leverage of TCE/TA for banks. Talk to management teams and look at peers with similar loan mixes, size, and geography; and see at what levels prior capital raises were done. Say the bank you are looking at is "overcapitalized" with a 12% TCE/TA ratio and the baseline you have established is 9%. We'd give a market multiple (say 1.5× TBV) to ¾ of TBVPS, and a 1× multiple to the remaining ¼ TBVPS since it has not been deployed, for a blended multiple of 1.375× of TBVPS.

ROE AND ROTCE

While a higher ROE and ROTCE are better, if the ROE and ROTCE are significantly higher than peers, there are a few quick things to consider. Check to see if the bank is taking on more leverage. Two banks may have the same ROA, but one of them can juice up ROE and ROTCE by driving up E/A and TCE/TA. If one has higher ROA, consider what are the drivers for the higher ROA. Look at earning asset yields. In particular, if these are higher than peers, check if their loans are riskier or if they are sacrificing on structure to make up on loan pricing.

EXHIBIT 5.2 P/TBV and ROTCE Heat Maps

P/TBV by State

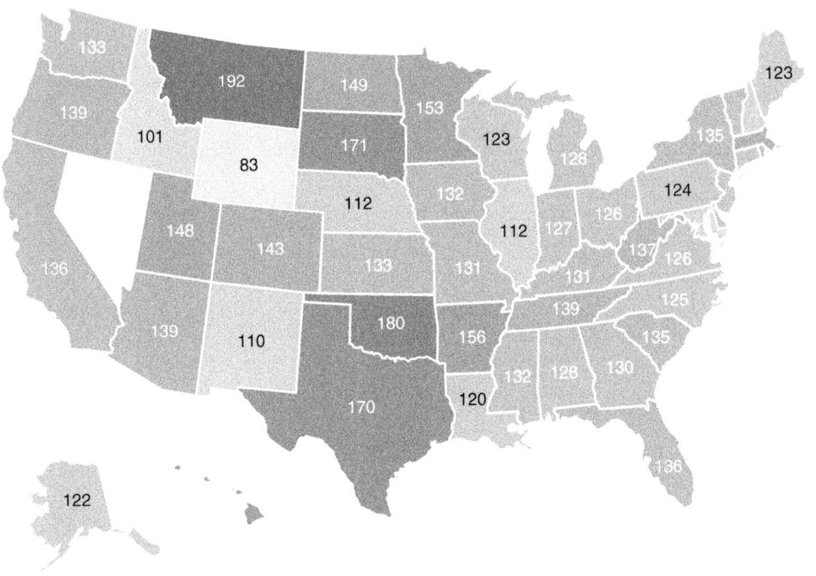

ROTCE by State

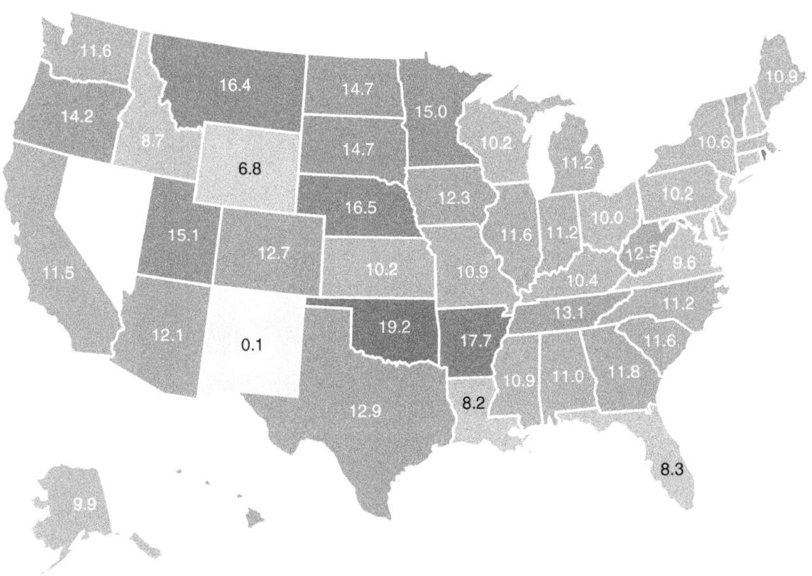

Source: S&P Market Intelligence

PRICE/EARNINGS

Price to earnings ratio is self-explanatory; however, a few caveats are in order. Consensus estimates are an okay place to start but prepare your own estimates. Always use forward estimates; make sure you are using a diluted EPS estimate (there are a few small banks that use basic EPS in their earnings press releases) and check the earnings growth. If the earnings growth looks to be too good to be true, it probably is unless there has been an acquisition, a new business line, cost take-outs, and so forth. Back into what an implied ROTCE and ROA for the bank would be. If that is out of line with the historical performance and comps, be wary. Remember: P/E is also a function of TBV and ROTCE. Specifically, P/E = P/ (TBV * ROTCE).

We direct the curious reader to a couple of good books on the topic of earnings:

1. *Quality of Earnings* by Thornton L. O'Glove,
2. *Earnings Management* by Thomas E. McKee
3. *Financial Shenanigans* by Howard Schilit

Forecasting Forward Estimates

An entire book could be devoted to modeling. We are going to provide the basic outline for gearing a very simple model. Most of the accounting concepts that need to be understood are covered in Chapter 2 on Financial Statement Analysis.

1. Starting drivers for a bank model would include the growth rate assumed for loans, securities, and other earning assets; the NIM assumed; and the fee and other non-interest income. This will get you to the operating revenue line item. Remember to use the average balances for use in the projection and not the end of period balances from the balance sheet.
2. Make growth assumptions for non-interest expense items such as salaries, data processing, occupancy etc. Subtracting the non-interest expense from the operating revenue gets you pre-provision net revenue (PPNR).
3. Estimate provisions for loan losses. This will have two components: net charge-offs of existing loans and provisions for new loan growth. The former is calculated based on a provision for loss rate as a

% multiplied by the average loans. The latter is calculated by multiplying the ratio of reserve/loan with the growth of loans in the period. Subtracting the provisions from the PPNR gets you to the pre-tax operating income.

4. Add nonrecurring items and gains/losses from securities to get you to pre-tax income. Subtract taxes to get to net income. Subtract any preferred dividends to get to net income to common shareholders.
5. Divide this by the average diluted shares to get to diluted EPS.
6. Derive capital and asset quality ratios to make sure these are in balance.
7. Compare the growth rates you are assuming and the NIM with street estimates, company guidance, peer metrics, and historical actuals. Check assumptions for earning asset yields and cost of funds with the rate environment and fixed/floating nature and term structure. What does the forward curve look like? Is it seeing steepening or flattening? What does the bank disclose as part of its parallel shock rate analysis? What is the implied probability for FOMC rate movements, and are you baking that in? Check growth rate of assets and if capital needs to be raised and if so, how much? If shares are being repurchased, what is the stock price you are assuming it to be purchased at?

Compare the P/E of the bank in question with its own historical P/E and the industry historically, the S&P 500, peer multiples in its geography, and its asset size band (Exhibits 5.3–5.5, and 5.6).

EXHIBIT 5.3 P/E Range for US Banks

Source: Bloomberg

EXHIBIT 5.4 P/E of Banks vs. S&P P/E Historically

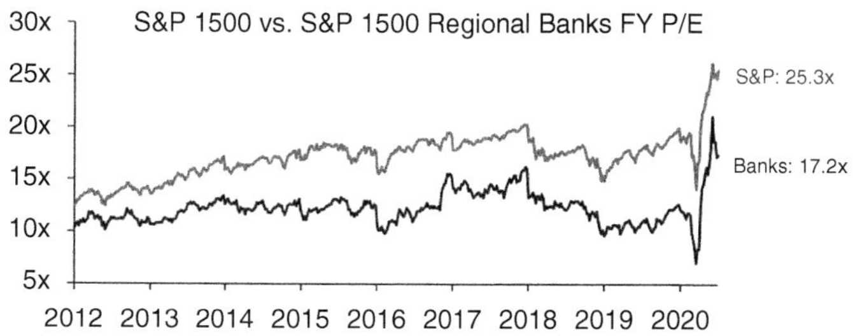

Source: Bloomberg

EXHIBIT 5.5 P/E Heatmap

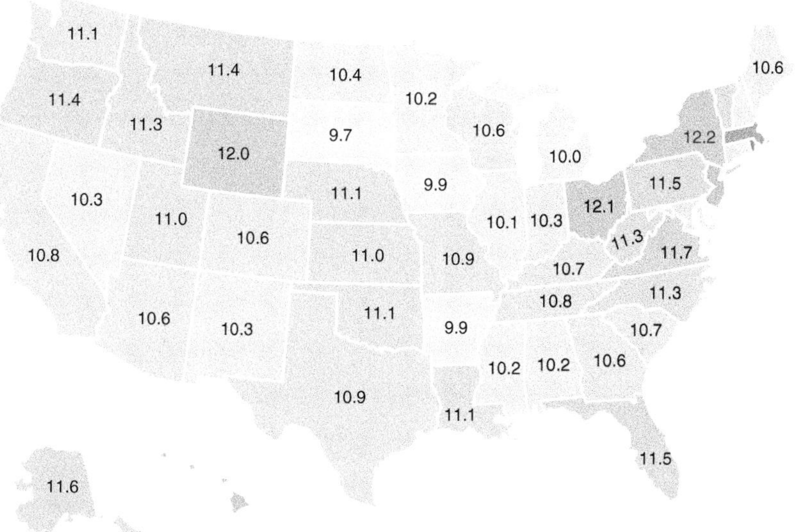

Source: S&P Market Intelligence

EXHIBIT 5.6 P/E of Banks Aggregate by Size

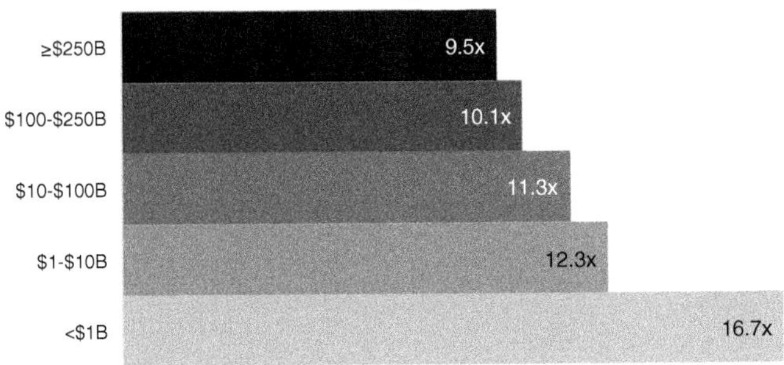

Source: S&P Market Intelligence

PRICE/PPNR

During the trough of the cycle, estimates are often depressed and negative. P/E at this point is generally less meaningful (you would be applying a trough multiple on trough estimates). PPNR is also sometimes called PTPP (Pre-tax Pre-Provision). A variation of this on an after-tax basis called Pre-Provision Earnings or Pre-Provision Profit may also be used (Exhibit 5.7).

EXHIBIT 5.7 Price to PPNR

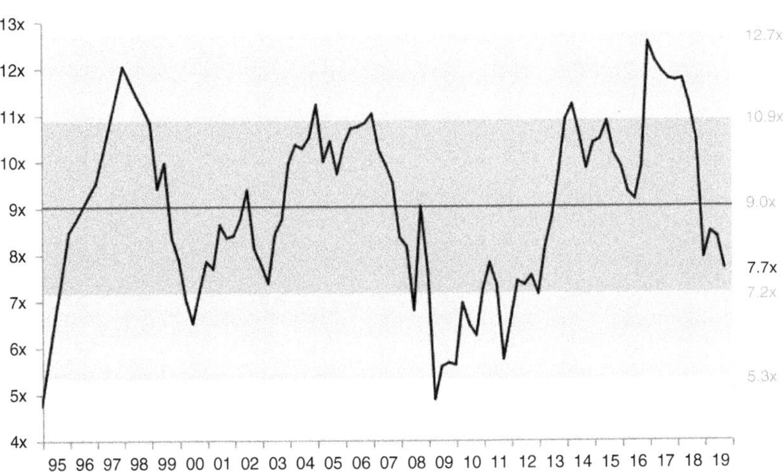

Source: FactSet financial data and analytics

DEPOSIT PREMIUM

The rationale behind Core Deposit Premium, a valuation metric we consider, requires some explanation.

We believe that one of the enduring aspects of a high-quality franchise is a strong core deposit base (Exhibit 5.8). These deposits are relatively sticky and have a lower deposit beta. A deposit beta is the sensitivity of the cost of deposits to the fed funds rate. Deposit beta is more formally defined as the change in the cost of deposits for every 100bps change in the fed funds rate. We would expect core deposit premiums to rise in periods of rising interest rates when a food fight for deposits could break out.

$$\textit{Core Deposit Premium} = \frac{\textit{Market Capitalization} - \textit{Tangible Common Equity}}{\textit{Core Deposits}}$$

Similarly, in an M&A transaction, one can look at the premium paid for the target as

$$\textit{Core Deposit Premium} = \frac{\textit{Purchase Price} - \textit{Tangible Common Equity}}{\textit{Core Deposits}}$$

Core deposits will explicitly exclude brokered deposits. The FDIC defines brokered deposits *as "any deposit that is obtained, directly or indirectly, from or through the mediation or assistance of a deposit broker."* The agency defines a deposit broker as *"any person engaged in the business of placing deposits, or facilitating the placement of deposits, of third parties with insured depository institutions, or the business of placing deposits with insured depository institutions for the purpose of selling interests in those deposits to third parties."*

In general, we value noninterest-bearing DDAs over interest-bearing DDAs over money market accounts over CDs.

EXHIBIT 5.8 Core Deposit Types

Demand Deposits	Negotiable Order of Withdrawal (NOW) Accounts	Automatic Transfer Service (ATS) Accounts	Money Market Deposit Accounts (MMDAs)	Other Savings Deposits & Time Deposits < $250K

PRECEDENT TRANSACTIONS

As the name implies, we are looking here at comparable prior M&A transactions. The key here is that not all banks are for sale, and hence one must be careful assuming a similar multiple for an otherwise equivalent peer, but with a board or management unwilling to sell. Change of control premiums in the 20%+ range are commonplace.

We primarily look at P/E, P/TBV, and Core Deposit Premium to establish what a bank could sell for in a takeout. While doing this it is important to look at precedent transactions where the target had similar profitability and geography and was within the same asset size band as the bank we are analyzing.

We analyzed all US M&A deals since 2002 and have the P/TBV, P/E (LTM), Core Deposit Premium, and the Day 1 Deal Premium in Exhibits 5.9, 5.10, 5.11, and 5.12.

We thought it was interesting that while the P/TBV deal multiple and Core Deposit Premiums never fully recovered back to their pre-GFC high,

EXHIBIT 5.9 P/TBV of Closed US M&A Transactions

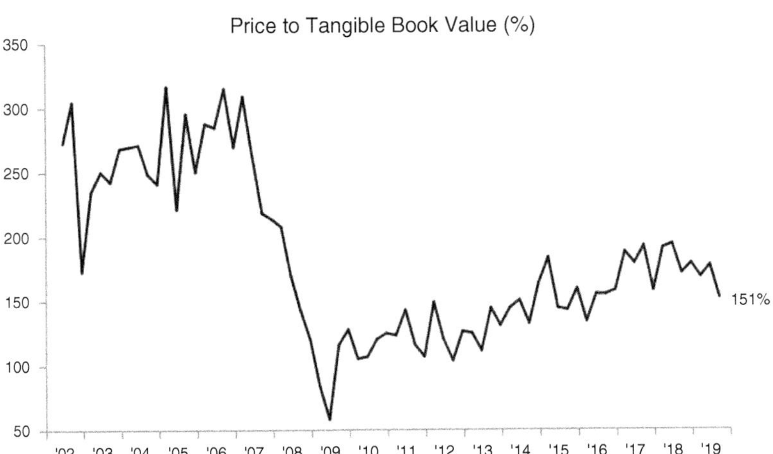

EXHIBIT 5.10 P/E (LTM) of Closed US M&A Transactions

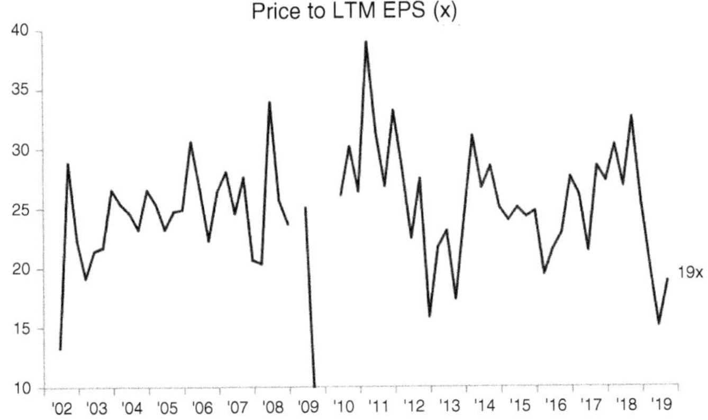

EXHIBIT 5.11 Core Deposit Premium

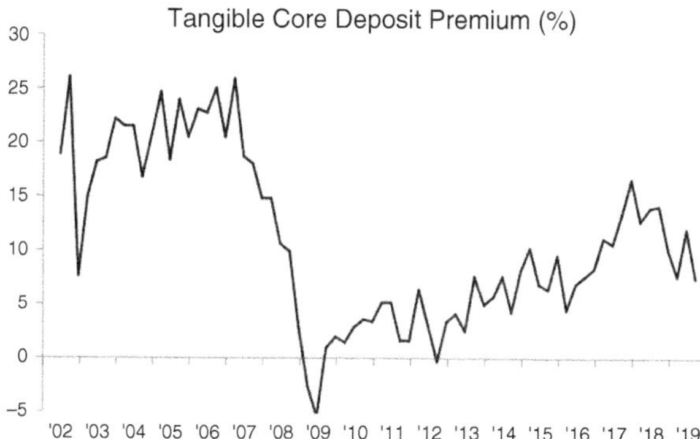

EXHIBIT 5.12 Day 1 Deal Premium

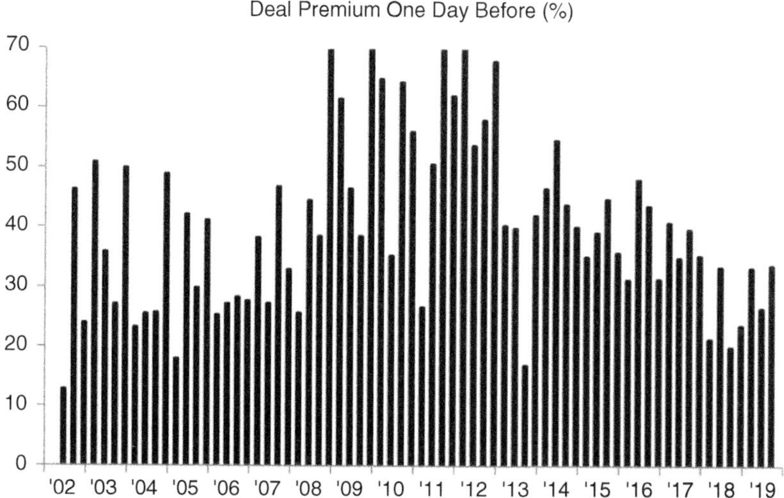

the average deal premium never dips much below 20% (Exhibit 5.12). This is intuitive as you would at least need that premium to get the board to agree and shareholders to vote for the deal. This stable premium, coupled with over 800 publicly traded banks in the US, has made investing in takeout candidates within the bank space a historically fruitful endeavor.

In low and no premium all-stock deals, one needs to understand the dilution (or sometimes accretion) to the acquiror's book, cost take-outs, and the combined earnings power on a go-forward basis. Though you might miss a one-day pop, remaining in the acquirer's stock may not be a bad idea, assuming you have gone through all other key checklist items.

EXHIBIT 5.13 50 Largest Transactions Since 2013

	Buyer Name/ Target Name	Announce Date	Deal Value ($MM)	P/TBV (%)	P/E LTM (x)	Tang. Core Deposit Premium (%)	1 Day Deal Premium (%)
1	BB&T Corporation/SunTrust Banks, Inc.	2/7/19	28,283	179	11.0	8.2	7.0
2	Royal Bank of Canada/City National Corporation	1/22/15	5,373	266	22.1	12.2	26.0
3	Canadian Imperial Bank of Commerce/PrivateBancorp, Inc.	6/29/16	4,918	270	23.5	22.1	5.0
4	Fifth Third Bancorp/MB Financial, Inc.	5/21/18	4,617	274	14.8		24.2
5	KeyCorp/First Niagara Financial Group, Inc.	10/30/15	4,007	167	19.3	6.7	9.8
6	TCF Financial Corporation/Chemical Financial Corporation	1/28/19	3,552				
7	CIT Group Inc./IMB HoldCo LLC	7/22/14	3,376	103	18.7	0.9	
8	Huntington Bancshares Incorporated/FirstMerit Corporation	1/26/16	3,371	165	15.1	6.9	31.0
9	Synovus Financial Corp./FCB Financial Holdings, Inc.	7/24/18	2,869	241	20.6	23.3	(1.8)
10	TIAA Board of Overseers/EverBank Financial Corp	8/8/16	2,517	152	21.7		4.6
11	BB&T Corporation/Susquehanna Bancshares, Inc.	11/12/14	2,507	173	16.6	9.0	38.9
12	PacWest Bancorp/CapitalSource Inc.	7/22/13	2,382	177	5.4	35.4	20.1
13	Sterling Bancorp/Astoria Financial Corporation	3/7/17	2,230	159	35.4	9.9	18.6
14	First Horizon National Corporation/Capital Bank Financial Corp.	5/4/17	2,190	210	28.2	16.8	(2.9)
15	Mechanics Bank/Rabobank, National Association	3/15/19	2,100	157	14.5	8.2	
16	Prosperity Bancshares, Inc./LegacyTexas Financial Group, Inc.	6/17/19	2,068	219	12.7	21.1	9.3
17	Umpqua Holdings Corporation/Sterling Financial Corporation	9/11/13	1,995	173	19.1		13.9
18	BB&T Corporation/National Penn Bancshares, Inc.	8/17/15	1,816	220	17.7	15.5	18.2
19	Pinnacle Financial Partners, Inc./BNC Bancorp	1/22/17	1,732	270	23.8	22.2	2.1
20	WSFS Financial Corporation/Beneficial Bancorp, Inc.	8/8/18	1,507	177	53.0	16.6	20.3
21	Cadence Bancorporation/State Bank Financial Corporation	5/13/18	1,504	273	28.7		16.0
22	F.N.B. Corporation/Yadkin Financial Corporation	7/21/16	1,487	235	22.3	19.2	9.9
23	Toronto-Dominion Bank/Scottrade Bank	10/24/16	1,300	100	11.2	0.0	
24	Chemical Financial Corporation/Talmer Bancorp, Inc.	1/26/16	1,118	158	19.3	10.4	(2.2)

25	Independent Bank Group, Inc./Guaranty Bancorp	5/22/18	1,037	319	23.7	25.5	15.2
26	BBCN Bancorp, Inc./Wilshire Bancorp, Inc.	12/7/15	1,032	227	16.1	23.0	10.4
27	IBERIABANK Corporation/Sabadell United Bank, N.A.	2/28/17	1,028	196	21.2	13.2	
28	First Financial Bancorp./MainSource Financial Group, Inc.	7/25/17	1,006	288	22.4		15.3
29	CIT Group Inc./Mutual of Omaha Bank	8/13/19	1,000	125	10.9	3.2	
30	Veritex Holdings, Inc./Green Bancorp, Inc.	7/24/18	1,000	259	24.2		15.1
31	BOK Financial Corporation/CoBiz Financial Inc.	6/18/18	978	290	25.6		4.0
32	United Bankshares, Inc./Cardinal Financial Corporation	8/18/16	929	231	19.5	20.2	1.5
33	Banco de Credito e Inversiones SA/CM Florida Holdings, Inc.	5/24/13	881	191	14.5	13.8	
34	CVB Financial Corp./Community Bank	2/26/18	878	250	32.5	21.0	48.9
35	PacWest Bancorp/Square 1 Financial, Inc.	3/2/15	856	283	23.3	20.1	(0.7)
36	Valley National Bancorp/USAmeriBancorp, Inc.	7/26/17	852	263	16.7	18.4	60.9
37	CenterState Bank Corporation/National Commerce Corporation	11/26/18	850	208	22.4	15.1	5.1
38	Bank of the Ozarks, Inc./Community & Southern Holdings, Inc.	10/19/15	800	193	38.4	17.5	
39	Home BancShares, Inc./Stonegate Bank	3/27/17	781	269	22.9	21.1	7.2
40	People's United Financial, Inc./United Financial Bancorp, Inc.	7/15/19	758	126	13.2	4.4	4.5
41	Ameris Bancorp/Fidelity Southern Corporation	12/17/18	757	184	16.0	8.8	27.1
42	Valley National Bancorp/Oritani Financial Corp.	6/26/19	744	140	13.7	10.2	0.5
43	Independent Bank Corp./Blue Hills Bancorp, Inc.	9/20/18	725	186	35.0	19.2	12.0
44	PacWest Bancorp/CU Bancorp	4/6/17	706	273	25.3	16.4	(0.1)
45	Banner Corporation/Starbuck Bancshares, Inc.	11/5/14	702	148	37.5	7.8	
46	Union Bankshares Corporation/Xenith Bankshares, Inc.	5/22/17	700	159	10.3		10.4
47	South State Corporation/Park Sterling Corporation	4/27/17	694	241	27.4		2.8
48	Columbia Banking System, Inc./Pacific Continental Corporation	1/9/17	661	325	30.0	21.4	36.1
49	MB Financial, Inc./Taylor Capital Group, Inc.	7/15/13	659	185	11.3	9.3	24.6
50	First Citizens BancShares, Inc./First Citizens Bancorporation, Inc.	6/10/14	645	118	14.2	1.5	40.4

Source: S&P Global Market Intelligence

6

Regulation

"On January 18, 1972, the Corporation announced that a financial assistance program designed to rehabilitate the Bank of the Commonwealth, Detroit, Michigan, had been developed jointly by the Corporation, the Board of Governors of the Federal Reserve System, and the Michigan State Bank Commissioner, and concurred in by the board of directors of the bank."

– Annual Report of the FDIC, 1972

The quote that we have used comes from the FDIC's annual report of 1972 and refers to the assistance provided to Bank of the Commonwealth. This bank has the dubious distinction of being the first "Too Big to Fail" bank.

We would like to re-stress here that nothing stated in this chapter or elsewhere in this book should be used as a legal reference document. We are providing a rough sketch of the regulatory framework under which banks operate. Needless to say, it does not purport to constitute legal advice.

As discussed previously in Chapter 3, banks benefit from access to low cost deposits which are insured by the FDIC for amounts under $250,000. However, this access comes with a set of handcuffs which imposes restrictions on bank activities. Banks are regulated not just by the FDIC, but the Federal Reserve, the OCC, state regulators, and an alphabet soup of regulators.

The pendulum of regulation has been shifted back and forth driven by various crises and concerns. As investors we believe that there needs to be a delicate balance. Having sensible regulations is important to provide strong guardrails and enable banks to better serve the needs of the community. That said, regulations that are complex, onerous, and costly can adversely impact economic growth and disproportionately hurt smaller banks by driving up the cost of compliance. This can limit new banks from forming. De novo bank applications since the GFC have been few and far between.

Many regulations are conceived in reaction to a crisis and are thus geared to fighting and preventing the last crisis which may not help predict or prevent the next crisis. Left un-curated these could lead to unintended consequences at best and distract risk managers at worst by focusing their attention elsewhere.

REGULATORY LANDSCAPE

Financial institutions in the United States have multiple regulators. Exhibit 6.1 maps various regulated financial entities to their regulators. Specifically, banks in the United States operate under a dual banking system of federal and state regulators for purposes of charter and regulation of safety and soundness.

EXHIBIT 6.1 Mapping of Regulators and Their Institutions

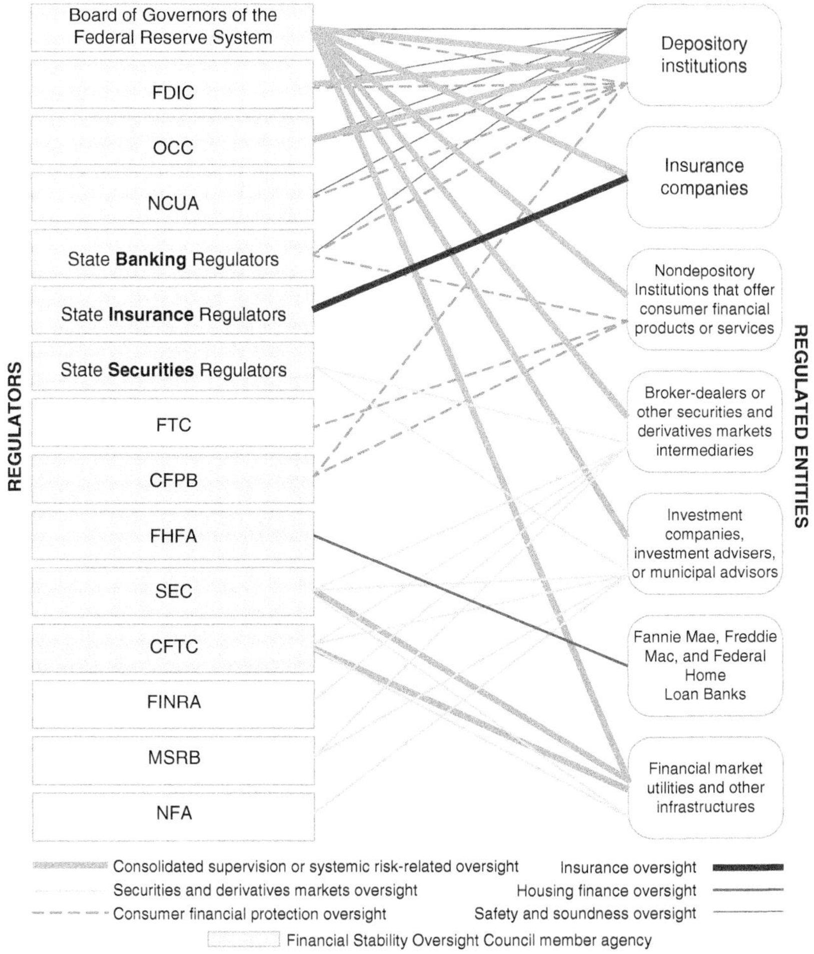

Note: This figure depicts the primary regulators in the U.S. financial regulatory structure, as well as their primary oversight responsibilities. "Regulators" generally refers to entities that have rulemaking, supervisory, and enforcement authorities over financial institutions or entities. There are additional agencies involved in regulating the financial markets and there may be other possible regulatory connections than those depicted in this figure. A list of acronyms is available on page iv. Source: GAD GAD-16-175

Source: US Treasury

Community Banks can be classified into two broad categories from a regulatory standpoint:

1. **National banks:** National banks obtain a national charter and are regulated by the OCC and have National or N.A. "National Association" in their name.
2. **State banks:** State banks obtain a state charter and have the home state's bank regulator as their primary regulator. They can choose one of two Federal regulators and be either (A) Member banks regulated by the Federal Reserve or (B) Non-member banks regulated by the FDIC.

HAVE REGULATIONS MADE THE BANKING SYSTEM SAFE?

We briefly delve into the various banking crises to answer this question. We looked at three US banking crises, including the great depression 1929–1932, the S&L crisis 1982–1995, and the Global Financial Crisis 2007–2008, and tabulated the costs in Exhibit 6.2.

While our table shows the cost of crises increasing, we note that our approach is not perfect since the data is not comparable across periods. We have used losses to unsecured depositors for the period 1921–1934 (a relatively narrow definition), cost to taxpayers and private sources (FHLB) during the S&L crisis, and loss of run rate GDP during the GFC (a relatively broad definition). Since the creation of the FDIC in 1933, no depositor has lost even a penny of insured deposits.

EXHIBIT 6.2 Cost of Banking Crises

Duration	Crisis	Loss/Cost	2017 Dollars
1921-1934	Great Depression	\$3.15 billion	\$45 billion
1982-1995	S&L	\$160 billion	\$316 billion
2007-2009	GFC	\$5.7 trillion	\$11.3 trillion

Note: The loss estimate in 2017 dollars is our estimate.
Source: CBO, GAO, and FDIC

1921–1935

From 1921 to 1935, 13,500 banks suspended operations. A bank suspension implies that it was either closed temporarily or permanently due to financial difficulties. This may be overstated since the count of suspensions included banks that were later reopened or whose operations were assumed by another entity. Depositors of suspended banks are estimated to have lost $3.15 billion, from 1921 to 1934 (Exhibits 6.3 and 6.4).

EXHIBIT 6.3 Losses to Depositors in Suspended Banks

Losses to Unsecured Depositors in Suspended Banks ($000s)	Total Deposits 1921-1930	Total Deposits 1931-1934	Losses to Unsecured Depositors 1921-1930	Losses to Unsecured Depositors 1931-1934	Losses as % of Deposits 1921-1930	Losses as % of Deposits 1931-1934
National Banks: No reopen	448,022	1,338,365	193,187	535,346	43%	40%
National Banks: Reopened	32,371	1,377,461	2,913	344,365	9%	25%
State and Private Banks: No reopen	1,608,623	2,663,568	581,035	1,065,427	36%	40%
State and Private Banks: Reopen	318,116	1,551,932	38,174	387,983	12%	25%
Total	**2,407,132**	**6,931,326**	**815,309**	**2,333,121**	**34%**	**34%**

Source: Annual Report of FDIC, 1934

EXHIBIT 6.4 Number of Bank Suspensions 1921–1935

		Member Banks		Nonmember Banks	
Year	All Banks	National	State	State	Private
1921	505	52	19	390	44
1922	366	49	13	281	23
1923	646	90	32	501	23
1924	775	122	38	578	37
1925	618	118	28	433	39
1926	976	123	35	766	52
1927	669	91	31	514	33
1928	498	57	16	406	19
1929	659	64	17	547	31
1930	1,350	161	27	1104	58
1931	2,293	409	107	1697	80
1932	1,453	276	55	1085	37
1933	2,737	941	103	1593	100
1934	57	1	0	43	13
1935	34	4	0	30	0
	13,636	**2,558**	**521**	9,968	**589**

Source: St. Louis Fed

1982–1995

The Federal Deposit Insurance Corporation (FDIC) was established under the Banking Act of 1933. After the founding of the FDIC, the next major series of bank failures hit during the eighties (Exhibit 6.5). We direct the reader to *History of the Eighties – Lessons for the Future* (FDIC, 1997) for an excellent review of this period. The S&L (Savings & Loan) crisis was the marquee banking crisis of the era. While there were a host of factors that precipitated the crisis, the proximate cause was a dramatic rise in interest rates. S&L assets were concentrated in long duration fixed-rate loans. Not only did the fair value of their loan portfolios decline, interest paid out to depositors began to eclipse the interest earned from loans issued in a lower rate environment (Exhibits 6.6 and 6.7).

EXHIBIT 6.5 Number of Bank Failures 1934–1995

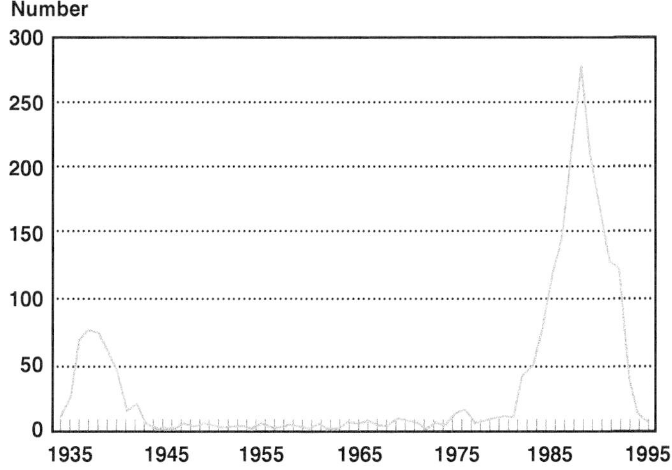

Source: *History of the Eighties – Lessons for the Future* (FDIC, 1997)
Note: This includes FDIC insured commercial and savings banks that were closed or received FDIC assistance.

EXHIBIT 6.6 Selected Statistics FSLIC Insured S&L 1980–1989 $B

Year	Number of S&Ls	Total Assets	Net Income	Tangible Capital	Tangible Capital/ Total Assets	No. Insolvent S&Ls*	Assets in Insolvent S&Ls*	FSLIC Reserves
1980	3,993	$604	$0.8	$32	5.3%	43	$0.4	$6.5
1981	3,751	640	–4.6	25	4.0	112	28.5	6.2
1982	3,287	686	–4.1	4	0.5	415	220.0	6.3
1983	3,146	814	1.9	4	0.4	515	284.6	6.4
1984	3,136	976	1.0	3	0.3	695	360.2	5.6
1985	3,246	1,068	3.7	8	0.8	705	358.3	4.6
1986	3,220	1,162	0.1	14	1.2	672	343.1	–6.3
1987	3,147	1,249	–7.8	9	0.7	672	353.8	–13.7
1988	2,949	1,349	–13.4	22	1.6	508	297.3	–75.0
1989	2,878	1,252	–17.6	10	0.8	516	290.8	*NA*

*Based on tangible-capital-to-assets ratio.
Source: *History of the Eighties – Lessons for the Future* (FDIC, 1997)

EXHIBIT 6.7 S&L Failures 1980–1988 $ '000s

Year	Number of Failures	Total Assets	Estimated Cost	Supervisory Mergers	Voluntary Mergers
1980	11	$ 1,348,908	$ 158,193	21	63
1981	34	19,590,802	1,887,709	54	215
1982	73	22,161,187	1,499,584	184	215
1983	51	13,202,823	418,425	34	83
1984	26	5,567,036	886,518	14	31
1985	54	22,573,962	7,420,153	10	47
1986	65	17,566,995	9,130,022	5	45
1987	59	15,045,096	5,666,729	5	74
1988	190	98,082,879	46,688,466	6	25

Sources: FDIC; and Barth, *The Great Savings and Loan Debacle*, 32–33.

Source: *History of the Eighties – Lessons for the Future* (FDIC, 1997)

2007–2009

The Global Financial Crisis was the worst since the depression and while costs for the financial system intervention have been mostly recouped on an accounting basis, the economic costs were heavy. See Exhibit 6.8 for the

EXHIBIT 6.8 Overview of Income and Losses for Selected Federal Government Interventions to Assist the Financial Sector During the 2007–2009 Financial Crisis

Program or Type of Assistance	Dollar Amount	Accounting Income / Losses
Programs with Broad-Based Eligibility		
Federal Reserve System's emergency credit and liquidity programs[a]	> $1 trillion peak loans outstanding[b]	Approximately $19.7 billion in gross interest and fee income as of June 30, 2012, according to estimates published on the Federal Reserve Bank of New York's (FRBNY) website.[c] The Federal Reserve has reported no losses on the programs that have closed. FRBNY protects that the remaining facility with loans outstanding will not incur losses.

EXHIBIT 6.8 *(Continued)*

Program or Type of Assistance	Dollar Amount	Accounting Income / Losses
FDIC's Temporary Liquidity Guarantee Program		Over $11 billion in total fee income is expected to exceed projected losses of around $2.4 billion.
• Debt Guarantee Program (DGP)	Approx. $345.8 billion (peak debt guaranteed)	All debt guaranteed by DGP was scheduled to mature by the end of 2012. FDIC collected $10.4 billion in DGP income from fees and surcharges. As of Dec. 31, 2011, FDIC reported estimated DGP losses of $152 million and projected that it would pay $682 thousand in interest payments on defaulting DGP-guaranteed notes in 2012.
• Transaction Account Guarantee Program (TAGP)	Approx. $834.5 billion (peak deposits guaranteed)	TAGP dosed on Dec. 31, 2010. FDIC collected $1.2 billion in fees. Cumulative estimated losses totaled $2.2 billion as of Dec. 31, 2011.
Treasury's Guarantee Program for Money Market Funds	> $3 trillion money market fund shares guaranteed at $1 per share	$1.2 billion of fee income and no losses. The program closed on Sept. 18, 2009.
Treasury's Capital Purchase Program (CPP)[d]	$204.9 billion disbursed	As of Oct. 31, 2012, Treasury had received almost $220 billion from its CPP investments, exceeding the $204.9 billion it disbursed. Of that disbursed amount, $8.3 billion remained outstanding as of Oct. 31, 2012. As of Sept 30, 2012. Treasury estimated that CPP would have a lifetime income of approximately $14.9 billion after all institutions exit the program.

Source: GAO

accounting income and losses for the intervention. See also Exhibits 6.9, 6.10, and 6.11. The CBO had previously estimated that the economic loss from the GFC was $5.7 trillion (there are other estimates that run into the low double digit trillion).

EXHIBIT 6.9 Failure Rate of Banks 1934–2017

Year	Bank Failures	Estimated Losses ($000s)	Total Deposits of Failed Institutions ($000s)	Total Assets of Failed Institutions ($000s)	Total Banks	Failure Rate
2017	8	1,132,364	4,683,360	5,081,737	4,918	0.16%
2016	5	47,114	268,516	277,182	5,112	0.10%
2015	8	866,542	4,870,464	6,706,038	5,340	0.15%
2014	18	392,245	2,691,485	2,913,503	5,607	0.32%
2013	24	1,247,973	5,132,246	6,044,051	5,847	0.41%
2012	51	2,461,603	11,009,630	11,617,348	6,072	0.84%
2011	92	6,617,073	31,071,862	34,922,997	6,275	1.47%
2010	157	16,359,499	79,548,141	92,084,987	6,519	2.41%
2009	140	26,957,643	137,835,208	169,709,160	6,829	2.05%
2008	25	18,160,993	234,321,715	371,945,480	7,077	0.35%
2007	3	161,851	2,424,187	2,614,928	7,279	0.04%
2006	0	0	0	0	7,397	0.00%
2005	0	0	0	0	7,523	0.00%
2004	4	3,917	156,733	170,099	7,628	0.05%
2003	3	62,646	901,978	947,317	7,767	0.04%
2002	11	415,314	2,512,834	2,872,720	7,887	0.14%
2001	4	292,465	1,661,214	1,821,760	8,082	0.05%
2000	7	32,538	342,584	410,160	8,315	0.08%
1999	8	590,861	1,320,573	1,592,189	8,582	0.09%
1998	3	223,051	260,675	290,238	8,777	0.03%
1997	1	5,026	27,511	27,923	9,144	0.01%
1996	6	60,615	230,390	232,634	9,530	0.06%
1995	8	112,664	1,191,079	1,225,943	9,943	0.08%
1994	15	190,521	1,524,526	1,600,689	10,453	0.14%
1993	50	900,240	8,390,802	9,976,901	10,961	0.46%
1992	179	6,965,419	74,694,534	89,554,183	11,467	1.56%
1991	268	15,228,449	118,115,433	143,444,562	11,927	2.25%
1990	381	18,833,879	114,049,222	146,585,865	12,347	3.09%
1989	530	53,353,918	137,759,203	163,862,508	12,715	4.17%
1988	232	5,377,743	37,321,949	48,363,949	13,137	1.77%
1987	217	1,862,603	15,367,551	15,823,491	13,723	1.58%
1986	162	1,682,540	14,062,855	15,307,286	14,210	1.14%
1985	139	0	8,910,855	9,901,523	14,417	0.96%
1984	83	0	3,219,560	4,188,925	14,496	0.57%
1983	50	0	3,044,826	3,833,144	14,469	0.35%
1982	34	0	3,749,157	4,652,702	14,451	0.24%
1981	9	0	1,147,715	1,377,910	14,414	0.06%
1980	10	0	219,890	239,316	14,434	0.07%
1979	10	0	110,753	132,987	14,364	0.07%
1978	7	0	854,150	994,034	14,391	0.05%
1977	5	0	34,577	42,358	14,411	0.03%
1976	16	0	865,108	1,039,292	14,410	0.11%
1975	13	0	339,597	419,950	14,384	0.09%

EXHIBIT 6.9 *(Continued)*

Year	Bank Failures	Estimated Losses ($000s)	Total Deposits of Failed Institutions ($000s)	Total Assets of Failed Institutions ($000s)	Total Banks	Failure Rate
1974	4	0	1,575,832	3,822,596	14,230	0.03%
1973	6	0	971,291	1,309,675	13,976	0.04%
1972	1	0	20,385	22,054	13,733	0.01%
1971	6	0	131,682	196,519	13,612	0.04%
1970	7	0	52,340	62,147	13,511	0.05%
1969	9	0	40,128	43,571	13,473	0.07%
1968	3	0	22,524	25,155	13,487	0.02%
1967	4	0	10,878	11,993	13,514	0.03%
1966	7	0	103,522	120,646	13,538	0.05%
1965	5	0	43,877	58,750	13,544	0.04%
1964	7	0	23,323	25,849	13,493	0.05%
1963	2	0	23,441	26,179	13,291	0.02%
1962	1	0	3,011	0	13,124	0.01%
1961	5	0	8,819	9,819	13,115	0.04%
1960	1	0	6,955	7,506	13,126	0.01%
1959	3	0	2,539	2,859	13,114	0.02%
1958	4	0	8,239	8,905	13,124	0.03%
1957	1	0	1,163	1,253	13,165	0.01%
1956	2	0	11,281	12,914	13,218	0.02%
1955	5	0	11,963	11,986	13,237	0.04%
1954	2	0	990	1,138	13,323	0.02%
1953	2	0	18,262	18,811	13,432	0.01%
1952	3	0	3,157	2,389	13,439	0.02%
1951	2	0	3,408	3,050	13,455	0.01%
1950	4	0	5,765	4,005	13,446	0.03%
1949	4	0	4,978	4,885	13,436	0.03%
1948	3	0	10,455	10,360	13,419	0.02%
1947	5	0	6,966	6,798	13,403	0.04%
1946	1	0	316	351	13,359	0.01%
1945	1	0	5,695	6,392	13,302	0.01%
1944	2	0	1,864	2,098	13,268	0.02%
1943	5	0	12,172	14,059	13,274	0.04%
1942	20	0	18,574	1,602	13,347	0.15%
1941	15	0	29,617	17,811	13,430	0.11%
1940	43	0	143,772	7,959	13,442	0.32%
1939	60	0	160,777	43,923	13,538	0.44%
1938	74	0	62,064	13,919	13,661	0.54%
1937	75	0	32,804	19,284	13,797	0.54%
1936	69	0	27,762	12,927	13,973	0.49%
1935	25	0	13,377	12,324	14,125	0.18%
1934	9	0	1,966	2,661	14,146	0.06%

Source: FDIC

EXHIBIT 6.10 Failure/Assistance as % of Banks 1934–2017

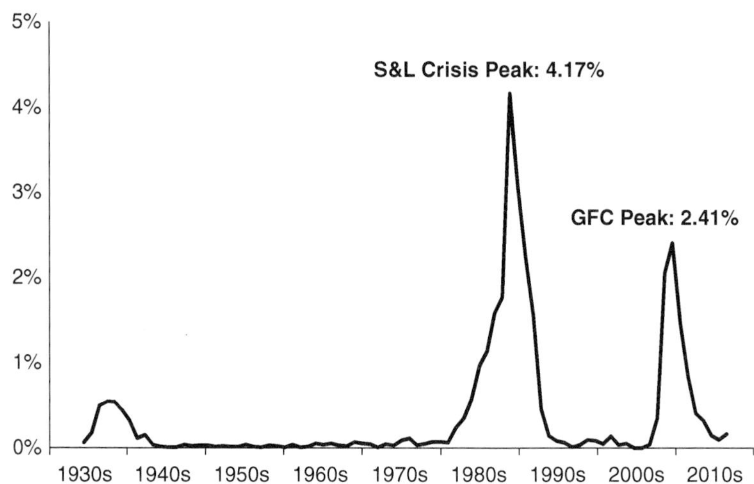

Source: FDIC
Note: Failure/Assistance – Failed institutions have had their charter rescinded because of insolvency, critical under-capitalization, or failure to meet deposit outflow demands. Assistance agreements are arrangements where the FDIC provides financial assistance to the institution or an acquiring institution, such as an agreement to purchase certain assets or the assumption of certain liabilities.

EXHIBIT 6.11 Estimated Losses 1986–2017

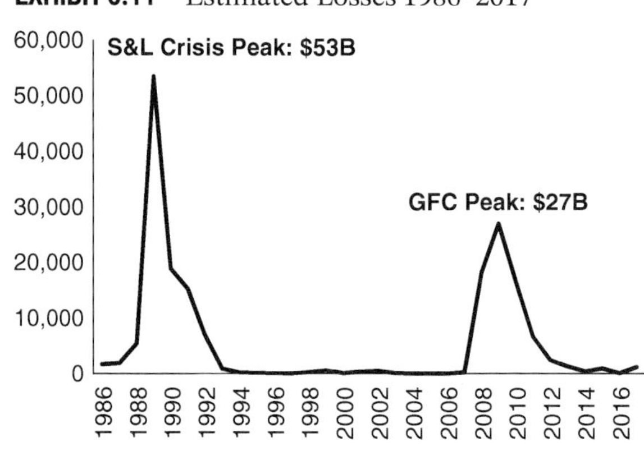

Source: FDIC
Note: Estimated Loss – The estimated loss is the difference between the amount disbursed from the Deposit Insurance Fund (DIF) to cover obligations to insured depositors and the amount estimated to be ultimately recovered from the liquidation of the receivership estate. Estimated losses reflect unpaid principal amounts deemed unrecoverable and do not reflect interest that may be due on the DIF's administrative or subrogated claims should its principal be repaid in full.

ARE WE SAFER?

We believe that in balance regulations have generally helped foster safety and soundness of the banking system and instilled a fair amount of discipline within banks. That said, we believe that increased regulatory complexity is not beneficial and can be counterproductive as we have seen mostly in cases from Europe (as was reviewed in Chapter 3 on capital). We view the current regulatory system as onerous and complex, given the number of regulatory agencies and the actual number of words in the code and the cost required to comply. We may truly need developments in artificial intelligence–fueled compliance technology to parse the complex web of regulations to ensure no inadvertent violations occur if the trend of increased regulation continues unabated.

"History doesn't repeat itself, but it does rhyme" as Mark Twain may or may not have said. As an aside, Quote Investigator has opined on the provenance of this quote. Irrespective of the provenance of the quote, this is true of banking crises as well. The precipitating factors of the next crisis are not always identical to the prior one. Banking regulations generated in response to a crisis are often well intentioned but will do little to prevent the next crisis.

TOO BIG TO FAIL

We believe that moral hazard has increased in recent times since the action by regulators has been to rescue large financial institutions and the Federal Reserve has been biased towards cutting interest rates in the wake of a crisis. These actions do decrease the fallout to the broader banking ecosystem from the implosion of a large financial institution and may help provide a softer landing for the economy; however, no one can deny that this implicit insurance from failure can encourage risky behavior. Participants will take on more risk since they now have the expectation that they will be bailed out upon failure. Regulators are well aware of this issue. We recommend readers to read *Too Big to Fail: The Hazards of Bank Bailouts* by Gary Stern and Rod Feldman for an excellent perspective on the moral hazard problem. Gary Stern was a former head of the Minneapolis Fed. We also direct readers to *Too Big to Fail: The Inside Story of How Wall Street and Washington Fought to Save the Financial System – and Themselves* by Andrew Ross Sorkin for an excellent review of the most recent crisis.

FEDERAL PRUDENTIAL REGULATORS

We do agree that guardrails and pragmatic regulations are needed to ensure the safety and soundness of the banking system by instilling risk management as a discipline among banks and taking steps to reduce procyclicality and to put in early warning systems that go off when the system starts to overheat. These are but some of the functions of regulators. The Federal Prudential regulators in the US are the OCC, the Federal Reserve, the FDIC, and the NCUA (Exhibit 6.12).

EXHIBIT 6.12 Federal Prudential Regulators and Functions

Table 1: Federal Prudential Regulators and Their Basic Functions

Agency	Basic function
Office of the Comptroller of the Currency	Charters and supervises national banks and federal thrifts.
Board of Governors of the Federal Reserve System	Supervises state-chartered banks that opt to be members of the Federal Reserve System, bank holding companies, thrift holding companies and the nondepository institution subsidiaries of those institutions, and nonbank financial companies designated by the Financial Stability Oversight Council.
Federal Deposit Insurance Corporation	Supervises FDIC-insured state-chartered banks that are not members of the Federal Reserve System, as well as federally insured state savings banks and thrifts, insures the deposits of all banks and thrifts that are approved for federal deposit insurance, and resolves all failed insured banks and thrifts and has been given the authority to resolve large bank holding companies and nonbank financial companies that are subject to supervision by the Board of Governors of the Federal Reserve System.
National Credit Union Administration	Charters and supervises federally chartered credit unions and insures savings in federal and most state-chartered credit unions.

Sources: OCC, Federal Reserve Board, FDIC, and NCUA.

FDIC INSURANCE

The FDIC was established in 1933 and depositors have not faced any losses on the insured deposits since then. The FDIC insurance covers all types of deposit accounts up to $250,000 per depositor, per insured bank, per account category (single, joint, trust, etc.)

If a bank fails, the FDIC would resolve it in one of two ways:

Do a P&A (Purchase and Assumption) transaction. If there is no acquirer for the deposits, the FDIC will pay the depositors by check up to the insured balance, which currently is $250,000. The IndyMac case is noteworthy. At the time that the Pasadena, California headquartered thrift failed in 2008, the FDIC limit was $100,000. Uninsured depositors were paid 50% on the balances above the limit. Congress subsequently raised the deposit insurance to $250,000 and made it retroactive with a start of January 1, 2008. Depositors lost balances above the new $250,000 limit. There has been speculation that following the failure of IndyMac and the optics surrounding it, the FDIC would step in to protect depositors above the $250,000 limit. We would not wager on that; we would use an insured cash sweep provided by Promontory to make sure deposits are covered by insurance. Please see a Q&A guide on IndyMac:

https://www.fdic.gov/resources/resolutions/bank-failures/failed-bank-list/indymac-q-and-a.html

The Deposit Insurance Fund (DIF) consists of the funds available to protect depositors. The DIF was formed in 2006 following the merger of the Bank Insurance Fund and the SAIF Savings Association Insurance Fund. The DIF's adequacy is measured by the reserve ratio which is the ratio of the fund balance to the insured deposits. The FDIC prices deposit insurance based on the risk profile of the bank in part based on the CAMELS rating (see next section).

CAMELS

Regulators evaluate banks on six components: capital adequacy, asset quality, management capability, earnings quantity and quality, liquidity adequacy, and sensitivity to market risk (CAMELS). Banks are rated on a 5-point scale on each of the six components, with 1 being the highest and 5 being the lowest (Exhibit 6.13). A composite rating is assigned, and some components may be given a higher weighting in the composite (the composite is not a simple average of the individual component ratings). The management component is given a higher weight. A bank rated 4 (deficient) or 5 (critically deficient) is placed on the problem bank list. The board of a bank rated 3 or higher consents to an agreement with regulators to correct the deficiencies. The cost of the insurance = assessment rate * assessment base. The FDIC establishes

EXHIBIT 6.13 Assessment Rates

Current Rates effective July 1, 2016 – Present

Rates first applicable on the invoice dated December 30, 2016

Total Base Assessment Rates for established Institutions (insured five or more years)* All amounts are in basis points annually.

	Established Small Institutions CAMELS Composite			**Large and Highly Complex Institutions****
	1 or 2	**3**	**4 or 5**	
Initial Base Assessment Rate	3 to 16	6 to 30	16 to 30	3 to 30
Unsecured Debt Adjustment***	-5 to 0	-5 to 0	-5 to 0	-5 to 0
Brokered Deposit Adjustment	N/A	N/A	N/A	0 to 10
Total Base Assessment Rate	1.5 to 16	3 to 30	11 to 30	1.5 to 40

*Total base rates that are not the minimum or maximum rate will vary between these rates. Total base assessment rates do not include the Depository Institution Debt Adjustment ("DIDA").
**See 12 CFR 327.8(f) and (g) for the definition of large and highly complex institutions.
***The unsecured debt adjustment cannot exceed the lesser of 5 basis points or 50 percent of an insured depository institution's initial base assessment rate; thus, for example, an insured depository institution with an initial base assessment rate of 3 basis points will have a maximum unsecured debt adjustment of 1.5 basis points and cannot have a total base assessment rate lower than 1.5 basis points. The unsecured debt adjustment does not apply to new institutions or insured branches.

an assessment rate based on the CAMELS rating, debt ratings, and selected financial ratios. A bank's official CAMELS ratings are confidential, and unauthorized disclosure is regarded as a criminal offense. That said, with publicly available data one can produce analysis that mirrors CAMELS criteria. In fact, the FDIC's Chair Jelena McWilliams has said that assessing the CAMELS system is one of her top priorities, and they are trying to understand if there is congruence in how the three agencies carry out the process. Unless a bank has been rated by all three, estimating congruence would be difficult. Measuring it from the outside would be even more difficult.

Assessment Rates for newly insured small institutions (those insured less than 5 years)*

	Risk Category I	Risk Category II	Risk Category III	Risk Category IV
Initial Base Assessment Rate	7	12	19	30
Brokered Deposit Adjustment (added)	N/A	0 to 10	0 to 10	0 to 10
Total Base Assessment Rate	7	12 to 22	19 to 29	30 to 40

Total base assessment rates do not include the depository institution debt adjustment.
Source: FDIC

KEY REGULATIONS

The key regulations for community banks are BSA/AML (Bank Secrecy Act/Anti Money Laundering), CRA (Community Reinvestment Act), Fair Lending, and HMDA (pronounced Humda, Home Mortgage Disclosure Act).

STRESS TESTING

Banks with consolidated assets over $10 billion are required to conduct certain annual tests to gauge if they have adequate capital to survive stress scenarios. These stress tests are run to estimate a bank's revenues, losses, reserves, and pro forma capital levels under typically three scenarios (baseline, adverse, and severely adverse). Banks that are between $10 and $50 billion conduct the Dodd-Frank Act Stress Test (DFAST) tests while those that are above $50 billion additionally conduct the Comprehensive Capital Analysis and Review (CCAR). We cover DFAST and CCAR in Chapter 3 on capital.

CROSSING THE $10 BILLION

$10 billion in assets is an important threshold; at least it was until the recently passed EGRRCPA legislation. A bank is deemed to have crossed $10 billion if it has an average of $10 billion in consolidated assets over the last four quarters. If the bank crosses this threshold on March 31st of a year, it must conduct the stress test the year after. If it crosses the threshold after March 31st, it gets extra time and can conduct the stress test two years after. Banks between $10 and $50 billion must conduct company run stress tests for scenarios issued by the Federal Reserve, submit the results to regulators and publish it between October 15th and 31st. The bank crossing $10 billion will also stand to lose revenue from debit card swipe fees. This is since the Durbin Amendment places a cap of 21 cents plus 0.05% of the transaction (plus an additional 1¢ if the issuer complies with fraud prevention standards) on these banks. Prior to Durbin, a bank with over $10 billion in assets may have earned $1.03 in swipe fees on a $100 transaction. Post Durbin, the bank would earn $0.26 (or $0.27 including a penny for fraud) on the same transaction. Given the significant costs entailed in crossing the $10 billion, banks considering M&A would look at deals that do not just cause them to merely step over the $10 billion but cross it meaningfully so they could potentially make up the lost revenues and offset the higher regulatory cost with scale. Banks crossing it organically would try to cross it after March to gain some extra time.

We provide below comments about the Durbin impact from a few banks as stated on their Q2:18 earnings calls. These estimates may have changed since; we are sharing these to illustrate the general impact from the Durbin Amendment. See also Exhibits 6.14 and 6.15.

South State Bank SSB – 7/31/18

As a reminder, during the second half of this year, we anticipate lower interchange income of approximately $8.5 million due to the impact of the Durbin amendment.

OceanFirst Financial OCFC – 7/27/18

And the Durbin amendment obviously is still in place and would still be a factor if we cross $10 billion. So, the way we think about $10 billion is if you're crossing it for a good reason then don't get hung up on the marginal incremental expense because you're going to keep growing your company, it will be okay, but certainly is a number.

First Interstate BancSystem FIBK – 7/26/18

As a reminder, the Durbin Amendment will take effect for us in the third quarter. We anticipate that this will reduce our payment services revenue by approximately $3.3 million per quarter.

Simmons First National SFNC – 7/24/18

As a reminder, now the total assets have surpassed $10 billion, we became subject to the interchange rate cap as established by the Durbin Amendment beginning July 1, 2018. We estimate that we will receive approximately $7 million less in debit card fees in 2018 and $14 million less in 2019 on a pre-tax basis.

Community Bank CBU – 7/23/18

We continue to expect the net reduction from Durbin mandated impacts on debit interchange revenues beginning this month of approximately $13 million to $14 million annually, negatively impacting quarterly earnings by $0.05 or $0.06 per share.

First Financial Bank FFBC – 7/20/18

So, the impact of Durbin will hit us starting in the beginning of the third quarter of 2019. And our estimate of the impact is that interchange income will be reduced by $3 million a quarter.

HomeBanc Shares HOMB – 7/19/18

We've been looking at it on a daily basis and it's real money that we're losing. I probably would up that closer to a little over $2 million a quarter pretax.

For an excellent take on the Durbin Amendment, we recommend readers review *The Dangerous Experiment of the Durbin Amendment* by Richard A. Epstein in the Cato Institute's *Regulation Magazine* Spring 2011.

EXHIBIT 6.14 Illustrative Example of Four-Party Network

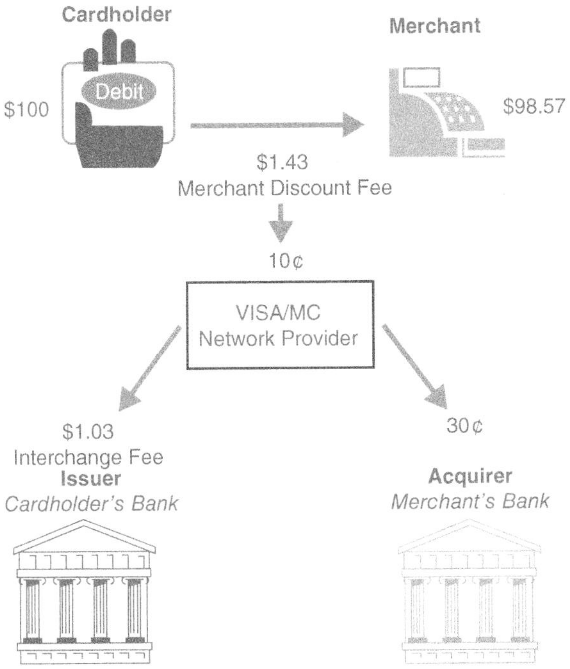

Cardholder

Merchant

Debit

$100

$98.57

$1.43
Merchant Discount Fee

10¢

VISA/MC
Network Provider

$1.03
Interchange Fee
Issuer
Cardholder's Bank

30¢

Acquirer
Merchant's Bank

Source: Congressional Research Service

EXHIBIT 6.15 Average Debit Card Interchange Fee

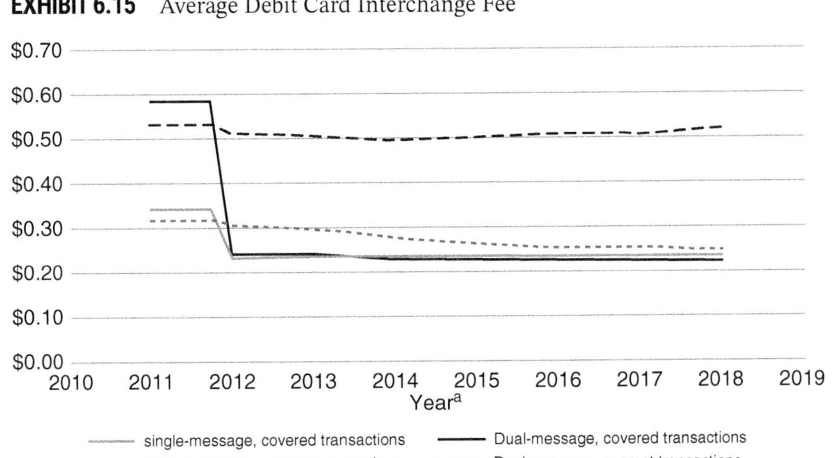

a. Data for years prior to 2013 reflect a split between covered/exempt issuers, rather than covered/exempt transactions.

Source: Federal Reserve

CHANGES FROM THE ECONOMIC GROWTH ACT

The Economic Growth Act of May 2018, also called by the unpronounceable EGRRCPA (Economic Growth, Regulatory Relief, and Consumer Protection Act), has scaled back portions of Dodd-Frank. The enhanced supervision threshold has been raised to $250 billion from $50 billion and the supervisory stress test for banks under $100 billion has been eliminated, while those with assets between $100 and $250 billion will conduct stress tests, but not every year. Thus, only banks with assets greater than $250 billion will be subject to CCAR going forward.

REGULATORY EXAMS

The OCC conducts an on-site exam annually. The exam cycle may be extended to 18 months in certain situations such as if the bank has under $1 billion in assets, has 1 or 2 CAMELS rating, or is not subject to enforcement from the FDIC or the Federal Reserve. Apart from the regular exam, a bank may be subject to a Target exam. This would target a particular area such as CRA or BSA/AML. A bank that is subject to an enforcement will likely have a Target exam around six months in to review their progress to addressing the situation.

SNC EXAM

Regulators also initiated a SNC (Shared National Credit) Exam beginning in 2016. Some banks have two SNC exams a year and others only one. These exams are conducted in Q1 and Q3. The results from both are published after the Q1 exam. We have looked at SNCs in Chapter 4 on credit.

WHEN IS A BANK DEEMED TO BE TROUBLED?

Here is what the prudential regulators have to say:

FDIC

Troubled condition means any insured state nonmember bank that:

1. Has a composite rating, as determined in its most recent report of examination, of 4 or 5 under the Uniform Financial Institutions Rating System (UFIRS), or in the case of an insured state branch of a foreign bank, an equivalent rating; or
2. Is subject to a proceeding initiated by the FDIC for termination or suspension of deposit insurance; or
3. Is subject to a cease-and-desist order or written agreement issued by either the FDIC or the appropriate state banking authority that requires action to improve the financial condition of the bank or is subject to a proceeding initiated by the FDIC or state authority which contemplates the issuance of an order that requires action to improve the financial condition of the bank, unless otherwise informed in writing by the FDIC; or
4. Is informed in writing by the FDIC that it is in troubled condition for purposes of the requirements of this subpart on the basis of the bank's most recent report of condition or report of examination, or other information available to the FDIC.

OCC

Troubled condition means a national bank that: (i) Has a composite rating of 4 or 5 under the Uniform Financial Institutions Rating System (CAMELS); (ii) Is subject to a cease and desist order, a consent order, or a formal written agreement, unless otherwise informed in writing by the OCC; or (iii) Is informed in writing by the OCC that as a result of an examination it has been designated in "troubled condition" for purposes of this section.

Federal Reserve

Troubled condition for a regulated institution means an institution that:

1. Has a composite rating, as determined in its most recent report of examination or inspection, of 4 or 5 under the Uniform Financial Institutions Rating System or under the Federal Reserve Bank Holding Company Rating System;
2. Is subject to a cease and desist order or formal written agreement that requires action to improve the financial condition of the institution, unless otherwise informed in writing by the Board or Reserve Bank; or
3. Is informed in writing by the Board or Reserve Bank that it is in troubled condition for purposes of the requirements of this subpart on the basis of the institution's most recent report of condition or report of examination or inspection, or other information available to the Board or Reserve Bank.

INFORMED IN WRITING?

The provision that a bank can be deemed troubled if it is informed in writing that it is troubled is somewhat tautological in nature. The regulatory language indicates that there is wide latitude for regulators in determining the troubled condition of a bank, and that banks can be considered troubled based on other information available to the regulator. See the last provisions for troubled condition determination by the FDIC, OCC, and the Board mentioned previously. This last criteria of informing the bank in writing does not give much for the bank to challenge or appeal through the appeal process or through the courts. This can cause some serious issues for a bank including that it cannot accept brokered deposits.

RELATIONSHIP WITH THE REGULATOR

Needless to say, having a good relationship with the regulator is paramount. We can think of at least a handful of situations where relationships were poor and proved costly to investors. Some banks remain in the penalty box longer and this can impact several things including their ability to participate in M&A.

By relationship we do not mean simply social chemistry, although that cannot hurt, but banks need to work on the relationship by taking the recommendations of the regulators seriously and working towards ameliorating any deficiencies. Banks need to ensure that they are not the poster child for being the "bad bank."

WHAT CAUSES A BANK TO FAIL?

We believe rapid growth of a bank should be monitored. The UBPR (Uniform Bank Performance Report) is a good place to start to review changes and look at where the bank ranks on a percentile basis versus the peer group. We recommend that readers read the reviews of specific failed banks done by the FDIC Office of Inspector General, especially the in-depth review reports done in some cases.

Apart from exogenous factors, such as economic conditions and internal factors that can be monitored from the outside (some of which we consider in Chapters 3, 4, and 9), we believe management quality and risk management (systems, processes, policies, exceptions, key personnel, and their length of professional experience) are the key areas to focus on. These are also tougher to gauge from the outside. This is more art and science and continual conversations with management teams of the bank and its peers as well as customers if possible are the only ways to gauge this.

MISCELLANEOUS TOPICS OF RELEVANCE TO INVESTORS

The following are important ownership and filing requirements of publicly traded SEC filing banks.

SEC FILING REQUIREMENTS

Ownership of equity securities comes with filing requirements once the ownership is above certain threshold limits. Ownership of banks comes with some added requirements.

If the beneficial ownership, which includes any person who directly or indirectly has voting or investment power (the power to buy or sell the security), is greater than 5% of a voting class of shares, a Schedule 13D has to be filed with the SEC within 10 days after the purchase.

Certain types of investors may be able to file the shorter Schedule 13G instead of the 13D. These include exempt investors (for example, those who accumulated the position prior to an IPO), qualified institutional investors (for example, a broker dealer who does not intend to exercise control), and passive investors (for example, an investor who certifies that they do not intend to exercise control).

CHANGE IN BANK CONTROL ACT (CBCA)

Under the CBCA any person (or group of persons acting in concert) must give the Federal Reserve (and the OCC if regulated by the OCC) notice of at least 60 days and obtain approval from the regulator prior to acquiring shares resulting in 25% or more of any voting class. The threshold for filing the notice and obtaining approval is 10%, if the bank is publicly traded and the person will own the largest position in the voting class.

Within 10 days of filing the notice the person also has to publish an announcement in a newspaper in the area where the bank operates and submit a copy of the announcement to the regulator.

If the regulator disapproves the request, the person may seek an appeal within 10 days of the disapproval. If the request is approved, the person has six months to complete the acquisition of the shares.

Additionally, if the bank has a state regulator, they also need to be given appropriate notice by the acquiror. There could be other onerous requirements; for example, the state law may require the entity to have a legal presence in the state.

BANK HOLDING COMPANY ACT (BHCA)

The acquiror of 25% or more of the voting shares of a bank becomes a *bank holding company* and becomes subject to regulatory supervision, capital requirements, safety and soundness exams, and so on. The acquiring entity may have to reorganize and divest its nonfinancial assets and operating entities.

One way to get around this requirement may be to ensure that the persons are not acting in concert and each person is under 10%.

Inadvertent crossing of the 5%, 10%, and 25% limits can occur especially if the acquiror was close to the threshold and the bank has repurchased shares. There needs to be continuous monitoring and a safety margin to prevent inadvertent crossing.

SWITCHING REGULATORS

Banks may opt away from a tougher regulator to one with a lighter touch. Most recently Bank of Tokyo-MUFJ switched its regulator from the State of NY Department of Financial Service (NYDFS) to the OCC. There are others that have switched the other way; for example, Bridge Bancorp was a federally chartered bank that became a NY State regulated bank in 2017. A change of regulators on its own should not be a cause for concern as long as the rationale is well articulated, and the motives are understood. A state regulator may be better situated to deal with the specific circumstances of a bank. For example, a bank with a high degree of loan concentration in one category, but one in-line with geographical peers, may be treated punitively by a national regulator versus a state regulator with a deep understanding of the local markets.

SHEDDING THE BHC

Under the prior Dodd-Frank regulations, bank holding companies with more than $50 billion in assets were classified automatically as a SIFI (Systemically Important Financial Institution). For example, Zions Bancorp shed its BHC and got around the requirements for SIFI banks. This may become less of a factor with the SIFI threshold being raised to $250 billion from $50 billion. The Bank of the Ozarks also had shed its BHC. One of the benefits of not having a BHC is that an acquiror would no longer need to wait for Federal Reserve approval on M&A. One of the side effects of not having a BHC is that the core systems conversion must be done on the same day as the date when the deal is consummated, whereas a BHC with multiple bank charters may run separate core systems for their banks.

S CORP BANKS

S Corps (Subchapter S corporations) have a tax advantage in being treated as partnerships for tax purposes. The profits are passed to the shareholders and taxed at the personal level. Since 1997 banks have been eligible to elect S Corp status. About a third of the banks in the country have opted to be treated as S Corps. This comes with a limitation that the number of shareholders be under 100. Apart from the tax status there are no other major regulatory differences for an S Corp bank.

FINTECH CHARTER

In 2019, the OCC commenced applications for national bank charters from fintech companies. This Special Purpose National Banks (SPNB) charter has been challenged by the NYDFS. In 2018, the OCC had granted a traditional charter to Varo, an all mobile bank partnered with The Bancorp Bank. Varo received FDIC approval on February 7, 2020 for deposit insurance.

UTAH INDUSTRIAL BANKS (INDUSTRIAL LOAN COMPANY ILC)

There are about 15 state-chartered industrial banks in Utah. These entities operate like banks with access to the discount window, Fed Wire, and FDIC insurance. They have one key difference in that the owner of the ILC may conduct nonfinancial activities that a regular BHC cannot. The state has low tax rates and also does not have an interest rate ceiling but has an "unconscionable" provision. An ILC charter has been a preferred route for fintechs that did not have a regular bank charter. These firms would apply to Utah's Department of Financial Institutions and to the FDIC. Two firms that recently received approvals include Square and Nelnet. Square had initially applied in September 2017, withdrew it July 2018, and reapplied in December 2018 and received approval on March 17th, 2020. Nelnet, a student loan servicer, also received approval on the same day. Square's bank is required to have an initial paid-in capital of $56MM and needs to maintain a leverage ratio above 20%. Nelnet is required to have an initial paid-in capital of $100MM and needs to maintain a leverage ratio above 12%. Rakuten, the Japanese e-commerce company, has an ILC application pending. SoFi (Social Finance) had previously dropped its ILC application.

REGULATION O

Reg O governs loans made to executive officers, directors, or principal shareholders of a bank. The amount of loan outstanding, the interest rate, and terms and conditions have to be reported. The loans may not exceed $100,000 and any loans above $25,000 (or 5% of the capital) must be approved by the board of directors.

KEY REGULATIONS FOR COMMUNITY BANKS

BSA/AML (Bank Secrecy Act/Anti Money Laundering), CRA (Community Reinvestment Act) and Fair Lending are key regulations that Community bankers spend considerable time on. Lapses in these areas can prove to be quite costly.

BSA/AML requires banks to collaborate with government agencies to report suspicious financial transactions.

CRA requires banks to serve the credit needs of all segments of their communities. The OCC conducts a CRA exam every three years and assigns banks four ratings (Outstanding, Satisfactory, Needs to Improve, or Substantial Noncompliance).

Fair Lending consists of the Fair Housing Act (FHA) and Equal Credit Opportunity Act (ECOA) and makes it illegal to discriminate in mortgage lending on the basis of race, color, religion, national origin, handicap, family status, or sex.

CANADA

While we were reviewing large banking crises globally, we could not help but notice that our neighbor to the north seems to have generally avoided major banking crises (at least thus far!). The Bank of Canada was only established in 1935. There was no deposit insurance until Canada Deposit Insurance Corporation (CDIC) was set up in 1967. Since 1967, there have been 43 bank failures.

EXHIBIT 6.16 G10 Banking Crises

Risk Type	Switzerland (91–96)	Spain (78–83)	UK BCCI (1991)	UK Small Banks (91–92)	UK Barings (1995)	Germany Herstatt (1974)	Norway (88–93)	Sweden (91–94)	Japan (94–02)	US Cont'tal Illinois (1984)	US S&L (82–95)	US New England (90–91)	US Sub-prime (98-00)
Credit	√	√	√	√	×	×	√	√	√	√	√	√	√
Market	×	×	×	×	√	√	×	√	×	×	√	×	×
Operational (Incl. fraud)	×	√	√	×	√	√	×	×	×	×	×	×	√
Shook													
Macro: real economy	√	√	√	√	×	×	√	√	√	×	√	√	×
asset prices	√	√	×	√	×	×	√	√	√	×	√	√	×
Banking system													
Financial liberalisation	√	√	√	√	×	√	√	√	√	×	√	×	×
Poor regulation/ supervision	×	√	×	×	×	×	√	√	√	×	√	×	×
Risk concentration	√	√	×	√	×	×	×	√	√	×	√	×	√
Bank specific	×	×	√	×	√	√	×	×	×	√	√	×	√
Impact													
Whole banking system	×	√	×	×	×	×	√	√	√	×	√	×	×
Small banks only	√	×	×	√	×	×	×	×	×	×	×	√	√
One bank	×	×	√	×	√	√	×	×	×	√	×	×	×
Systemic risk	×	√	×	√	×	√	√	√	√	√	√	×	×
Crisis resolution													
Speed of resolution	quick	quick	quick	slow	quick	quick	quick	quick	slow	quick	slow	quick	quick
Mainly closures	×	×	√	√	√	√	×	×	×	×	×	×	√
Main type of support	private	public/ private	×	private/ public	×	×	public/ private	public/ private	public	public	public	public	public
Fiscal cost of resolution (% of annual GDP)*	< 1	6	NII	0.007	NII	NII	3.1	4.0	(a)	.0003	2.1	NII	NII
Regulatory changes	√	√	√	×	√	√	√	√	√	√	√	×	√

Notes: X denotes no or not a cause of failure. NII denotes that the failure cost was either zero or close to zero.
Sources: Fiscal data from Swiss National Bank; Cuerve, Alvaro: "La crisis bancaria en España" Ed. Ariel, 1985; UK Small Banks: Bank of England Annual Report, 2000; Norwegian Ministry of Finance; Sverlges Riskbank; FDIC and FDIC respectively.

Prior to 1967 the major bank failure was Home Bank of Canada in August of 1923. Canadian banks have a single regulator in the OFSI (Office of the Superintendent of Financial Institutions).

There has been a lot of work done on the topic of fewer bank failures in Canada, and the consensus seems to be that the banking system above the 49th parallel is not as fragmented and their mortgage lending is different than in the US. The assets in Canada's banking system are highly concentrated in the "big five" banks: Royal Bank of Canada (RBC), Toronto-Dominion Bank (TD), Bank of Nova Scotia (Scotiabank), Bank of Montreal (BMO), and Canadian Imperial Bank of Commerce (CIBC), with one regulator to oversee them (OSFI). Meanwhile, not only was the development of the banking system more fragmented in the US, we also have a robust securities market and more developed shadow bank system which often operates outside of the jurisdiction of traditional banking regulators.

Of course, the flip side of this is one could argue the Canadian banking sector is less innovative, less dynamic, and more oligopolistic in terms of pricing than its US counterpart.

See Exhibit 6.16 for a list of banking crises in the G10 countries.

7

Role of the Central Bank and Interest Rates

"Interest rates are to asset prices what gravity is to the apple. When interest rates are low there is little gravitational pull on asset prices. Interest rates power everything in the economic universe."

– Warren Buffett at the Berkshire Hathaway Annual Meeting May 4, 2013

ROLE OF THE CENTRAL BANK

The Federal Reserve is the central bank of the United States. Though its existence feels perennial, it is actually the *third* central banking system implemented in the United States, preceded by the aptly named First Bank of the United States (1791–1811) and the Second Bank of the United States (1817–1836), as well as a rather messy period that involved a network of national banks.

Founded by Congress in 1913 following a secretive meeting on Jekyll Island between members of the government and some of the most important bankers of the time, the Federal Reserve is the monetary authority that manages the *currency*, *money supply*, and *interest rates* in the United States, and serves as a primary regulator in the banking industry.

The Federal Reserve is comprised of two main entities (Exhibit 7.1): a central authority known as The Board of Governors, based in Washington, D.C., and a network of 12 Federal Reserve Banks with different geographical domains – Boston, New York, Philadelphia, Cleveland, Richmond, Atlanta, Chicago, St. Louis, Minneapolis, Kansas City, Dallas, and San Francisco. These districts were set up many years ago, and thus reflected the economic and demographic realities of the time.

There are endless books and opinion pieces on the wisdom of an autonomous and rather opaque institution that wields so much power; however, this chapter will not focus on that. Instead, we are interested in how the Federal Reserve interacts with and influences regional and community banks.

EXHIBIT 7.1 The Federal Reserve Map

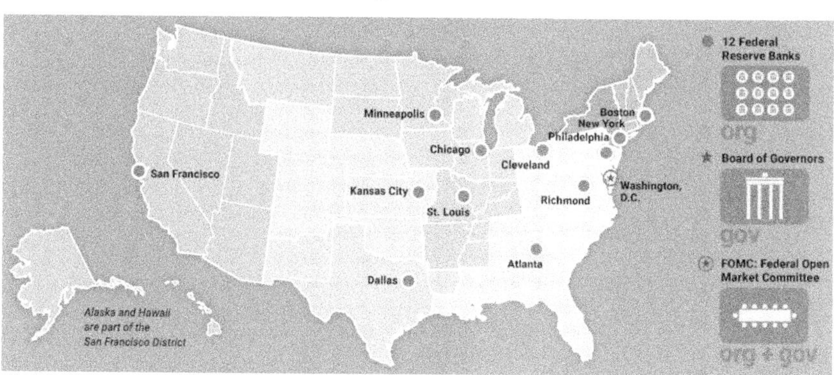

Source: Federal Reserve Bank of San Francisco

Whether the relative autonomy of the Fed is a good or bad thing is beyond the purview of this book. However, this independence has certainly allowed the Fed to remain comparatively un-politicized and has allowed the Fed to make longer-term though perhaps less popular decisions.

The Federal Reserve's relationship with banks is a deep and multifaceted one, from targeting interest rates, to implementing and enforcing regulation, to providing many bank-like services for depositories (Exhibit 7.2).

EXHIBIT 7.2 The Federal Reserve Structure

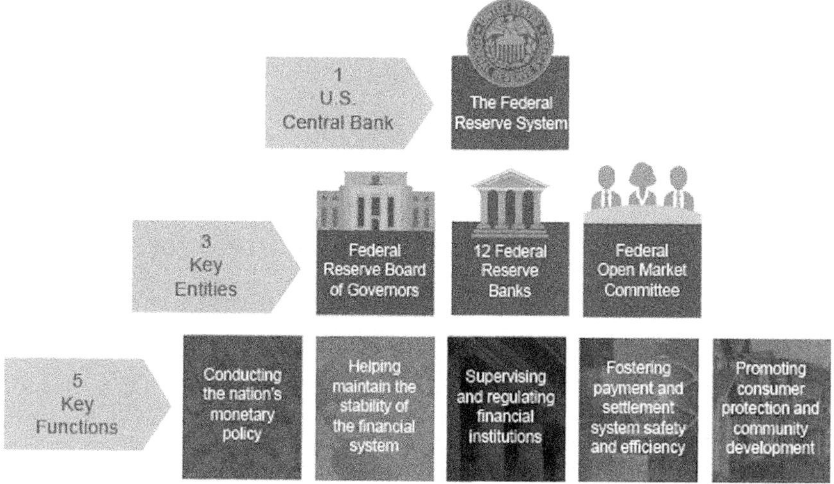

Source: Federal Reserve

THE FEDERAL OPEN MARKET COMMITTEE (FOMC)

The Federal Open Market Committee is the Fed's ultimate monetary policy-making body. The FOMC has 12 voting members: the seven members of the Board of Governors, the President of the Federal Reserve Bank of New York, and a rotating group of four Reserve Bank presidents (Exhibit 7.3).

The tools that the FOMC have at their disposal include the fed funds target range (which is manipulated through a number of tools), other open market operations, the rate on interest on required and excess reserves, the discount rate, and the reserve requirement. The FOMC meets eight times a year to assess economic conditions and to adjust monetary policy as they see fit. These policies influence the availability and cost of money and credit, and thus have a meaningful impact on the operating environment for banks.

Since the late 1970s, the Fed has been instructed to carry out what is known as the "dual mandate" of promoting "price stability" as well as "maximum employment." The former was defined relatively recently (2012) as a 2% year-over-year increase in the personal consumption expenditure (PCE) price index. "Maximum employment" is a much more complex topic, and thus does not have an explicit target. Indeed, even the appropriate metric to use to gauge "maximum employment" is a topic of much debate, though a U3 unemployment rate in the 4 to 5% range has been referenced in the past. The dual mandate started with the Federal Reserve Reform Act of 1977,

EXHIBIT 7.3 The FOMC Structure

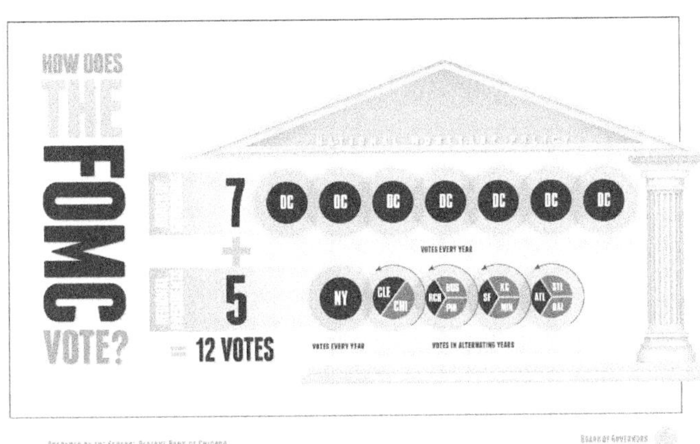

Source: Chicago Fed

which followed a period of stagflation in the late 1970s. It should also be noted that while called the dual mandate, there were three explicit goals, with the third goal being to promote moderate long-term interest rates. The Act stated: "*The Board of Governors of the Federal Reserve System and the Federal Open Market Committee shall maintain long run growth of the monetary and credit aggregates commensurate with the economy's long run potential to increase production, so as to promote effectively the* ***goals of maximum employment, stable prices, and moderate long-term interest rates****.*"

Since we now have a holistic understanding of the general goals of the Fed, let us delve deeper into some of the Fed's more important tools.

The Fed Funds Rate is perhaps the highest profile tool at the FOMC's disposal. Indeed, when looking at the policy statements put out by the FOMC, the fed funds rate target will be the first policy metric provided. This rate represents the rate at which depositories will lend their reserve balances (i.e., balances held at the Federal Reserve) to other depositories on an overnight and uncollateralized basis in order for the borrowing bank to fulfill reserve requirements. An increase in the fed funds rate represents a tightening of monetary policy, as it makes credit incrementally more expensive, while the converse is true for a decrease in the fed funds rate.

An important aspect is that the federal funds market is very much a market influenced by market forces, and is expressed as a target with a 25-bps range. The Federal Reserve works hard to influence this market to reach its proposed target through various means including open market operations by the trading desk of the Federal Reserve Bank of New York. In this case, open market operations usually refer to overnight repos (adds liquidity if fed funds are too high) and reverse repos (removes liquidity if fed funds are too low) of Treasuries, agency debt, and mortgage-backed securities. Setting the interest on reserves is another tool in the Fed's pocket that we go into later. Generally, when there are excess reserves in the system, the interest on reserves is used to manipulate effective fed funds; when there is a shortage of cash, repo operations are effective.

Once upon a time, the fed funds market was a good deal larger than what it is today. Pre-crisis, the interbank market was robust, and the largest suppliers and demanders of fed funds were the domestic commercial banks. A couple of drivers caused a dramatic shrinkage in the size of the fed funds market (Exhibit 7.4). One, the Fed purchased vast amounts of securities in the open market (more on that later), which flooded the entire banking system with excess liquidity. Banks held so much in reserves that the *demand* for fed funds declined. Two, the Fed started paying interest to banks on funds that were held in their reserve accounts, giving banks an alternate option to earn money on their reserves and thus decreasing the *supply* for fed funds as well.

EXHIBIT 7.4 Size of the Fed Funds Market

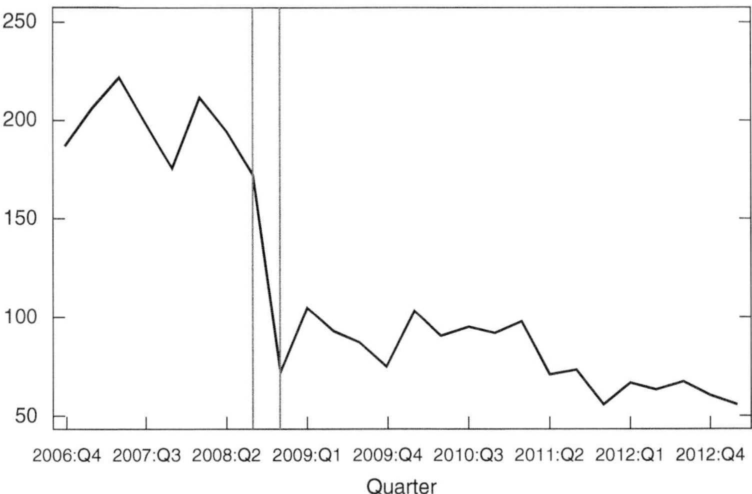

Notes: The vertical lines denote filings for the third and fourth quarters of 2008. The chart reflects fed funds sold by bank holding companies, stand-alone commercial banks, foreign banking organizations, and Federal Home Loan Banks. Fed funds sold by thrifts are included only after the first quarter of 2012, when they become publicly available. Data do not include lending by Fannie Mae or Freddie Mac, as historically those agencies report federal funds jointly with repo transactions in their regulatory filings, although additional information on their fed funds activity is often included on an ad hoc basis in the text and footnotes of their 10-Q and 10-K filings.

Source: NY Fed

Regardless of the diminished size of the fed funds market, the fed funds rate remains a benchmark rate that all market participants will pay close attention to (Exhibit 7.5). There is also a robust fed funds derivatives market as well, which provides a positive feedback loop for its prominence. The fed funds rate in many ways is seen as the core "risk free rate" that other short-term rates, such as LIBOR, react to.

The fed funds rate has a meaningful impact on the short end of the yield curve, and thus impacts things such as yields on short-term loans (such as C&I) and cost of deposits.

An important concept related to the fed funds rate is *the natural (or neutral) rate of interest*, frequently denoted as **r*** when in reference to the fed funds rate (Exhibit 7.6). It represents the rate of interest that leads to the economy operating at its full potential excluding any transitory shocks to aggregate supply and demand, which also means it exerts no pressure, up or down, on the

EXHIBIT 7.5 History of Fed Funds Rate

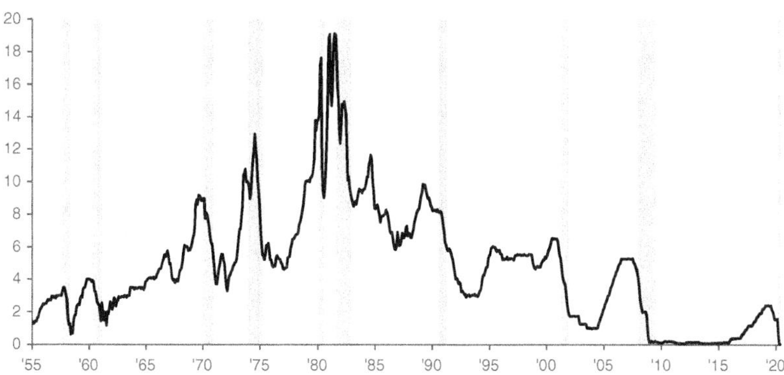

Source: St. Louis Fed

EXHIBIT 7.6 Fed Funds Rate: Actual vs. Natural

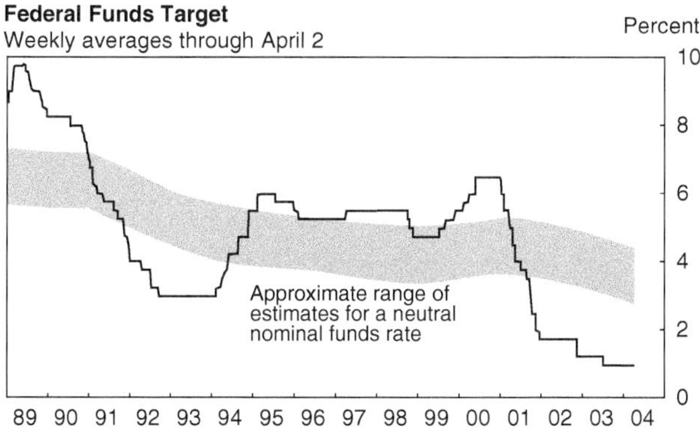

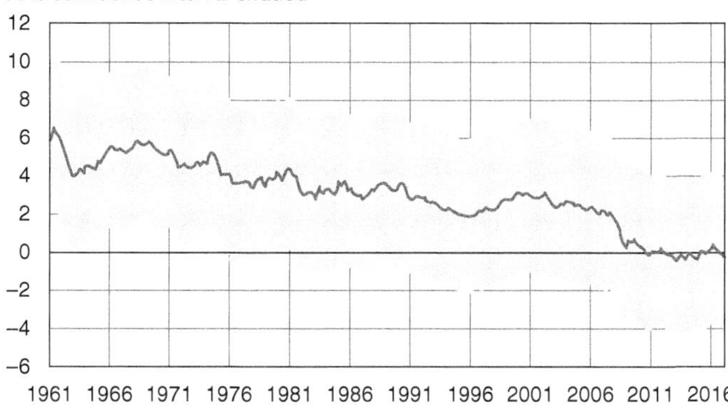

Source: Federal Reserve Bank of San Francisco

natural rate of inflation. The neutral rate is a *real* rate, which means it excludes inflation. This concept is important as over a long period of time, interest rates should revert to the neutral rate of interest. However, this rate is easy to define, but hard to estimate. A lot of academic horsepower has been focused on this topic recently. Thomas Laubach and John Williams are two economists that publish thoughtful pieces and estimates on this rate. This concept is important as it gives us an idea if monetary policy is currently accommodative or not, and which direction rates will go if there is an expectation for the rate to revert to the neutral rate over the long term.

Temporary Open Market Operations are operations conducted by the trading desk of the New York Fed to manipulate liquidity and short-term interest rates (Exhibit 7.7). As mentioned before, this overwhelmingly consists of repo (RP) operations and reverse repo (RRP) operations. These agreements can either be overnight or term.

In a repo operation, the Fed acts as a counterparty in the repo market by buying an asset (injecting cash) and simultaneously entering into a forward sale agreement. This effective injects liquidity into the system, with the NY Fed creating new reserves for the counterparty. Repo transactions are only conducted with primary dealers.

Conversely, in a reverse repo operation, the Fed *sells* an asset (takes cash out of the system) and simultaneously enters into an agreement to buy it back.

EXHIBIT 7.7 NY Fed O/N RP and RRP Operations

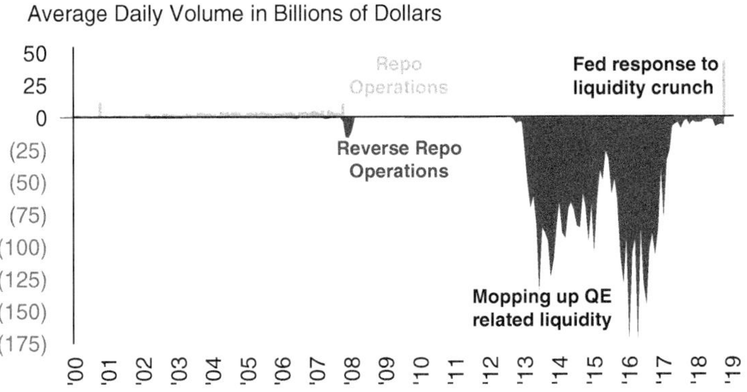

Source: New York Fed

The counterparties for RRP include primary dealers, money market funds, GSEs, and banks. Reverse repo operations help create a "floor" for rates as it would be irrational for financial institutions to lend at a rate below what the Fed would pay.

We see that pre-financial crisis, the NY Fed was steadily supplying liquidity to the repo market in a controlled manner. Following the financial crisis and the massive amount of quantitative easing, the entire financial system was flush with liquidity. In September 2013, the Fed implemented a standing reverse repo operation to mop up excess liquidity and provide a floor for interest rates. We can see the huge amount of liquidity taken out of the market by the NY Fed starting in 2013. Money market funds were by far the largest user of this facility.

After the Fed began the process of unwinding and normalizing the size of its balance sheet, excess liquidity began to drain out of the system. We see that beginning in 2018, financial institutions that were no longer awash in excess cash stopped tapping the NY Fed RRP operation, with liquidity in the repo market seemingly "in balance."

In September 2019, overnight repo rates spiked to 10%, far exceeding the fed funds 2–2¼ target range. The market became "out of balance" with the market having an oversupply of securities and a lack of cash to finance those securities. What caused this cash crunch? Some factors included a large settlement for a recent Treasury auction, quarter end tax payments, a general lack of cash, and the desire to hoard reserves at the tightly regulated primary dealers.

The Federal Reserve stepped in quickly to stabilize the market, providing liquidity to the repo markets for the first time since the financial crisis. Thus far, the operations have been fairly large in scale (north of $75B a day) and have been mostly oversubscribed. This additional liquidity was successful in stabilizing repo rates.

Interest on Reserves (IOR) represents the rate at which the Federal Reserve Banks pay interest on reserve balances that banks have deposited at their local Reserve Bank. There are technically two rates at play here, the interest on required reserves (IORR) and the interest on excess reserves (IOER). The Fed only started paying interest on reserves in October 2008 with the *Emergency Economic Stabilization Act of 2008* after a vigorous and long debate over the pros and cons of such an action. This ability to pay interest on reserves gave the Fed yet another tool to fine tune monetary policy.

As the Federal Reserve engaged in quantitative easing and pumped liquidity into the system, one risk was that this money would be recirculated via the fractional reserve system (remember the money multiplier?) and trigger unintended amounts of inflation. Strict capital requirements and paying banks to maintain reserves prevented this. We can see excess reserves by the banking system shot up following the implementation of paying interest on reserve balances (Exhibit 7.8).

We see excess reserves spike following the implementation of interest payments on excess reserves in 2008, and another spike in 2020 as the Fed temporarily reduced required reserves to 0 and pumped liquidity into financial markets in response to COVID-19. Excess Reserves are magnitudes of order higher than required reserves.

One justification for paying banks interest on their reserve balances is that by requiring banks to hold a certain amount of reserves, banks would be "taxed" by not earning interest on those balances. As a result, banks worked hard at minimizing the amount of reserves it would be required to hold, utilizing tricks such as "sweep accounts," whereby a bank would "sweep" checking account balances, which have a reserve requirement, into say a savings account, which does not. Banks would hold the absolute minimum amount of reserves possible, and frequently tapped the fed funds market to fulfill their reserve requirements (Exhibit 7.9).

The total amount of excess reserves has also been a topic of debate recently. At about $1.8 trillion, excess reserves make up about 50% of the entire monetary base of the United States. In a nutshell, there are arguments that such a significant amount of excess reserves has the potential to increase liquidity in an uncontrolled way.

EXHIBIT 7.8 Bank Excess Reserves

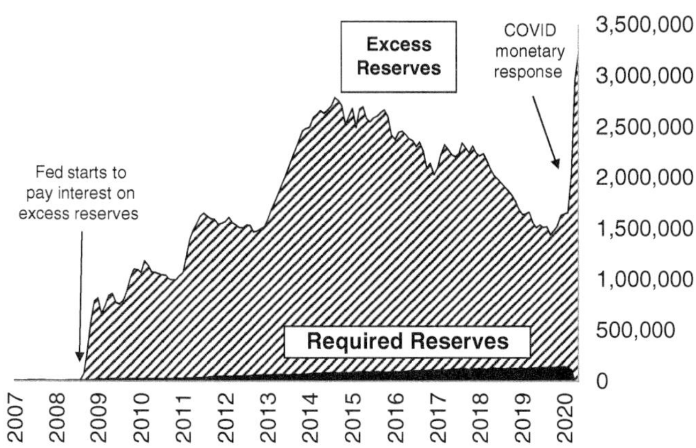

Source: Federal Reserve

EXHIBIT 7.9 How Interest on Reserves Affects Interest Rates

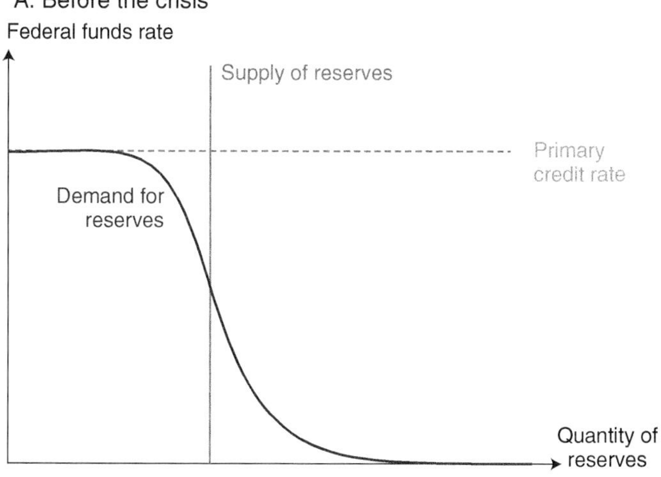

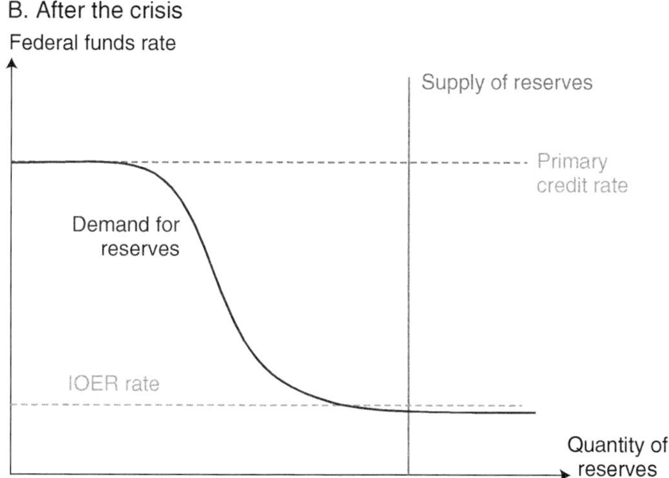

Source: Federal Reserve Bank of San Francisco

As mentioned before, adjusting the IOER is now a critical way for the FOMC to implement the fed funds target range. As the IOER is directly determined by the Fed, they have the unilateral ability to change it as they see fit. Prior to this, the Fed had to carefully forecast and adjust the *quantity* of reserves through open market operations to adjust short-term rates; however,

EXHIBIT 7.10 IOER vs. Fed Funds

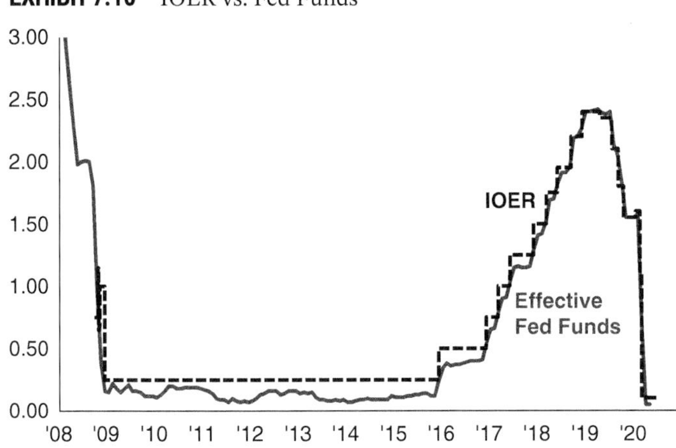

Source: St. Louis Fed

IOER gave the ability for the Fed to directly price reserves. For entities that meet the requirements to earn the IOER, there will be little incentive for them to lend at a rate below the IOER, thus creating an "anchor" for fed funds (Exhibit 7.10).

Permanent Open Market Operations represents the outright purchase of Treasury and mortgage-backed securities by the Fed, which are accounted for in the System Open Market Account (SOMA). This stands in contrast to the *temporary open market operations* (i.e., repos and reverse repos) that the Fed uses to influence the fed funds rate. Permanent Open Market Operations recently came into prominence in the United States following the financial crisis. The Federal Reserve drastically increased its purchase of Treasuries and mortgage-backed securities through three rounds of "Quantitative Easing" (QE) starting from December 2008 to October 2014 in order to lower longer-term interest rates, and once again in 2020 following the COVID-19 pandemic related economic disruptions (Exhibit 7.11).

Collectively, the Federal Reserve accumulated around $4.5 trillion in Treasuries and MBS. This drastic accumulation was unprecedented for the United States, and thus the long-term future effects are still analyzed to this day. A consensus is, however, that QE did manage to lower longer-term interest rates and improve the availability of credit (Exhibit 7.12). The Federal Reserve estimates that open market operations decreased the 10-Year Treasury yield by ~100 bps at its peak.

Indeed, mortgage application volumes post-crisis proved to be quite robust as mortgage rates declined dramatically.

EXHIBIT 7.11 Size of Fed Balance Sheet

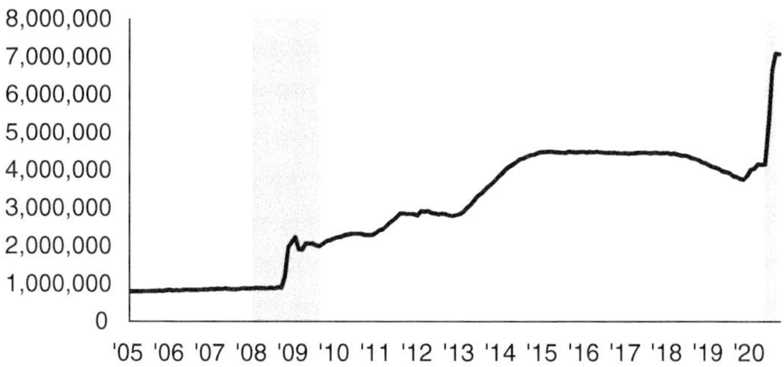

Source: St. Louis Fed

EXHIBIT 7.12 Estimated Effect of QE

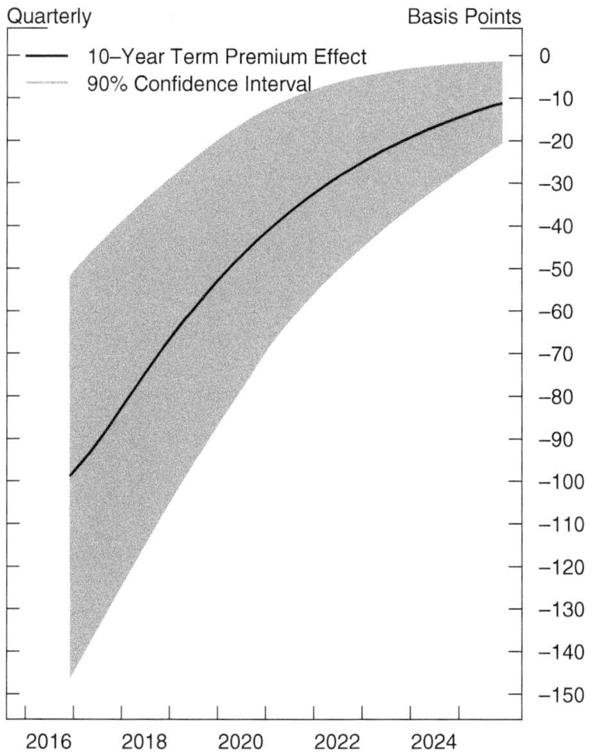

Source: Federal Reserve

After peaking at around ~$4.5T in assets, the Fed maintained that level of assets for a while before announcing the orderly reduction of its balance sheet by allowing securities to mature without reinvesting proceeds. The Fed allowed about $50B in assets to mature a month, while economists discussed what the ultimate size of a "normalized" balance sheet would look like. Many believed it would end up in the ~$3.5T range.

In July 2019, the Federal Reserve announced the discontinuation of the reduction of its balance sheet by September 2019, leaving the balance sheet in the ~$3.75T range. However, the committee remixed its balance sheet by allowing MBS holdings to mature and to reinvest proceeds into Treasury securities.

Similar to the fed funds target, permanent open market operations influence the operating environment for banks. Higher longer-term rates will naturally benefit yields on certain loans benchmarked to those rates (like mortgage and CRE). However, the offset is that a tighter environment could dampen demand for those types of loan products, making growth incrementally harder.

The Discount Rate and Discount Window represents the interest rate charged to banks on collateralized loans they receive from their regional Federal Reserve Bank's lending facility, known as the discount window. There are actually three separate rates at play here: primary credit, secondary credit, and seasonal credit. The primary credit program is usually an overnight loan, made to banks in sound financial condition. The rate is set at 50 bps over the fed funds target. Secondary credit is used to meet short-term liquidity needs or to resolve severe financial difficulties for those depositories ineligible for primary credit. The rate is set at 50 bps over the primary credit rate (i.e., 100 bps over the fed funds target). Seasonal credit is usually extended to small banks that deal with some form of seasonality in their business (i.e., agriculture). There is some stigma for financial institutions that tap the discount window, as the implication is that a bank tapping the discount window is suffering from liquidity issues and is unable to access other funding.

The Reserve Requirement is one of the oldest tools available to central banks, and represents the amount of funds that a bank needs to hold in either vault cash or deposited at the Federal Reserve against deposits (Exhibit 7.13). This is to ensure that banks will have sufficient liquidity to handle depositor withdrawals. Fractional reserve banking is possible because banks are not required to hold a 100% reserve against their deposits. Thus, the reserve ratios are an important lever for the Federal Reserve to control credit. Higher reserve ratios will mean less lending activity, while lower reserve ratios will mean more lending activity.

The Money Multiplier is a fundamental concept necessary to understand the impact that reserve ratios can have on monetary policy. In short, the money multiplier is the inverse of the reserve ratio and represents the

EXHIBIT 7.13 Reserve Requirements

Reserve Requirements		
	Requirement	
Liability Type	**% of Liabilities**	**Effective Date**
Net transaction accounts [1]		
$0 to $16.0 million[2]	0	1-18-18
More than $16.0 million to $122.3 million[3]	3	1-18-18
More than $122.3 million	10	1-18-18
Nonpersonal time deposits	0	12-27-90
Eurocurrency liabilities	0	12-27-90

Source: Federal Reserve

multiplicative effect that an initial increase in bank deposits will have on the total money supply. For example, if banks are required on average to hold 10% of their deposits in reserve, it means that 90% of the deposit can be lent out. Thus, if a bank receives $100 of new deposits, it will be able to lend out $90. That $90 will eventually end up as $90 in fresh deposits somewhere else, where $81 will be subsequently lent out. Ultimately, $100 in new deposits with a 10% reserve ratio will lead to $\$100 \times (1/0.1) = \$1{,}000$ increase in money supply.

Reserve requirements are tweaked much less frequently by the Federal Reserve in comparison to the other tools that it has at its disposal. Reserve requirements were, however, suspended during the COVID-19 pandemic.

EXTRAORDINARY MONETARY MEASURES

The 2008 Financial Crisis brought unprecedented levels of stress to the most complex financial system to date. A complex web of financial derivatives and products built upon a foundation of unsound subprime mortgages had a cascading effect through the financial system. The evaporation of liquidity as market participants lost confidence in counterparties, and underlying collateral was arguably the most disruptive aspect of the crisis. The Fed's established playbook going into the crisis involved the short end of the curve. It took the Fed only a little over a year to take fed funds from 5 1/4 (September 2007) to zero (December 2008). Other monetary tweaks involved reducing the spread of the discount rate over federal funds, lengthening loans to banks from overnight to 90 days. The Fed also created a range of liquidity facilities for key non-bank market participants, including broker-dealers and money market funds. However, as the crisis deepened, the Fed needed to bring additional firepower. Enter quantitative easing.

Quantitative Easing (QE) involved large-scale asset purchases (LSAPs), which were done in three "waves" between late 2008 and October 2014. In the secondary market, the Fed purchased longer-dated Treasuries, agency debt, and MBS, which bid up the prices for those assets and in turn lowered yields.

This had a cascading effect as other investors looked to other asset classes for yield. This hyper accommodative stance also gave confidence and diminished concerns about tail risks such as deflation. A study done by the Fed suggested the first two rounds of LSAPs (cumulatively $2.325 trillion) boosted aggregate output by almost 3% and increased private payrolls by more than 2 million jobs (Chung et al. 2011). However, as Fed Chair at the time Ben Bernanke has written, "we can't know exactly how much of the US recovery can be attributed to monetary policy, since we can only conjecture what might have happened if the Fed had not taken the steps it did."

For the banks, the LSAPs ended up supplying *trillions* of excess reserve balances to the banking system – versus virtually zero in excess reserves the few years just prior to the crisis.

Meanwhile, lower rates helped induce borrowing, but banks had to grapple with declining yields weighing on their profitability. They managed to mitigate a lot of this through reducing deposit and funding costs. One study (Di Maggio, Kermani, and Palmer (2018)) drew a relationship between the Fed buying MBS and a boom in refinancing in existing mortgages. Another study (Darmouni and Rodnyansky (2017)) showed that banks that owned more MBS prior to QE saw faster growth in loans than banks that had little or no MBS holdings.

Although the scale of the Fed's LSAPs was unprecedented, they were not completely in uncharted territory. Up until the 2008 financial crisis, The Bank of Japan (BoJ) had the most high profile LSAP program and coined the phrase "quantitative easing." In brief, the BoJ introduced quantitative easing in 2001, after unsuccessfully battling deflation and a sluggish economy for 15 years. Interest rates in Japan were lowered to virtually zero in an attempt to combat the economic headwinds, and the country fell into a liquidity trap in which the rates are so low that actors prefer holding cash to debt. Thus, the BoJ moved to more unconventional tools and expanded the size of its monetary base by an unprecedented 60% in just two years through open market purchases of government bonds, ABS, and eventually equities. Unfortunately, CPI in Japan seemed to be largely unchanged through this period, though one could argue it could've been even worse sans QE. One issue was the signaling of commitment from the BoJ as the inflationary force of money expansion was offset by the deflationary force of the *expectation* for future money contraction. Indeed, most of the expansion was reversed by 2006.

Of note, the Fed has characterized these LSAPs as "credit easing" rather than "quantitative easing." The former being characterized as focused on the mix of loans and securities purchased in order to manipulate credit spreads and credit markets, while the latter being focused asset purchases in order to expand the quantity of bank reserves.

Finally, the inverse of quantitative easing is appropriately called **quantitative tightening**, and revolves around the unwinding of the massive pool of assets accumulated by the Fed, which was done by simply allowing these assets to mature without subsequently reinvesting the proceeds.

NEGATIVE INTEREST RATES AND THE EVENT HORIZON

The Federal Reserve drew the line at zero for fed funds. Simply, the unknown effects of such an unconventional move and a range of other more palatable tools prevented the Fed from crossing that threshold. However, other central banks around the world have adopted negative interest rate policies (NIRP) to inconclusive results. In the modern era, negative rates were first deployed by Sweden in 2009 when it cut its overnight deposit rate to –0.25%. The ECB followed in 2014 when it lowered its deposit rates to –0.1%. The Bank of Japan adopted negative rates in January 2016, while Switzerland has the deepest negative policy rates. There are some nuances to implementation, but the end goal is to support easier financial condition and to expand the extension of credit beyond what was possible with rates at zero. Like crossing the event horizon of a black hole, the countries that have adopted NIRP after the financial crisis have not been able to escape back into a more normal monetary environment.

Generally, countries with NIRP also have banks with extremely low profitability. Thus, any indications that the US might adopt NIRP in the future will most likely be coupled with a mass exodus by investors out of bank stocks. The market rates have gone negative in several markets, and we estimate that about 29% of the outstanding developed market sovereign debt now trades at a negative yield.

EXTRAORDINARY MONETARY MEASURES PART II

The outbreak of the COVID-19 pandemic in early 2020 brought the global economy to a grinding halt. Unlike the great financial crisis, the genesis of this crisis was not in the financial sector. Despite this, the Federal Reserve moved swiftly and pre-emptively to stabilize the financial markets. Broadly, the actions by the Federal Reserve can be categorized by their role as either a regulator or as a central bank. Exhibit 7.14 expounds upon the latter.

EXHIBIT 7.14 Pandemic Fed Programs

Program	Size	Description
Municipal Liquidity Facility	Up to $500B	This facility aims to help state and local governments. The NY Fed created an SPV to purchase eligible notes directly from issuers (municipalities).
Main Street Lending Program	Up to $600B	To support lending to small and medium-sized businesses, the Boston Fed created an SPV to purchase participations in loans from eligible lenders.
Paycheck Protection Program Liquidity Facility	$68B as of 7/8/2020	This program was implemented to enhance the SBA's Paycheck Protection Program (PPP) by extending credit to eligible financial institutions that originate PPP loans. Properly underwritten PPP loans guaranteed by the SBA are eligible to serve as collateral.
Money Market Mutual Fund Liquidity Facility	$19.6B as of 7/8/2020	This facility aims to keep the money market mutual funds liquid and functioning in the event of large investor redemptions. The Boston Fed provides advances for eligible borrowers to purchase certain MMMF assets. Eligible participants include all US banks.
Commercial Paper Funding Facility	$12.8B as of 7/8/2020	This New York Fed facility purchases (via an SPV) eligible commercial paper through primary dealers to provide liquidity and support for the short-term funding markets. Eligible paper consists of 3-month unsecured and asset-backed commercial paper directly.
Primary Dealer Credit Facility	$2.3B as of 7/8/2020	The facility provides 90-day credit to primary dealers (the largest US broker-dealers) in exchange for a broad range of collateral. On an individual level, dealers can borrow up to the margin-adjusted collateral amount.
Primary Market Corporate Credit Facility	$750B combined with SMCCF	This facility is open to investment grade companies whereby the Fed provides credit through making loans and purchasing bonds directly.
Secondary Market Corporate Credit Facility	$1.3B as of 5/19/2020	This facility supports the secondary credit markets purchasing investment grade corporate bonds in the open market.
Term Asset-Backed Securities Loan Facility	$8.7B as of 7/8/2020 Up to $100B	The TALF provides support for the ABS market by making three-year loans fully secured by eligible ABS.

Note: As of July 2020

THE U.S. TREASURY MARKET

The U.S. Treasury Market is incredibly liquid and is the "backbone" for many fixed income instruments. In 2018, the U.S. Treasury issued approximately $10.2 trillion in securities, while SIFMA reported average *daily* trading volume of $594.1 billion in the secondary markets. The Treasury market mostly consists of marketable T-Bills, Notes, Bonds, and Treasury Inflation Protected Securities (TIPS), which are auctioned regularly by the Federal Reserve Bank of New York. Because these securities are backed by the full faith and credit of the United States, they are the closest instruments we have to "risk-free." Their pricing and yields are foundational when it comes to the pricing of other securities.

The U.S. Treasury publishes upcoming auction schedules several days before an auction. An auction announcement will disclose the amount offered by maturity, the auction date, and the issue date among other pertinent information. Competitive bids, which are submitted by large financial institutions, are the pricing mechanism. Primary dealers, banks, and broker-dealers are the largest group of buyers. Their job in this context is to make markets and allocate Treasuries to their underlying clients. Other important competitive bidders include large investment funds, pensions and retirement funds, foreign accounts, and insurance companies that directly interact with the Treasury market. The Treasury collects all competitive bids and determines the lowest yield that would "clear" the auction (Exhibit 7.15).

These auctions are important price discovery mechanisms for the market. Important ratios to pay attention to include the bid-to-cover ratio, which represents the ratio of bids to total amount offered, and the percentage of the offering that goes to primary dealers, who are responsible for absorbing any supply not bought by other bidders (Exhibit 7.16).

The Treasury also publishes estimates on the total required issuance of net marketable securities on a quarterly basis based on budget projections. This is helpful in providing us a general guideline on how much supply is "coming down the pipe."

Holders of Treasury securities can be broadly broken down into three categories: Government Accounts, Domestic Entities, and Foreign Entities. Each group owns roughly a third of the Federal debt (Exhibit 7.17).

EXHIBIT 7.15 Treasury Auction Schedule Example

Tentative Auction Schedule of U.S. Treasury Securities

Security Type	Announcement Date	Auction Date	Settlement Date
3-Year NOTE	Wednesday, May 06, 2020	Monday, May 11, 2020	Friday, May 15, 2020
10-Year NOTE	Wednesday, May 06, 2020	Tuesday, May 12, 2020	Friday, May 15, 2020
30-Year BOND	Wednesday, May 06, 2020	Wednesday, May 13, 2020	Friday, May 15, 2020
13-Week BILL	Thursday, May 07, 2020	Monday, May 11, 2020	Thursday, May 14, 2020
26-Week BILL	Thursday, May 07, 2020	Monday, May 11, 2020	Thursday, May 14, 2020
4-Week BILL	Tuesday, May 12, 2020	Thursday, May 14, 2020	Tuesday, May 19, 2020
8-Week BILL	Tuesday, May 12, 2020	Thursday, May 14, 2020	Tuesday, May 19, 2020
13-Week BILL	Thursday, May 14, 2020	Monday, May 14, 2020	Thursday, May 21, 2020
26-Week BILL	Thursday, May 14, 2020	Monday, May 18, 2020	Thursday, May 21, 2020
52-Week BILL	Thursday, May 14, 2020	Tuesday, May 19, 2020	Thursday, May 21, 2020
10-Year TIPS	Thursday, May 14, 2020	Thursday, May 21, 2020	Friday, May 29, 2020
20-Year BOND	Thursday, May 14, 2020	Wednesday, May 20, 2020	Monday, June 01, 2020
4-Week BILL	Tuesday, May 19, 2020	Thursday, May 21, 2020	Tuesday, May 26, 2020
8-Week BILL	Tuesday, May 19, 2020	Thursday, May 21, 2020	Tuesday, May 26, 2020
13-Week BILL	Thursday, May 21, 2020	Tuesday, May 26, 2020	Thursday, May 28, 2020
26-Week BILL	Thursday, May 21, 2020	Tuesday, May 26, 2020	Thursday, May 28, 2020
2-Year FRN	Thursday, May 21, 2020	Wednesday, May 27, 2020	Friday, May 29, 2020
2-Year NOTE	Thursday, May 21, 2020	Tuesday, May 26, 2020	Monday, June 01, 2020
5-Year NOTE	Thursday, May 21, 2020	Wednesday, May 27, 2020	Monday, June 01, 2020
7-Year NOTE	Thursday, May 21, 2020	Thursday, May 28, 2020	Monday, June 01, 2020

Source: U.S. Treasury

EXHIBIT 7.16 Treasury Auction Results Example

TREASURY NEWS

Department of the Treasury • Bureau of the Fiscal Service

For Immediate Release
June 23, 2020

CONTACT: Treasury Auctions
202-504-3550

TREASURY AUCTION RESULTS

Term and Type of Security	2-Year Note
CUSIP Number	912828ZX1
Series	BC-2022
Interest Rate	0-1/8%
High Yield [1]	0.193%
Allotted at High	94.81%
Price	99.864327
Accrued Interest per $1,000	None
Median Yield [2]	0.160%
Low Yield [3]	0.080%
Issue Date	June 30, 2020
Maturity Date	June 30, 2022
Original Issue Date	June 30, 2020
Dated Date	June 30, 2020

	Tendered	Accepted
Competitive	$112,848,740,000	$45,799,187,500
Noncompetitive	$100,925,300	$100,925,300
FIMA (Noncompetitive)	$100,000,000	$100,000,000
Subtotal [4]	**$113,049,665,300**	**$46,000,112,800[5]**
SOMA	$6,291,525,900	$6,291,525,900
Total	**$119,341,191,200**	**$52,291,638,700**

	Tendered	Accepted
Primary Dealer [6]	$69,861,000,000	$14,302,827,500
Direct Bidder [7]	$11,955,000,000	$7,669,620,000
Indirect Bidder [8]	$31,032,740,000	$23,826,740,000
Total Competitive	**$112,848,740,000**	**$45,799,187,500**

Source: U.S. Treasury

EXHIBIT 7.17 Holders of Treasury Securities

Federal Reserve & Other Government Accounts ($7,999 / 36%)
Mutual Funds ($2,012 / 9%)
China ($1,121 / 5%)
Japan ($1,078 / 5%)
Depositories ($769 / 3%)
State & Local Governments ($648 / 3%)
Private Pensions ($440 / 2%)
State & Local Pensions ($395 / 2%)
Insurance Companies ($202 / 1%)
US Savings Bonds ($155 / 1%)
Other Countries ($4,275 / 19%)
Other Investors ($2,934 / 13%)

Billions of USD

MONETARY THEORIES

It is difficult to fully grasp the workings of the central bank without first capturing some essentials of macroeconomics. While this book is not about macro, we felt it important to cover some key topics to help the reader.

Benjamin Franklin, whose portrait adorns our hundred-dollar bills, was a major proponent and theorist of paper money. In 1729, while he was publisher of *The Pennsylvania Gazette*, he anonymously published a seminal piece entitled *"A Modest Enquiry into the Nature of a Paper Currency"* after observing the effects that a lack of gold and silver coinage had on the local Philadelphia economy and the subsequent increase in economic activity following the modest issuance of paper money. At the time, Philadelphia was lacking gold and silver coinage due to the acquisition of large manufacturing goods from Europe. Pennsylvania itself did not produce gold or silver, and thus was dependent on trade to replenish their stock of coins. It became very problematic for the internal economy when there was not enough coinage to support economic activity. Franklin noted the alternative at the time, barter, was extremely limiting.

Further, Franklin posited that paper currency got its value *not* from a fixed exchange rate with precious metals (in contrast to paper money in Europe), but with the quantity of paper money relative to the volume of internal trade. An excess of paper money relative to the volume of internal trade causes it to lose value. Franklin also promoted backing paper money to land, as the value of land was much more fixed and would not suffer from supply shocks like the discovery of New World gold.

David Ricardo, one of the most influential classical economists of all time, was also a tremendously successful stock and loan broker. His contribution to monetary theory was his thoughts on England's bullion controversy of the early 1800s. In 1797, the Bank of England suspended the convertibility of gold-backed banknotes into gold to prevent a bank run. David Ricardo was a major proponent of reinstating the convertibility of gold, publishing *The Price of Gold* and *The High Price of Bullion*, arguing that paper money should be backed 100% by gold in order to avoid inflation. His other important contributions to economic thought include comparative advantage in trade and his theory of rents.

Milton Friedman famously said that inflation "is always and everywhere a monetary phenomenon." A celebrated economist and free market proponent, Milton Friedman was also awarded a Nobel Prize in Economics in 1976 for his work in the fields of consumption analysis, monetary history, and policy. Though the *quantity theory of money* had been around for centuries, Friedman was responsible for reviving interest in money supply and nominal output. This was timely, as it was during a period in the 1970s plagued by high inflation. Friedman, who was very much distrustful of central governments, warned that irresponsible fiscal spending would be effectively paid for through debt monetization and ultimately inflation. Friedman was a proponent of an algorithmic, and thus predictable, method of controlling the money supply.

Spending and Keynes

The Keynesian multiplier is the concept that government deficit spending would have a multiplicative and cascading effect on the economy. Say for instance, the government borrows $100MM to improve the highway system. That $100MM would be paid out to contractors and laborers, who in aggregate would save a certain percentage and re-inject the remainder into the economy by buying goods and services. Mathematically, we can conceptualize the Keynesian Multiplier in this simplified geometric equation:

$$\textbf{\textit{Keynesian Multiplier}} = \frac{\mathbf{1}}{\mathbf{1} - \textbf{\textit{Marginal Propensity to Consume}}}$$

where the *marginal propensity to consume (MPC)* is the percentage of received money that is used to purchase goods and services. We can see as the MPC increases, so does the Keynesian Multiplier (Exhibit 7.18).

EXHIBIT 7.18 MPC & The Keynesian Multiplier

Marginal Propensity to Consume	Keynesian Multiplier
10%	1.1×
25%	1.3×
50%	2.0×
75%	4.0×
90%	10.0×

Phillips Curve

The Phillips curve describes the relationship between inflation and unemployment. The logic goes that as unemployment declines, the labor market tightens, and firms must raise wages to attract increasingly scarce labor. As wages increase, so does inflation. When Phillips developed this framework, the empirical evidence was very strong in the short-run. Thus, monetary and fiscal policymakers had a tool to estimate the tradeoff between inflation and employment (Exhibit 7.19).

EXHIBIT 7.19 Phillips Curve in the 1960s

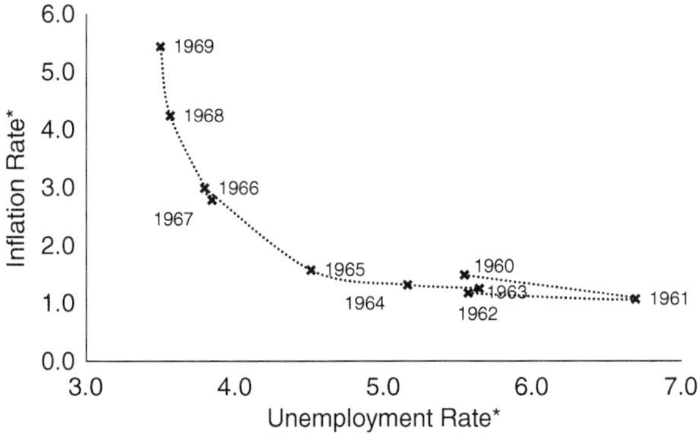

Source: St. Louis Fed
*Annual Averages

However, in the early 1970s, high inflation and high unemployment plagued the economy in a phenomenon known as "stagflation." The accepted explanation was that when workers and firms begin to *anticipate* inflation due to policy decisions, the Phillips curve shifts upwards as workers and firms would start to take inflation into account during wage negotiations, causing workers' wages and firms' costs to rise more quickly, thus further increasing inflation. Thus, a modified framework, known as the Long-Run Phillips Curve, was introduced. In it, there is a long-term natural rate of unemployment that the economy will revert to as the short-term curve shifts up and down in reaction to inflation *expectations* (Exhibit 7.20).

In this example, an economy heats up from a long-term equilibrium (point A) and experiences an unsustainably low unemployment rate coupled with higher inflation (point B). This higher inflation impacts labor input costs and creates a new short run Phillips Curve shifted to the right.

EXHIBIT 7.20 The Long Run Phillips Curve

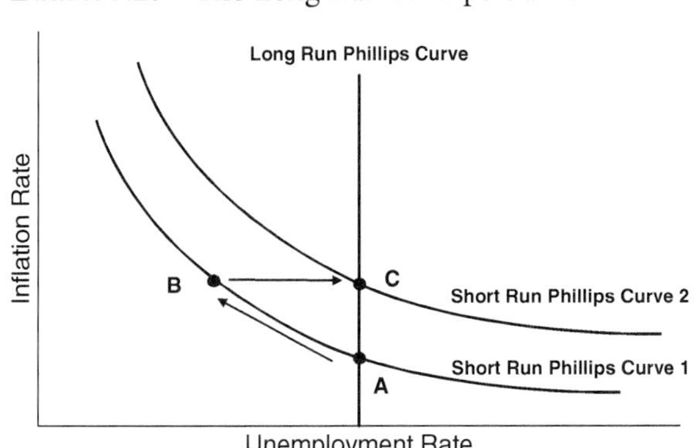

The Taylor Rule

The Taylor Rule, proposed by John B. Taylor, is a framework to determine how interest rates *should* be based on changes in economic conditions such as inflation and output:

$$i_t = r^* + \pi_t + a_\pi(\pi_t - \pi_t^*) + a_y(y_t - \bar{y}_t)$$

where the target short term interest rate (i_t) is equal to the real natural equilibrium rate (r^*) plus the current rate of inflation (π_t) plus some proportion of the difference between actual and target inflation ($\pi_t - \pi_t^*$) plus some proportion of the difference between actual and target output (logarithm) ($y_t - \bar{y}_t$). Normally, these two factors are equally weighted $a_\pi = a_y = 0.5$. We can see the intuition behind this. If inflation or economic output is running above their targets, the Taylor Rule would prescribe a higher interest rate to cool the economy (Exhibits 7.21 and 7.22).

EXHIBIT 7.21 Prescribed Interest Rate for a "Hot" Economy

Natural rate of interest	r^*	1.0%
Current inflation rate	π_t	**3.0%**
Inflation target	π_t^*	2.0%
Inflation gap (50% coefficient)	$a_\pi(\pi_t - \pi_t^*)$	**0.5%**
Logarithm of actual output ($19.5T)	y_t	13.29
Logarithm of potential output ($19.0T)	$\bar{y}_t$	13.28
Output gap (50% coefficient)	$a_y(y_t - \bar{y}_t)$	**0.6%**
Target short term interest rate		**5.1%**

EXHIBIT 7.22 Fed Funds vs. Taylor Rule Estimated Rate

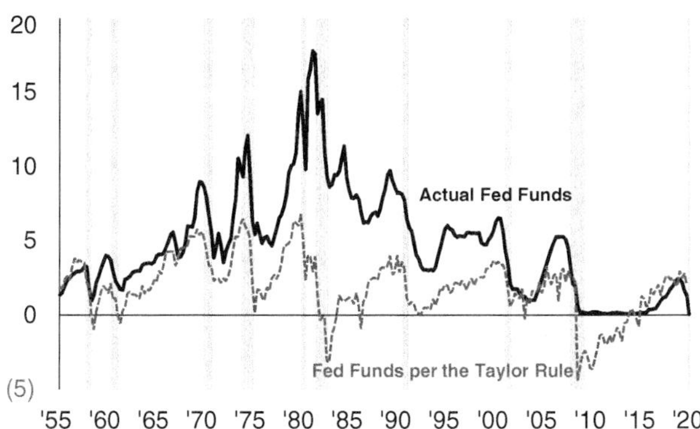

Source: St. Louis Fed

Money Supply and The Monetary Base

The money supply broadly describes the total amount of money, whether it be physical, or bank account balances, in circulation. In the past, economists such as Milton Friedman have noted the close relationships money supply has with important economic variables such as inflation, though recently this relationship has been somewhat unstable. Still, money supply growth does appear to still have some explanatory power for variance in inflation rates (Exhibit 7.23).

The **monetary base** (also known as base money and narrow money) is one metric that is particularly relevant for banks (Exhibit 7.24). It represents

EXHIBIT 7.23 Money Supply and Inflation Tightly Correlated

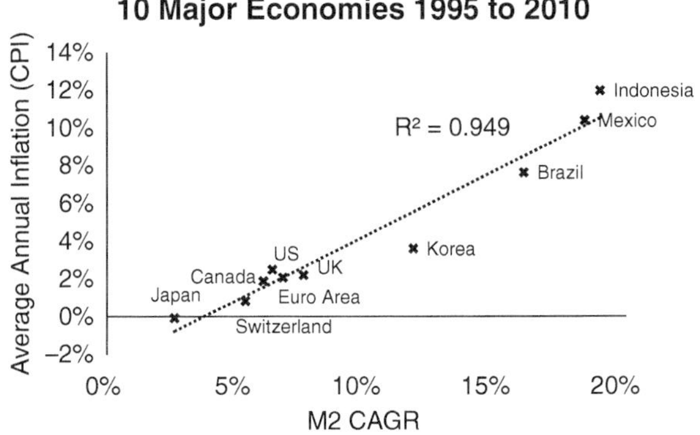

Source: St. Louis Fed

EXHIBIT 7.24 US Monetary Base

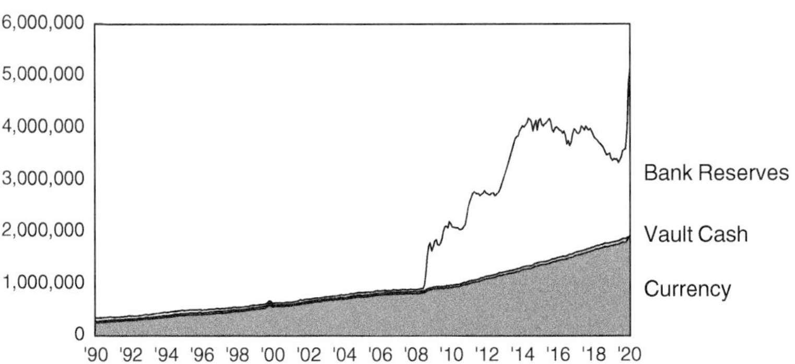

Source: Federal Reserve

the sum of physical currency in circulation plus physically held bank deposits plus reserve balances.

We can see the effect that QE had on the monetary base, with the explosion in bank reserves practically doubling the monetary base.

Quantity Theory of Money

The **Quantity Theory of Money** states that the general price level (P) is directly proportional to the amount of money (M) in circulation. In its simplified state, the **equation of exchange** is as follows:

$$M \times V = P \times T$$

The right side of the equation represents price level (P) multiplied by the real value of aggregate transactions (T). Usually this is estimated with *real GDP*, making the right side of the equation ($P \times T$) simply *nominal GDP*.

On the left side, M represents money supply multiplied by V, which is known as the velocity of money. The velocity of money represents the number of times a certain unit of money is circulated within the economy over a certain period of time. It is usually measured as a ratio of GDP to a country's M1 or M2 money supply. Thus, we can see this relationship is tautologically true as V is defined as a ratio of the other variables (P, T and M).

What the quantity theory of money postulates, then, is that V is relatively stable so that an increase in money supply leads to an increase in price levels given the same level of aggregate real output.

We know a static velocity of money is not the case empirically, but the equation of exchange gives us a helpful framework in thinking about the relationship between money supply and price.

$$\%\Delta P \approx \%\Delta M + \%\Delta V - \%\Delta T$$

How do banks play into this? M2 money supply is a multiple of the monetary base (MB), and that multiple is greater than one whenever banks operate under a fractional reserve framework.

$$M2 = MB \times m$$

Where m equals the money multiplier.

Specifically, the money multiplier is inversely related to the reserve ratio.

$$m = \frac{1}{Reserve\ Ratio}$$

Putting it all together, we have

$$P = \frac{MB \times \frac{1}{RR} \times V}{T}$$

which concludes that price levels are inversely correlated to the reserve ratio, all else being equal. Stated another way, if the reserve ratio were to decrease (monetary loosening), price levels would increase (inflation); an intuitive conclusion.

INTEREST RATES

Interest rates are naturally one of the most important factors to consider when assessing a bank. For most companies, interest rates have implications for financing costs. Not only is this true for financial intermediaries like banks, but topline revenues are linked to prevailing interest rates as the underlying benchmark of pricing of all credit instruments are rates.

$$Required\ Rate = \underbrace{\underbrace{RRFR + IP}_{Nom.\ Risk\text{-}Free\ Rate} + MRP}_{Benchmark\ Rate} + \underbrace{LP + DRP}_{Credit\ Spread}$$

$RRFR = Real\ Risk\text{-}Free\ Rate$

$IP = Inflation\ Premium$

$MRP = Maturity\ Risk\ Premium$

$LP = Liquidity\ Premium$

$DRP = Default\ Risk\ Premium$

A common way to price debt instruments is through layering risk premia over a risk-free rate. The *real risk-free rate* plus the *inflation premium* make up the *nominal risk-free rate*, something akin to the fed funds rate.

Investors then must be compensated for *maturity risk*; this is also called the *term premium*, the additional return for being locked into a fixed income instrument over a longer period of time. Combined with the nominal risk free rate, this composes the benchmark yield that risky credit is generally priced on.

EXHIBIT 7.25 Yield Curve by Decade

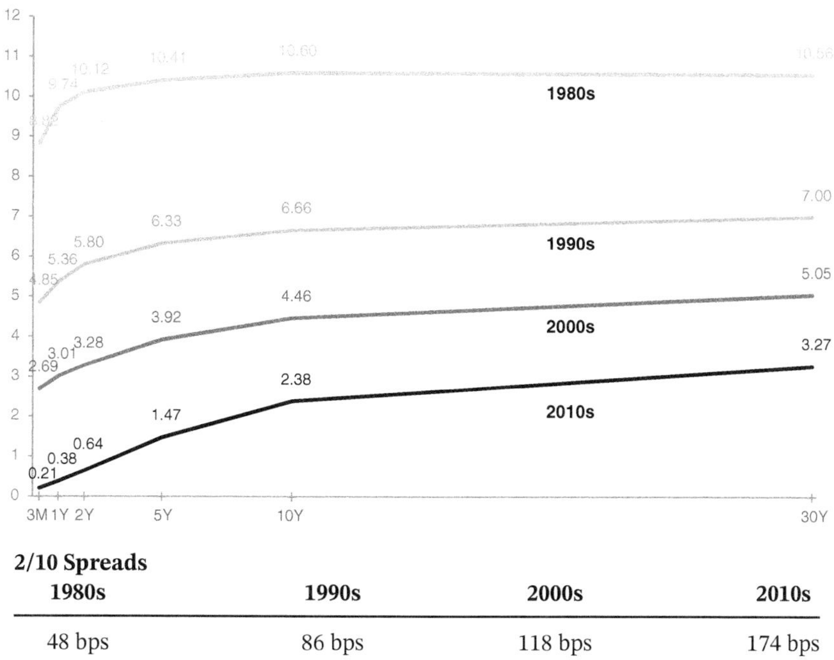

2/10 Spreads

1980s	1990s	2000s	2010s
48 bps	86 bps	118 bps	174 bps

From parallel yield curve shifts to yield curve steepenings to complete inversions, the multitude of possible environments affects different bank models in dramatically different ways. Generally, bank investors are interested in both the *absolute level* of interest rates, and the *relative* level of interest rates between different maturities. The *yield curve*, which plots the interest rates of bonds (usually Treasuries) across different maturities, is an invaluable visualization. For reference, we show the average yield curve by decade using U.S. Treasuries (Exhibit 7.25). Though yields have generally moved lower, it is interesting to note that average yield curve steepness has actually increased.

Banks that benefit from a rising rate environment are known as *asset sensitive*. As in, interest earned on assets increase *more* than the interest cost on liabilities. Conversely, banks that benefit from a falling rate environment are known as *liability sensitive*. According to aggregated management disclosures, the banking industry as a whole skews towards being asset sensitive. Generally, disclosures provide NII or NPV through parallel shifts in the yield curve (either shocks or 12-month change), which may or may not be a realistic scenario.

ARE HIGHER INTEREST RATES BETTER FOR BANK STOCKS?

Intuitively it makes sense that they would. Since banks are lenders, they *should* benefit from lending money at a higher rate, to the detriment of borrowers. Is it as simple as indiscriminately piling into bank stocks ahead of anticipated rate hikes? The answer is, not really, this has not been a layup strategy. Compared to the S&P 500, the banks stocks in that index do not exhibit any unusually high correlation with short- or long-term rates (Exhibit 7.26).

EXHIBIT 7.26 Interest Rates and Stock Correlation

R^2 of Rates and S&P 500 Sectors		
1990–2020	**Fed Funds**	**10-Year**
S&P 500	**0.24**	**0.59**
Consumer Discretionary	0.26	0.56
Consumer Staples	0.40	0.74
Energy	0.42	0.62
Financials	**0.04**	**0.26**
Health Care	0.30	0.63
Industrials	0.28	0.62
Information Technology	0.14	0.43
Materials	0.35	0.65
Real Estate	0.01	0.26
Telecom	0.02	0.02
Utilities	0.19	0.56
Banks	**0.00**	**0.10**

Even if we exclude recessions, we get a similar result:

R^2 of Rates and S&P 500 Sectors Excluding Recessions		
1990–2020	**Fed Funds**	**10-Year**
S&P 500	**0.25**	**0.56**
Consumer Discretionary	0.36	0.59
Consumer Staples	0.47	0.74
Energy	0.40	0.66
Financials	**0.01**	**0.17**
Health Care	0.35	0.62
Industrials	0.30	0.60
Information Technology	0.12	0.35
Materials	0.37	0.61
Real Estate	0.04	0.06
Telecom	0.04	0.01
Utilities	0.14	0.47
Banks	**0.00**	**0.06**

Source: Bloomberg

This is actually good news for active investors, as there is an opportunity to pick bank stocks that will outperform the market given certain interest rate expectations. Further, for those of us that have a strong view on the interest rate environment, we can express those views through specific bank stocks. Stock performance should correlate to future expectations on earnings, which is a function of ROA. For community banks heavily reliant on spread income, ROA is highly dependent on NIMs, which finally is driven by the dynamics between the yield on earning assets and the cost of funding behind them.

HOW DO INTEREST RATES AFFECT PROFITABILITY?

The correlation matrix in Exhibit 7.27 calculates the relationship between important benchmark interest rates and bank profitability metrics. What we find is that yields on earning assets and costs of funding are both *highly* correlated to short and long rates. However, these are *offsetting* sensitivities. As rates increase, yields on earning assets increase, but so does the cost of funding those assets, and thus industry NIM, pre-tax ROAA, and ROE show very little sensitivity to short rates, long rates, and the spread between them.

However, other exogenous variables, such as a rapidly changing economic environment or regulatory changes, could cause our R^2 to be low. So, let us look at a historical time series to isolate certain periods of pronounced rate moves to see if there are any trends to bank profitability metrics.

Let's first look at profitability on a pre-tax ROAA basis, as it strips out the effects of leverage and taxes. Exhibit 7.28 suggests comparing it to the 10-year yield.

However, we see that the largest shocks to profitability are credit quality related (the 2007 crisis and the S&L crisis of the late 1980s and 1990s). Even in relatively benign times, the general decline in long-term rates has little effect on profitability from the 1990s to 2000s.

Perhaps there are too many "non-interest" related factors at play, such as general improvements in efficiency through technology and refinements in fee income streams. We can try to zero in on just the "rate sensitive" drivers of profitability by looking at NIM (Exhibit 7.29). In this case, we'll compare it to the 3-month to 10-year spread. Conventional wisdom says that banks "borrow

EXHIBIT 7.27 R^2 of Interest Rates and Profitability Metrics

	Fed Funds	10-Yr Yield	2/10	3M/10Y
Yield on EA	0.903	0.913	0.180	0.022
Cost of Funding	0.924	0.914	0.193	0.028
NIM	0.000	0.003	0.005	0.011
PT ROAA	0.070	0.118	0.018	0.050
ROE	0.001	0.003	0.024	0.022

Source: FDIC, St. Louis Fed. 1984 – 2019

EXHIBIT 7.28 Pre-tax ROA and 10-Year Yield

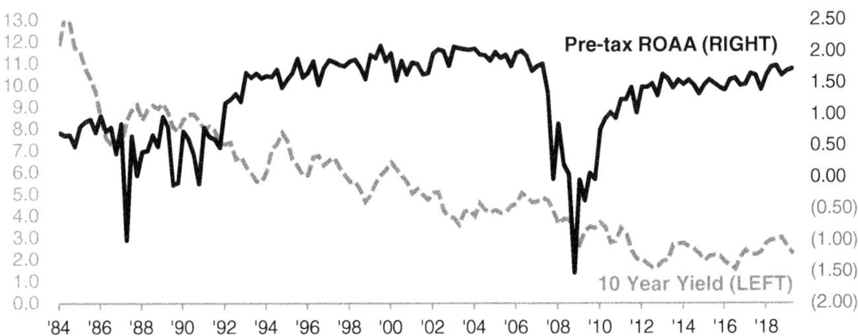

Source: FDIC, St. Louis Fed.

EXHIBIT 7.29 NIM and 3M/10Y Spread

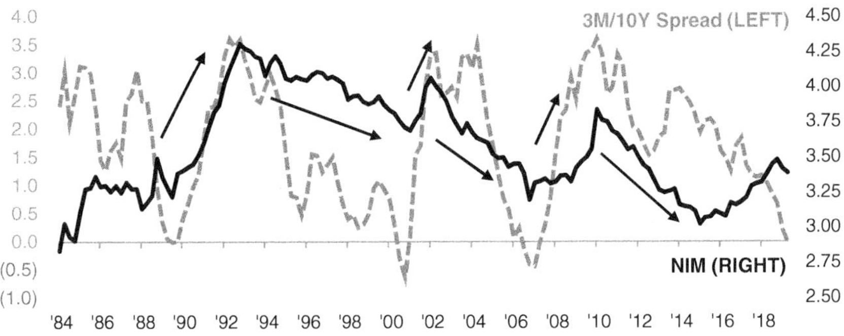

Source: FDIC, St. Louis Fed.

short" and "lend long," taking advantage of the term premium to earn returns. This is also commonly called "maturity transformation."

Here we can clearly see that in a steepening yield curve environment, NIMs generally expand, while a flattening yield curve is correlated to NIM erosion. This relationship appears to break down over the last few years given the extraordinary monetary policies that were put in place at the time (i.e., ZIRP and QE).

PARALLEL SHOCKS AND A NOTE ON MANAGEMENT DISCLOSURES

Most bank management teams will provide in the MD&A section a table that serves as a helpful guideline to rate sensitivity. Generally, the analysis is done by performing a parallel "shock" to interest rates anywhere from 50 to 200 bps and projecting the effects on market value and NII. The plus side to this analysis is that banks have much more granular information on their loan book and deposit base than what is given in public disclosures, and thus the analysis is much more accurate than what an outside investor could hope to achieve. However, the negative is that rates rarely move in the way used in their analysis. Yield curve twists, where the steepness of the curve changes, occur constantly.

Exhibit 7.30 is an example of an interest rate sensitivity disclosure for FNBG.

Unusually, we see that both rising *and* declining rates would negatively impact NII. This occurs when there is beta asymmetry, when deposit pricing is more sensitive to hikes in rates than cuts (this can happen near the zero bound). With a cost of total deposits of only 27 bps, FNBG would not have much room to lower deposit pricing. However, since the decline in NII from

EXHIBIT 7.30 Interest Rate Risk for FNBG

TABLE 17

(Dollar amounts in thousands)	**Interest Rate Risk Simulation Change in Economic Value of Equity As of December 31, 2017**				
	Rates Decline			**Rates Increase**	
Rate change	(2%)	(1%)	Current	+1%	+2%
Projected market value of equity	$ 99,814	$ 112,398	$ 119,280	$ 118,648	$ 115,773
Change from current	$ (19,466)	$ (6,882)		$ (632)	$ (3,507)
	Change in Annual Net Interest Income 12-Month Time Period				
(Dollar amounts in thousands)	**Rates Decline**			**Rates Increase**	
Rare change	(2%)	(1%)	Current	+1%	+2%
Projected net interest income	$ 45,267	$ 46,092	46,347	44,206	41,888
Change from current	$ (1,080)	$ (255)		(2,141)	(4,175)

Source: FNB Bancorp 2017 10-K

+1% to rates is much more severe than the decline in NII from -1% to rates, we'd categorize FNBG as being more liability sensitive.

INTEREST RATE SENSITIVITY AND BUSINESS MIX

Generally, more commercially oriented banks are more asset sensitive. Their shorter-term loan books, predominately C&I and CRE loans, are benchmarked to short-term rates such as LIBOR or Prime, and reprice much quicker. We pulled interest rate risk disclosures from 141 publicly traded banks and regressed them against C&I exposure. As one would expect, higher C&I exposure correlates to more asset sensitivity (Exhibit 7.31).

EXHIBIT 7.31 Interest Rate Risk vs. Loan Mix

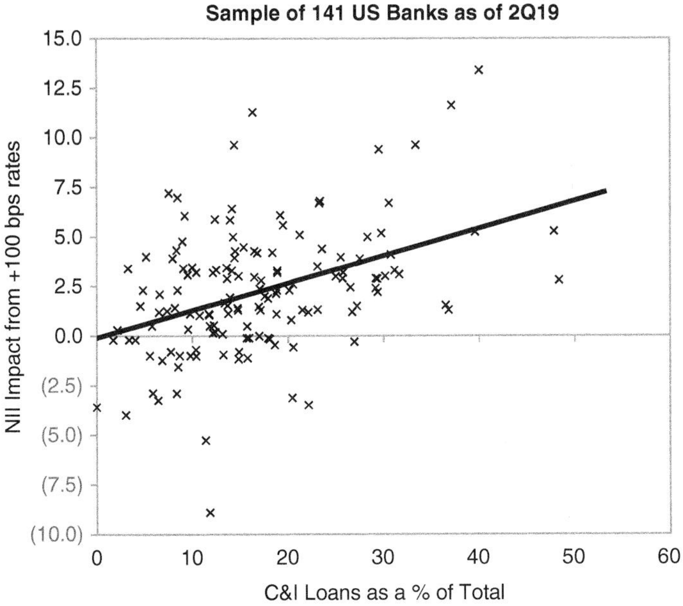

Source: S&P Global Market Intelligence

INTEREST RATES AND LOANS

Different loans are priced off of different parts of the yield curve. Generally, the term of the loan gives us a good idea of what underlying rate the yield will be benchmarked to (Exhibit 7.32).

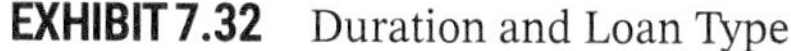

EXHIBIT 7.32 Duration and Loan Type

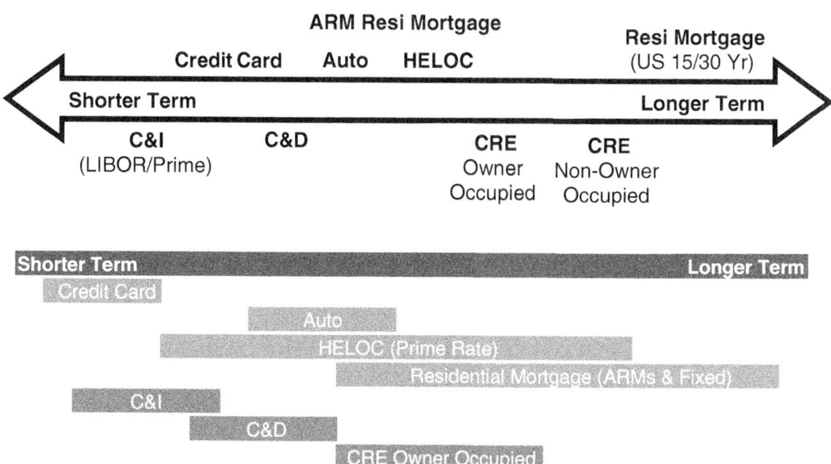

Loan Beta is a simple metric that estimates the change in loan yields for a given change in rates. For instance, if Fed Funds moved from 100 bps to 75 bps, while loan yields moved from 450 bps to 430 bps, the loan beta would be calculated as:

$$\frac{\Delta Loan\ Yields}{\Delta Rates} = \frac{450 - 430}{100 - 75} = 80\%$$

However, we would be very cautious in using historical data for specific entities to calculate loan betas and draw forward looking conclusions. First, as we see in Exhibit 7.32, there are multiple benchmark rates used to price loans, and thus picking just one to estimate a loan beta would be an oversimplification. Shifts in loan portfolio composition would also skew any loan yield time series. Finally, changes in the risk profile (aka, widening or tightening credit spreads) introduce another variable that can explain changes in loan yields that could be misattributed to changes in benchmark rates.

Instead, management teams will have the most granular and up-to-date information with how their loan portfolios are positioned, and what sensitivities, or betas, these assets will have to different benchmark rates. Combined with a look at the general composition of their loan portfolio, an investor can better understand a bank's sensitivities to benchmark rates.

Interest Rate Floors are another important consideration, particularly when benchmark rates are relatively low. A floor is simply an agreed upon rate that an adjustable rate loan cannot fall below. It is most common in C&I

EXHIBIT 7.33 Lowering Asset Sensitivity Through Swaps

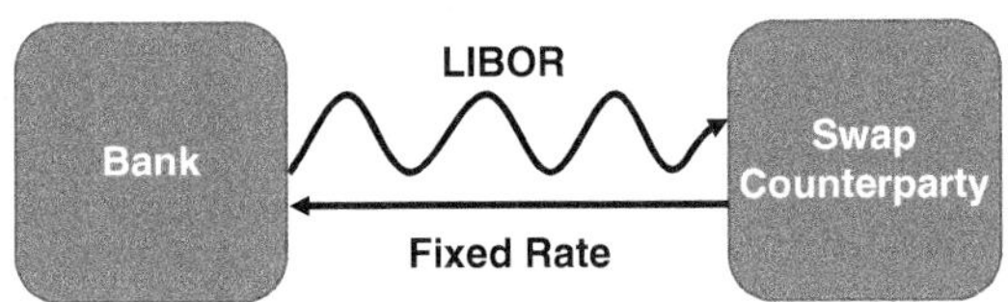

loans as well as adjustable rate mortgages. For example, a C&I loan could be priced at LIBOR+200 with a 350 bps floor. If LIBOR was at 100 bps, the adjustable rate of 300 bps would be below the 350 bps minimum. This is an important point. In a scenario where a large portion of a bank's loans are significantly below their floors, a shift higher in benchmark rates could negatively impact deposit costs without an associated benefit in loan yields.

Hedges are used to effectively manipulate the *duration* of a bank's assets. This is typically executed through derivatives, namely, interest rate swaps (Exhibit 7.33). For instance, in a falling interest rate environment, where monetary policy is clearly loosening, a very asset sensitive bank could pursue a strategy to *reduce* its asset beta. It could enter into a *pay floating receive fixed swap*. Effectively transforming whatever floating rate assets into fixed rate assets (aka, extending duration).

When evaluating the effectiveness of a swap, management will *usually* disclose what the impact would be in a parallel shift scenario. Otherwise, we can gauge the impact by looking at the *size* and *term* of the swap. It follows that a *larger* and *longer* swap would generally have a larger impact.

As an aside, swaps are priced off the *swap forward curve* so that the present values of the future cash flows from *both* legs of the swap are equal. Swaps are zero-sum: If rates evolve in a way that is different from the forward curve (which typically happens), one side of the swap wins at the other side's expense.

INTEREST RATES AND DEPOSITS

Sensitivity of a bank's assets to benchmark rates tells only half of the story. Remember, banks are funded predominately through liabilities, and thus are extremely sensitive to the rate environment. If one were to describe the most valuable qualities a deposit franchise should have, it would be one that is low cost and stable.

Stability could mean one of two things: (1) predictable and minimal outflows and (2) stable cost. We will remind readers that *deposit betas,* the change in costs for a given change in rates, is a popular concept used to describe deposit price sensitivity.

Often the elements of cost and stability are at odds with each other. Deposits that have low and stable costs, like business demand deposit accounts (DDAs), could have zero cost and zero beta, but could also see large swings as a business will need their deposit "on demand" for payroll and other expenses. This can stress a bank's liquidity and force them to invest a smaller portion of those deposits into relatively more liquid instruments. However, these deposits are generally thought to be more additive to deposit franchise value.

On the other end of the spectrum, time deposits, such as certificates of deposit (CDs), are stable in terms of pricing (fixed over the term) and flows. However, these deposits are very commoditized, making them ultra price competitive and not as additive to deposit franchise value. Also, due to the fact that a portion of time deposits are always rolling off, from the *bank's* perspective, these deposits are actually quite sensitive to changes in market rates.

Somewhere in between we have savings accounts and money market accounts (note: not to be confused with money market *funds)* that offer higher rates that are more sensitive to prevailing benchmark rates but with more restrictions on withdrawals.

It follows then, that under the expectation of *rising rates* one would increase exposure to banks with *low deposit betas* (i.e., high DDAs), while in a *falling rate* environment, one would search for *higher deposit beta* names (i.e., high CDs) (Exhibit 7.34).

As we can see in Exhibit 7.35, overall cost of funding in the bank industry is highly correlated to fed funds, and clearly has an aggregate deposit beta <1.

EXHIBIT 7.34 Deposit Spectrum

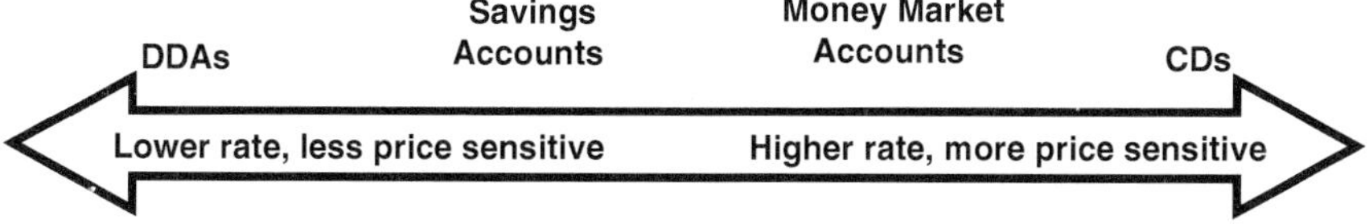

EXHIBIT 7.35 Cost of Funding vs. Fed Funds

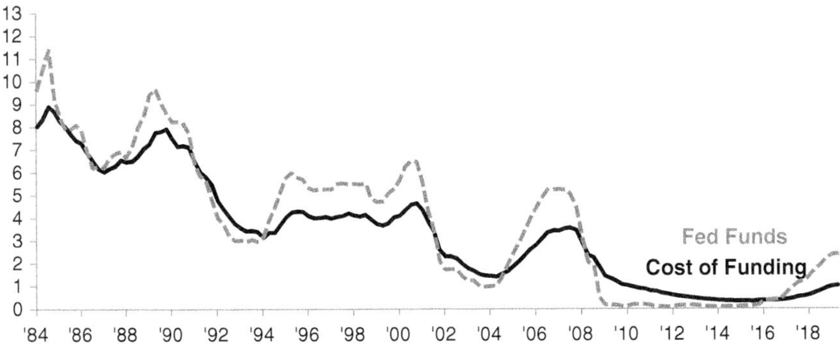

Source: S&P Global Market Intelligence

Copper-Gold ratio as an indicator for the direction of interest rates.

Given the sensitivity of banks to rates, getting a sense of the direction of rates is important. The ratio of the price per pound of copper to the price per troy ounce of gold is a contemporaneous indicator of the direction of interest rates. This is one of the market gauges tracked by DoubleLine Capital. We recommend readers to review their white paper on the topic:

https://doubleline.com/dl/wp-content/uploads/ThePowerofCopper-Gold_Mayberry2019.pdf

8

M&A

"Banks are sold, not bought."

– Wall Street saying, provenance unknown

Before we start this chapter, we'd like to remind our readers of the important human aspect of mergers and acquisitions. The exciting cost synergies in an excel model often come at the expense of people's livelihoods, and we should always remain compassionate towards the potential dislocations and disruptions that a merger can bring.

Consolidation has been a meaningful industry trend since the mid-1980s. The number of bank charters has come down from a peak of over 18,000 in the mid-1980s to just over 5,000 (Exhibit 8.1).

Continued consolidation seems like an inevitable trend. To put it bluntly, there are still too many banks and too much legacy banking infrastructure (Exhibits 8.2 and 8.3). An extreme example: The state of Iowa has over 270 commercial and savings banks and a population of just 3.2 million! And from a branch perspective, the United States has approximately 31 bank branches per 100,000 adults, nearly 50% higher than the OECD average.

Other secular trends are at play as well. New paradigms and financial technologies introduce economies of scale opportunities and open new paths for generating positive operating leverage. Regulation and compliance expenses have also created a "sweet spot" for scale that most banks have yet to achieve. The number of banks and branches seems destined to decline, while inversely, the total assets and deposits per bank seem primed to rise.

The astute investor can capitalize on this trend. According to the FDIC, there have been over 200 bank mergers *every year* for the past few years (FDIC QBP). Meanwhile, acquired companies have historically been taken out at healthy control premiums. Owning a basket of likely take-out candidates has proven to be a benchmark beating strategy (Exhibit 8.4).

EXHIBIT 8.1 Steady Consolidation

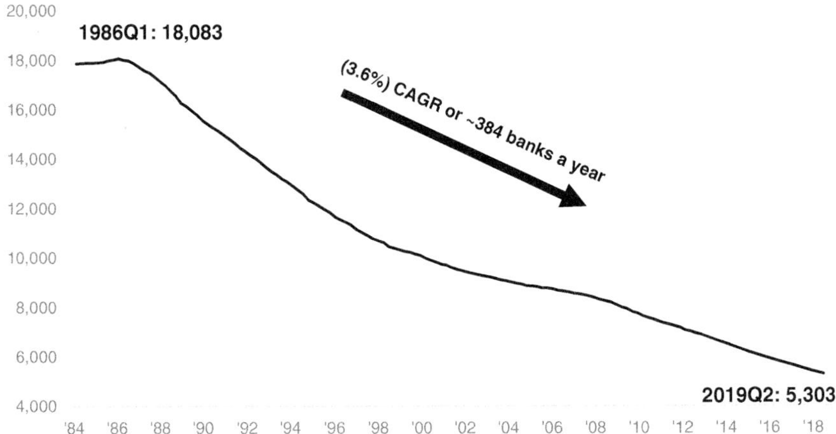

Source: FDIC

EXHIBIT 8.2 Most Crowded Banking States

	State	Banks	Population	Population per Bank
1	ND	72	762,062	10,584
2	NE	171	1,934,408	11,312
3	IA	276	3,155,070	11,431
4	KS	221	2,913,314	13,182
5	SD	65	884,659	13,610
6	MN	283	5,639,632	19,928
7	OK	196	3,956,971	20,189
8	WY	28	578,759	20,670
9	MO	248	6,137,428	24,748
10	MT	42	1,068,778	25,447
...				
	Total	5,153	331,494,238	64,330

Source: FDIC, US Census Bureau

EXHIBIT 8.3 Too Many Branches

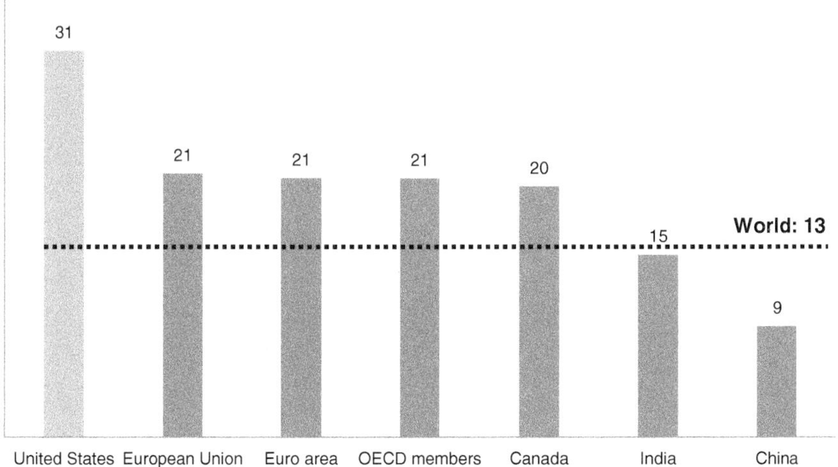

M&A DRIVERS

Banks are indeed for the most part sold not bought, and we believe qualitative factors are a key item to be considered. These factors are not unique to banking but are an important consideration. These factors include age and tenure of the CEO and board, succession planning and bench strength, the shareholder base (look for insider ownership and activists), change of control provisions found in proxy filings (DEF14A), a management's historical proclivity to sell banks, and social factors like trust in potential buyer's currency, affinity with the buyer (i.e., shared interests), and similarity of cultures at the two banks.

One can never be too certain of these factors as they are fairly subjective, but the astute long-term investor will be able to assess the overall mosaic and discount the odds. Other considerations, including scarcity value and quality of the franchise, impact the premium paid, but absent the willingness to sell, no transaction is consummated and the potential premium remains a moot point.

EXHIBIT 8.4 Reliable Deal Premiums

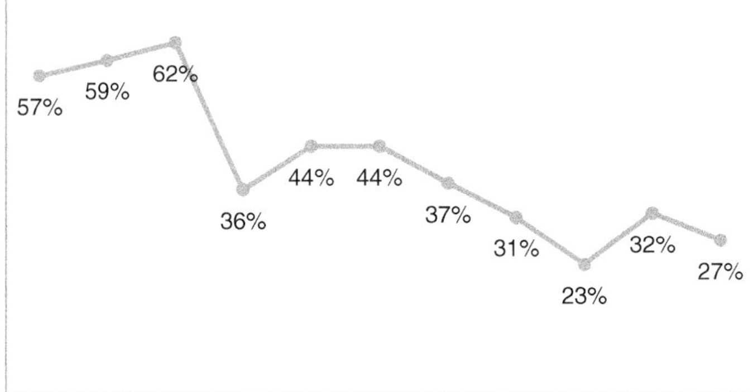

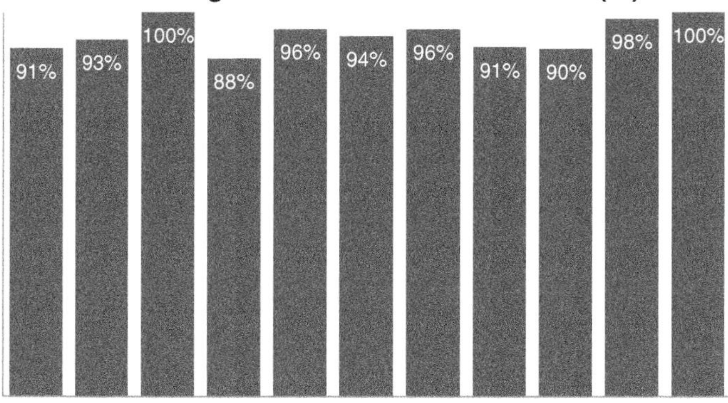

Source: S&P Global Market Intelligence

M&A ARGOT

There are many *types* of transactions – whole bank, branch, FDIC-assisted, 363 sale (bankruptcy), and S-Corp asset sales. The focus of this chapter is on whole bank acquisitions, perhaps the most exciting and common, but we will touch upon other types of combinations for our reader's edification.

Whole bank business combinations can generally be described as acquisitions, mergers, and mergers of equals (MOEs). The main differentiator is the relative size and influence of the two parties involved.

At one time, "mergers" and "acquisitions" had stricter definitions: mergers being defined as two entities combining to form a new entity, while acquisitions were strictly defined as when one company absorbed another into its existing structure. These legacy definitions are still used for their connotations. Colloquially, mergers imply some form of collaboration and input from the acquired entity and have "friendlier" connotations, while acquisitions can imply anything from more dominating decision-making from the acquiring management to an outright hostile takeover. Typically, a regular merger or acquisition is when the buyer retains 60% or more of the combined pro forma equity base.

Merger of Equals

A merger of equals (MOE) once had a stricter definition too. MOEs used to only occur when two similarly sized entities legally combined into a new entity, retiring its old shares and issuing new shares. The board and management team would technically be "new," but made up of an equal mix of legacy board members and management. Recently, we've found transactions described as MOEs where the economic, management, and board interests are pretty much evenly split; however, one entity is allowed to survive as the "legal" acquiror, and one existing share class is used as the currency for the combined entity. Often times, these deals are structured as zero to low premium deals for the acquired institution. This makes the "merger math" pencil out easier, as we will see later in the chapter.

Branch Deals

As the name suggests, these are transactions involving the transfer of bank branches. Branch sales not only include the physical branches (which could include the underlying real estate or the assumption of the lease), but also the deposits, and could include loans and employees associated with the branch.

Why would a bank sell its branches? The specific branches might not be meeting certain financial targets, which could stem from the geographic location, the product mix not being in demand within those markets, and a bank simply exiting a subscale geography. On the other hand, a divestiture of branches could be necessitated to assuage antitrust concerns over a proposed merger.

The metrics to know here are the core deposit premium, the deposits that leave around the time of the announcement, and the deposits at the branch one year following the transaction based on the FDIC annual survey.

FDIC-assisted Deals

When bank failures occur in the wake of periods of severe financial stress, the Federal Deposit Insurance Corporation (FDIC) helps to market and sell these failing banks to healthy depositories.

The FDIC aims to use the least costly option to resolve troubled institutions if a recapitalization is not feasible. Qualified bidders (a healthy bank) may participate in a process to bid for the assets. The bidders are predominately interested in the deposits, as the toxic assets of a failing bank are usually what caused issues in the first place. The winning bidder assumes the insured deposits and may purchase *certain* loans and other assets of the bank.

The marquee feature of an FDIC-assisted deal is a Shared Loss Agreement (SLA), usually referred to as a "loss share agreement," which was introduced in 1991. In a loss share agreement, the FDIC agrees to absorb a portion of the loss *and recoveries* on a specified pool of assets in order to make their acquisition more palatable to credit sensitive acquirors. The losses and recoveries generally are shared on an 80/20 (buyer/FDIC) basis. Loss share agreements last on average 8 to 10 years depending on the asset class.

363 Sale

Under section 363 of Chapter 11 of the bankruptcy code, a bank holding company may sell the subsidiary bank with the approval of the bankruptcy court and without the approval of the creditors. This is a likely approach if the bank is impaired and a recapitalization is difficult due to holding company debt.

S-Corp Asset Sale

Recall a Small Business Corporation (S-Corp) is a corporation structure that does not pay income taxes, instead electing to pass corporate income, losses, deductions, and credits directly to its shareholders. Around a third of all banks are organized as S-Corps, hence their relevance for bank M&A.

In an acquisition of an S-Corp, both the seller and the buyer must make the election, and every single holder of the S-Corp has to consent. The result is a stepped-up cost basis for the buyer and a taxable transaction for the seller, but the tax gains for the buyer exceed the tax loss for the seller.

CONSIDERATION AND CURRENCY

Consideration can take the form of stock, cash, or a mix of both. Most deals are some mix of cash and stock. An acquiror's stock is often referred to as its "currency." In bank investing, P/TBV is the most commonly used way to measure an acquiror's currency, and if that currency trades at a significant P/TBV premium, it gives the acquiror a leg-up in acquisitions.

Financially, cash deals tend to be more dilutive to tangible book value, doubly so when an acquiror has a premium currency but doesn't get to use it. However, due to the lack of issuance of new shares (notwithstanding when the acquiror taps the equity capital markets for fresh capital), the EPS accretion tends to be higher.

Exhibit 8.5 illustrates the wide range of TBV and EPS accretion percentages depending on the consideration mix (from all-stock to all-cash) and the buyer's currency. We run the model assuming the target is an identical institution that is 10% of the buyer's size, is acquired for 150% of TBV, no deal-related costs, no FV (Fair Value) adjustments to the target's balance sheet, and net income of the combined firms is equal to the two separate firms.

As we can see, using cash is most dilutive to TBV, and the impact is accentuated when the buyer has a rich currency that it does not utilize. Conversely, EPS accretion is greatest when all cash is used, as it does not dilute share count. However, when the buyer's currency trades at a relative premium, EPS accretion is still achievable in an all-stock transaction.

EXHIBIT 8.5 TBV and EPS Accretion/Dilution

TBV Accretion/(Dilution)

		% Cash				
		0%	**25%**	**50%**	**75%**	**100%**
Buyer P/TBV	**100%**	**(4.3%)**	**(4.5%)**	**(4.7%)**	**(4.8%)**	**(5.0%)**
	125%	**(1.8%)**	**(2.5%)**	**(3.3%)**	**(4.1%)**	**(5.0%)**
	150%	**0.0%**	**(1.2%)**	**(2.4%)**	**(3.7%)**	**(5.0%)**
	175%	**1.3%**	**(0.2%)**	**(1.7%)**	**(3.3%)**	**(5.0%)**
	200%	**2.3%**	**0.6%**	**(1.2%)**	**(3.1%)**	**(5.0%)**

EPS Accretion/(Dilution)

		% Cash				
		0%	**25%**	**50%**	**75%**	**100%**
Buyer P/TBV	**100%**	**(4.3%)**	**(1.1%)**	**2.3%**	**6.0%**	**10.0%**
	125%	**(1.8%)**	**0.9%**	**3.8%**	**6.8%**	**10.0%**
	150%	**0.0%**	**2.3%**	**4.8%**	**7.3%**	**10.0%**
	175%	**1.3%**	**3.4%**	**5.5%**	**7.7%**	**10.0%**
	200%	**2.3%**	**4.1%**	**6.0%**	**8.0%**	**10.0%**

Generally, all-stock and cash+stock deals are most common. All cash deals typically are only viable when the targets are relatively small.

THE EXCHANGE RATIO

In a transaction that involves stock as part of the consideration, the exchange ratio refers to the number of the acquirer's shares the selling shareholder will receive per share held. There are a number of exchange ratio options:

- **Fixed Ratio** – As the name suggests, the parties agree, at the time of signing, on a specific number of acquiror shares the selling shareholders will receive (Exhibit 8.6). This exposes the seller to market risk (both upside and downside). However, fixed ratios allow the buyer to know with certainty the amount of forthcoming dilution. Finally, if the consideration is a cash-stock mix, the cash portion is fixed while the stock portion will fluctuate, thus more often than not the stock and cash consideration will be of unequal value at close. This can be accentuated by a lengthy period between deal announcement and closing. Fixed ratios are often seen in MOEs or significant transactions, in which the sellers will represent a significant influence on the combined entity.
- **Fixed Ratio with Collar** – A collar in a fixed ratio transaction is primarily implemented to protect the seller by adjusting the exchange ratio so that the deal value stays within a certain band. This reduces the market risk by the seller at the expense of introducing dilution risk for the buyer (although it can also benefit the buyer through less dilution if their stock rallies through the upper threshold).
- **Fixed Value (floating ratio) –** In contrast to fixed *ratios*, fixed *value* deals "lock in" a price for the seller, and it is the buyer's responsibility to deliver that value to the sellers at close (Exhibit 8.7). Usually fixed value deals are implemented when the acquired company is relatively small compared to the buyer. In small deals, the probability of significant dilution is low, as it would require a significant movement by the buyer's stock. Generally, sellers will seek a fixed value if the owner/operators want a "cleaner" exit or monetization of their bank.
- **Fixed Value with Collar –** In contrast to a *fixed ratio collar*, a *fixed value collar* is for the *buyer's* protection, preventing unacceptable dilution in the event of adverse price action of the buyer's stock, and moving the incremental price risk to the seller.

EXHIBIT 8.6 Fixed Exchange Ratios

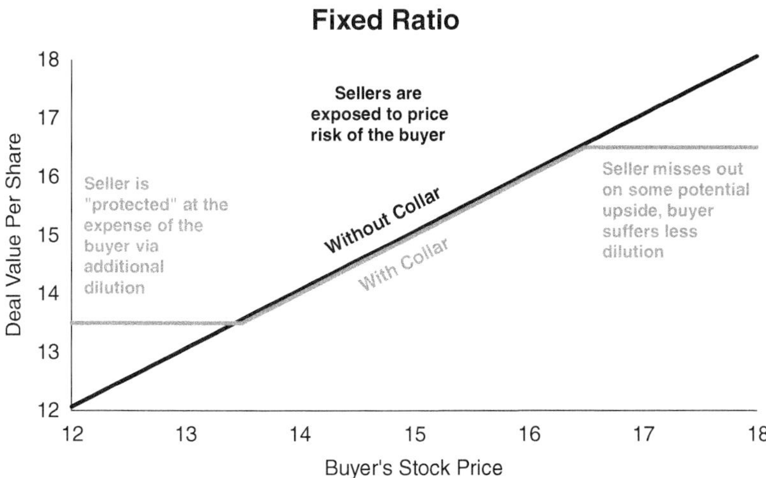

EXHIBIT 8.7 Fixed Value (Floating Ratios)

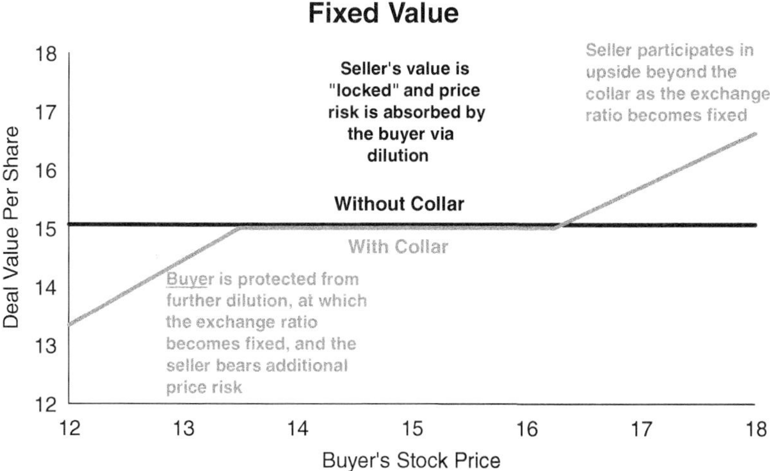

EPS ACCRETION AND DILUTION

In its most generalized framework, pro forma EPS equates to the *combined* net income inclusive of all synergies, divided by the pro forma share count, taking into account any new shares issued to consummate a transaction:

$$\text{Pro Forma EPS} = \frac{\text{Acquiror's Net Income} + \text{Target's Net Income} + \text{Net Synergies}}{\text{Original Sharecount} + \text{Issued shares}}$$

It goes without saying that at a minimum, a transaction should be EPS accretive, but it is not quite as straightforward as just considering the percentage increase in EPS of the combined institution, and applying the historical earnings multiple of the buyer.

The oldest trick in the book, EPS accretion via bootstrapping, in which a high P/E company buys a low P/E company, is well understood by the market. A high P/E firm acquiring a low P/E firm will increase the EPS of the acquiror, but the combined value of the firm is theoretically the same as the two separate parts if there are no synergies to be had. Thus, the combined earnings stream *must* be assigned a lower blended multiple on earnings. A prime example in bank land would be if a high-quality bank with strong credit quality and exposure to strong geographies acquires a cheap but troubled institution in a noncontiguous and unfavorable geography with credit issues. Although the transaction could be EPS accretive, the market will discount the combined P/E multiple to reflect the less attractive earnings stream of the target.

In Exhibit 8.8, an acquiror trading at 13.5× P/E acquires a smaller institution in an all-stock transaction at 9.9× P/E. Although the transaction is 5.6% EPS accretive, we're not assuming any synergies; thus, the combined market value must be equal to the separate parts, and there must be P/E compression to the extent that there is no per share price improvement.

EXHIBIT 8.8 EPS Bootstrapping in an All-stock Transaction

	Acquiror		**Target**		**Adj.**		**Combined**
Market Value ($MM)	$135.00	+	$24.75			=	$159.75
Net Income ($MM)	$10.00	+	$2.50			=	$12.50
Share Count (MM)	3.00	+	0.75	+	(0.20)	=	3.55
EPS ($)	3.33		3.33				3.52
P/E (x)	13.5x		9.9x				12.8x
Share Price ($)	**45.00**		**33.00**				**45.00**

EXHIBIT 8.9 EPS Accretion in an All-cash Transaction

	Acquiror		Target		Adj.		Combined
Market Value ($MM)	135.00	+	24.75			=	159.75
Net Income ($MM)	10.00	+	2.50			=	12.50
Share Count (MM)	3.00	+	0.75	+	(0.75)	=	3.00
EPS ($)	3.33		3.33				4.17
P/E (x)	13.5x		9.9x				12.8x
Share Price ($)	**45.00**		**33.00**				**53.25**

Let's contrast this by walking through an identical transaction but using all cash. We see the same multiple compression, but the lack of share dilution means theoretical price appreciation, even if combined market value does not improve.

EPS accretion is usually given as a percentage of the most recent year's EPS. Since deals usually close mid-year, it is more helpful to look at EPS accretion for the first full-year of the combined franchise (Exhibit 8.9).

SYNERGIES AND VALUE CREATION

This brings us to synergies, the value that is created by bringing two institutions together. Synergies can range from explicit cost saves (i.e., elimination of overlapping branches) to more strategic (i.e., pairing a great deposit franchise with a differentiated asset generator). It is then our job to assess whether the synergies communicated by management are reasonable or not, and more importantly, if the market is over- or under-estimating the synergy opportunities.

Cost synergies are the easiest one to judge. The most helpful way to assess it is as a percentage of the target's expense base. Expense saves can come in many forms: branch overlap, management overlap, back office duplication, and consolidation of technology vendors. When it is a small in-market deal with lots of branch overlap, this number can be north of 50%. High cost save assumptions on an out-of-market acquisition is an aggressive assumption that should be scrutinized. Management will also give guidance on the timeline that cost saves are expected to be implemented, and those assumptions should be analyzed as well.

Revenue synergies usually do not get as much immediate credit by the market. Rarely does management give quantitative guidance, and almost never is it incorporated into their EPS accretion calculations. However, understanding the cross-selling opportunities and ways to leverage the strengths of each company in an acquisition can give us an edge in better valuing the combined institution.

Dis-synergies can occur too, particularly as bank regulation is often stricter for larger institutions. The clearest example of this is the Durbin amendment, which limits fees charged to retailers for debit card processing. This limit applies to banks with over $10 billion in assets.

TANGIBLE BOOK VALUE DILUTION AND EARNBACK

As banks are balance-sheet focused entities, bank investors are very sensitive to tangible book value dilution, and investors are keen to understand the tangible book value ramifications of a transaction. From an investing perspective, dilution is most important on a per share basis. This is relatively straightforward to calculate, given we've been provided with the necessary inputs; however, most of the time the calculation will be provided by management. As we saw earlier, broadly speaking, a higher cash consideration and a higher P/TBV premium will all be more dilutive to TBV.

Just looking at the TBV "hole" is only part of the story. A wildly accretive deal would pay for itself in short order, while a deal that permanently impairs earnings would permanently destroy value. Holistically, "earnback" represents the time it would take (normally expressed in years) for a company to "earnback" the dilution incurred during an acquisition. Unfortunately, "earnback" can be defined in multiple ways, and can vary wildly depending on the definition used. It is then our job to normalize the earnback into a comparable form so that the earnback numbers we look at are more-or-less apples-to-apples. The methods commonly used are the **crossover method, the accretion (or "simple") method**, and **the static method.**

The **crossover method** is perhaps the most theoretically justified way to calculate earnback, but also the most complex method that requires the most inputs and assumptions. Essentially, it requires modeling two TBV projections, one with the deal and one without the deal. The earnback period is defined as when the TBVPS of the combined entity exceeds that of what was projected of the standalone company. In this way, the crossover method gets closer to measuring the real time it would take for a deal to pay for itself as compared to if the company chose not to do a deal.

In Exhibit 8.10, we assume 5% TBV dilution but 25% EPS accretion (simplifying assumptions include no dividends or buybacks, steady earnings growth, and immediate earnings accretion). In this case, the earnback occurs slightly before year 4. The disadvantage to the crossover method is that it is more labor intensive to calculate, and the relatively larger number of subjective assumptions and inputs reduces comparability.

EXHIBIT 8.10 Crossover Method

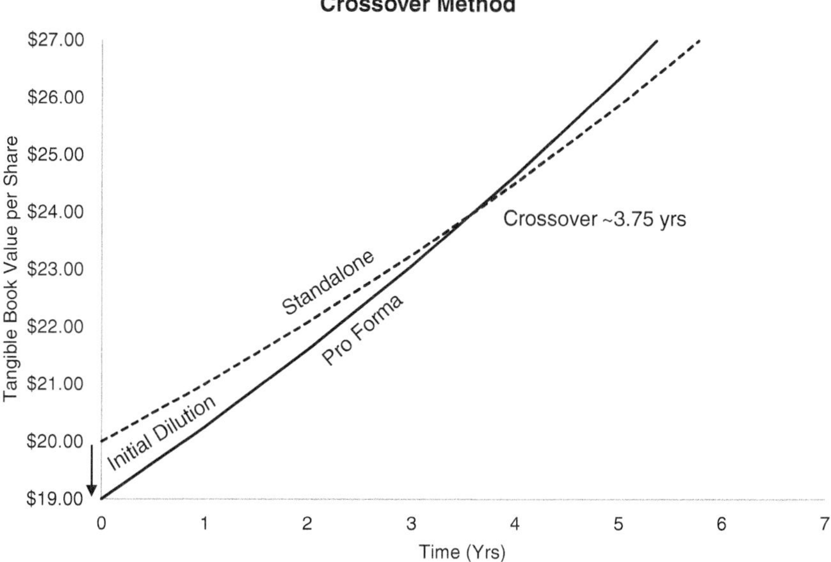

The **accretion method**, also referred to as the **simple method,** divides the dollar value of the tangible book value dilution by the fully phased-in incremental EPS.

$$Earnback = \frac{TBV\ Dilution}{EPS\ Accretion}$$

In our prior example, with 5% TBV dilution (on $20 TBV) and 25% EPS accretion (on $1.00 of EPS):

$$\frac{Current\ TBV \times Dilution}{Current\ EPS \times Accretion} = \frac{\$20 \times 0.05}{\$1 \times 0.25} = \frac{1.00}{0.25} = 4\ yrs$$

The advantage of this method is that it is easy to calculate, requires less assumptions than the crossover method, and is thus more comparable across deals.

The **static method** is the least popular way to estimate earnback and is rarely used in practice. It measures the time it takes for the combined company's TBV to exceed where it was before the combination. The issue with the static method is that even if a transaction is dilutive to earnings, as long as earnings are *positive* the static method will yield a positive earnback. However, it is clear that the company would have been better off going it alone rather than permanently impair earnings through an acquisition.

The market's tolerance for lengthy earnbacks depends on a number of factors, but ideally one would want TBV to be earned back in a reasonable period. We would prefer three years or sooner, but there can be compelling deals where the earnback is much longer.

PURCHASE ACCOUNTING

Purchase accounting can be frankly a complex and confusing topic. At its highest level, when a merger occurs, the balance sheet of the target is marked to fair value and combined with the acquirors, while certain premiums and discounts are then amortized or accreted back through income over time. When there is a difference between fair value and the actual price paid for a target, the difference is recorded as goodwill, or in the case where FV exceeds purchase price, a bargain purchase gain will be recorded.

Step 1: Mark the target's balance sheet to fair value.

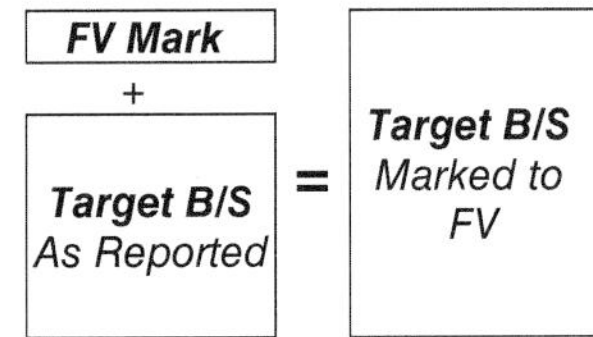

Step 2: Record the excess purchase price as goodwill.

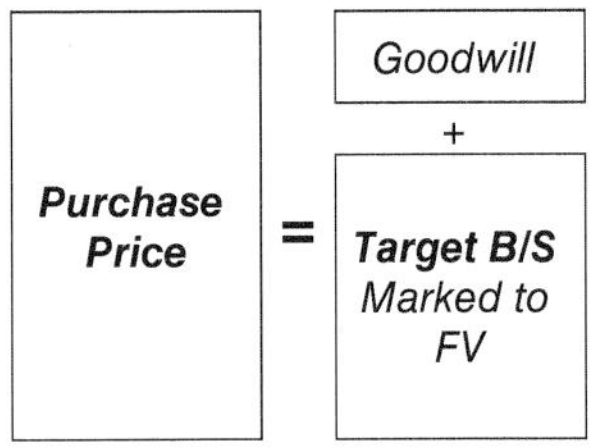

Goodwill = Purchase Price – (FV of Tang. Assets + FV of Intang. Assets).

Goodwill is a balance sheet "plug" in a business combination.

Purchase accounting can add considerable noise to financial results, and we'll need to understand what the primary sources of noise are to get a cleaner picture of bank's financial condition.

Purchase Accounting Accretion

When the fair value (FV) of a loan (or financial asset) is determined to be different from the expected contractual cash flow or unpaid principal balance of the loan, the fair value is recorded on the balance sheet, and that difference flows through the income statement over the life of the financial asset. In fact, for yielding debt instruments, accretion income will flow through *net interest income*, which is an input for calculating NIMs. Thus, banks that have been historically acquisitive can have inflated NIMs due to accretion income from past deals flowing through interest income. Most of the time, management teams will point out what "core" NIMs are after stripping out accretion income.

Why would the fair value of a loan differ from the expected cash flow of a loan? The two primary sources are interest rates and credit.

Interest marks can occur when prevailing rates differ from rates when the loan was originally underwritten. Remember, rates and bond prices are inversely related. When rates rise, prices on debt instruments should fall, all things being equal, in order to improve the yield on the instrument to the point where they become competitive with new paper. Interest rate marks can be positive or negative. If rates decline, a book of loans would trade at a premium to their UPB (Unpaid Principal Balance). Conversely if rates rise, that book of loans would trade at a discount to their UPB.

Credit marks are the other major type of mark taken on loan portfolios, representing discounts to reflect management's best estimate of loss content for a financial asset. Note that we touch upon how credit marks are applied under the new CECL paradigm later in this chapter. In short, CECL's new treatment of purchased credit deteriorated (PCD) loans does not allow for credit mark accretion. Instead, the credit discount is reflected in a reserve allowance.

In Exhibit 8.11, $100,000 of performing loans is acquired and the fair value is determined to be $95,000. Day 1, the loans would be brought onto the balance sheet at fair value; the discount (or premium) is accreted (or amortized) through income for the life of said asset.

Bargain Purchase Gain and Negative Goodwill

A related concept, not unique to banks, but still important, is the bargain purchase gain. A bargain purchase gain is a gain recorded on the income statement when assets are acquired at less than fair value. This typically happens for distressed sellers that require immediate liquidity. Remember that purchase accounting requires balance sheet items to be brought over at fair value. Thus, if the cash outflow from the purchase is less than the recorded value of the purchased asset brought onto the balance sheet, a gain must be recorded.

EXHIBIT 8.11 Acquired Non-PCD Loans

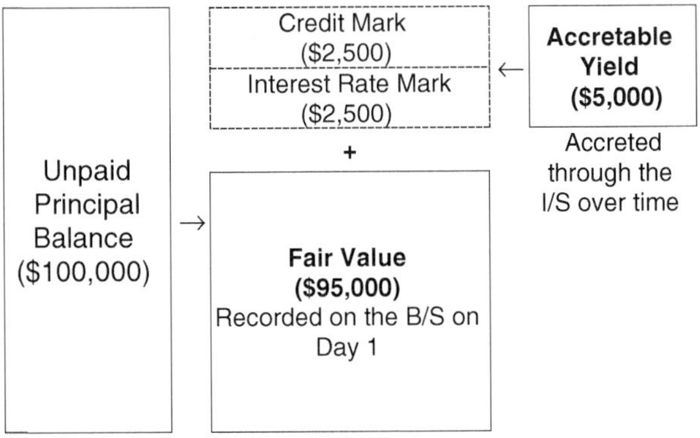

EXHIBIT 8.12 Bargain Purchase Gain

Bank A	As Reported	Acquisition	Pro Forma
Cash	*200*	*(90)*	*110*
Loans	*800*	*+95*	*895*
Total Assets	*1,000*	*+5*	*1,005*
Total Liabilities	*900*		*900*
Total Equity	*100*	*+5*	*105*

In Exhibit 8.12, a pool of loans with $95 in fair value is acquired for only $90; a bargain purchase gain of $5 is recorded (and reflected in an increase in retained earnings) to account for the +$5 increase in total assets.

Core Deposit Intangibles

From an accounting standpoint, deposits are liabilities. They are balances that are contractually owed to the deposit holder. However, bank deposits are not a typical liability. They are the franchise of a bank and gives the bank a major funding advantage over non-banks. Remember that a bank's profitability hinges on the spread between money lent and money borrowed. Thus, a stable, low-cost, sticky deposit franchise is a significant advantage.

In that vein, purchase accounting dictates that banks can record something called a core deposit intangible, which reflects an estimation of the economic value of those deposits.

EXHIBIT 8.13 Purchase Price Allocation and CDI

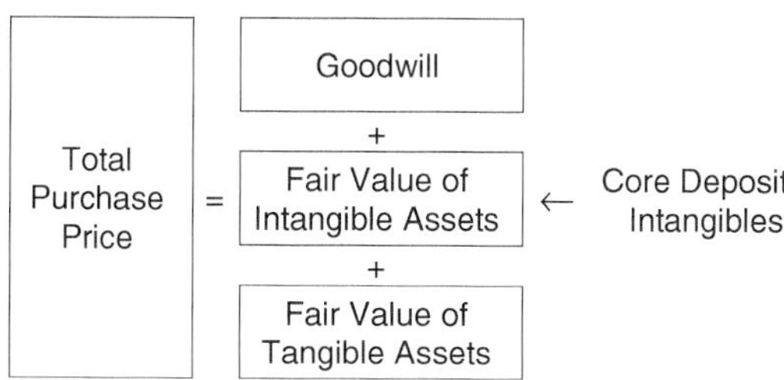

In an acquisition, the core deposit intangible is recorded as an intangible asset when marking the target's balance sheet to fair value (Exhibit 8.13).

The estimation of what the core deposit intangible should be is a highly detailed process best left to full-time professional accountants. At a high level, an acquiror would segment the target's deposits by type and estimate the deposit rate, sensitivities, life, decay, and associated non-interest fees and expenses tied to such accounts. This is compared to the acquiror's marginal borrowing rate, which would allow a DCF analysis to be conducted to estimate the core deposit value.

As investors, the metric we usually look at to assess CDIs is the core deposit intangible to core deposit ratio. This typically sits in the 1–3% range and is dependent on the quality of the deposit franchise as well as prevailing interest rates (Exhibit 8.14).

EXHIBIT 8.14 CDIs Tightly Correlated to Interest Rates

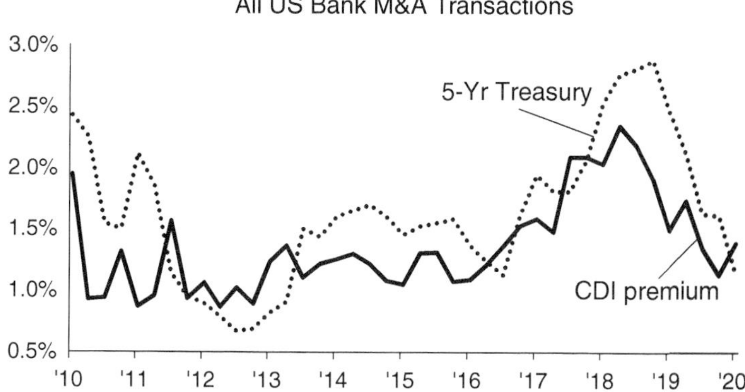

After a CDI has been established, it is amortized over its useful life. This is typically done in an accelerated fashion over a 10-year useful life.

Deferred Tax Liabilities

Acquisitions usually lead to the creation of Deferred Tax Liabilities (DTL) or Assets (DTA). This is one of the trickier topics in purchase accounting.

In GAAP purchase accounting, the target's assets are marked to fair value and those differences are amortized or depreciated over time. However, tax accounting does not allow the revaluation of these assets. Thus, an asset that's been marked up will have an associated amortization expense in the GAAP books that is not present in the tax books. These additional GAAP expenses will depress pre-tax income and understate what the actual taxable income is (Exhibit 8.15).

EXHIBIT 8.15 Explaining Merger Related DTLs

GAAP Accounting	**Year 0**	**Year 1**	**Year 2**
1 Operating Income	100.0	110.0	120.0
2 Less: Amortization of Intangibles Created in Acquisition	(10.0)	(10.0)	(10.0)
3 Book Pre-tax Income	90.0	100.0	110.0
4 Implied Tax Expense (25%)	**22.5**	**25.0**	**27.5**

In this example, the amortization of the intangible created through merger accounting decreases pre-tax income, and implied taxes

Tax Accounting	**Year 0**	**Year 1**	**Year 2**
1 Operating Income	100.0	110.0	120.0
~~2 Less: Amortization of Intangibles Created in Acquisition~~	~~(10.0)~~	~~(10.0)~~	~~(10.0)~~
3 Taxable Income	100.0	110.0	120.0
4 Actual Tax Expense (25%)	**25.0**	**27.5**	**30.0**

However, tax accounting will not have the amortization expense as the tax-basis of the asset was not written up. Thus, actual tax expenses are higher than what is implied in the GAAP books.

EXHIBIT 8.16 FNBG's Acquisition Related DTL

FNB Bancorp and Subsidiary
Notes to Consolidated Financial Statements
December 31, 2017, 2016 and 2015

(In thousands)	America California Bank September 4, 2015
Book value of net assets acquired from	
Book value of net assets acquired from America California Bank	$ 18,138
Fair value adjustments:	
Leans	2,171
Cure deposit intangible asset	727
Time deposits	(1,732)
Other liabilities	(243)
Total purchase accounting adjustments	19,061
Deferred tax liabilities	(300)
Fair value of net assets acquired from America California Bank	$ 18,761
Merger consideration	21,500
Less fair value of net assets acquired	(18,761)
Goodwill	$ 2,739

Thus, a DTL is created to account for the temporary difference in taxes.

Note that the tax basis for various assets are not publicly disclosed. It is usually impossible for an outside analyst to calculate merger-related DTLs and DTAs. However, it is important to understand where these deferred taxes arise from (Exhibit 8.16).

Here we see FNB Bancorp's acquisition of America California Bank generated a DTL, driven by the fair value mark-up of America California.

In Exhibit 8.17 we walk through the balance sheet combination of a whole-bank acquisition. Our acquiror acquires the target for $89.7MM, or 130% of TBV for 50/50 cash-stock consideration.

- * Transaction Expenses for the acquiror are estimated to be 2% of total deal value, or $1.8MM. This expense is tax deductible so a DTA is created.

EXHIBIT 8.17 Merger Model Balance Sheet

$MM Except Per Share	Acquiror	Target	Transaction Expenses*	Purchase Accounting	Pro Forma
Cash + Equiv.	150.0	10.0	(1.8)	(44.9) **A**	113.4
Securities	600.0	120.0			720.0
Total Gross Loans	3,000.0	600.0		(5.1) **B**	3,594.9
Loan Loss Reserve	(30.0)	(6.0)		3.3 **C**	(32.7)
Net Loans	2,970.0	594.0			3,562.2
Goodwill	-	-		10.0 **D**	10.0
Core Deposit Intang.	100.0	-		13.6 **E**	113.6
Deferred Tax Asset	10.0		0.4	- **F**	10.4
Intangibles	110.0	-			134.0
OREO		45.0			145.0
Other Assets					-
Total Assets	**3,930.0**	**769.0**			**4,674.5**
Core Deposits	3,000.0	680.0			3,680.0
Other Deposits	400.0	20.0			420.0
Other Liabilities	-	-			-
Deferred Tax Liability				1.1 **F**	1.1
Total Liabilities	3,400.0	700.0			4,101.1
Preferred Equity	-	-			-
Noncontrolling Interests	-	-			-
Common Equity	530.0	69.0	(1.4)	(24.2) **G**	573.4
Total Equity	530.0	69.0			573.4
Total Liabilities & Equity	**3,930.0**	**769.0**			**4,674.5**
Tang. Equity	420.0	69.0			439.5
Tang. Common Equity	420.0	69.0			439.5
Tang. Assets	3,820.0	769.0			4,540.6
TCE Ratio	11.0%	9.0%			9.7%
Reserve Ratio	1.00%	1.00%			0.91%

Deal Terms		**Financial Assumptions**	
Deal Value (% TCE)	130%	Tax Rate (%)	21.0%
Deal value ($M)	89.7	PCD Loans (%)	15.0%
Stock Consideration (%)	50.0%	Non PCD Credit Mark (%)	1.0%
Cash Consideration (%)	50.0%	PCD Credit Mark (%)	3.0%
		Assumed CDI (%)	2.0%
		Merger Charges (% of DV)	2.0%
		Merger Charges ($M)	1.8

A. Represents the cash component of the transaction:

$$(\$89.7 \times 50\% = \$44.9)$$

B. Non PCD loans are marked to fair value:

$$(\$600 \times 85\% \times 1\% = \$5.1)$$

C. The targets LLR is eliminated ($6.0), and a reserve is created for PCD loans:

$$(\$600 \times 15\% \times 3\% = \$2.7)$$

D. Goodwill is purchase price less fair value of net assets. Note that goodwill can only be calculated *after* marking the target's balance sheet to fair value:

$$(\$89.7 - (\$780.8 - 701.1) = \$10)$$

E. Core Deposit Intangibles are estimated to be 2% of core deposits:

$$(\$680 \times 2.0\% = \$13.6)$$

F. In this example, a net DTL is created as the DTL generated from the CDI mark up ($13.6MM) exceeds the DTA generated by the loan mark downs ($1.8MM).

G. Target's common equity is reversed ($69MM) and partially offset by the issuance of new shares ($\$89.7 \times 50\% = \$44.9$).

INTERNAL RATE OF RETURN

Internal Rate of Return (IRR) should be a well-known term for those familiar with corporate finance. It is a bit less emphasized in bank land, and requires a number of inputs that make it difficult for us to analyze. Formally, the IRR is the discount rate that makes the NPV of all future cash flows of the acquisition equal to zero. In its most generalized form:

$$NPV = \sum_{n=0}^{N} \frac{CF_n}{(1 + IRR)^n} = 0$$

Rearranged in a more helpful form, the IRR equals the discount rate that makes all future cash flows equal to the initial investment.

$$Initial\ Investment = \sum_{n=1}^{N} \frac{CF_n}{(1 + IRR)^n}$$

Going one step further, if we make the assumption that the acquisition can be modeled by a growing perpetuity of cash flows, we can simplify the expression. Recall the present value of a perpetuity can be expressed as:

$$PV\ of\ FCF = \frac{CF_1}{R - g}$$

Since we are solving for the rate (R) that makes the PV of future cash flows equivalent to the initial investment:

$$Initial\ Investment = \frac{CF_1}{IRR - g}$$

$$\therefore IRR \approx \frac{Incremental\ Earnings}{Initial\ Investment} + g$$

This can provide you with a simple back-of-the-envelope way to ballpark IRRs.

The rule of thumb is that the *IRR* must exceed *cost of capital* in order for it to create value. *IRR* disclosures tend to be vague and high level within bank merger presentations.

A single bullet point like "IRR greater than 15%" is the typical level of disclosure one would find.

STRATEGIC CONSIDERATIONS

There are a bevy of other strategic considerations that can meaningfully impact the stock reaction of the acquiror that aren't necessarily reflected in pro forma financials.

For instance, a highly asset sensitive franchise neutralizing its asset sensitivity by acquiring a liability sensitive target would improve the combined franchise through a more durable earnings stream that's less sensitive to external factors. Diversifying the loan portfolio by acquiring loans and loan generation capabilities that an acquiror did not have before would also decrease the concentration risk of a franchise. Pairing up an urban lending franchise where there is healthy loan demand, with a low-cost sticky rural deposit franchise is another good example of good strategic rationale.

CURRENT EXPECTED CREDIT LOSSES (CECL) AND M&A

A recently implemented accounting standard, ASU 2016-13, introduced the current expected credit losses (CECL) methodology, which replaces the existing incurred loss methodology. Although the principal concept of fair value acquisition accounting remains, there are broad changes to that which in turn affects several concepts covered in the chapter, like EPS accretion and TBV dilution.

Day 1 refers to immediately after a transaction is consummated and the businesses combined. Under CECL, the loans are classified into two groups: **purchased credit deteriorated (PCD)** and **non-purchase credit deteriorated (non-PCD)** financial assets. This is analogous to the previous accounting standard's **purchased credit impaired (PCI)** and **non-purchase credit impaired (non-PCI)** categories, respectively.

FASB defines **PCD** loans as loans that "have experienced a more-than-insignificant deterioration in credit quality." Under the new accounting standards, the buyer estimates and records an allowance for credit loss, which is then *added* to the purchase price. This is colloquially the "gross-up" approach. Said another way, PCD loans are effectively marked to fair value, with the credit mark showing up in the **allowance** for loan losses. This contrasts to PCI marks, which are reflected directly on the gross loan balance by a "credit related loan mark" contra-asset. Thus, *net* loan balances are the same, but the reserve ratio will be higher under CECL. The benefit of this approach is that it makes pools of originated and acquired loans more comparable, as the credit quality "mark" shows up in the ALLL for both.

In Exhibit 8.18, a $100MM portfolio of credit-deteriorated assets are purchased at 95 cents on the dollar (aka have a 5% credit mark). Net loan balances are the same under PCD and PCI, but the discount is reflected under the ALLL under CECL.

EXHIBIT 8.18 PCD Accounting

	(Old Methodology) PCI	(New Methodology) PCD
Loans (Par Value)	$100,000	$100,000
Credit Mark	($5,000)	$0
Gross Loan Balance	$95,000	$100,000
ALLL	$0	($5,000)
Net Loan Balance	$95,000	$95,000

EXHIBIT 8.19 Non-PCD Accounting

	(Old Methodology) Non-PCI	(New Methodology) Non-PCD
Loans (Par Value)	$5,000,000	$5,000,000
Credit Mark	($50,000)	($50,000)
Gross Loan Balance	$4,950,000	$4,950,000
ALLL	$0	($50,000)
Net Loan Balance	$4,950,000	$4,900,000

Non-PCD loans are loans that have not experienced significant credit quality deterioration. The implementation of CECL has created a somewhat strange interaction with existing accounting rules. Under CECL, non-PCD assets are recorded at fair value on the balance sheet, same as the prior standard. However, CECL requires a provision to also be recorded, with the expense running through the income statement, which represents the best estimate for all future expected credit losses for the acquired portfolio. Thus, this results in a "double dip" credit mark that is essentially counted twice.

In Exhibit 8.19, a $5B portfolio of performing assets is acquired with a 1% credit mark. The acquiror records these balances at fair value, and then records a provision expense to establish a reserve against the acquired assets.

Day 2 accounting for periods after a business combination are important as well. In short, the marks taken on loans for non-PCD loans are accreted through income over time. Note, due to no credit mark being taken on PCD loans, there is no credit-related accretion income for PCD loans.

BUYBACKS OR DEALS?

From a financial leverage perspective, a bank with excess capital can lever up by growing via a deal or shrink via a buyback. Of course, there is a proclivity for management to want to grow versus shrink. However, one should carefully gauge the relative attractiveness of a deal by asking ourselves, would we be better off by just buying back stock?

The exercise is relatively straightforward. We estimate the EPS accretion and TBV dilution of a deal and compare it to a buyback that would leverage the balance sheet to a similar degree. Generally, when a bank's stock trades near TBV, the opportunity cost of doing a buyback rises. Further, the lower execution risk of a buyback compared to an acquisition makes buybacks an incrementally more attractive option.

EXHIBIT 8.20 Acquisition or Buyback

	EOP Balance	PF Acquisition	PF Buyback
Tangible Equity	90.00	85.50	77.73
Tangible Assets	990.00	1,075.50	977.73
TE/TA	9.1%	7.9%	7.9%
Shares Outstanding	3.00	3.00	2.63
Net Income	10.00	11.00	10.00
TBV per Share	30.00	28.50	29.58
EPS per Share	3.33	3.67	3.81

In Exhibit 8.20, our bank in question could choose to either:

(a) Buy a bank for $13.5MM cash at a valuation of 150% of TBV, or
(b) Buy back $12.3MM in stock at 110% TBV.

Pro forma leverage is the same, but the buyback yields higher EPS accretion and less TBV dilution.

CHAPTER 9

Cycle

"When the music stops, in terms of liquidity, things will be complicated. But as long as the music is playing, you've got to get up and dance. We're still dancing."

– Charles O. Prince III, July 2007

The comments above made by Charles "Chuck" Prince, the former Chairman and CEO of Citigroup did not age well. Chuck Prince got a lot of flak for these comments that had a rather unfortunate timing in that they were made to the *Financial Times* in mid-2007. In a later interview with the Financial Crisis Inquiry Commission, he clarified that his comments were in relation to leveraged lending to private equity firms and not the mortgage business.

In defense of Mr. Prince not many people in similar seats in 2007 were prescient to figure out how long the music would play. This is true at any point in a business cycle; no one can tell when the cycle ends. We had been constantly hearing investors ask "where are we in the cycle?" and we have been hearing responses ranging from "7th or 8th innings," "two years left," "late cycle," or something similar for the last five years preceding the COVID-19 pandemic. There were crickets as the markets made its ascent towards the mid-February 2020 peak, brushing off news of COVID-19 cases in Wuhan, China in December 2019 and the first US case in the state of Washington in January 2020.

What should a prudent investor do apart from buying left tail protection in the form of options and credit default swaps – which can be a drag during normal times, buying bonds, Gold, and investing in long short funds. We believe investors need to pay close attention to the indicators and investor psychology surrounding cycles.

BANK SENSITIVITY TO CYCLES

Bank investors need to pay extra attention since banks have higher leverage than most other entities and this makes them more sensitive to cycles. At a macro level bank lending is the lifeblood of the economy, and lending is highly

EXHIBIT 9.1 Strong Correlation Between GDP and Loan Growth

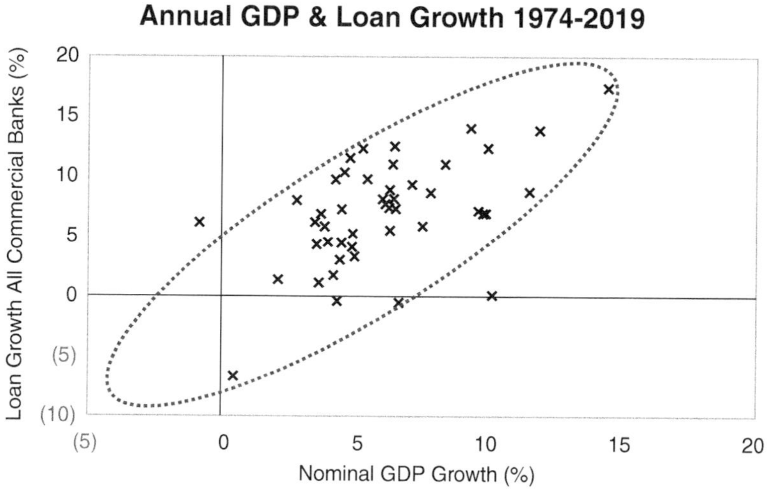

Annual GDP & Loan Growth 1974-2019

Loan Growth All Commercial Banks (%)

20	
15	
10	
5	
0	
(5)	
(10)	

(5) 0 5 10 15 20

Nominal GDP Growth (%)

Source: Federal Reserve, BEA

correlated to GDP as seen in Exhibit 9.1. Given this tight connection between banks and cycles, bank investors, like other investors, have to pay attention to cycles.

No one needs reminding that financials and banks especially were the epicenter of the last crisis, and it was called the Global "Financial" Crisis. The pandemic induced crisis of 2020 is largely outside the banking system, and banks are in much better shape from a capital standpoint. However, affected industries will draw down lines of credit and thus increase a bank's exposure to the impacted industries. Knowing your bank's credit underwriting and on- and off-balance sheet exposure to sectors is key at a micro level. We cover this in Chapters 3 and 4.

BULL MARKETS DO NOT DIE OF OLD AGE

The last bull market, which commenced March 9th, 2009, ended around March 11th, 2020. This eleven-year run was the longest in US history. As the old Wall Street adage suggests, the length of the recovery does not determine its end. We recall that Reinhart and Rogoff, in their work analyzing 100 systemic bank crises, determined that it took eight years on average (median of 6.5 years) to get back to the pre-crisis level of income.

The recovery from March 23rd, 2020 has been the fastest on record fueled by monetary and fiscal stimulus but that is a topic for another day, as we are focused here more on the end of cycles.

If they do not die of old age, what causes a cycle to end? The factors that contribute to cycle mortality include the start of a recession (or the increased odds of a recession which can serve as a self-fulfilling prophecy), market exuberance (silly to egregious valuation going on to even more egregious valuation), geopolitical tensions, systemic bank and debt crises, increasing inflation and tightening actions by a central bank to quell inflation, and yes, pandemics. In short, anything that can convince enough market participants to move from FOMO (Fear of Missing Out) to FOLE (Fear of Losing Everything). During FOMO, the market moves up on positive news flow and shrugs off negative news. During FOLE, the market is no longer whistling past the graveyard. Good news is disregarded while anything negative is immediately dissected and the worst possible scenario gets priced in despite the odds.

NBER – THE CYCLE'S TIMEKEEPER

The National Bureau of Economic Research (NBER) is the accepted record keeper for the timing of business cycles. The last expansion commenced June 2009 according to the NBER. We would note that the NBER's identification of the dates of inflection in the business cycle are retrospective and not prospective as they carefully collect and analyze backwards looking data. The identification of the current recession's peak as having occurred in February 2020 was made on June 8, 2020. The identification of the prior peak as having occurred in December 2007 was made on November 28, 2008. In short, do not wait for the NBER, or for that matter anyone else, to ring a bell to alert you about inflection points (Exhibit 9.2).

EXHIBIT 9.2 Inflection and Announcement Dates

Turning Point	Peak/Trough	Announce Date (Days After Turning Point)
February 2020	Peak	Jun 8, 2020 (128)
June 2009	Trough	Sep 20, 2010 (476)
December 2007	Peak	Dec 1, 2008 (366)
November 2001	Trough	Jul 17, 2003 (623)
March 2001	Peak	Nov 26, 2001 (270)
March 1991	Trough	Dec 22, 1992 (662)
July 1990	Peak	Apr 25, 1991 (298)
November 1982	Trough	Jul 8, 1983 (249)
July 1981	Peak	Jan 6, 1982 (189)
July 1980	Trough	Jul 8, 1981 (372)
January 1980	Peak	Jun 3, 1980 (154)

Source: NBER

EXHIBIT 9.3 US Business Cycle Duration

(Months)

Peak Month	Trough Month	Contraction (Peak to Trough)	Expansion (Trough to Peak)	Cycle Duration (Trough to Trough)	Cycle Duration (Peak to Peak)
	Dec 1854				
Jun 1857	Dec 1858	18	30	48	
Oct 1860	Jun 1861	8	22	30	40
Apr 1865	Dec 1867	32	46	78	54
Jun 1869	Dec 1870	18	18	36	50
Oct 1873	Mar 1879	65	34	99	52
Mar 1882	May 1885	38	36	74	101
Mar 1887	Apr 1888	13	22	35	60
Jul 1890	May 1891	10	27	37	40
Jan 1893	Jun 1894	17	20	37	30
Dec 1895	Jun 1897	18	18	36	35
June 1899	Dec 1900	18	24	42	42
Sep 1902	Aug 1904	23	21	44	39
May 1907	Jun 1908	13	33	46	56
Jan 1910	Jan 1912	24	19	43	32
Jan 1913	Dec 1914	23	12	35	36
Aug 1918	Mar 1919	7	44	51	67
Jan 1920	Jul 1921	18	10	28	17
May 1923	Jul 1924	14	22	36	40
Oct 1926	Nov 1927	13	27	40	41
Aug 1929	Mar 1933	43	21	64	34
May 1937	Jun 1938	13	50	63	93
Feb 1945	Oct 1945	8	80	88	93
Nov 1948	Oct 1949	11	37	48	45
Jul 1953	May 1954	10	45	55	56
Aug 1957	Apr 1958	8	39	47	49
Apr 1960	Feb 1961	10	24	34	32
Dec 1969	Nov 1970	11	106	117	116
Nov 1973	Mar 1975	16	36	52	47
Jan 1980	Jul 1980	6	58	64	74
Jul 1981	Nov 1982	16	12	28	18
Jul 1990	Mar 1991	8	92	100	108
Mar 2001	Nov 2001	8	120	128	128
Dec 2007	Jun 2009	18	73	91	81
Feb 2020			128		146
	1854–2020	17	41	56	59
	1854–1919	22	27	48	49
	1919–1945	18	35	53	53
	1945–2020	11	64	69	75

Source: NBER

The FAQs on the business cycle dating procedure (Exhibit 9.3) make for an interesting read and are accessible at:

https://www.nber.org/cycles/recessions_faq.html

THIS TIME IS "RARELY" DIFFERENT

We focus our attention on a few indicators that have worked in the past and are good ones to keep track of. We would be wary of anyone that looks at these indicators flashing red and tells you that "this time is different." Look at the data to understand if this time is really different and bring a healthy dose of skepticism since, while there can be false positives in our experience, "this time is rarely different." That said, remember these are indicators; there are bound to be false positives and false negatives.

Here are a few key ones that we focus on:

1. Inversion of the yield curve
2. High Yield spreads
3. TED spread
4. FRA-OIS (Libor-OIS) spread
5. Repo rates
6. Unemployment crossing its moving average

INVERSION OF THE YIELD CURVE

As we've written about in Chapter 7, the yield curve is a graph obtained by plotting yields on the Y axis and the term on the X axis. A normal yield curve is upward sloping, with yields increasing with maturity. The treasury yield curve is commonly considered "inverted" when the yield of the 10-year Treasury note is below that of the 1-year Treasury bill (Exhibit 9.4).

This idea that the inversion of the yield curve and the economic cycle were connected had its genesis in Professor Campbell Harvey's 1986 dissertation at the University of Chicago entitled "Recovering Expectations of Consumption Growth from an Equilibrium Model of the Term Structure of Interest Rates."

The dissertation is accessible at: https://faculty.fuqua.duke.edu/~charvey/Research/Thesis/Thesis.htm

All 10 recessions since 1955 have been preceded by an inverted yield curve. During this period there has been only one false positive when there was a slowdown but not an NBER defined recession. The lag between the

EXHIBIT 9.4 Yield Curve Inversions Preceding Recessions

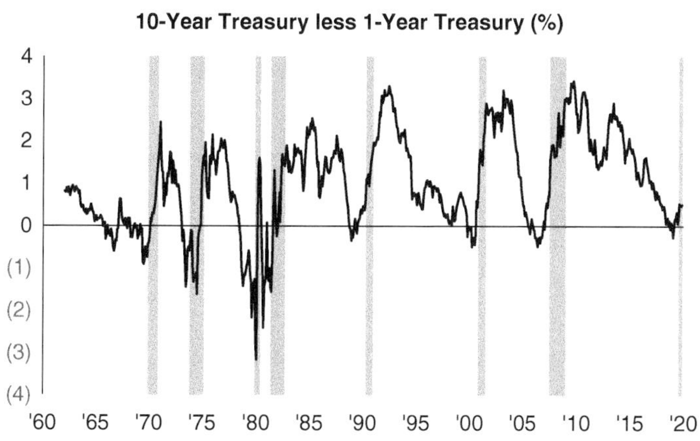

Source: St. Louis Federal Reserve

yield curve inversion and the start of a recession has ranged between 6 and 24 months.

Recommended Reading:

1. *Economic Forecasts with the Yield Curve* by Michael D. Bauer and Thomas M. Mertens – Federal Reserve Board of San Francisco, March 5, 2018.
2. Glenn D. Rudebusch and John C. Williams (2009): "Forecasting Recessions: The Puzzle of the Enduring Power of the Yield Curve," *Journal of Business & Economic Statistics*

The research paper concludes that a "*simple model for predicting recessions that uses only real-time yield curve information would have produced better forecasts of recessions at horizons beyond two quarters than the professional forecasters provided.*" It also goes on to state, "*Finally, it is interesting to note that many times during the past 20 years forecasters have acknowledged the formidable past performance of the yield curve in predicting expansions and recessions but argued that this past performance did not apply in the current situation. That is, signals from the yield curve have often been dismissed because of supposed changes in the economy or special factors influencing interest rates.*"

May we all have the intellectual honesty to stick to yield curve reading and not ascribe the inversion to other factors so as to fit to a narrative. Always remember "this time is rarely different."

EXHIBIT 9.5 The Term Spread Jan 2019–Jul 2020

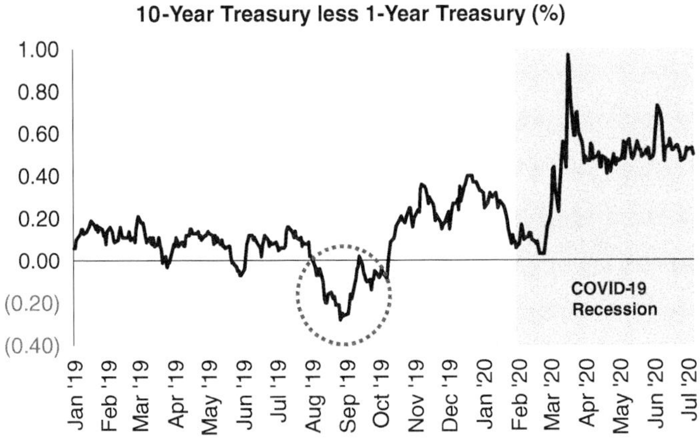

Source: St. Louis Federal Reserve

Was There a Yield Curve Inversion Prior to the COVID-19–fueled Recession?

The yield curve was inverted from early August 2019 to October 2019, as can be seen in Exhibit 9.5. There was also an inversion for a much shorter period in late May to early June 2019. We believe that this was a canary in the coal mine moment. To be clear we believe that COVID-19 was the proximate factor that drove the markets into bear territory. However, we believe there were signs ahead of the arrival of the pandemic that the overall macro environment was fragile, and it would not have taken a lot to serve as a tipping point.

HIGH YIELD SPREADS

High yield spreads widen ahead of and during recessions and have been good leading indicators (Exhibit 9.6). They do, however, generate false positives, typically when there are other factors contributing to financial stress:

HY spreads widened by about 350 bps from March to September 1998. This coincided with the Russian Financial Crisis and LTCM (Long Term Capital Management) collapse.

HY spreads widened by around 400 bps from April to August 2011. The Eurozone debt crisis, S&P's downgrade of the US sovereign debt rating, and general concern over the fragility of the global economy drove investors out of risky assets.

EXHIBIT 9.6 HY Spreads and Recessions

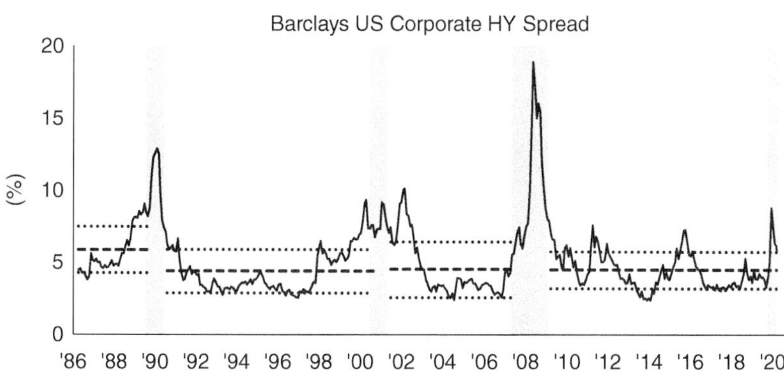

Source: Bloomberg

There was a spike again in late 2015 and 2016, which was driven by spreads blowing out in the metals, mining, and energy complex, and the expectations of an FOMC rate hike cycle.

The market always has a narrative around what is driving the blowing out of high yield spreads just like it does with yield curve inversion. When this narrative does not pass the smell test, one needs to delve into considering if the credit market is flashing a signal of the end of the business cycle.

HY spreads blew out to over 17 in December 2008. Note that changing the periodicity (daily, weekly, monthly, quarterly, yearly) has an effect on the spread measures in charts. Thus, we will see some different measures depending on the periodicity used. The key is to get the concept of the excess spread.

Naturally, implicit in higher level of spreads is an expectation of a higher default rate and hence loss rate.

An excess spread of 17% implies a default rate of around 24%, assuming a loss given default of 70%. We give these simple steps to calculate this:

$$Loss\ Rate = Default\ Rate \times Loss\ Given\ Default$$

$$Loss\ Given\ Default = (1 - Recovery\ Rate)$$

$$Loss\ Rate = Default\ Rate \times (1 - Recovery\ Rate)$$

The Excess Spread is the Compensation for the Loss Rate

$$\therefore Excess\ Spread = Default\ Rate\ \times\ (1 - Recovery\ Rate)$$

EXHIBIT 9.7 Excess Spread of 17% – Default and Recovery

Default Rate	(1-Recovery Rate)
17.0%	100.0%
18.9%	90.0%
21.3%	80.0%
24.3%	**70.0%**
28.3%	60.0%
34.0%	50.0%
42.5%	40.0%

Plugging in excess spread of 17% and estimated Recovery Rate of 30%, and solve for default rate:

$$17\% = \textit{Default Rate} \times 70\%$$

$$\textit{Default Rate} = 24.3\%$$

Calculating for default rate would yield 24.3%.

Since there were two variables and one equation, we made an assumption about one variable to calculate the other. Exhibit 9.7 shows the default rate for recovery rates ranging from 0% to 60% for excess spread of 17%.

HY default rates spiked to 6.3% in 2008 and 12.1% in 2009, compared to the LT average HY default rate of around 3.3%.

At a macro level, the excess spread in 2009 proved to be adequate to cover for the actual default rate. In other words, buy when spreads widen and blow out. This is easier said than done. Why is this difficult to execute in the fog of war? We have an anecdote to share which can help illustrate the predicament with a live example.

If we look at the daily moves during the first two months of the Pandemic bear market of 2020, HY spreads increased to close to 11 on March 23, 2020 and since then receded with the announcement of the Fed backstop with the Corporate Credit Facilities. As of early May 2020, HY spreads were in the mid 7s. An excess spread of 11% implies a default rate of around 16%, assuming a loss given default of 70%. This coincided with the market bottom of March 23, 2020 (as of May 4, 2020, the time of writing this).

A person covering one of the authors from the sell side had asked in the lead-up of the crisis as to where would spreads need to blow out to before one should step back and buy, and in response we said 10 (Exhibit 9.8). However, as it went past 10, we did not heed our own advice but continued to remain in a more defensive posture. Why were we hesitant? (1) We were no longer sure if 10 was the appropriate level of excess spreads, if the GFC was an appropriate prologue, and if we should be seeing spreads blow out past

EXHIBIT 9.8 HY Spreads in the Lead-up to the Pandemic

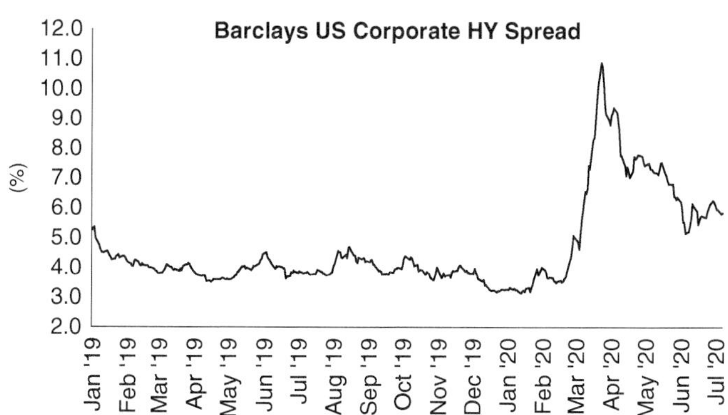

Source: Bloomberg

the 17 level seen during the GFC; and (2) The quick intervention by the Fed (especially the terms of the Corporate Credit Facility allowing them to buy HY were extremely accommodative) distorted what would be a normalized market reaction. When it comes to Fed action, the signaling of the intent is often adequate to produce the desired outcome.

This was a long-winded way of saying that, like with all inflection points, one does not know where the turn is when it comes to level of spreads. One needs to look at the sensitivity of spread levels versus recovery rates and implied default rates and determine the course of action (Exhibit 9.9).

Spreads across the credit markets are interconnected as investors look at them using a relative value framework, and it is instructive to look at some other spreads.

TED SPREAD

The TED spread is the spread between the 3-month LIBOR and the 3-month Treasury bill (Exhibit 9.10). A bit of trivia: TED is a contraction for *T-Bill* (the risk-free benchmark) and *ED* or *Eurodollar* contract tied to LIBOR. It spiked in August of 2007 and was a good early indicator for the GFC. LIBOR is a loan pricing benchmark for seven different periods (overnight, 1-week, 1-month, 2-month, 3-month, 6-month, and 12-month) in five different currencies (USD, GBP, EUR, JPY, and CHF). It is the rate at which banks borrow from each other on an unsecured basis. The 3-month is used due to its liquidity and data rich history. It makes intuitive sense that in times of stress this would widen in relation to the Treasury bill, a relatively risk-free asset.

EXHIBIT 9.9 Implied Default Rates

Loss Given Default (%)	Excess Spread (bps) 500	600	700	800	900	1,000	1,100	1,200	1,300	1,400	1,500	1,600	1,700	1,800	1,900	2,000
100%	5.0%	6.0%	7.0%	8.0%	9.0%	10.0%	11.0%	12.0%	13.0%	14.0%	15.0%	16.0%	17.0%	18.0%	19.0%	20.0%
95%	5.3%	6.3%	7.4%	8.4%	9.5%	10.5%	11.6%	12.6%	13.7%	14.7%	15.8%	16.8%	17.9%	18.9%	20.0%	21.1%
90%	5.6%	6.7%	7.8%	8.9%	10.0%	11.1%	12.2%	13.3%	14.4%	15.6%	16.7%	17.8%	18.9%	20.0%	21.1%	22.2%
85%	5.9%	7.1%	8.2%	9.4%	10.6%	11.8%	12.9%	14.1%	15.3%	16.5%	17.6%	18.8%	20.0%	21.2%	22.4%	23.5%
80%	6.3%	7.5%	8.8%	10.0%	11.3%	12.5%	13.8%	15.0%	16.3%	17.5%	18.8%	20.0%	21.3%	22.5%	23.8%	25.0%
75%	6.7%	8.0%	9.3%	10.7%	12.0%	13.3%	14.7%	16.0%	17.3%	18.7%	20.0%	21.3%	22.7%	24.0%	25.3%	26.7%
70%	7.1%	8.6%	10.0%	11.4%	12.9%	14.3%	15.7%	17.1%	18.6%	20.0%	21.4%	22.9%	24.3%	25.7%	27.1%	28.6%
65%	7.7%	9.2%	10.8%	12.3%	13.8%	15.4%	16.9%	18.5%	20.0%	21.5%	23.1%	24.6%	26.2%	27.7%	29.2%	30.8%
60%	8.3%	10.0%	11.7%	13.3%	15.0%	16.7%	18.3%	20.0%	21.7%	23.3%	25.0%	26.7%	28.3%	30.0%	31.7%	33.3%
55%	9.1%	10.9%	12.7%	14.5%	16.4%	18.2%	20.0%	21.8%	23.6%	25.5%	27.3%	29.1%	30.9%	32.7%	34.5%	36.4%
50%	10.0%	12.0%	14.0%	16.0%	18.0%	20.0%	22.0%	24.0%	26.0%	28.0%	30.0%	32.0%	34.0%	36.0%	38.0%	40.0%
45%	11.1%	13.3%	15.6%	17.8%	20.0%	22.2%	24.4%	26.7%	28.9%	31.1%	33.3%	35.6%	37.8%	40.0%	42.2%	44.4%
40%	12.5%	15.0%	17.5%	20.0%	22.5%	25.0%	27.5%	30.0%	32.5%	35.0%	37.5%	40.0%	42.5%	45.0%	47.5%	50.0%
35%	14.3%	17.1%	20.0%	22.9%	25.7%	28.6%	31.4%	34.3%	37.1%	40.0%	42.9%	45.7%	48.6%	51.4%	54.3%	57.1%
30%	16.7%	20.0%	23.3%	26.7%	30.0%	33.3%	36.7%	40.0%	43.3%	46.7%	50.0%	53.3%	56.7%	60.0%	63.3%	66.7%
25%	20.0%	24.0%	28.0%	32.0%	36.0%	40.0%	44.0%	48.0%	52.0%	56.0%	60.0%	64.0%	68.0%	72.0%	76.0%	80.0%
20%	25.0%	30.0%	35.0%	40.0%	45.0%	50.0%	55.0%	60.0%	65.0%	70.0%	75.0%	80.0%	85.0%	90.0%	95.0%	100.0%
15%	33.3%	40.0%	46.7%	53.3%	60.0%	66.7%	73.3%	80.0%	86.7%	93.3%	100.0%					
10%	50.0%	60.0%	70.0%	80.0%	90.0%	100.0%										

EXHIBIT 9.10 TED Spread

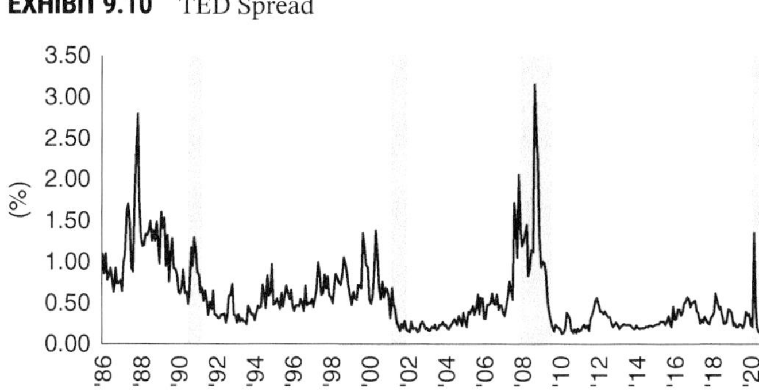

Source: St. Louis Federal Reserve

FRA–OIS

FRA–OIS spread is the spread between a *Forward Rate Agreement* (FRA) rate and an *Overnight Indexed Swap* (OIS) rate and is an important stress indicator for the banking system.

Recall FRAs are contracts to exchange future fixed payments for floating ones *in advance*. In the US, the key rate is again 3-month LIBOR, thus making it the "risky" component of the spread. Similarly, the OIS rate is the fixed rate leg of a fixed-for-floating rate swap (however, recall swaps are a *series* of payments settled in *arrears*). The OIS rate in this case is constructed with the geometric mean of the annualized expected effective fed funds rate. The important takeaway is that the OIS rate is the "risk-free" benchmark component of the spread because (1) it represents expectations of the "risk-free" rate, and (2) swap structures have lower default risk due to no exchange in principal and only net interest payments being exchanged at maturity.

The LIBOR–OIS spread is viewed as a canary in the coal mine for predicting bank insolvencies and funding stress (Exhibit 9.11). Indeed Former Fed Chair Alan Greenspan has oft been quoted saying, "LIBOR–OIS remains a barometer of fears of bank insolvency."

Recall that the Effective Fed Funds Rate (EFFR) is the volume-weighted median of the actual rates paid on overnight fed funds. The FOMC sets a 25-bps target for the EFFR.

EXHIBIT 9.11 LIBOR–OIS

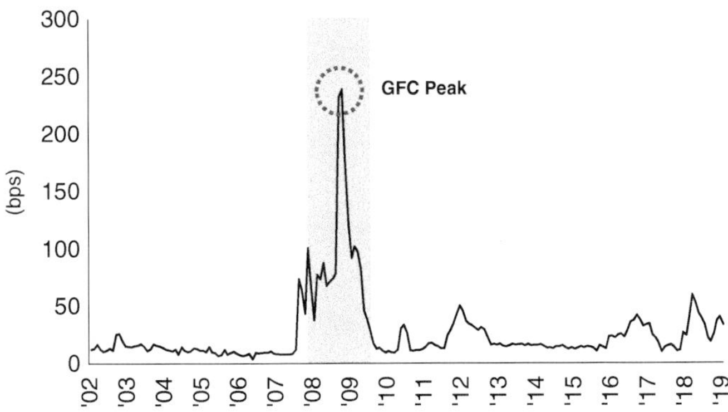

Source: Bloomberg

REPO RATES

Effectively a collateralized loan, a borrower sells securities to a lender with an agreement to repurchase (Repos) it later. These securities serve as collateral, and the repo rate is the difference between the sale price and the repurchase price (aka a zero-coupon loan). Given the phase out of LIBOR, the Kansas City Fed replaced LIBOR with the Repo rate in the TED Spread, which is one of the 11 variables used in constructing the KCFSI Kansas City Financial Stress Index. Repo rates are important to monitor.

The repo rates published are based on three reference rates: TGCR (Tri-Party General Collateral Rate), based on data collected from BNY Mellon; BGCR (Broad General Collateral Rate), based on the TGCR data and general collateral financing repo rates from DTCC; and SOFR (Secured Overnight Financing Rate), which is the broadest measure, including the BGCR data and rates from the DVP (Delivery versus Payment) market where counterparties can identify specific securities (Exhibit 9.12). SOFR is the heir apparent for LIBOR, as LIBOR gets phased out in 2021. SOFR–OIS will not have the same predictive power as LIBOR–OIS since it is through a centralized party and reduces the counterparty risk component.

Unlike the fed funds rate, the repo rate is secured and as such should be lower than the fed funds rate in normal circumstances. September 2019 saw repo rates spike significantly. During that time there were a variety of explanations, some of which made sense. September 16, 2019, was the deadline for quarterly corporate tax payments. The settlement of a large treasury auction also took place on the same day. As a result, reserves declined by \$120B over a two-day period. Large banks that would normally lend to the repo market

EXHIBIT 9.12 SOFR Repo Rates

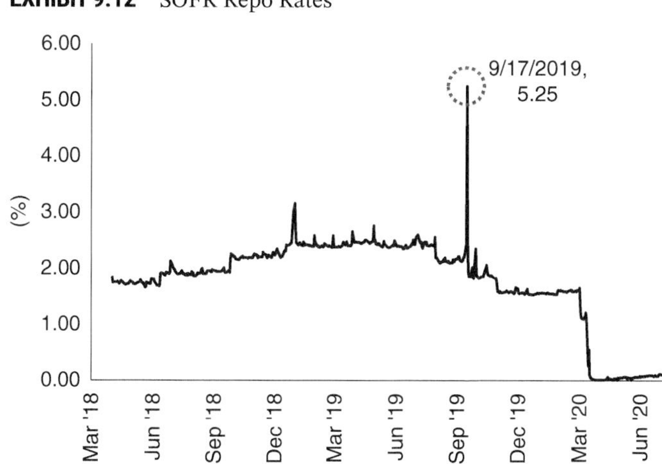

Source: St. Louis Federal Reserve

to take advantage of the higher rates were not able to do so due to resolution planning and liquidity requirements. Additionally, there were likely increased requirements from hedge funds for secured funding.

Jamie Dimon, on the J.P. Morgan earnings call said in reference to the repo rate spike and the bank's account with the Fed: "*But now the cash in the account which is still huge, it's $120 billion in the morning, it goes down to $60 billion during the course of the day and back to $120 billion at the end of the day, that cash we believe is required on the resolution and recovery and liquidity stress testing. And therefore, we could not redeploy it into repo market which we would have been happy to do. And I think it is up to the regulators to decide they want to recalibrate the kind of liquidity they expect us to keep in that account.*"

We believe the repo rate spike was a function of the mechanics of the market in conjunction with a confluence of factors rather than a precursor of the events of March 2020. The spike was a cry for help emanating from participants accessing a plumbing mechanism that had started to creak even without any significant issue. The repo distribution is clearly in need of reform to ensure that a cascade of events contributing to sequential increase in stress and financial contagion is not set off. One way this could be achieved would be for the Fed to provide repo directly to non-banks. However, this may be fraught with political risk as the optics of the Fed lending to hedge funds may not go down well with certain constituencies.

UNEMPLOYMENT RATE

The unemployment rate crossing and going above its own 12-month Moving Average has historically been a good indicator that a recession has commenced (Exhibit 9.13). This technical indicator, similar to using stock moving averages as support and resistance lines, helps frame the velocity and magnitude of changes in employment. We heard this originally on a call hosted by DoubleLine Capital and view it as a good metric to track.

EXHIBIT 9.13 Unemployment Rate vs. the 4 Quarter M.A.

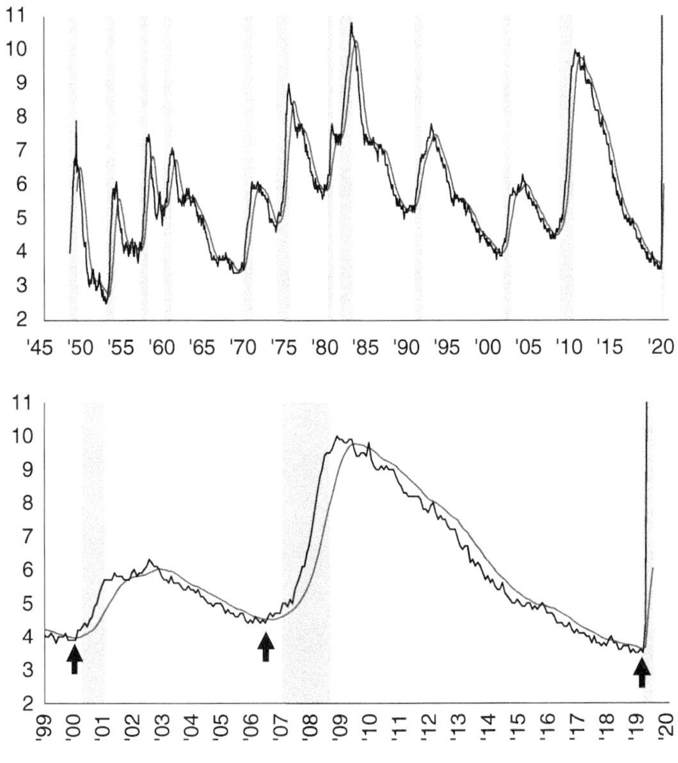

Source: St. Louis Federal Reserve

OTHER INDICATORS TO TRACK

There is a long list of indicators that an investor needs to keep an eye out for. We present next a short list of some other important indicators.

BUSINESS CYCLE INDICATORS

There are numerous other indicators that market participants should continually look at including money supply, real GDP growth, housing starts, unemployment, jobless claims, S&P 500, manufacturing PMI (purchasing managers index), consumer confidence, Market Capitalization to GDP.

CREDIT CYCLE INDICATORS

Apart from these business cycle indicators, we believe participants should also monitor a few credit cycle indicators: Covenant Lite issuance trends, LBO issuance as % of HY issuance, M&A issuance as % of HY issuance, EBITDA/Interest Expense trends, overall HY Debt/EBITDA (ex Energy, Metals, and Mining), Senior Loan Officer Survey % Tightening (this is correlated with HY spreads), overall M&A and LBO Volume, Debt as % of GDP, spread per unit of leverage, NY Fed Consumer Debt stats, Credit Card NCOs and Delinquencies, subprime mortgage and auto originations, IG leverage, New Issue leverage, and CDS spreads.

INFLATION MEASURES

Pay close attention to inflation measures, specifically the change in Headline and Core (excludes Food and Energy) PCE (Personal Consumption Expenditures), Headline and Core CPI (Consumer Price Index), average hourly earnings, and the price of Copper (we believe that Dr. Copper still has some efficacy despite its relevance as an inflation measure being called into question by some). We believe that the BLS (Bureau of Labor Statistics) inflation measures understate inflation due to some anomalies, chief among which is that healthcare is a much lower percentage of the basket than it is a percentage of GDP. That said, it is important to focus on this since the FOMC watches inflation closely (PCE is the FOMC's favorite), and thus watching these headline inflation numbers could give insights into future Fed actions.

REFLEXIVITY AND SELF-FULFILLING PROPHECIES

While monitoring metrics it is important to keep some theories from the social sciences in mind. Two in particular are useful.

Karl Popper's reflexivity theory, which George Soros has expounded on and is similar to the Observer Effect in physics, has two principles: fallibility and reflexivity. Fallibility holds that human participants are fallible and thus their perception of the market and the actual market may be at variance. Reflexivity holds that the market observers will take action based on their perceived view of the market and these actions in effect change the market.

Robert K. Merton (father of Robert C. Merton of the Black Scholes Merton model fame) illustrated his concept of the self-fulfilling prophecy with a run on a hypothetical bank. The bank was solvent, but when depositors assumed it was not, there was a run which made their original false assumption come true. This can be extended to a scenario of talking oneself into a recession.

VALUATION

No discussion of business cycles would be complete without discussing valuation in some form. We have an entire chapter dedicated to that topic. We have decided to eschew placing in a chart here showing multiples at various market peaks and troughs over time. Stocks and the broader market are bound to be expensive at a peak and cheap at a trough. However, a stock and by extension the market does not go down merely because it is expensive, and it does not go up merely because it is cheap. That may have well been the case in a pre-Internet age where access to filings and call transcripts were difficult to come by or delayed. In the current environment, where the market is continually digesting these and numerous other tidbits of information, the mere understanding that a stock is expensive or cheap does not offer much of an edge. That said, one should look at valuation multiples of individual stocks and assess how many standard deviations it is away from the historical mean. If a stock is significantly more expensive or cheap versus not just peers but the historical mean, one needs to understand why that may be the case. Are the estimates off? Are there aspects of the franchise that are not fully reflected in the estimates? And in the case of an expensive stock, can the entity use its currency to make accretive acquisitions? Also, never use trough multiples on trough estimates or the other way around.

It is important to realize that charge-offs occur with a lag to the phase of the business cycle. Exhibit 9.14 shows net charge-offs as a percentage of the average loans. Given the lag, it is important to assess if estimates reflect credit costs appropriately from a magnitude and timing standpoint.

Be intellectually curious as to why valuations are where they are, but never be dogmatic about selling expensive names and buying cheap names. In doing so you are just assuming that the entire market is wrong. That may very well be the case, but the burden of proof and the amount of due diligence

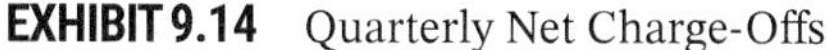

EXHIBIT 9.14 Quarterly Net Charge-Offs

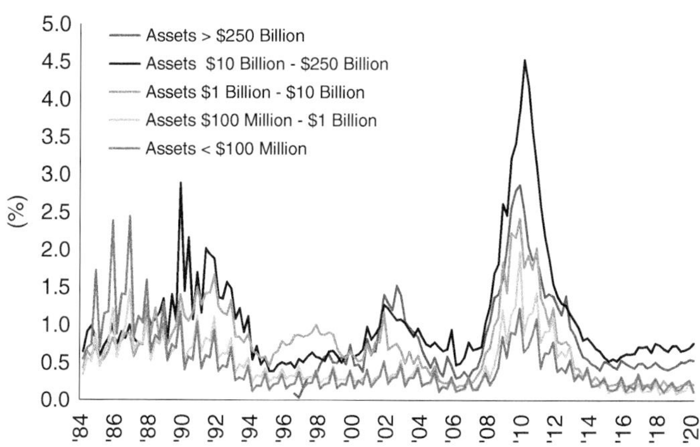

Source: FDIC

should be high. As an anecdote in the Fintech Catalyst strategy, which one of the authors has managed since May 31, 2015, we saw 20 acquisitions over 19 quarters. However, we saw M&A premium erode over that time frame. We took that to be a sign that valuations were stretched when even well thought out strategic M&A was receiving a tepid reception in the market.

10

Conversations

"I believe in the discipline of mastering the best that other people have ever figured out. I do not believe in just sitting down and trying to dream it all up yourself. Nobody is that smart."

– Charlie Munger

ALWAYS BE LEARNING

We believe that reading and continually learning from others is important to hone investing skill. Learning from a book is essential for the basics, but to improve one's craft it is important to be immersed in continuous conversations with management teams, investors, analysts, and all market and industry participants. One of the authors, Suhail Chandy, meets with over 150 bank management teams a year (in addition to fintech, real estate, financials and technology management teams) and has benefited immensely from the cross pollination of ideas, thoughts and learnings. The following thirteen conversations are with a diverse set of accomplished industry leaders and investors. These conversations reflect the thinking as of a certain point in time. The experience set of these individuals includes:

Founders: Five founders who between them have founded three banks and four investment management firms.

C-Suite: Five public company C-Suite members including one fintech CEO, two bank CEOs, one chairman, and one vice chairman.

Investors: Seven investors, including the deputy CIO of a $150B AUM firm, a bank investor from a trillion-dollar AUM firm, a founder of a $3B AUM investment firm focused on complete capital structure analysis, two founders of financial services–focused investing firms, a CIO of credit at a $3B AUM firm, and an activist.

Rates Strategist: One top-ranked rates strategist.

CONVERSATION PARTICIPANTS

Management

1. Matt Flake; CEO and President, Q2
2. Dale Gibbons; Vice Chairman and CFO, Western Alliance Bancorporation
3. Vernon W. Hill II; Chairman, Republic First Bancorp
4. Christopher T. Holmes; President & CEO, FirstBank
5. Dennis "Denny" S. Hudson III; Chairman and CEO, Seacoast Banking Corporation

Investors

6. Abbott Cooper; Founder and Managing Member, Driver Management Company LLC
7. Fred Cummings; President and Founder, Elizabeth Park Capital Management
8. Peter Duffy, CFA; CIO of Credit, Penn Capital Management
9. Chris Fortune, CFA; Vice President, T. Rowe Price
10. Martin Friedman; Co-Founder, Managing Member and CEO, FJ Capital Management
11. Rich Hocker; Founder and CEO, Penn Capital Management
12. Jeffrey Sherman, CFA; Deputy Chief Investment Officer, DoubleLine

Rates Strategist

13. Ian Lyngen, CFA, Managing Director, Head of US Rates Strategy, BMO Capital Markets

Matt Flake

CEO AND PRESIDENT, Q2

Matt currently serves as Chief Executive Officer and President of Q2 and is a member of the Board of Directors. He has been with Q2 since its founding in 2005.

During his tenure at Q2, he's been a significant contributor to the growth and strategic direction of the organization. With more than 20 years of experience in the financial services industry, including sales and banking operations, Matt is intensely determined to help regional and community-focused financial institutions compete with megabanks and

(continued)

(continued)

money center banks. He is a recipient of the esteemed EY Entrepreneur of the Year Award in the Central Texas region and was an EY Entrepreneur of the Year national finalist.

Matt received his degree from Baylor University and is currently a member of the Dell Children's Hospital Board of Trustees.

1. **Matt, prior to Q2, you were also at Q-Up and S-1 with Hank Seale. Take us through the history of Q2's founding and evolution?**

   Hank founded Q2 in 2004 because he wasn't happy with the way things had gone after S1's acquisition of Q-Up, and he ultimately didn't believe there was an online banking company approaching the space in the right way to really help community financial institutions. Hank, a deep believer in the importance of community financial institutions, saw that technology had the power to be the great equalizer for community banks. With the right digital partner, technology could put community banks on as close to a level playing field with the megabanks as they'd ever been. So, he founded Q2 with a mission: to build stronger communities by strengthening their financial institutions.

   At that time, almost every bank in the country had an online banking system already, and many viewed it as a commoditized market. To this day Hank often quotes something he heard many, many times upon founding Q2: "There just isn't enough room for another online banking company. There's no way you'll succeed."

   What Hank saw early on was that vendors in the space continued to develop a unique system every time a new feature, product, or channel came about. Meanwhile, the pace of technological change was growing considerably in the early 2000s. This meant that for community banks to keep up, they'd be forced to continue bolting on new technologies and managing an ever-growing pile of systems, integrations, and the processes to support them. Hank believed they'd be buried under the weight of technology, rather than being able to leverage it to operate more efficiently and compete with the megabanks.

   Hank's proposed solution, totally novel at this time, was a single platform architecture that would allow a bank to have and maintain a single digital banking system that could serve as the hub for all of their digital activity; that could handle the burden of integrating to other third-party systems for the bank, rather than subjecting the bank to manage all of that technology and all of those integrations on their own. The idea was that we could reduce the complexity of managing technology for banks, make it infinitely more scalable, and run all of their digital functionality through a single user experience.

We started pitching this idea to Texas banks in 2005, and today we have more than 400 banks and credit unions of all shapes and sizes using our digital banking platform.

2. **What do banks need to do to embrace digital banking and become future proof?**

Embracing digital banking is really about a cultural or mindset shift. It starts by thinking about digital as more than just a self-service channel for account holders. Technology should not merely replace every physical product and service a financial institution offers; it should enable financial institutions to do things that were never possible in the old brick-and-mortar banking model. For example, with the right technology, a financial institution can acquire customers anywhere in the country – meaning they're no longer restricted to their traditional geographic footprint. This is the kind of game-changing outcome that technology can create for financial institutions who think about using it for more than just self-service.

From a pure technology perspective, to become future proof we encourage financial institutions to focus on open platform technologies that "play nice" with other systems; that share data and create a cohesive user experience, even as the user navigates from one underlying technology to another.

3. **Digital banking is seeing competition from large incumbents and smaller venture backed start-ups. What does Q2 do to stay competitive and maintain a refreshed stable of products given the pace of change in technology stack as well as expectations on user experience?**

We always start by listening to our customers. They know better than anyone what challenges they, and the industry at large, are facing, even if they don't know the perfect technology solution to those challenges. That's what we believe our job is.

One of the biggest things we've learned in recent years is that the definition of digital banking has changed. It's no longer just an online service channel; technology pervades every area of the financial institution's business and every interaction they have with account holders. While continued innovation within conventional online and mobile banking is important, we don't believe there is one magic feature that will suddenly solve all financial institutions' digital challenges. Account holders are looking for a single, cohesive experience across every digital interaction, from the moment they become a customer to the daily management of their finances, to how quickly and easily they can apply for – and receive – a loan. The customer doesn't care, or need to know, that these are separate functions, products, or business units within the bank.

Historically, these experiences have been extremely fragmented; some are digital, some are in-branch or on paper, and some are a mix of both.

And very few of them work cleanly together to create or share a single view of the account holder's financial information and position.

It's because of this that we've made investments over the past few years in modern, open, platform-based technologies in each of these areas. Our portfolio, centered around our digital banking platform, now includes differentiated technologies for account opening and customer acquisition, risk management and compliance, digital lending for multiple asset classes, and sales and relationship management tools. And it is critical that each of these technologies is modern and designed to work tightly with other systems; most legacy banking technology is old and closed loop, which creates a fragmented experience for account holders. The end goal is that we will integrate these technologies and give our customers the ability to offer a completely integrated and cohesive technology stack that spans their relationship with account holders.

4. **Anecdotally, based on banks we have spoken with, we have seen big ramps in usage of mobile banking once a customer starts using Q2. Can you give us a sense of what the ramp across the board is for Q2 customers in years 1 and 2 after adoption?**

   The ramp in number of mobile banking users can vary pretty substantially depending on the specific financial institution, how digitally enabled their customer base is, how sophisticated their marketing and communications efforts are around transitioning to a new online and mobile system, and so on. It's difficult to isolate the factors that influence numbers like this and attribute growth specifically to Q2.

   We do believe it's meaningful to look at other measures of digital engagement and usage and how they change over time. Metrics like how many times users log in in a month on average, how much time a user spends in the mobile channel once they've logged in, number of transactions or volume of dollars moved through the system in a given period, and so on start to paint a fuller picture of digital usage for our customers. We generally see improvement in these numbers over time as customers move over to our systems, and I believe it's easier to attribute some of this growth to how we design and deliver our software than pure mobile user growth.

5. **How do you see traditional banks and neobanks competing and co-existing? Does each side need to emulate some of the best practices on either side? Perhaps neobanks need to adopt the approach to credit and underwriting done by traditional banks while traditional banks need to embrace open banking and integrate more APIs into their infrastructure?**

   In general, we take the stance that traditional financial institutions and newcomer neobanks and fintech companies each have their strengths and weaknesses, and that the success of one group does not have to come at the expense of the other.

Fintechs, or neobanks, have proven to be very good at creating digital-first financial products. Generally speaking, these are companies who have been born in the digital age, so they have the distinct advantage of getting to build their products from scratch with all the modern technology and user experience expertise available today. Meanwhile, traditional financial institutions have the much tougher job of trying to port legacy products and services into the digital channel that have deep dependencies on the traditional brick-and-mortar, 9-to-5 banking model.

Financial institutions, however, still have a massive advantage in terms of breadth of products and services. Most fintechs achieve success by picking a single product or service in the financial services ecosystem and perfecting it; once they've done that, though, they feel immense pressure to expand their offering. And that's where financial institutions' biggest advantage comes into play: their regulatory standing and infrastructure. The bottom line is, you still need a bank (or credit union) charter in order to offer some of the most fundamental banking products, like a checking or savings account. So while fintechs are nibbling around the edges of financial services – some with impressive success – they are generally challenged to move more towards the center of the ecosystem, and that's where the real value lies for companies looking to enter the financial services space.

These factors create an environment where financial institutions and fintechs/neobanks are naturally suited for partnership with one another. We see a new hybrid model gaining serious traction, where fintechs are building front-end experiences that most traditional financial institutions couldn't, while partnering with financial institutions to provide the regulatory infrastructure that powers these products in the background. We have a line of business called Q2 Open that's aimed at facilitating these partnerships via a common technology that helps these two groups communicate and partner effectively.

Dale Gibbons

VICE CHAIRMAN AND CFO, WESTERN ALLIANCE BANCORPORATION

Dale M. Gibbons is Vice Chairman of Western Alliance Bancorporation and has been Chief Financial Officer since May 2003. Mr. Gibbons has more than 30 years of experience in commercial banking, including serving as Chief Financial Officer and Secretary of the Board of Zions Bancorporation from August 1996 to June 2001. From 1979 to 1996, he worked for First Interstate Bancorp in a variety of retail banking and financial management positions. Mr. Gibbons is a summa cum laude graduate of Arizona State University and a CPA.

1. **How do you see the pandemic-induced crisis play out versus the GFC?**

   The current crisis is a lot different than the GFC on three elements.

   (a) *The event itself:*

   The event is a self-induced economic downturn to mitigate the health costs of the worst pandemic in a century. However, dramatic strides in medical technology appear likely to drive the development of effective therapeutics and a vaccine in far less time than ever before. These successes will affect the shape of the recovery curve. The GFC was an L; we can argue what letter the current crisis takes whether it could be a V, a W, or a U but we see an end to it.

   (b) *Secondly, the fiscal response:*

   The dramatic fiscal response providing trillions in economic relief through PPP, direct payments to families, and enhanced unemployment benefits has sharply deferred, if not precluded, much of the financial hardship that would have otherwise taken place. For financial institutions, loss expectation has historically correlated highly with unemployment. However, these programs have propped up household income despite much higher unemployment levels, which will reduce credit losses.

   (c) *Lastly, monetary policy:*

   The Fed cutting rates to zero and massive balance sheet expansion from bond purchases has moved the needle on system liquidity. The bond purchases have collapsed spreads and thus they have quenched the thirst for funding by preventing credit markets from seizing up. At the end of the day, I expect there is a cost to all of this money printing, but expect that reckoning is further out after inflation has been rekindled.

2. **Talk to us about the credit and underwriting process at WAL that allows you to generate very high risk-adjusted loan yields versus peers?**

   Most significant is that we have self-selected business lines with fewer competitors and better loss metrics. We do not attempt to offer a complete array of financial products. Instead, we've focused on our strengths and where we can obtain expertise in a particular business line. Case in point is when we acquired Bridge. We saw that Silicon Valley Bank was enjoying superior risk-adjusted returns in its business model, but rather than try to develop this business in house, we acquired an organization that had demonstrated that they can effectively execute.

   Through this process we assimilated several national business lines in areas that are not commoditized and operate efficiently without a high-cost infrastructure. Consumer banking is a particularly challenging area and one we largely avoid as it is most susceptible to commoditization, which will flatten margins over time. Consumer-focused regional banks will have a difficult time as the megabanks with better AI decisioning and mobile apps have a sustained competitive advantage in servicing this sector. On the other hand, AI is not as effective for commercial underwriting, as clients are more heterogeneous and require far more complex AI systems to be developed for smaller populations than the consumer space.

3. **What is your philosophy towards ALCO and balance sheet management? What are the overarching goals in balance sheet management and what tools have you used to accomplish those goals?**

   The primary goal of ALM is to have sufficient liquidity and capital: liquidity to meet client demand for credit needs and depositor withdrawals, and capital to cover for a black swan event that would be in excess of credit loss models. However, a well-managed balance sheet will also be a substantial contributor to net interest income that is well balanced to produce stable revenue, even during periods of substantial interest rate volatility.

   We assess interest rate risk through simulation and economic value of equity models. EVE is more theoretical and assumption reliant, but if one just looks at just simulation, they will miss tail risk. You can capture the tails better with economic value of equity.

4. **What is your take on CECL? Is it procyclical, impactful on M&A, etc.?**

   While CECL is certainly procyclical, I think the biggest flaw in the methodology is that it abandons the matching principle of accounting that revenue should be recognized in the same period as the cost to produce that revenue was incurred. This is Accounting 101. The FASB knows this as demonstrated with the promulgation of FAS 91 some years ago that defers loan origination costs and amortizes them by reducing interest revenue over the life of the loan. With CECL they have walked away from this and require registrants to provide for cumulative losses on day 1 of origination. This does not reflect market value of the credit and impairs comparability across companies as a growing enterprise reports lower earnings, while one harvesting market share may show provision reversals and greater income. This reduces the relationship between EPS and franchise value. I expect analysts will start looking at some variant of EPS such as PPNR less net charge-offs on a per share basis since GAAP EPS has become a less useful indicator with CECL.

5. **Talk to us about your tech spending priority over the next five years?**

   Security is number one. The relentless bombardment of cyber attacks mandates constant vigilance. Treasury services are also very important for us, enhancing ease of use and providing intuitive features and functions. We look at things to see what the MVP (minimum viable product) is and pick our battles for entry into new verticals. Not all product arrays will be highly competitive, but our products will be deep where we focus.

6. **What are the key attributes of high-quality bank franchises?**

   I have long believed that bank value is primarily derived from its funding base. Creating a low-cost, stable deposit base gives the organization optionality to do the best for shareholders for asset selection.

   A bank with low loans to deposits may not be maximizing shareholder returns, but has much more opportunity to improve its performance than one with a weak funding structure. Insufficient liquidity is often the first symptom of serious financial mismanagement.

7. **Anything else that you would like to share with readers?**

   While I applaud the fiscal and monetary response to COVID-19, I fear the precedents set by these actions and the salve they provided will encourage continued use even when future circumstances are not as dire as the pandemic. Modern monetary theory suggests that one can do everything one desires with money printing so long as you control the printing press and inflation is managed. Not to be flip, but my view is you can until you can't. Ultimately it is all about confidence in pieces of paper. At some point in time that belief and reliance can come to an end and if the public perception turns that the emperor has no clothes, I don't think it'll be possible to regain monetary confidence.

Vernon W. Hill II

CHAIRMAN, REPUBLIC FIRST BANCORP

Vernon W. Hill II is the Chairman of Republic First Bancorp, Inc. He is also the Founder of Metro Bank, London, Britain's first new retail bank in 100+ years. Often credited with reinventing American banking, Vernon was the founder and former Chairman and President of Commerce Bank, which he founded in 1973.

1. **Identifying great locations and branch design and signage is one differentiating attribute of your banks. We have seen that in the way you have breathed life into and improved the visibility of the Republic Bank branches, the brand recognition for Metro in the UK, and the success enjoyed by Commerce (Exhibits** 10.1 **and** 10.2**). What are the characteristics of great locations? How can locational advantages be leveraged in a digital age?**

EXHIBIT 10.1 Commerce Bank Growth

Date	Assets ($ millions)	Deposits ($ millions)	Deposit Growth %	Comp Store Deposit Growth	Stock Price	Market Cap ($ millions)	Market Cap / Deposits %	# of Years in Business
12/31/1995	$ 3,022	$ 2,789	33%		$ 3.47	$ 237	8.5%	23
12/31/1996	$ 3,593	$ 3,252	17%	10%	$ 5.43	$ 486	14.9%	24
12/31/1997	$ 4,388	$ 3,785	16%	11%	$ 8.81	$ 835	22.1%	25
12/31/1998	$ 5,424	$ 4,929	30%	26%	$11.90	$ 1,573	31.9%	26
12/31/1999	$ 6,636	$ 5,609	14%	14%	$ 9.63	$ 1,145	20.4%	27
12/31/2000	$ 8,297	$ 7,388	32%	15%	$17.09	$ 2,172	29.4%	28
12/31/2001	$ 11,364	$ 10,186	38%	27%	$19.67	$ 2,582	25.3%	29
12/31/2002	$ 16,404	$ 14,549	43%	29%	$21.60	$ 2,930	20.1%	30
12/31/2003	$ 22,712	$ 20,701	42%	27%	$26.34	$ 4,030	19.5%	31
12/31/2004	$ 30,502	$ 27,659	34%	32%	$32.20	$ 5,147	18.6%	32
12/31/2005	$ 38,466	$ 34,727	26%	25%	$34.41	$ 6,148	17.7%	33
12/31/2006	$ 45,272	$ 41,288	19%	17%	$35.27	$ 6,649	16.1%	34
10/2/2007	$ 49,994	$ 46,534			$42.37*	$ 8,500	18.3%	35
	Average Annual Comp Store Growth			31%				
	Rate over 5-Year Period (2002–2006)							

*Represents CBH stock value on date of announced merger.

0.4142 shares of TD stock exchanges for each Commerce Share

TD Stock Value	$ 31.87
Cash	$ 10.50
Total Value	$ 42.37

Source: Vernon Hill

EXHIBIT 10.2 Top 50 Banks Ranked by 10-Year Return as of 12/31/2006

Symbol	Bank	HQ	Assets ($bn)	Market Cap ($bn)	10-Year Return	5-Year Return	1-Year Return
IFIN	Investors Financial Corp.	Boston, MA	11.6	2.8	28.77%	5.41%	16.14%
CBH	Commerce Bancorp, Inc.	Cherry Hill, NJ	45.3	6.3	22.67%	13.97%	3.89%
COF	Capital One	McLean, VA	150	33.6	20.73%	7.52%	−11.00%
BOKF	BOK Financial	Tulsa, OK	18.1	3.5	17.69%	14.18%	22.41%
C	Citigroup	New York, NY	1882.6	262.3	17.19%	6.74%	19.52%
USB	U.S. Bancorp	Minneapolis, MN	219.2	63.3	17.16%	16.27%	26.39%
MTB	M&T Bancorp	Buffalo, NY	57.1	13.4	17.09%	12.67%	14.23%
STT	State Street Corp	Boston, MA	107.4	22.7	16.58%	6.63%	23.29%
CBSS	Compass Bancshares	Birmingham, AL	34.2	8	16.57%	19.64%	27.22%
UB	Union BanCal	San Francisco, CA	52.6	8.9	16.25%	12.88%	−8.30%
MRBK	Mercantile Bancshares	Baltimore, MD	17.7	6	15.89%	13.57%	28.00%
CFR	Cullen Frost	San Antonio, TX	13.2	3.2	15.68%	15.36%	6.46%

Source: Vernon Hill

Your brand is who you are, what you are, what the customer expects.
- *Design is a competitive weapon.*
- *In retailing and banking your store is your brand identity.*
- *We have learned that the best site is almost always worth the price. Roughly, for each $1 million we pay in extra land costs, we need only $1 million in added deposits.*
- *Today, delivery is about the experience, i.e. Apple, where all delivery channels and products are unified and reinforcing.*

2. **Prior to your storied career as a bank founder you had a background in real estate, where you helped Ray Kroc of McDonald's in finding sites. What were some things you learned from that experience?**
   - *Your mission is to create fans not customers.*
   - *Your brand is your greatest asset.*
   - *Great sites produce higher sales (deposits).*
3. **The banks that you have founded ushered in exemplary levels of customer service. How does customer service need to adapt when a cellphone delivers on many of the tasks people conducted at a branch?**
   - *Customers want the best of every channel, and they all must deliver a unified experience.*
   - *Apple stores deliver the highest sales per square foot of any retailer, and they do not need stores.*
   - *The customer wants a choice, not forced into any channel.*
   - *Online only banks have yet to succeed.*
4. **Your book *Fans! Not Customers: How to Create Growth Companies in a No Growth World* is something we recommend to our readers in this book. There is a lot of sage advice there on strategy, branding, customer service, and culture. What are some of the things a bank needs to do to differentiate and grow?**

   MODEL:
   - *Creating fans is #1.*
   - *Must be value added and differentiated.*
   - *No stupid rules.*

   CULTURE:
   - *Must be persuasive and supporting the model.*
   - *Culture has no meaning without a clear model.*

   EXECUTION:
   - *Fanatic execution.*
   - *No stupid rules.*
   - *Renewed success.*

5. **What are the key attributes of high-quality bank franchises?**
    - *Create fans.*
    - *Low-cost deposit base.*
    - *Local banks serving local communities.*
    - *Leadership from the top.*
6. **Anything else that you would like to share with readers?**

    Focus on answering the following questions:
    - *What is your model?*
    - *What is your value added?*
    - *Am I creating fans?*
    - *Do I have a growth machine?*
    - *Successful entrepreneurs develop informed instinct.*
    - *Everyone has a unique talent.*
    - *Stars are those who match their unique talent with their profession.*

Christopher T. Holmes

PRESIDENT AND CEO, FIRSTBANK

Chris Holmes was named President of FirstBank in 2012 and CEO in 2013 as part of a planned transition of the bank's executive leadership. While his career has included work in 14 countries around the world, his global view of economics includes an understanding that banking is driven by local needs and providing individual service to customers. Originally from Lexington, Tennessee, Chris has a background in both rural communities and urban metro centers that is uniquely suited for leadership at FirstBank. As President and CEO, Chris is responsible for leading and managing all facets of the bank's operations, including establishing its long-term goals, strategies, and corporate vision.

In 2016, Chris led FirstBank's transition from a privately held, single shareholder bank to a publicly traded company listed on the New York Stock Exchange. FB Financial Corp.'s initial public offering, which closed with $128.5 million in proceeds, was the largest IPO in Tennessee banking history. Chris also led the 2015 acquisition of Northwest Georgia Bank and the 2017 acquisitions of Clayton Bank and Trust and American City Bank, which expanded the bank's footprint across Tennessee. Most recently, Chris negotiated the purchase of 14 retail branch locations from Atlantic Capital Bank, which further increases the bank's presence in the Knoxville, Chattanooga, and North Georgia markets.

Prior to joining FirstBank in 2010 as Chief Banking Officer, Chris served as the Director of Corporate Financial Services and the Chief Retail Banking Officer for Greenville, South Carolina–based South Financial Group. Previously, he worked for 20 years in the Memphis-area market, first with EY and then in several management positions for National Bank of Commerce, which was acquired by SunTrust, and Trustmark National Bank. Currently, Chris serves as a Director on the following boards: FB Financial Corporation (FBK), FirstBank, Delta Dental, Hospital Hospitality House, Nashville Area Chamber of Commerce, Nashville Symphony Association, Nashville Zoo at Grassmere, Tennessee Bankers Association, Vice Chairman, Executive Committee, Tennessee Hospital Association, YMCA of Middle Tennessee, Executive Committee.

In addition, Chris serves as a founding member of the Coalition for Better Health Steering Committee, which is a subgroup of the Governor's Foundation for Health and Wellness. He is a 2014 graduate of Leadership Nashville.

Away from the office, Chris enjoys traveling and spending time with his wife, Susan, and three daughters, Hayley, Hannah, and Hope. He also enjoys hunting, biking, snow skiing, and playing golf.

1. **Walk us through First Bank's evolution from $14MM to $6B in assets.**

   You can find a good summary of our story in the Prospectus that we filed with our initial public offering in September of 2016. The inception of the bank was in rural Tennessee, as a community bank in a small town with less than 1,000 people. From 1906 through 1984 the bank had amassed a robust $14 million in total assets. In 1984 the bank was purchased by two partners: Steve White who supplied half of the $1.5 million purchase price and managed the bank, and Jim Ayers who supplied the other half of the purchase price. The two partners set out to grow the bank, and in 1986 the bank expanded into the county seat of Lexington, Tennessee, as branching was only permitted in the county where the bank was chartered. The new owners instilled a growth culture and the bank had tripled in size in four years. The bank then seized on the opportunity to buy the two branches of one of the two competitors in town. Shortly after the purchase, Ayers bought the interest of his partner and became the sole shareholder. The bank continued to grow organically and through small acquisitions in rural West Tennessee over the next decade. In 2000, the bank made its initial entry to metropolitan markets by opening branches in Memphis and Nashville. Over the next decade, the bank continued to grow organically and branch across Tennessee including entering the Knoxville and Chattanooga markets. The bank used a familiar model of accumulating deposits in small communities and making loans in *metropolitan communities. Unfortunately, the bank suffered the same fate of many community banks that branched into metro markets during the early 2000s when the great recession of the late 2000s caused substantial loan losses. The bank survived the recession, and in 2010 developed a strategy to become a full-service community bank in both its metropolitan and community markets. The strategy changed from simply making loans in the metropolitan markets to becoming the leading community bank in each of its markets, including Nashville, Memphis, Knoxville, and Chattanooga. Once the goal was set and the capital commitment was made, the bank set out to attract the talent, build the delivery systems, and acquire the technology needed to become a market dominating bank. The last ten years, the bank has stuck to that strategy with some minor adjustments as we have grown. We have been successful because we simply amplified our existing community banking culture versus changing the culture. The community approach resonated with people in the larger markets. When you have 60 competitor banks in the market (Nashville has 60 banks in the market), you have to be able to differentiate your brand and get scale. We created a differentiated strategy with our community approach in an urban market, and when it was successful, set out to make it scalable. Today, we talk about being a scalable community bank. The community approach operates according to a set of values. For instance, when we entered Nashville, we divided the MSA by communities and hired a leader in each community. We hired a president in each community with local community knowledge who went to high school in the community, is a member of the Rotary club, attends the PTA meetings, and goes to the local high school football games. Today we get calls and resumes from experienced bankers in Atlanta, Charlotte, and other places who want to move to Nashville because it has become a hot market. These are solid, seasoned bankers. We do not even interview them because our model requires someone with local knowledge. We are hiring folks with local contacts and to develop local customer relationships. This community ethos is designed into our strategy and decision making.*

2. **First Bank has industry leading metrics on NIM and Efficiency. Tell us how about you manage the franchise to achieve these metrics given competitive pressures?**

   This is managed through an active management process. We teach people what is important for us and compensate them accordingly. Several of our executives and all of our directors are successful investors and have successful careers outside of the bank. We get business intelligence in real time. Competitive intelligence is very useful. Recently, we saw a bank offer an unsecured loan to our director at 1.76%. This bank also paid the borrower 1.05% for their deposits. The same officer at the bank is handling both the loans and deposits. The banker obviously has an incentive system to drive balances and not profitability. By our definition, that bank, which is a large regional bank, does not operate using sensible metrics. We are focused on revenue growth, credit quality, margins, efficiency, and return on capital. We are not afraid to walk away from business that does not meet the hurdles that drive those metrics for us. There is no magic formula. It is about being focused on the right measures and the discipline to stick to your values, goals, and metrics when you see others making bad decisions but winning business. They may benefit in the short term, but we will win the long game.

3. **You have done four whole bank deals and one branch deal in five years. What criteria do you set for M&A?**

   Some people consider us acquisitive. Our focus is really on organic growth and elite financial performance. All of our acquisitions were made to improve our financial performance. They were all in-market deals that improved our scale and operating leverage. The Kentucky transaction was in a contiguous market, but the bank was a family-owned bank and we got a great shareholder as a result. We are always trying to increase our market density, improve operating leverage, and enhance franchise value with in-market or contiguous deals. With that strategy, we get approached about a lot of transactions that we never consider. Financial metrics are very important. We don't want dilution to our tangible book value and the transaction has to be EPS accretive. We look at the culture and organizational fit. The deposit side of the balance sheet is also very important. We prefer banks with strong legacy core deposit customers. Deposit generation is harder than loan growth and takes longer to do organically. You don't grow core deposits quickly. When we can acquire solid, core deposit franchises, that is valuable to us. We can make loans faster than we can grow deposits. All of our transactions have stuck to this approach.

4. **You have one foot in the growing metro markets of Tennessee and the other in the community markets. What are some of the lessons you have learned as you straddle both markets?**

   In a community market of 15–20 thousand people, where we are one of the dominant banks, our bankers will know everyone in the community. Our bankers literally know everyone that walks into the bank. The large banks have an impersonal model that doesn't work in these smaller communities. We have basically used the same model in metropolitan markets, by subdividing the metro markets into communities and hiring people from those communities that understand the market and know the people. Folks like to know that there is someone they can reach out to by phone, email, or text. Even if they never come into the branch, someone at the bank who knows them and values their relationship is always within reach.

5. **Talk to us about your tech spending priority over the next five years?**

   We went through a core system change four years ago. We went to Jack Henry. Previously, we were on a smaller core system, not a big three core system, with significant limitations. The move to Jack Henry has allowed us to systematically upgrade all of our applications. We recently upgraded our treasury management system and have a strong treasury management team. We consistently win treasury management business head to head against the large national banks. We are currently doing an online and mobile conversion to the Banno platform. We have to be really good but haven't had to be leading edge. That is changing because our model is unique, we are finding things that we want to do that others aren't doing. That is causing us to hire more associates with technology expertise and look at additional spending. We are watching the evolution of core systems and open platforms. We are thinking about how we can further adapt the customer experience to what is unique to us. If we give a credit card to one of our customers with our brand and another company's 1-800 number, they will probably have a bad experience. The same can be said with the merchant services product. We are thinking about technologies to allow us to control every aspect of the customer experience. It is important for us to eventually have that ability. It is also important to have high quality data about your customers. When you have very good data, in some cases you know more about people than they know about themselves and can help them understand what is coming in their financial lives before they have thought about it.

6. **What are the key attributes of high-quality bank franchises?**

   Having a differentiated customer value proposition is important. So many banks that we compete with have a strategy that is purely driven by financials or simply copies the large regional banks. The customer value proposition never gets consideration. We don't believe there are that many great operators out there today in the small and midcap bank space. It is important to have a distinct customer value proposition and for bank employees to be able to understand it, articulate it, and have a laser focus on delivering it. The other key attribute is strong core deposits. We believe that a bank's market value is most directly correlated with the quality of the bank's core deposit portfolio. The advantage of being a bank is being able to offer FDIC-insured deposits. It is the one product that the non-banks can't offer.

7. **Anything else that you would like to share with readers?**

   We need more people with solid business acumen in banking today. There are a lot of good bankers and people that have financial acumen, but not enough with good business acumen.

Dennis "Denny" S. Hudson III

CHAIRMAN AND CEO, SEACOAST BANKING CORPORATION

Dennis "Denny" S. Hudson III was named Chairman of Seacoast in July 2005, and has served as Chief Executive Officer of the Company since June 1998. Mr. Hudson has also served as Chairman and Chief Executive Officer of the bank since 1992. He was President of Seacoast from June 1998 to July 2005, after serving in various positions with the company and the bank since 1978.

Mr. Hudson also serves on the board of directors, the audit committee, and the compensation committee of Chesapeake Utilities Corporation (ticker: CPK), a public gas and electric utilities company headquartered in Dover, Delaware. In November 2015, Mr. Hudson was appointed as an independent director to PENN Capital Funds, a mutual fund group managed by PENN Capital Management. Mr. Hudson also serves on the board of Martin Health System and the Community Foundation for Palm Beach and Martin Counties. From 2005 through 2010, he also served as a member of the board of directors of the Miami Branch of the Federal Reserve Bank of Atlanta.

Mr. Hudson is actively involved in the community, having served on the boards of the Martin County YMCA Foundation, Council on Aging, The Pine School, the Job Training Center, American Heart Association, Martin County United Way, the Historical Society of Martin County, and as chairman of the board of the Economic Council of Martin County. He has been recognized for his achievements with several awards including the Florida Senate Medallion of Excellence Award presented by Florida Senator Ken Pruitt in 2001. Mr. Hudson is a graduate of Florida State University with a Bachelor's degree in Finance, and a Master's degree in Business Administration.

1. **Seacoast is a franchise that has withstood the test of time over its 87-year history. What are some of the learnings over time that you would like to share?**

   Our mission has never changed – we help people improve their lives and build stronger communities. And yet the way we do that has changed many times over the last 87 years. Our leadership team sees great value in making sure we are consistent and disciplined in our focus on helping our customers while also innovating around how we do that. Compared to 10 years ago, today we rarely see our customers and so we have created new ways to support and maintain contact in order to meet their needs and deepen relationships.

2. **Seacoast has been a digital innovator to the extent that you have other banks coming to you to tap into your expertise. Take us**

through your digital journey: What has worked and what more needs to be done?

More than any other industry, banks have access to extremely valuable information about their customers. Everything a customer does is recorded and time-stamped in a bank's core processing system. At Seacoast we have compiled behavioral information over time as well as other data and are able to use it to better meet customer needs with timely, relevant conversations. Those conversations happen in our branches, on the phone and also through our digital channels. When you combine this capability with our understanding of the drivers of customer profitability, we have been able to serve customers better while also improving shareholder returns. The backbone of digital innovation for a bank is building an advanced analytics capability to take advantage of a bank's most valuable asset – its customer data. Without it, a bank cannot be successful as a digital innovator.

Over the last couple of years, we have added more analytics resources into support areas including credit, risk, and operations for example. This is helping us control costs by avoiding mistakes and has improved throughput using robotic process automation. There is much more to do here on the cost side.

3. **As you look at M&A opportunities, what are the key characteristics you seek and criteria you set?**

   At the front of that list would be a strong deposit franchise. Next would be robust customer relationships. And finally exposure to growth markets. The first and last items are fairly apparent while the middle one requires some work to value, which is where our analytics competency becomes valuable. When you have all three, we can usually rapidly build additional value beyond the value at purchase.

4. **Talk to us about your tech spending priority over the next five years?**

   The vast majority of our tech spending is outsourced to other scale players. Core processing costs continue to fall fairly rapidly as we increase spend around additional customer capabilities. So, most of our increase in spend is related to adding new capabilities via partners. Most of our internal spend is focused on enabling the use of customer insights by our people and digital channels, something none of our partners seem to care about because most of our peers haven't discovered how valuable it is.

5. **What are the key attributes of high-quality bank franchises?**

   The same attributes that are part of our M&A criteria, which are: strong deposit franchise, robust customer relationships, and exposure to growth markets. Add to these a sustainable ability to grow customers without taking on too much credit risk. The ability to achieve that last characteristic means the leadership team has a balanced and long-term focus on creating real value for customers and shareholders.

6. **Anything else that you would like to share with readers?**

   Lowering the cost to serve our customers will be an important goal for banks in the next few years. Low-cost digital channels will continue to expand across more services, as the branch channel will continue to play a smaller role in our customers' lives. While banks that get this right will find themselves with a distinct advantage, it will be in-market M&A that will accelerate many banks toward this important goal. Using the right M&A to quickly adjust what I believe is a massive oversupply in branches will, when combined with the shift to digital, create real value for shareholders over the next few years.

Abbott Cooper

FOUNDER AND MANAGING MEMBER, DRIVER MANAGEMENT COMPANY LLC

Abbott Cooper is the founder and managing member of Driver Management Company LLC. Prior to founding Driver, Abbott founded and was the senior portfolio manager of the Financial Opportunity Strategy at Hilton Capital Management. Prior to that, Abbott was a senior investment banker covering depository institutions at Jefferies and Bank of America Merrill Lynch. Abbott began his career as a corporate lawyer, focusing on public and private company mergers and acquisitions, corporate governance, contests for corporate control, and capital markets. Abbott has a JD from the University of Montana School of Law and a BA from the University of Virginia.

1. **What does it mean to be an activist in a regulated space with multiple regulators and multiple regulatory schemes? Banks are perceived to be special, and some consider themselves to be quasi utilities. How does one balance service to the community versus shareholder returns?**

   Unlike a widget company, banks are highly regulated industries and the goals/objectives/priorities of both lawmakers who enact legislation dealing with bank regulators and the regulators who implement that legislation (including through rule making) are not the same (and in many cases not consistent with) the goals/objectives/priorities of investors. An example is the focus on "control" of a bank or bank holding company, which is a status that comes with significant burdens and costs and can occur at significantly lower ownership thresholds than a normal person would consider evidence of "control." In addition, there are usually two regulators (and two different regulatory schemes) at play – the Federal Reserve at the bank holding company level and either the OCC (if the subsidiary bank is a federally chartered bank) or state regulators (if the subsidiary bank is state chartered) – and these regulators can have inconsistent interests. In particular, state regulators can be highly protective of the banks they regulate, since it is those banks' continued existence as independent entities that provides justification for the regulators' continued existence. Unlike the Federal Reserve, who has taken pains to outline clear rules of the road for equity investment in bank holding companies, many state banking laws and regulations are extremely vague, which can lead to unpredictable outcomes as well as the strong sensation of arbitrary and capricious enforcement driven by the desire of banks to entrench themselves and implemented by pressuring their state regulators.

In addition, due to a mixture of a strong lobby as well as the popular perception (reinforced by such films as It's a Wonderful Life), many community banks tend to view themselves as quasi-utilities, whose obligations are first and foremost to their customers, then to the communities in which they operate, and only after that are shareholder concerns and objectives taken into account. Not surprisingly, many of the banks with that type of mindset are among the worst performers in terms of shareholder return and important metrics such as return on equity. Nevertheless, this appeal to "serving the community" is often used as a rationale for actions that result in less optimal shareholder returns – particularly when a bank bases a decision not to seek a buyer out of a "concern for the community." Lost in this mindset, however, is the fact that the stronger a financial institution is (in terms of profitability, growth, etc.) the better it is able to serve customers, provide opportunities to employees, positively impact the communities in which it operates, and so on.

2. **This sector has a lot of M&A but no unsolicited bids. How do you convince the board to run a sale process?**

   Ultimately, the board has to realize that (i) the banking organization's stand-alone prospects are less than robust (due to the markets in which it operates, competition, deposit franchise, expense base, strength (or lack thereof) of management, etc.), (ii) shareholders are unhappy with returns and are looking for greater value, and (iii) there are other banks that are likely to pay a far greater price than where the bank's stock could reasonably be expected to trade on its own over the near to medium term. As a practical matter, it takes a lot of pushing to force board members to take a hard, objective look at the particular bank's performance and prospects relative to peers as well as to assess the market, economic, and other risks that lie ahead.

3. **Engagement process can be long but during lulls in M&A what do activists focus on?**

   The engagement process takes a lot of work and time — even when the M&A market is closed, it remains a good time to remind boards that windows of opportunity come and go and missing one can have a real adverse effect on shareholder value.

4. **Break down for the reader the nuts and bolts of an activist campaign? Most investors notice it when the first letter gets sent. What happens before that during the process? What are the state laws that allow for access to the shareholders?**

   At its core, an activist campaign at a bank is all about trying to provide a compelling case for change to different audiences. Given the restrictions on ownership with banks, it is even more important for a bank activist to be a catalyst for other shareholders to take a stand as well. Part of that is showing the market the value that can be obtained by shareholders through a particular course of action (generally through a sale) versus another (continuing on a stand-alone path). Being so dependent on other shareholders creates a lot of discipline – the activist's premise must be sound and the value to be created must be significant, otherwise other investors won't support the activist's objectives. Similarly, a reluctant board has an easier time dismissing an activist's demands if they are unreasonable, unrealistic, or unlikely to create value, so there is a tremendous amount of time and effort spent on identifying the right opportunities and rigorously testing a particular investment thesis, as well as the analysis that backs it up and the message that will get it across. There is also a lot of "lobbying," whether trying to demonstrate the merits of a course of action to a board or other shareholders, media outlets, and so on — whatever is necessary in order to create a situation where the board cannot hide from its shareholders and their expectations regarding value and value creation. State laws can vary a lot. Maryland law requires you to be a record holder of 5% or more of the common stock and for a period greater than six months for access to the stock ledger and obtain a list of shareholders. Delaware law requires you to be a record holder or beneficial owner, but does not specify the ownership amount or duration.

5. **How do you compare corporate governance at banks versus other sectors?**

   I don't have any empirical evidence, but banks generally seem behind the curve as far as adopting what are now considered "best practices" in corporate governance and the smaller the bank is, the more behind the curve it is likely to be.

Fred Cummings

PRESIDENT AND FOUNDER, ELIZABETH PARK CAPITAL MANAGEMENT

Fred Cummings is the President and Founder of Elizabeth Park Capital Management. He serves as Portfolio Manager for the privately-held, alternative asset management firm focused on long/short equity, event-driven, and customized investment opportunities in the banking sector. Mr. Cummings is a nationally-recognized investment and banking portfolio manager with 30+ years' industry experience leading disciplined, client-focused investment practices. His esteemed performance establishes him as a principled bellwether across the investing and banking industry. His singular focus on banks paired with his curated approach to investing, M&A, and risk analysis transcends the Elizabeth Park mission to be the best bank investment firm in the country.

Prior to founding Elizabeth Park, Fred achieved a distinguished 17-year career at KeyBanc Capital Markets as one of the sell-side's foremost Senior Analysts covering the banking sector. He additionally served as a Senior Analyst for FSI Group, a $150M hedge fund. He launched his career at McDonald & Co. as a sell-side Junior Analyst.

Fred earned his BA in Economics with honors from Oberlin College. He has actively supported Oberlin's Connect Cleveland Initiative and Business Scholars Speaking Program as an honored guest speaker for 23 consecutive years. He is an alumnus and ardent supporter of Western Reserve Academy (WRA). Fred dedicates his time serving on several boards, including The Marshall Project, Strategic Value Bank Partners, and Nirvana Analytics. He serves as an investment committee member for Laurel School and WRA.

Fred was named to 2017's Crain's Cleveland Business Who's Who and Cleveland.com*'s People to Watch in 2015. As an industry expert, he has been featured on various media outlets, including* The Wall Street Journal, INC Magazine, Crain's Cleveland Business, *and* CNN Money. *Fred lives in the Cleveland area with his wife and two daughters.*

1. **What is something in your background that may be of interest to the reader that is not in your profile?**

   I played football at Oberlin College and hold the record for the longest rushing touchdown from scrimmage of 99 yards.

2. **How did you get into investing, and specifically investing in banks?**

   In June 1989, I started my career as a junior bank analyst with McDonald & Company Securities in Cleveland, where I supported three senior analysts. I was promoted to the senior analyst position in May 1991.

3. **What would you be doing if you were not a professional investor?**

   A schoolteacher at some level.

4. **What are the salient aspects of your investment process and philosophy?**

   Invest in banks that we understand, which means we don't invest in the ten largest banks in the country. Emphasize a fundamental, bottom-up approach, with a focus on soundness, profitability, growth, and management quality. Identify attractive risk/reward opportunities. In general, we believe the banks with the best risk-adjusted returns on tangible common equity will trade at the highest multiples, both on tangible book value and forward EPS. Our investment style has remained consistent over time.

5. **How do you evaluate management?**

   We believe in having face-to-face meetings before initiating a position. We normally meet with over 200 banks each year in which we focus on their credit approval process and risk appetite, business model, profitability goals and growth targets, incentive compensation structure (cash/stock mix) across the bank, inside ownership, and capital management priorities.

6. **Do you derive any value from the sell side?**

   Yes. Sell side is helpful with providing management access, timely information on M&A appetite, and near-term changes in fundamental trends.

7. **Does fintech help (augment capabilities) or harm (disintermediate) banks? Does the impact differ between large versus small or consumer versus commercial?**

   Overall, my sense is that fintech has helped to augment or even level the playing field for small to mid-sized banks that don't have the resources to develop technological capabilities internally. The small to mid-sized banks need functionality, not customized solutions, and the fintech providers allow them to accomplish this.

8. **Consolidation has been a major theme in the bank space. How does it play into your investment strategy? Does bank consolidation increase, stay on pace?**

   Identifying likely sellers is a key aspect of our investment strategy since it allows us to generate uncorrelated returns. Our M&A focus is primarily reflected in the micro-cap banks (market-caps less than $250M) that we buy. At times, micro-cap banks have comprised 30% of our portfolio. These smaller banks generally are less profitable than their bigger competitors and have higher inside ownership, which provides alignment of interest. We have found that small banks with clean balance sheets, an attractive and low-cost deposit mix, and solid profitability have commanded significant change of control premiums over time. The stocks are routinely mispriced relative to their fundamentals based on the lack of trading liquidity.

9. **What are some of the cycle inflection indicators you pay attention to?**

   Early stage delinquencies and criticized/classified assets are the two key fundamental indicators we monitor closely. We also look at the slope of the yield curve.

Peter Duffy, CFA

CIO OF CREDIT, PENN CAPITAL MANAGEMENT

Mr. Duffy has been with Penn Capital since 2006. As CIO of Credit, he is responsible for guiding the firm's credit strategies. Mr. Duffy serves as a Senior Portfolio Manager for Penn Capital's Defensive, Short Duration High Yield, and Multi-Credit Spectrum strategies. He is also a member of the firm's Executive Team, which oversees the firm's overall corporate strategy and management.

Prior to joining Penn Capital, Mr. Duffy was a Director for Deutsche Asset Management's global high yield debt team. Previously, he was with GE Capital and was a management consultant at Arthur Andersen LLP. He received a BS in Finance summa cum laude from Villanova University and an MBA from The Wharton School of the University of Pennsylvania.

1. **Bank investors need to have a good understanding of credit analysis. What is your approach to credit analysis and investing?**

   We have a regimented checklist of items. We take a bottom up look at each individual credit by reviewing the fundamentals, the industry, and the documentation – bond indentures and loan creditor agreements. We layer this with a macro overview where we look at several items including the SLOOS (Senior Loan Officer Opinion Survey). Tightening and loosening standards are correlated with spreads. Overall valuation boils down to where we are in the cycle. Expected default rates drive spreads, and that is driven by the age of the lending cycle. This influences us on which types of credits we spend time on.
2. **What are some of the key items for credit analysis on your checklist (Exhibit 10.3)?**

   Understand the business model first, most importantly pricing power and capital intensity. Do they have pricing power, are there competitors, and what are the barriers to entry are important questions. How much capital do they need to deploy? E&P companies for example have a difficult business model. To get oil out of the ground they need capex continually. To make

EXHIBIT 10.3 Abbreviated Checklist

Story: Real BUSINESS MODEL?	Comments
Barriers to Entry	High capital entry, regulatory support, trademarks, unique technology, processes
Pricing Power	Raise prices if necessary, or too competitive; watch anti-predatory and/or anti-monopoly lawsuits
Purchasing Power	Ability to negotiate prices with vendors; high vendor concentration is a risk
Substitutes	Commodity good or truly unique and value added
Competition	Fierce competition or duopoly/monopoly structure
Market Share	Dominant; shrinking or growing; growing with price and volume
First to Market	First often wins the game
Product Lifecycle	Growth or mature; cash cow; constant reinvention or minimal investment required
Product Concentration	Prefer broad
Customer Concentration	Prefer broad, under 10% of total revenue from one customer at minimum; customer concentration may be a good thing if certain customer is different/better than all other potential customers
Geographic Concentration	Prefer global or national versus regional or local
Equity Sponsorship	Large, better rated backers; significant position in company both in % terms and value to equity sponsor
Management Equity Ownership	More the merrier, but could lead to share repo or other bondholder unfriendly acts
Management Quality	Years in business, track record of execution
Disclosure	Timing and detail of financial reports, management discussions
Years in Business	Longer the better, unless truly market moving invention; relationships should be strong
Brand Recognition	Every little bit helps
Capital Intensity	High for technology; match maint capex to depreciation
Cyclical	Look through it; prefer minimal cycle, unless fundamental improvement is clear
Risk/Regulatory Factors	Other key risks, including environmental, lawsuits, govt. investigations, etc.
Systems	Integrated; same platform
Story	Composite of above qualitative points and other fundamental factors; strong business model, break trends down by segment

EXHIBIT 10.3 *(Continued)*

Financials: COULD they file?	Comments
FCF	Positive; growing
CFO	Look for differences with FCF, working capital usage, non-cash items
Cash Conv Cycle	Slow cash conversion; working capital intensive; large DSOs or inventory days
Organic Rev Growth	Without need for acquisitions; through market share gains or pure demand growth
Revenue Accounting	Potential for "channel stuffing," large customer financings, etc. versus true cash
Margin Growth	Through price increases (that stick), scale or operating efficiency; layoffs are nice, but could signal problems deeper or in long term
Credit Stats	Strong; improving
Margin Sensitivity	Fixed vs. Variable cost structure
Acquisition Spending Risk	Acquisitive; use of equity; strategic or bolt on
Acquisition Integration Risk	Watch multiples paid, amount of equity in acquisition, international issues, systems plan
Share Repo Program	Kind of a nice problem to have, but for borderline credits this could push them over the edge
Cash FX Expos	Translation is less problematic, but watch mismatch of revenues and costs in periods of significant FX volatility (i.e., Euro, Yen, and AUD getting beaten up)
Interest Rate Refi Risk	Increase rates if credit has deteriorated since last financing
Float vs. Fixed Debt	Give benefit to those with high floating rate debt in decreasing interest rate environment, and vice versa; tie in with refi risk, given credit deterioration and changes in LIBOR
Subordination/Corp Structure	Operating subsidiary guarantees, generally the source of cash flow and assets, is preferred (upstream guarantee); watch for just holding company

(continued)

EXHIBIT 10.3 *(Continued)*

Financials: COULD they file?	Comments
Callable	Watch for near term callability, low call price (esp. on new issues), expiring or low equity clawbacks
Covenants Protective	Limit additional senior or secured debt; limit capex or acquis or other payments; leverage, coverage; change of control; equity clawback; require paydown from asset sales, etc.
Major Event Risk	Acquisition integration, economic cyclically, major lawsuits, etc.
Downgrade/Outlook Risk	Unless already priced in, watch for negative sentiment from rating agencies; try to understand what they are thinking and how they analyze credit
Fraud Risk	High amounts of capex versus depreciation or high amounts of borrowing but no cash build

Flexibility: WILL they file?	Comments
Cash on Hand	Watch for restricted/escrowed cash earmarked for other purposes; also, be careful when looking at cash equivalents and make sure they are truly short-term marketable securities
True Availability	Availability may be limited by borrowing base assumptions (maximum % of A/R, Inventory, and PPE), LCs, or for specific uses (i.e., capex, acquisitions)
Maturity Schedule	Desire back end loaded; want ability to refi if not, including operational progress, positive FCF, coverages north of 1x; may increase if availability decreases (usually at % rate) and fully drawn
Asset Coverage	Prefer tangible assets, unencumbered; real estate/mortgage paper, limited senior debt in front; always PV this back for time in liquidation; can also use EBITDA multiple to find TEV if company is deemed to be ongoing entity; don't forget to factor in cancelled operating leases into general unsecured claims

EXHIBIT 10.3 *(Continued)*

Flexibility: WILL they file?	Comments
Unencumbered Assets to Pledge	Understand amount of unencumbered assets; this can provide cushion if needed
Actual Default	CFO, Cash on Bal, Availability, and other sources of liquidity versus amortization schedule; don't forget to factor in acceleration of A/P if vendors demand it
Technical Default	Look at covenants (current and step downs) versus projections
Amount of Bank Debt	Top heavy or none?; switching from unencumbered to secured bank debt could be option too
Ability to Buy Back Bonds	If can buy at a discount, perhaps cash on balance sheet or bank flexibility
Access to Covenant Relief	Willingness of banks to waive or amend; adjust interest for higher rate
Access to Refi Debt	Must see positive FCF, at least 1x on EBIT and EBITDA-MaintCapex coverage, therefore ability to service debt in future
Equity/Convertible Access	IPO, Strong private equity partners, strong stock price, strong stock/convert market
Exchange Offer	Can they get this done to extend maturity?
Someone to Acquire Them	Do they have a strategic market niche and leadership position? Perhaps buy bonds at discount
Someone to File Them	Who will file? Maybe more relief if cap structure is all bonds; is situation desperate?

Source: Peter Duffy

things worse it is a naturally depleting asset and the E&P company is a price taker. Secondly, model out the financials three years out. Key items are to check the level of cash flow, capex, and pricing power. Commodity companies like energy have less predictable cash flow streams. Project the level of cash flow and do a scenario and sensitivity analysis. Be skeptical of adjustments to EBITDA made by underwriters. Do not include non-recurring add backs. If underwriting a merger, cost savings and revenue synergies are to be expected but estimates can be too high. Reduction in G&A costs and physically getting rid of headquarters can be real factors but understand how much of the rest are real reductions in cost on an ongoing basis. Third, look at liquidity. You can have a good business with a good forward cash flow stream but that is constrained by liquidity. On the flip side there could be a poor business with weak cash flow but a ton of liquidity. Watch out for zombie companies: companies that are over-levered but have stable cash flow or are a melting ice cube with a slowly declining revenue stream and business model that is slowly going away. These companies have a lot of leverage, so they kind of proceed knowing that someday they will be a failure.

Cash flow and leverage help determine risk of solvency. Some companies may look troubled with debt and not enough cash flow but have access to liquidity. In liquidity analysis look at revolver capacity, exchanging bonds, selling assets, and raising equity

3. **What are the salient aspects of your investment process and philosophy? Has your investment style evolved over time? How so and why?**

If you had your druthers, you would be slower and deliberate in doing due diligence. In the past every deal came with a weeklong roadshow, and we would meet with them and have a couple of days to complete the analysis. Nowadays you have to make a quick decision. In a drive-by issuance you have a couple of hours to decide after an online roadshow. The modeling process and rigor with checklist needs to be condensed. Also, today there is more access to information with industry-based research and news flow. More information and less time to ingest it means the process has to adapt to keep up.

4. **War stories/case studies? Any interesting names current or past investments?**

JC Penney credit trade was a win. We invested in a bond where we knew that we did not like the business. It was a structurally challenged melting ice cube. But we liked the short-term liquidity and in 2017 bought the 2019 bonds. The play was not that we liked JCP but it was strictly about the pace of deterioration we expected. They did a sale leaseback of their corporate HQ and then tendered for the bonds.

We bought the bonds in the low 90s and got taken out at well north of par. Their demise was hastened with the closures following the COVID-19 pandemic.

With a short dated loan or bond you may not always like the company. This is the difference between being a lender and a stock investor. To own the stock you need to get behind the story; to be a lender, the question to be addressed is can I get my money back in six months or a year over a defined time.

There could be a situation where you like the credit characteristics and buy the bonds but don't like the story and are short the stock. Don't confuse the criteria you seek as a stock investor with the criteria you seek as a lender.

CEDC (Central European Distribution Corporation) was a negative credit story. They were a Polish vodka company headquartered in New Jersey. Then they levered up to buy a Russian facility to distribute in Russia. One day the Russian government raided the facility and shut it down. Essentially cut the cash flow after you had levered up.

Learning from that was to be careful investing outside the developed world (U.S., Canada, and Western Europe). Governmental corruption, rule of law, and bankruptcy laws outside these markets can vary from developed market expectations. In hindsight we should not have stuck with CEDC and should have sold the credit when they bought the facility in Russia.

5. **Do you derive any value from the sell side?**

We do not value the opinions of sell side credit analysts, but we value the information they can provide quickly. They typically focus on fewer names and will be more of an expert on certain companies and credits, and having a quick summary with high-level projections is useful as a starting point for a quick look.

Chris Fortune, CFA

VICE PRESIDENT, T. ROWE PRICE

Chris Fortune is a Vice President for T. Rowe Price. He has covered the regional and community bank stocks since 2005 and serves as an investment officer for select mutual funds. He has been quoted for his expertise in financial publications including Barron's, Businessweek, and SmartMoney. *Prior to working at T. Rowe Price, Fortune was a technical manager for Ciena Corp. He also co-founded and was vice president of software development for wireless start-up AppReach Inc.*

Previously, Fortune was a senior sales engineer and business consultant for USinternetworking and a technical lead and software engineer for ARINC. Fortune holds the Chartered Financial Analyst designation and an MBA in finance and accounting from The Wharton School at the University of Pennsylvania, where he was the head fellow and head trader for the Wharton Investment Management Fund. He earned bachelor's degrees in electrical engineering at Dartmouth College and physics at Colby College.

1. **What is something in your background that may be of interest to the reader that is not in your profile?**

I'm a true geek that loves finding ways to leverage new technologies. As a middle schooler in the mid-1980s, I'd spend hours on my Apple //e computer and my 1200 baud modem communicating on dial-up bulletin boards. This was well before any widespread use of the Internet and even prior to AOL. I studied physics and electrical engineering in undergrad, and my first job out of college was as a software engineer where I coded using C on a UNIX platform. I still tinker with coding on the side and have written a proprietary program on my Mac to help crunch market data for insights on bank stocks and the economy.

My wife and I recently purchased some land where we've built a modern farmhouse. I now have about ten acres that I'm trying to learn how to farm. So, you'll often see me riding on my John Deere on weekends. You might also find me skateboarding with my 11-year old son, watching my 9th grade daughter play soccer, or my 11th grade daughter dance.

2. **How did you get into investing, and specifically investing in banks?**

   I've been generally interested in the stock market ever since high school based on the idea that you could make money by analyzing numbers better than the next guy. My dad also taught me the basic ideas of diversification, risk/reward, and compounding early on. After college, I worked at high-flying tech companies like USinternetworking and Ciena during the Internet boom of the late 1990s and realized that I spent a lot of my free time watching CNBC and trying to figure out what drove these stocks. So, I ended up going back to get my MBA at Wharton in 2003 to switch my career from a software engineer/consultant to an investment analyst.

   For my summer internship between my first and second years at Wharton, I landed at a very small investment firm in Annapolis, MD, called Hillman Capital. They didn't have anyone covering bank stocks for them at the time since the sector "was so different than the rest of the stock market." So, they asked me to spend the summer figuring out bank stocks. That was my first introduction to bank stock investing. Once I graduated from Wharton, I landed a job as an analyst at T. Rowe Price, which coincidentally, was looking for a new bank analyst at the time and perfectly matched my summer intern experience. So, I was able to leverage my summer intern experience to hit the ground running at T. Rowe just a few years prior to the GFC.

3. **What would you be doing if you were not a professional investor?**

   I'd probably still be involved in software or technology in some capacity. Likely working at a smaller entrepreneurial start-up rather than a larger firm – I like that energy. Either that or maybe a farmer!

4. **What are the salient aspects of your investment process and philosophy? Has your investment style evolved over time? How so and why?**

   When I first started covering bank stocks, I focused on things like valuation, sentiment, and quarterly trends. However, I've since shifted my focus to what I feel matters more in determining which banks can compound alpha over many years. As a result, I now focus more of my time on things like management quality/incentives, strategy, geography, and balance sheet. I don't spend too much time on trying to figure out if a bank if going to beat or miss any given quarter, other than maybe to help make a tactical call on when to build or trim a position within the scope of a longer-term perspective.

I believe that banks tend to trade on Forward P/Es. You could argue there's also a relationship between ROEs and P/B, but the slope of that line actually just simplifies down to P/E. My sense is that sell-side analysts spend 90% of their time trying to pinpoint the exact future EPS, and then spend only a few seconds pairing it with a P/E. Put another way, they spend all their time figuring out the future ROE, without much thought for the appropriate cost of capital. I've found that you can gain an edge by better understanding a bank's appropriate P/E (or Cost of Capital) over the long term. This leads to many factors beyond just EPS growth, and circles back to things like understanding management quality/incentives, strategy, geography, balance sheet, etc. An appropriate P/E is not just about EPS growth – in fact, that's often not even the main factor. I feel this aspect often gets overlooked by the sell-side and shorter-term investors.

In addition, when I first started analyzing banks, I focused on 1-year upside %'s. However, I've learned to take a more balanced perspective by balancing the 1- and 3-year upside potential with the downside risk. Having lived through the Financial Crisis, I spend a fair amount of time contemplating what a worst-case scenario might look like and what that would mean for any given stock.

Also following the financial crisis, I now spend more time finding and monitoring what I feel are decent leading indicators for the economy. However, I'm not going to outline exactly what they are here.

5. **Do you have a checklist approach? If you did, what are some of the key items on it?**

   I don't have a hard checklist approach by any means. However, there are certain things that I feel are very important in any investment thesis. Most of these items come back to the core issue of looking for a capable management team that is likely to be a good steward of capital with a high probability of making intelligent capital allocation decisions. So if I had a checklist, some of the things I would include might be things like decent insider ownership/incentives, a track record of making intelligent capital allocation decisions, a strong credit culture, and a general plan/understanding of how to compound shareholder value over many years without taking excessive risk.

6. **How do you evaluate management?**

   I like to ask management questions that give them a chance to share their insights into how they think about generating shareholder returns over many years. I also like to ask questions to gain their understanding of their cost of capital or P/E. For instance, one common discussion with bank management teams is around "NII vs. NIM." For example, many management teams will say, "Doing XYZ will be NII accretive even though its NIM dilutive." I'd ask them to unpack that a little bit more – as the implicit assumption is that NII accretion will translate to EPS accretion, which will translate to a higher stock price. Maybe. However, there could also be an equal (or worse) offset from an increased cost of capital and lower P/E – due to the dynamics of thinner capital ratios, taking on more credit risk, or paying up for incremental funding. Seeing if management understands these concepts (or can at least have an intelligent conversation around the ideas) can help gauge the depth of management. Do they really dig into concepts that drive their own stock – or are they simply parroting what their investment bankers may have practiced with them earlier? Another good question is asking where they deploy excess capital and why – and asking them how their answers might change in a flat yield curve environment, or if their stock price was much higher or lower.

7. **What was your best/favorite investment idea and how did you find the opportunity? Conversely, what has been your worst/least favorite idea and what went wrong?**

I can't talk about specific names but can discuss themes. In general, some of my best investment ideas have come when you have long-term confidence/visibility into steadily improving ROEs. In these cases, you can get the benefit of a growing TBV plus an expanding P/TBV multiple over many years, while the market will be focused on paying a peer-like Forward P/E. This typically comes back to a quality management team with the right incentives and levers to pull. It can come from either an underperforming bank (often trading closer to P/TBV) where there is a real catalyst that gives visibility into steadily improving ROEs for years to come (often a CEO upgrade). Or it can even come from an already outperforming bank (higher P/TBV) where quality management has the ability to consolidate their geographies with multiple shareholder friendly accretive deals. The commonality between the two is a quality management team that is self-aware of its starting point and understands the levers it needs to pull to improve returns in a shareholder friendly manner for the long term. A management with a long history of subpar returns is unlikely to change its stripes unless something significant has changed.

In general, some of my worst recommendations have come when a cheap stock valuation has lured me into overlooking a poor management team or a weak balance sheet. I used to do this more often early in my career than I do now. Sometimes lightning does strike, and you can get a takeout at a premium, but this feels more like gambling than investing. Meanwhile, there's an opportunity cost of being committed to that investment and, in my experience, it's more likely that you are holding a multi-year underperformer in these cases with a management/board that is deeply entrenched and in reality unwilling to consider a sale. The worst mistake is overlooking a weak balance sheet that can completely collapse (capital too thin, assets too risky, liquidity crisis) if the environment degrades.

8. **Do you derive any value from the sell side?**

   Sell side analysts help me understand the landscape from their unique perspective – namely gauging investor sentiment and sharing any chatter that might be circulating among the investor community. They also help me ramp on new names more quickly and understand the Bull/Bear arguments on those names.

9. **How do you view the fintech space both from niche start-up challengers and large tech incumbents? Does fintech help (augment capabilities) or harm (disintermediate) banks? Does the impact differ between large versus small or consumer versus commercial? Does digital banking help level the playing field, or does it make it worse for smaller banks?**

   I view fintech as having a potentially symbiotic relationship with the banks. At a high level, most fintech products seem to help customers with the simpler and more common banking functions. These are often the more commoditized lower margin/higher volume transactions. Using technology to address these types of more common customer demands can help free up bank personnel to tackle the more complex, higher margin relationships – such as understanding a small business' specific needs well enough to recommend new products and deepen the relationship. Also, most SMid banks that I follow are commercially focused, where much of the value relies on the local relationships with decision-making authority rather than a new mobile app to perform common functionalities. Local relationships with both the option of offering a simple tech-enabled solution as well as the ability to help navigate the more complex relationships/products would be the home run.

10. **Consolidation has been a major theme in the bank space. How does it play into your investment strategy? Does bank consolidation increase, stay on pace?**

    I like to invest in banks where I feel that the management and board is open to pursuing a sale if it was the right decision for shareholders. However, an actual takeout is never core to my investment thesis for any bank. In fact, the few times where my thesis relied on a takeout have been some of my worst recommendations. I've often made much better returns investing in quality management teams that execute year-in and year-out rather than a potentially subpar bank with any degree of takeout speculation already baked in.

Regardless of whether I view the management team as a likely seller or not, I do analyze what value the bank might have for a potential acquirer. Whether or not the bank actually sells, I believe the market will price the stock to some degree based on how valuable it might be to a potential buyer. Someone told me early on in my bank analyst career that I should determine a bank's value by starting with TBV, adding a deposit premium dependent on the quality and mix of the deposit base, and then subtracting any risks in the earning assets. I still think there's something to that simple approach, especially in understanding a bank's potential takeout value. For instance, I often hear people say, "the all-in deposit costs for an online bank is actually similar to a traditional bank after you add in the branch overhead costs." While this might be true, it doesn't mean the stocks should trade at similar values. An acquirer could acquire low-cost deposits from a traditional bank, shut down branches, and still be left with some valuable low-cost deposits. However, if an acquirer purchased an on-line deposit platform, it has only acquired market-rate sensitive deposits that it could have raised on its own. This helps explain why the former trades at a better valuation than the latter, even if the all-in cost of deposits were exactly the same.

If I had to guess, I'd imagine M&A increases slowly in coming years as long as the economy remains healthy.

11. **What are some of the cycle inflection indicators you pay attention to?**

    I look at a lot of the traditional indicators that many analysts monitor – such as the yield curve, tightening/loosening of credit, and so on. I also monitor some proprietary leading indicators, but I don't really want to share any of those here.

12. **Has the rise of passive management changed the way you invest? Are we close to peak passive?**

    I'm not going to speculate on whether we are close to the peak in passive or not; however, I have witnessed passive funds having a much larger impact on the individual stocks over the past year. For instance, stocks that have a higher percentage of passive ownership versus average daily liquidity tend to have exaggerated movements – both up and down. Understanding this dynamic can help active investors add another tactical tool to their toolbox by understanding which stocks may be overshooting or undershooting fundamentals depending on the current market sentiment.

Martin Friedman

CO-FOUNDER, MANAGING MEMBER AND CEO, FJ CAPITAL MANAGEMENT

Mr. Friedman founded FJ Capital Management LLC in 2007 and is the portfolio manager for the flagship Financial Opportunity Fund, an event-driven strategy focused on the US community and regional bank sector. Mr. Friedman established the Financial Opportunity Fund and has successfully navigated the fund, creating substantial alpha since inception. He also created in the spring of 2015, the Financial Opportunity Long/Short Fund, a lower net, broader financial services fund with lower market volatility and beta.

Mr. Friedman currently serves on the Board of Directors for Dogwood State Bank based in Raleigh, North Carolina, since May 2019. He served on the Board of Directors of Silvergate Bank in San Diego, California, from February 2019 to January 2020, and served on the Board of Directors of Denver, Colorado, –based TIG Bancorp from December 2017 until October 2019. In 2013, as part of the recapitalization of Anchor Bank, Madison, Wisconsin, Mr. Friedman was elected to the Board of Directors where he served on the Board of the bank holding company and compensation committee until 2015. Mr. Friedman served on the Board of Directors of Guaranty Savings Bank in Metairie, Louisiana, from 2008 to 2009, and Access National Bank (ANCX) in Reston, Virginia, from 2009 to 2019. Mr. Friedman brings over 30 years of experience in and around the commercial and investment banking industries, in which he applied and developed skills in financial analysis with an expertise in financial institutions, corporate finance, SEC and banking compliance, and management.

He was previously Director of Research for Friedman, Billings, Ramsey Group, a research and securities trading firm, from 1998 to 2007. Prior to that, he was a securities analyst, focusing on the financial services industry with the same firm from 1992 to 1998. Mr. Friedman graduated from the University of Maryland with a Bachelor of Science in Finance.

1. **What is something in your background that may be of interest to the reader that is not in your profile?**

   From an early age, I was always fascinated by the stock market and how it works. Also, I'm an avid gardener and love to plant and watch things grow.
2. **How did you get into investing, and specifically investing in banks?**

   I was always interested in business and got my break in 1987 when my Uncle Emanuel Friedman offered me an opportunity to move from home, New Orleans, Louisiana, and come work for him at the institutional DC-based firm Johnston, Lemon. He specialized in banks and taught me how to analyze both risk and opportunity within the bank sector. In 1989, he formed Friedman, Billings, Ramsey, and I was one of the dozen people who were there from day one. After an eight-year career as a senior analyst covering banks and financial service companies, I finished the balance of my sixteen-year career at FBR as their Director of Research where I oversaw all of the research efforts and managed over 140 research professionals. My passion was always on the investment side, so in late 2007 I formed FJ Capital with my partner Andy Jose to focus on what I knew best – analyzing and investing in financial services with an emphasis on banks.

3. **What would you be doing if you were not a professional investor?**

   I would likely be running another business. Really doesn't matter what, always had the ambition of leading people and creating a business.

4. **What are the salient aspects of your investment process and philosophy? Has your investment style evolved over time? How so and why?**

   Our investment approach is a bottom-up fundamental sizing up of the business and a qualitative view of management skills. Our philosophy is to invest in banks where management owns a lot of stock and cares more about their stock than earning W-2 income. We want to invest with owners with real skin in the game that know how to evaluate risk and manage the business for the benefit of shareholders. Our approach is to invest in a business for the long term unless the thesis changes or there is a risk we did not underwrite. Of course, we have to be thoughtful on the entry and make sure we have a sufficient return for the risk we are assuming. We like to look at companies for at least three years and thus tend to be longer-term shareholders. We also incorporate a macro view of both the national and local economies where the companies operate. It's our view that community banks are microcosms of their local economy. I would say my style has evolved over time and incorporates other factors, but has stayed true to fundamental long term investing. Another important aspect is diversification and not investing with too much leverage. We are after all investing in companies that employ leverage, so it's important not to double lever.

5. **Do you have a checklist approach? If you did, what are some of the key items on it?**

   We do incorporate a checklist that includes several management items and fundamental checks. We seek to understand and evaluate the risk and see if the skill set matches with that risk. Understanding what's in the loan book and the underwriting is a must and getting a feel of how the banks fit into the two major themes in our space:

A. *Consolidation – is the bank interested in buying or selling? Or both? We view this as a major structural trend in the US that will last another 10 to 15 years as the number of banks goes from 5,400 currently to around 2,000 – still more than the rest of the major economies of the world.*

B. *We look for banks in good markets that are able to take share from larger banks that no longer service small business well.*

Because of all the mega mergers over the last 30 years, we have a three-tier banking system. All of the consolidation will now take place in small to mid-size banks where we focus our investing.

6. **How do you evaluate management?**

   This is the key to investing in banks. We never invest in a bank without meeting management and understanding their motivations. We look at their track record in this company and in past ventures. We build relationships in order to understand the risk they are taking and if they built a deep enough bench to underwrite that risk.

7. **What was your best/favorite investment idea and how did you find the opportunity?**

   I analyzed and invested in so many banks over the years. My best ideas come from being patient and waiting for "the pitch." We seek to build relationships over time and invest when the entry price is attractive relative to the risk. Most of the opportunities I find are from meeting management teams. My team and I meet with over 700 banks a year to find the right 50 to 60 to invest in.

8. **Do you derive any value from the sell side?**

   We do derive value from sell side. I spent 16 years as lead financial services analyst and director of research on the sell side, so I understand their value proposition. Our space has some fine investment banks and analysts that have thoughtful research. They provide consensus estimates that we can compare to our own earnings view. They also host management visits and calls, which add tremendous value to a firm like ours.

9. **How do you view the fintech space both from niche start-up challengers and large tech incumbents?**

   The fintech space has been funded well and has created some innovative technology. In order to assess this, you first have to look at the bank's business model. The largest 30 banks in the US have a heavy retail model where community banks have less brick and mortar and compete based on service and responsiveness to small and mid-size business needs. Large banks are spending billions to defend their retail turf while community banks compete on service and build relationships with small and mid-size businesses that may have a non-cookie cutter loan need that requires human intervention. Thus, we do not see technology displacing banks, rather we view fintech as ultimately partnering with banks to serve the needs of their respective customers.

10. **Consolidation has been a major theme in the bank space. How does it play into your investment strategy? Does bank consolidation increase, stay on pace?**

    One of our core strategies is to identify candidates that want to participate in this consolidation theme. We think owning both sides of the equation can create value for long-term shareholders: owning sellers and collecting one-day premiums; or owning the combined company as they create efficiencies that take earnings and return on equity higher.

    My view is that consolidation will continue until there are about 1,000–2,000 banks left in the US. At that level we will be closer to the world mean. We clearly have too many banks and credit unions in the US competing for fewer loans and navigating tough margins and low-growth environments for the next several years.

11. **What are some of the cycle inflection indicators you pay attention to?**

    Credit is the biggest factor in investing in banks. Therefore, either a perceived or actual recession is an inflection indicator. Typically, we see yield curve flattening or inversion followed by a recession. Banks' stocks lead the market down going into recession and can have strong returns before the end of recessions. So, we track leading economic indicators for recession risk.

12. **Has the rise of passive management changed the way you invest? Are we close to peak passive?**

    Our investment process remains the same, but we have to be mindful of passive funds and their effect on liquidity and trading. We track all our companies and which ETFs own them and track the flows. Hard to know if we are at a peak passive, but it's another variable you have to take into account around investing.

Rich Hocker

FOUNDER AND CEO, PENN CAPITAL MANAGEMENT

Mr. Hocker founded Penn Capital in 1987 and serves as Chief Investment Officer and Chief Executive Officer, guiding overall portfolio strategy. His investing and institutional non-investment grade corporate lending experience spans over 40 years. While serving as a Partner for Delaware Investment Advisors (DIA) from 1977 to 1987, he was responsible for building the investment side of DIA's fixed income operation. During this period, Mr. Hocker developed and managed one of the nation's first high yield mutual funds, the

(continued)

(continued)

Delchester High Yield Bond Fund. He also served as the first high yield bond manager for several institutional clients including General Motors, State of Vermont Teachers Retirement Association, and Colorado Fire and Police.

Prior to DIA, Mr. Hocker trained as a corporate lender and supported key senior lenders at Provident National Bank, which is now PNC Bank, a top 20 US banking institution. He later rose to serve as head of the investment division. Mr. Hocker also founded and served as CEO of Covenant Bank, a New Jersey–based regional bank which grew to 16 branches and $500MM in deposits before being acquired by First Union in 1997.

He and his wife, Marcia Hocker, are the founders of the Ethel Mae Hocker Foundation which provides scholarship opportunities to less fortunate, deserving Greater Philadelphia-area elementary and high school students who have demonstrated leadership abilities, academic success, and commitment to the community, and need financial support. Mr. Hocker received both his BS in Accounting and an MBA in Finance from the Kogod School of Business at American University.

1. **What is something in your background that may be of interest to the reader that is not in your profile?**

   One of the goals in my life is to address the inequalities in education in our major cities. My faith in America is underpinned by the belief that everyone has the opportunity to excel if they have equal access to education. The Ethel Mae Hocker Foundation helps achieve this goal. The focus of our foundation is to assist the children in Philadelphia and Camden to have a choice in education. On a yearly basis we help 90 children to have that opportunity.

2. **You founded Covenant bank and sold it to First Union for 3.5× TBV in 1997. Take us through the founding, growth, and sale of the bank.**

   The philosophy of the business model was to serve the needs of the small and medium-sized businesses in Southern New Jersey. The lack of competition in the market aided superior returns to the shareholders of the bank. The uniqueness of the model caught the eye of First Union, who wanted to enter the market. This helped the shareholders obtain a very satisfactory premium in a sale.

3. **How did that experience of managing a bank shape your views on credit?**

   One needs to be fully engaged in the credit process when running a bank and understand the customer. Engaging with the customer is what helps build strong long-term relationships and profitable accounts.

4. **You managed one of the first high yield mutual funds from 1977 to 1987. That was an interesting period in the Volcker years during which the rate on the 10-year went from 6.8 to 15.8 before going back down. What are some things that stood out to you during a period of interest rate volatility?**

   Volcker's actions had the most impact on small and medium-sized businesses that needed access to the banks and to the capital markets. They were overcome by the drastic rise in interest rates which could not be accommodated by their profit margins. This caused tremendous distress in the markets and helped to create opportunities which produced returns in excess of equity returns. This tactical strategy coupled with credit analysis led to the outperformance of the style that I managed.

5. **Are there any war stories you would like to share with readers from investing in high yield during the age of Michael Milken?**

   In the late 70s, I had the opportunity to meet Mike and he inspired me to go into the high yield world. The first high yield bond that I bought was from Mike directly; this was before Drexel became the king of high yield. Mike was living in Cherry Hill, New Jersey, when I first met him at the Tavistock Country Club for dinner with a friend. It was definitely interesting times and created a great opportunity for the markets and me.

Jeffrey Sherman

DEPUTY CHIEF INVESTMENT OFFICER, DOUBLELINE CAPITAL LP

Jeffrey Sherman, CFA, is Deputy Chief Investment Officer of the asset management firm DoubleLine Capital LP. Mr. Sherman also serves as lead portfolio manager for multisector and derivative-based strategies. He is a member of DoubleLine's Executive Management and Fixed Income Asset Allocation committees. He can be heard regularly on his podcast "The Sherman Show" (@ShermanShowPod), where he interviews distinguished guests on investment, market, macroeconomic, and monetary issues. Mr. Sherman has appeared as a guest himself on CNBC, Bloomberg Television, and FOX Business, and his comments have been quoted by many other news sources, including *the New York Times, the Financial Times, the Wall Street Journal, Barron's, Investor's Business Daily, Reuters, Bloomberg News, Yahoo Finance, Business Insider*, and *ZeroHedge*.

1. **GFC versus the 2020 pandemic crisis, how is it playing out?**

The key distinction between the GFC and the 2020 pandemic crisis is the velocity of the decline in markets and economic data. The GFC unfolded over many quarters – from the time home prices started to decline in the latter half of 2006 to the 2008 implosions of Bear Stearns and Lehman Brothers, to the Federal Reserve's introduction of quantitative easing in November of that year to the bottom in risk markets in March 2009 and so on. However, the speed and magnitude of the market's response to the health pandemic was unprecedented. Over the course of one month, the S&P 500 shed more than 31% (Feb. 20, 2020 to March 20, 2020).

The monetary response followed the "traditional" path, the "previously non-traditional, but now accepted" path, and the "unprecedented" path.

The traditional path of cutting rates was enacted early by cutting the Federal Funds Rate by 150 basis points over two weeks in early to mid-March, followed by the announcement that interest rates will remain near zero for the foreseeable future. At a news conference following the Federal Open Market Committee meeting on June 10, Fed Chairman Jerome Powell said, "We're not thinking about raising rates. We're not even thinking about thinking about raising rates."

The Fed further unleashed its "non-traditional, but now accepted" policy of quantitative easing, announcing unlimited firepower in the purchases of Treasuries and Agency mortgage-backed securities and has continued to commit to the purchase of up to $120 billion per month (up to $80 billion in Treasuries and up to $40 billion in Agency mortgage-backed securities). To put the size of this program into perspective, the Fed bought up to $80 billion per month during its peak purchases during its third session of quantitative easing (QE3) throughout 2013.

Lastly, the Fed is pursuing "unprecedented" policies through liquidity facilities focusing on credit markets, both by tapping legacy programs launched to address the GFC and creating new ones. These include the Term Asset-Backed Securities Loan Facility (TALF), the Commercial Paper Funding Facility (CPFF), the Money Market Mutual Fund Liquidity Facility (MMLF), the Municipal Liquidity Facility (MLF), direct loans to a chosen list of small businesses via the Main Street Lending Program (MSLP) and, more importantly, two facilities to acquire U.S. corporate bonds: the Primary Market Corporate Credit Facility (PMCCF) and the Secondary Market Corporate Credit Facility (SMCCF).

These monetary responses coupled with the fiscal response via the CARES Act appear to have put a floor under the price of risk assets. Weighing at $2 trillion in nominal dollars and equal to 10% of nominal GDP, the CARES Act was the largest economic stimulus in U.S. history. Although I refer to this as stimulus, most of these transfer payments were used to cover lost wages during the health pandemic and economic *shutdowns – not to increase money velocity as with traditional stimulus packages. Two months after the passage of the CARES Act, an economic recovery appears to be underway. The durability and strength of this recovery are predicated on the consumer. As of July 2, 2020, more than 31 million Americans were receiving some form of supplemental unemployment insurance: 19 million from continuing unemployment claims and 12. 8 million from claims under the Pandemic Unemployment Assistance (PUA) program. Prior to the health pandemic, 1.7 million Americans were receiving unemployment benefits. Given these estimates, the unemployment rate is probably just shy of 20%.*

Part of the CARES Act provides an incremental payment of $600 per week as part of the unemployment benefit; that is set to expire at the end of July. This incremental benefit has allowed the consumer to continue to spend near pre-COVID-19 levels, but its scheduled expiration leaves consumption at risk should these benefits expire amid no resumption of employment. So although the economic data has improved as of late, there is the risk of the economy rolling over if those receiving unemployment benefits do not get back to work in the near term. This makes a W-shaped recovery possible and keeps a cloud over the recovery until we get more clarity on the virus in the form of vaccines, therapeutics, or herd immunity, or some set of those factors. More likely than a V- or W-shaped recovery is one which takes the outlines of the sign of the square root function: After the initial rebound, the recovery slows and becomes more drawn out as we cope with the ramifications of a post-COVID-19 economy (lack of business travel, less airline demand, less hotel demand, and the resculpting of the workplace dynamic) on the back of elevated private- and public-sector debt.

2. **What are the cycle inflection indicators you track and high-frequency indicators that you focus the most on?**

In this environment, we are focused on the consumer. Typically, we watch the current unemployment rate versus its 12-month and 36-month moving average. When the rate exceeds the 12-month average, it is time to be "on watch" for an impending recession. This is usually a good indicator, although it has given a couple of false positives in the past. When the rate exceeds its 36-month average, a recession is usually imminent. In the current recession, both indicators were triggered simultaneously as the jobs losses were extremely heavy and quick.

Right now, a few of the higher-frequency data that we are focusing on are in the airline, automotive, restaurant, and hotel industries. For airlines, the TSA provides checkpoint throughput each day and compares that metric to its reading one year ago. Most recently, 725,000 individuals were going though security versus the nadir of 87,500 on April 14, 2020. While an improvement, the most recent readings remain a fraction of the year ago reading of 2.8 million. This is an important metric to focus on: mobility and the resumption of business travel, a major driver of economic activity.

For the automotive data, we are not focused on automobile sales but rather on gasoline consumption. This is another mobility metric; given the slack in airline demand, gasoline consumption may increase as people decide to travel via automobile. Over the past two years, daily consumption has been roughly 10 million barrels; that number plummeted to 5,800 barrels in early April 2020. Demand has rebounded to 9 million barrels per day. This is encouraging, but daily consumption is still nearly 1.5 million barrels less than a year ago.

Restaurant demand, which was decimated by closing businesses in March/April, has started to revive. OpenTable provides a demand estimator by looking at year-over-year changes in online/phone/walk-in reservations in various states. This data set was down 100% due to the closures but started to uptick in early May when some states reopened. Using a seven-day moving average of the year-over-year demand change, we saw improvement in Texas and Georgia, which were first to reopen, to almost half from last year's level, but those have rolled over given the recent spike in cases and are now down more than 60% from last year's level. However, New York, which recently started to allow in-person dining, is continuing its uptrend, but the state is off around 80% from last year.

The hotel industry has suffered immensely given the shutdown of the economy and lack of travel, either for business or leisure. We focus on monthly occupancy instead of revenue per available room (RevPAR) as that should provide better guidance to activity and not reflect discounts designed to attract visitors. Over the last five years, May hotel occupancy has vacillated between 62% to 70% and was 31% in May 2020, off its recent low of 24.5% in April.

Combining the reading of all of these indicators, it appears that some of the worst may be behind us, but we are far from out of the woods, and pre-pandemic economic levels are still distant.

3. **What are some of the potential consequences of the unprecedented actions by the Fed?**

To be clear, the Fed doesn't print money, at least not yet; the Treasury does. So if you want to discuss the budget deficit's impact on the economy, significant increases typically lead to either inflation, a devaluation of the currency, or both.

The direction of the trade-weighted dollar is inversely correlated to the direction of the magnitude of the twin deficits (budget deficit and trade deficit). This relationship implies that the next big move in the dollar is likely lower. The dollar benefited in this recent bout of volatility from a global shortage of dollars, a development which the Fed eased by opening swap lines with various central banks. So if the economy makes another leg down, and Congress responds by funding significant measures through more borrowing, the dollar could persist in its most-recent downtrend.

To date, Jerome Powell has leaned against negative interest rate policy and continues to dismiss its alleged merits. We feel this is the correct response as there is no evidence that negative interest rates stimulate the economy. Indeed, the contrary appears to be the case: Regions that implemented negative interest rates have suffered massive weakness within their banking sectors. We do think that there are additional, significant consequences to the U.S. targeting negative interest rate policies, given the dollar's prominence as the global reserve currency. Also, there is a significant investor need for positive-yielding, high-rated sovereign debt. The global financial system would experience a significant disruption were U.S. Treasuries to offer a negative yield for a prolonged period of time.

We believe that the Fed has increased its moral hazard by violating the Federal Reserve Act of 1913 through the creation of its facilities to purchase corporate bonds. On March 23, 2020, when the Fed announced these facilities, it put a local bottom in risk asset prices, especially for assets which the Fed supports through these programs. These programs increase the moral hazard risk for markets since there is a perception of the "Fed put." In other words, issuers and investors believe that default becomes a remote risk because they believe the Fed will buy the assets from investors or provide liquidity beyond the underlying asset's solvency. Fed interventionism also distorts the market pricing function. As a result, asset prices may deviate significantly from fair value, leaving the market vulnerable to a repricing shock if the Fed ever steps away. This market repricing did take place, starting in May 2013, when then-Fed Chairman Ben Bernanke alluded to the idea of "tapering of bond purchases" during QE3. The resulting sell-off in many risk assets is now colloquially referred to as the "Taper Tantrum." So even though investors rejoice when there is artificial support from extraneous sources, they can as quickly step away when that source is taken away or people anticipate the removing of the source.

4. **Yield curve control (YCC) is increasingly coming into focus. Do you believe that this will be effective in the U.S.? Are there lessons to be learned from Japan on YCC?**

Yield curve control (YCC) is another form of market manipulation since it sets the market-clearing price (yield) versus letting supply and demand set the price. In addition to Japan, the U.S. does have experience with YCC. Starting in 1942, during World War II, the Fed and Treasury coordinated YCC, whereby the Fed would purchase any Treasury that yielded above a certain level. This lasted until 1947, when the Fed became concerned about inflation, raised short rates, and significantly expanded its balance sheet through buying the long end of the curve, where there was less demand given the attractiveness of short-term rates relative to long-term rates. YCC is essentially an extension of quantitative easing: Instead of targeting a dollar amount of securities, the central bank, in this case the Fed, targets the price of the securities at which it is a buyer. There is a potential benefit to YCC. If the market trusts the Fed's commitment to buy securities at a certain price, it may require less "balance sheet" from the Fed to support the market. This is something that the Bank of Japan has experienced since implementing YCC in 2016. The nominal amount of Japanese government bonds (JGBs) purchased each quarter has been less than was the case under its direct quantitative easing regime. YCC is not without risk, as it is predicated on the Fed's commitment to the program as well as its ability to implement YCC. Given the global economy is more inextricably linked than it was in 1942, it is hard to extrapolate from a sample size of one (the BoJ experience). Thus far, it is unclear whether the Fed will embrace YCC; it has already taken a step in that direction. The Fed's pledge of low rates for the foreseeable future has effectively done YCC on the front end of the curve (say out to two or three years), given that longer rates are interpolated from a series of short-end rates. One could argue that a credible Fed with strong forward guidance – delivering on its promises – does not need to engage in the direct act of YCC. After all, the Fed has already jawboned the market into pricing in its policy objective. As with all of these programs, the crux is to maintain credibility, as without it, the market will find its own price of risk.

Ian Lyngen, CFA

MANAGING DIRECTOR, HEAD OF US RATES STRATEGY, BMO CAPITAL MARKETS

Ian is a Managing Director and Head of US Rates Strategy in the BMO Capital Markets Fixed Income Strategy team. His primary focus is the US Treasury market with specific interests in monetary policy and economic and technical analysis. He was recently ranked first in the 2019 Institutional Investor Survey's for US Rates Strategy, Fixed Income Strategy, and Technical Analysis. Ian also ranked first in 2018 Institutional Investor Survey's for US Rates Strategy and Technical Analysis.

Ian joined BMO from CRT Capital Group, where he was part of an award-winning strategy duo, ranking first in the Institutional Investor Survey's US Government Bond Strategy category for 11 consecutive years, first in the fixed income Technical Analysis category for five consecutive years, and runner-up in the general Fixed-Income Strategy category for seven consecutive years. Prior to CRT Capital, Ian served as Senior Interest Rate Strategist at RBS Greenwich Capital.

Ian earned an MBA from Yale School of Management and a Bachelor of Science in Finance from the University of Minnesota. He is a Chartered Financial Analyst and member of the New York Society of Security Analysts.

1. **What are some of the high frequency indicators that you recommend bank investors keep a close eye on?**

   Given the uncertain macroeconomic backdrop and rapidly evolving Federal Reserve balance sheet, we are paying increased attention to higher-frequency indicators than before. On the economic side, weekly releases such as initial jobless claims (for the labor market) and the New York Fed's Weekly Economic Index as a near real-time growth gauge have become more relevant. For financing conditions, we're watching the Fed's weekly H41 table release – which provides updates on liquidity facility take-up and aggregate reserves – as well as daily benchmark funding rates such as SOFR, LIBOR, EFFR, and TGCR. Finally, given financial conditions are so heavily reliant on COVID-19 risk, the daily case/death patterns across states and countries also should be monitored.
2. **What are things bank investors should look out for during the transition from LIBOR to SOFR?**

   During the transition from LIBOR to SOFR, bank investors should be attentive to process of deepening SOFR-related markets (indexed FRNs, futures, swaps, etc.) and any regulatory guidance/developments. There has been some speculation that the transition could get delayed, but that has yet to be confirmed by the official sector. As such, we're closely watching for any clarification surrounding the LIBOR transition, specifically whether the timeline may be adjusted.
3. **What are the implications of yield curve control and do you believe it helps central banks achieve their goals?**

   In practical terms, yield curve control would be a commitment by the Fed to purchase all Treasuries yielding above a certain threshold out to a certain maturity date. Hypothetically, the central bank would purchase any Treasury out to 5 years yielding above 25 bp, and that would augment their forward guidance and cement the reality that it will be several years (at a minimum) before monetary policy is normalized. While this policy would bolster already implemented forward guidance via both Fed speeches and the SEP dotplot, it is a bit redundant given 5-year yields are only at 27 bp. Nonetheless, should the economic situation deteriorate, we would not be surprised to see this policy come to pass later this year or in 2021.

4. **What is your opinion on negative rates as a policy measure?**

   The Fed has made it clear they will not be taking policy rates negative this cycle. Given the realities of the domestic money market complex as well as the NIRP experience in Europe, the cons of negative rates have outweighed any potential benefits. Growth and inflation on the Continent were suppressed even before the pandemic, and arguably the ECB is now trapped in a negative rate regime with little hope of normalization in the near term. Additionally, a variety of FOMC members have expressed a preference for level specific forward guidance, more aggressive balance sheet expansion, or YCC as policies rather than negative rates.

Appendix

"An investment in knowledge pays the best interest."

– Benjamin Franklin

CONVERSIONS

No book on investing in banks would be complete without a section on Thrift Conversions. This was a topic discussed by Seth Klarman in the investing classic *Margin of Safety* as well as by Peter Lynch in *One Up on Wall Street.*

WHAT IS A THRIFT?

A thrift is a depositary institution that mostly makes residential mortgage loans. They are also called a Savings Bank or a Savings and Loan Association. They can be owned by their depositors or members (Mutual Ownership) or by their shareholders (Stock Ownership). They can have a Federal Charter (regulated by the OCC) or a State Charter (regulated by a State Regulator). Credit Unions, while they share some resemblance, are not thrifts. Credit Unions are owned by their members (Mutual Ownership) and regulated by the NCUA (National Credit Union Administration) if they have a Federal charter or alternatively by a state regulator. Their deposits are insured not by the FDIC but by the NCUSIF (National Credit Union Share Insurance Fund).

Thrifts have to pass the QTL (Qualified Thrift Lender) test under which the thrift must maintain at least 65% of its portfolio assets in qualified thrift investments (primarily residential mortgages and mortgage backed securities). Since a rule change in 2019, a Federal Savings Association with total assets over $20 billion can opt to become a covered savings association and avoid meeting the QTL test and not be required to obtain a national bank charter. State-chartered savings associations will need to obtain a national charter unless they had converted to a federal savings association prior to 12/31/2017.

Prior to the GFC, federal-chartered thrifts were regulated by the OTS (Office of Thrift Supervision). The agency was dissolved in 2011 and superseded by the OCC. The OTS itself was established in 1989 in the aftermath of the S&L crisis and had replaced the Federal Home Loan Bank Board (FHLBB). In the lead-up to the GFC, it was not just thrifts that were regulated by the OTS, but organizations as complex as AIG came under its purview.

MUTUAL CONVERSION

A thrift that is a mutual is owned by the depositors or members of the Savings and Loan Association. A mutual becomes a publicly listed entity by going through an IPO conversion and converts from a mutual owned by depositors to a publicly listed entity owned by shareholders.

Depositors get subscription rights to the conversion IPO. Several investors track mutual thrifts and maintain deposits in the hopes of a conversion which can sometimes prove to be an attractive investment. Depositors who have qualifying deposits as of an eligible record date receive the rights. The rights are tiered with the first priority being depositors who maintained deposits at least one year prior to the date when the board of the thrift adopts its plan of conversion. The next tier would be the ESOP (employee stock ownership plan), which typically gets a 5 to 8% allocation of the offering. Subsequent tiers would be based on other record dates as of which deposits were maintained.

The conversion rights are nontransferable, so a depositor cannot transfer it to a third-party investor; and many thrifts now have rules in place to encourage only depositors that reside in the community. Thrifts around NYC have considerable deposits from investors, and thus smaller depositors may not get an adequate allocation as it can get prorated based on the amount of deposits.

There are three conversion types:

Standard: This is a full conversion where 100% of the ownership is transferred from depositors to the shareholders.

MHC (Mutual Holding Company) or First Step or First Stage: This is a partial conversion, where less than 50% converts to public shares, and the MHC owns the remaining greater than 50%.

Second Step or Second Stage: The MHC portion, the greater than 50% portion after the first step MHC, converts to public shares.

While there were a few that broke price on the first day of trading, on average thrift conversions over the last five years saw a median 18.5% IPO day one pop (Exhibit A.1).

EXHIBIT A.1 IPO Day 1 Pop

Company	Ticker	HQ	Type	Year	IPO pop (%)
Provident Bancorp, Inc. (MHC)	PVBC	Amesbury, MA	Second Step	2019	8.2
HarborOne Bancorp, Inc. (MHC)	HONE	Brockton, MA	Second Step	2019	0.2
Pioneer Bancorp	PBFS	Albany, NY	MHC	2019	47.5
First Seacoast Bancorp	FSEA	Dover, NH	MHC	2019	−2.5
Eureka Homestead Bancorp	ERKH	Metairie, LA	MHC	2019	21.0
Richmond Mutual Bancorporation	RMBI	Richmond, IN	MHC	2019	36.5
TEB Bancorp (MHC)	TBBA	Wauwatosa, WI	MHC	2019	−10.0
Rhinebeck Bancorp, Inc. (MHC)	RBKB	Poughkeepsie, NY	MHC	2019	17.5
1895 Bancorp Of Wisconsin, Inc. (MHC)	BCOW	Greenfield, WI	MHC	2019	−4.0
CBM Bancorp, Inc.	CBMB	Baltimore, MD	Standard	2018	28.0
Sidney Federal Savings and Loan Association	SFSA	Sidney, NE	Standard	2018	0.0
Mid-Southern Bancorp, Inc.	MSVB	Salem, IN	Second Step	2018	24.5
Columbia Financial, Inc. (MHC)	CLBK	Fair Lawn, NJ	MHC	2018	54.2
SSB Bancorp, Inc. (MHC)	SSBP	Pittsburgh, PA	MHC	2018	−5.5
Seneca Financial Corp. (MHC)	SNNF	Baldwinsville, NY	MHC	2017	18.0
FFBW, Inc. (MHC)	FFBW	Brookfield, WI	MHC	2017	15.3
PDL Community Bancorp (MHC)	PDLB	Bronx, NY	MHC	2017	49.0

EXHIBIT A.1 *(Continued)*

Company	Ticker	HQ	Type	Year	IPO pop (%)
Eagle Financial Bancorp, Inc.	EFBI	Cincinnati, OH	Standard	2017	49.2
Heritage NOLA Bancorp, Inc.	HRGG	Covington, LA	Standard	2017	22.2
Community First Bancshares, Inc. (MHC)	CFBI	Covington, GA	MHC	2017	32.9
PCSB Financial Corporation	PCSB	Yorktown Heights, NY	Standard	2017	64.6
HV Bancorp, Inc.	HVBC	Doylestown, PA	Standard	2017	36.7
Community Savings Bancorp, Inc.	CCSB	Caldwell, OH	Standard	2017	30.0
Bancorp 34, Inc.	BCTF	Alamogorda, NM	Second Step	2016	27.5
Ottawa Bancorp, Inc.	OTTW	Ottawa, IL	Second Step	2016	15.7
FSB Bancorp, Inc.	FSBC	Fairport, NY	Second Step	2016	22.3
WCF Bancorp, Inc.	WCFB	Webster City, IA	Second Step	2016	9.9
Randolph Bancorp, Inc.	RNDB	Stoughton, MA	Standard	2016	21.9
Best Hometown Bancorp, Inc.	BTHT	Collinsville, IL	Standard	2016	10.0
HarborOne Bancorp, Inc. (MHC)	HONE	Brockton, MA	MHC	2016	29.2
Central Federal Bancshares, Inc.	CFDB	Rolla, MO	Standard	2016	4.5
PB Bancorp, Inc.	PBBI	Putnam, CT	Second Step	2016	12.5
New Bancorp, Inc.	NWBB	New Buffalo, MI	Standard	2015	19.0
Cincinnati Bancorp (MHC)	CNNB	Cincinnati, OH	MHC	2015	0.0
MSB Financial Corp.	MSBF	Millington, NJ	Second Step	2015	19.8
Provident Bancorp, Inc. (MHC)	PVBC	Amesbury, MA	MHC	2015	28.5

EXHIBIT A.1 *(Continued)*

Company	Ticker	HQ	Type	Year	IPO pop (%)
Equitable Financial Corp.	EQFN	Grand Island, NE	Second Step	2015	8.5
Kearny Financial Corp.	KRNY	Fairfield, NJ	Second Step	2015	72
First Northwest Bancorp	FNWB	Port Angeles, WA	Standard	2015	21.8
MW Bancorp, Inc.	MWBC	Cincinnati, OH	Standard	2015	15.0
Ben Franklin Financial, Inc.	BFFI	Arlington Heights, IL	Second Step	2015	3.0
Beneficial Bancorp, Inc.	BNCL	Philadelphia, PA	Second Step	2015	8.2
Median					**18.5**

Source: Bloomberg

THREE-YEAR ANNIVERSARY

Regulators do not approve an acquisition of a thrift prior to the three-year anniversary of its IPO; hence, that anniversary date is something investors keep track of. This three-year clock turns on when they are fully public, which means the thrift would have had to do a standard conversion or already be an MHC and do their second step.

STANDARD CONVERSION

Let us assume that a thrift with equity value of $50MM adopts a plan of conversion and hires bankers. To keep the math simple assume they appraise the value at $100MM, and the ESOP, MRP/RRP (management recognition plan/ recognition and retention plans), and expenses cost $10MM. As the calculation in Exhibit A.2 shows, the pro forma book value per share is $14. The depositors essentially got it at a discount to book of 29%. Assuming no other quirks, this could see a day 1 pop of close to 30% and eventually drift up to peer valuation. Not a bad day for the depositor turned shareholder as he realizes the value of the pre-conversion equity in addition to their contribution.

The valuation for an MHC conversion can be complicated due to the structure, since only less than 50% of the shares are in the float. To simplify matters, value the thrift on a fully converted basis and make assumptions on the pricing of the second stage conversion.

EXHIBIT A.2 Mutual Conversion

$MM	
Pre-Conversion equity	50
IPO Raise	100
ESOP, MRP/RRP, and expenses	10
Pro forma post conversion equity	140
Outstanding shares	10
Book value	14
IPO price discount to book	29%

RUSSELL RECONSTITUTION

The FTSE Russell indexes go through an annual reconstitution ("Russell recon") in June (Exhibit A.3), and these rebalancing changes are worth following since several index funds track these indexes. There are about $9 trillion in assets that are benchmarked to these indexes. The indexes add IPOs on a quarterly basis, but the recon event is only once a year. The process starts with a ranking date in early May (last done on May 8th, 2020).

EXHIBIT A.3 Russell 2020 Calendar

Friday, May 8 – "rank day" – Russell US Index membership eligibility for 2020 reconstitution determined from constituent market capitalization at market close.
Friday, May 22 – "query period" begins – preliminary shares and free float information for Russell 3000 Index constituents are published daily and queries welcomed (query period runs through June 12).
June 5 – preliminary US index add and delete lists posted to the FTSE Russell website after 6 p.m. US eastern time.
June 12 & 19 – US index add and delete lists (reflecting any updates) posted to the FTSE Russell website after 6 p.m. US eastern time.
June 15 – "lock down" period begins – US index add and delete lists are considered final.
June 26 – Russell Reconstitution is final after the close of the US equity markets.
June 29 – equity markets open with the newly reconstituted Russell US Indexes.

Source: FTSE Russell

THE RECON PLAY

The Russell recon is a weighting game but definitely not a waiting game. What do we mean? Most of the price action occurs in the lead-up based on the expectation. The primary threshold for small banks is to estimate the market cap cutoff for entry into the Russell 2000. This cutoff was $94.8MM in 2020,

$152.3MM in 2019, and $159.2MM in 2018. There are four actions possible: 1. New name gets added to the index; 2. Existing name gets deleted from the index; 3. Stays in the index but has a lower weight; and 4. Stays in the index and has a higher weight. Typically, the most play is to be had with 1 and 2. After estimating the weight, calculate the projected demand after the indexes are reconstituted. Divide this by the average daily volume to see how many normal days of buying or selling there needs to be or how much additional volume there needs to on one day. You would need access to the Index provider or to a sell-side firm that tracks it to check the accuracy of the process.

EXHIBIT A.4 Banks Added to Russell 3000 Performance vs. KRE (Quartiles)

Reconstitution Year	Quartile	6-Mo Prior vs. KRE (%)	3-Mo Prior vs. KRE (%)	May 31 vs. KRE (%)	6-Mo After vs. KRE (%)	1-Year After vs. KRE (%)
2016	Top	18%	8%	4%	6%	14%
	Bottom	6%	3%	−5%	−20%	−13%
2017	Top	30%	2%	11%	9%	6%
	Bottom	7%	−5%	−2%	−10%	−14%
2018	Top	18%	8%	8%	15%	5%
	Bottom	0%	0%	−8%	−3%	−3%
2019	Top	19%	−1%	2%	1%	9%
	Bottom	5%	−6%	−4%	−8%	−13%

Source: Hovde Group

COMPENDIUM OF BANK STATS

EXHIBIT A.5 Number of Community Banks

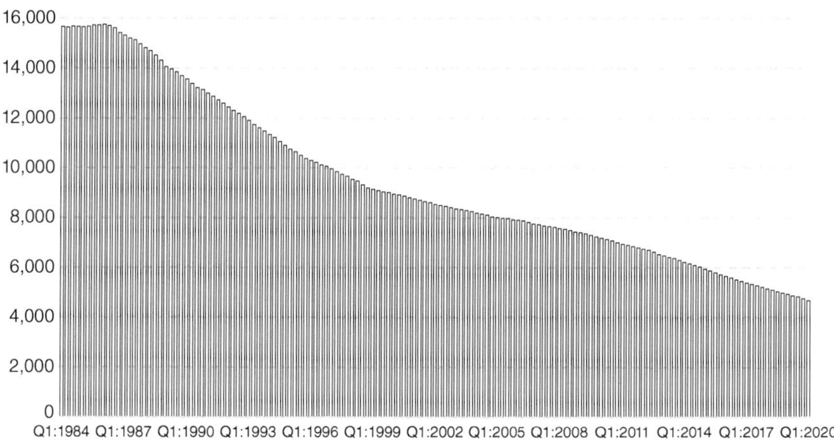

Source: FDIC

EXHIBIT A.6 Number of Total Insured Institutions

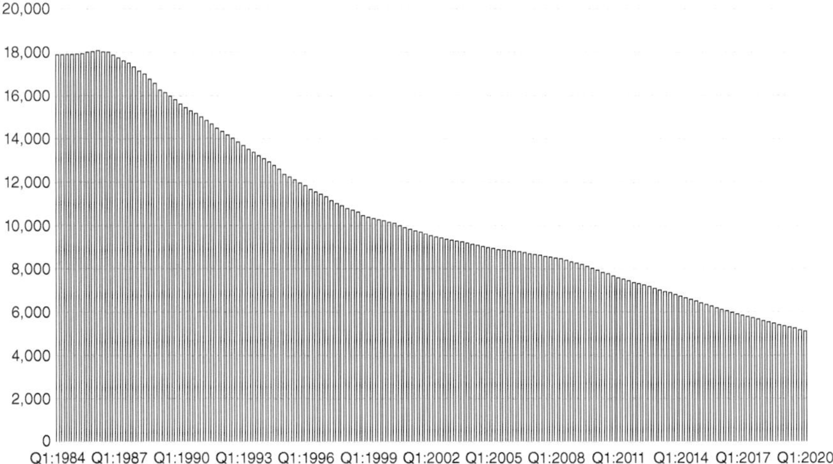

Source: FDIC

EXHIBIT A.7 Number of Bank Charters Approved

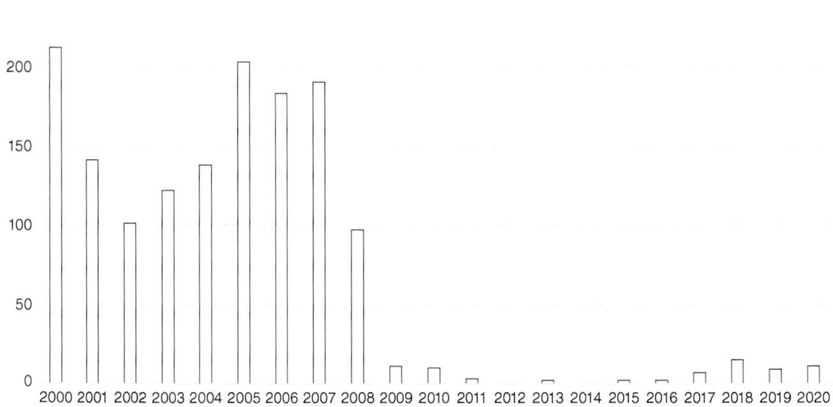

Source: FDIC

Note: This includes shelf charters: 2 in 2009, 8 in 2010, and 3 in 2011 to acquire failed banks.

EXHIBIT A.8 Number of De Novo Applications Filed and Withdrawn

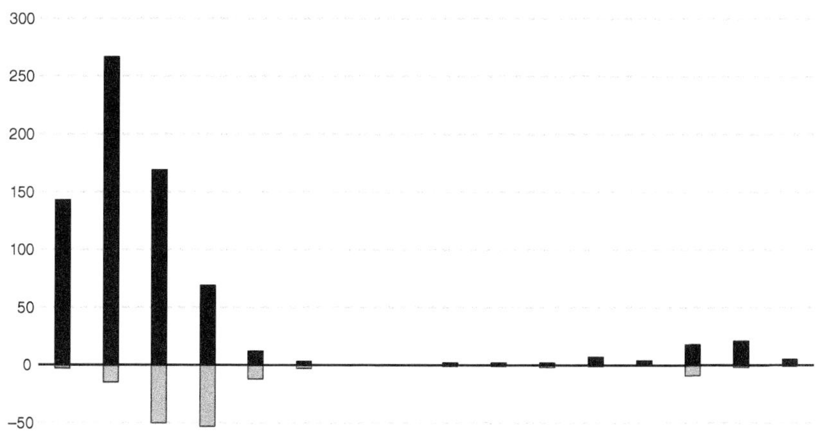

Source: FDIC

EXHIBIT A.9 Number of Problem Banks

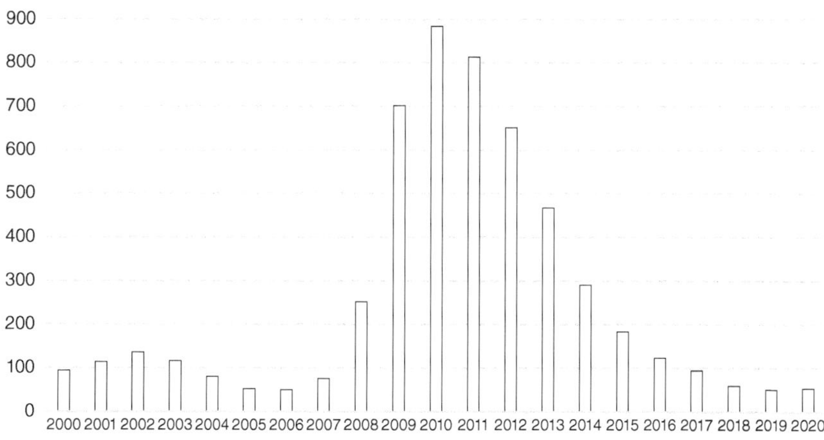

Source: FDIC. YTD March 31st, 2020

EXHIBIT A.10 Number of Failed Banks

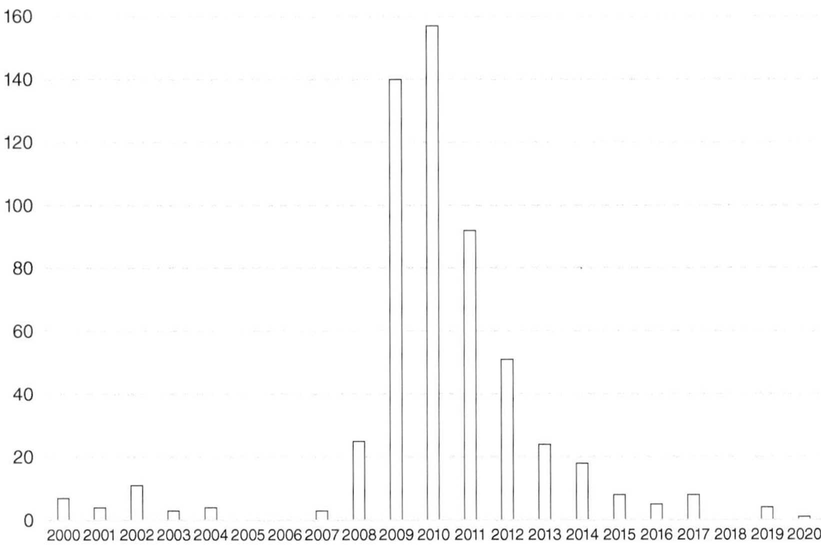

Source: FDIC. YTD March 31st, 2020

EXHIBIT A.11 Number of Branches

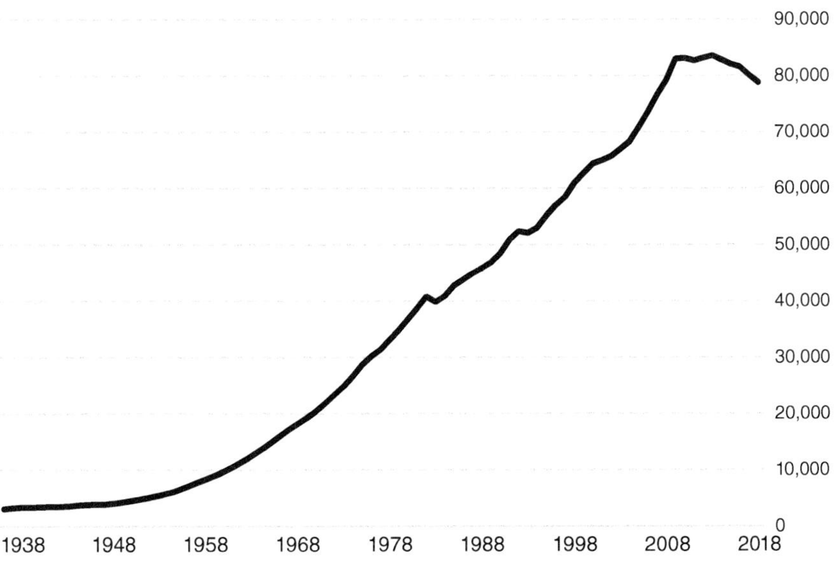

Source: FDIC

EXHIBIT A.12 Employees

Source: FDIC
Note: Data prior to Q1:1990 does not include institutions filing TFRs (Thrift Filing Reports).

EXHIBIT A.13 Assets

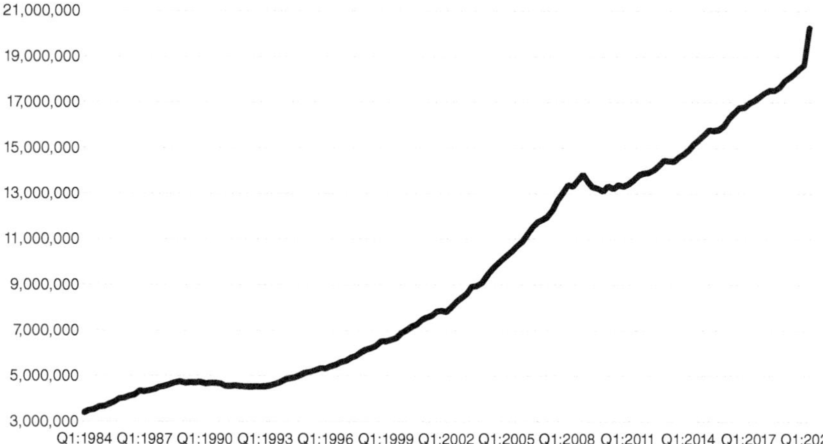

Source: FDIC

EXHIBIT A.14 ROA

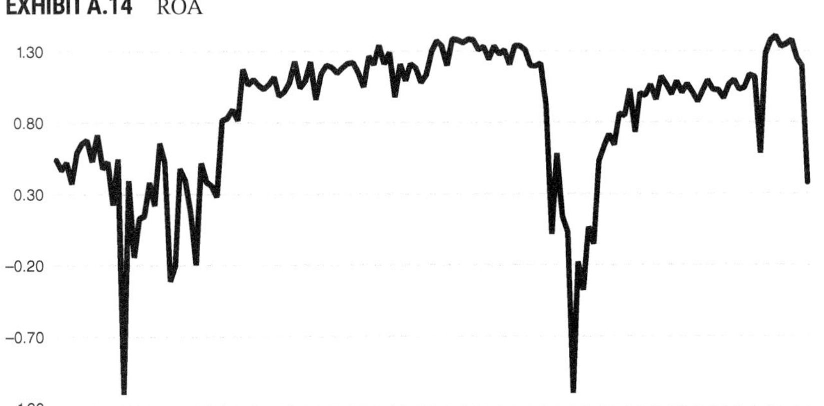

Source: FDIC

EXHIBIT A.15 ROE

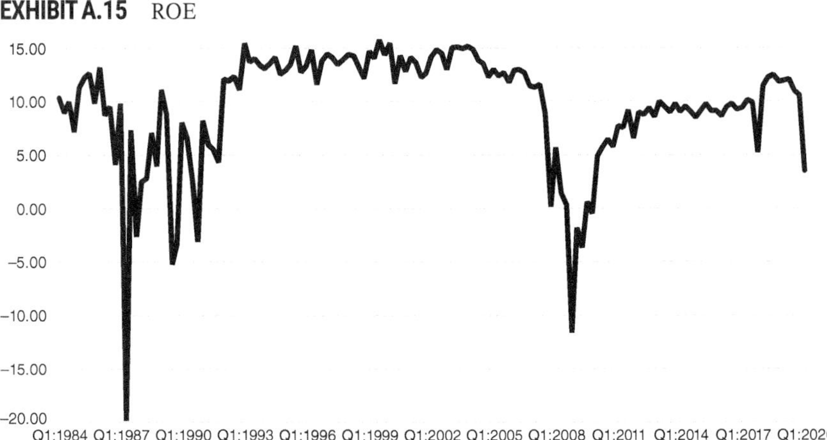

Source: FDIC

EXHIBIT A.16 AEA Yield

Source: FDIC

EXHIBIT A.17 Cost of Funding

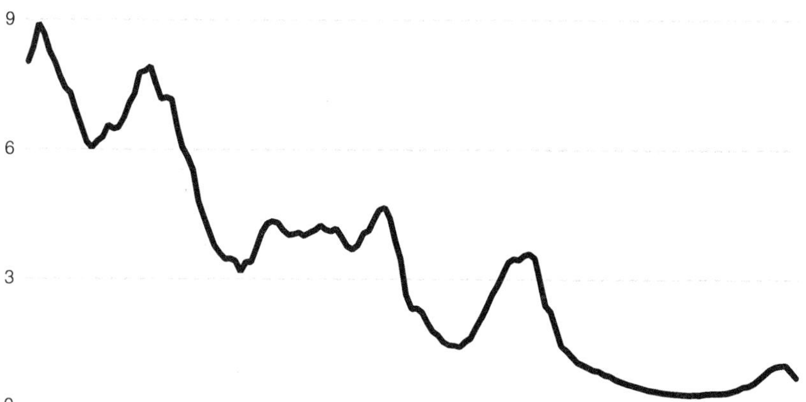

Source: FDIC

EXHIBIT A.18 10-Year US Treasury

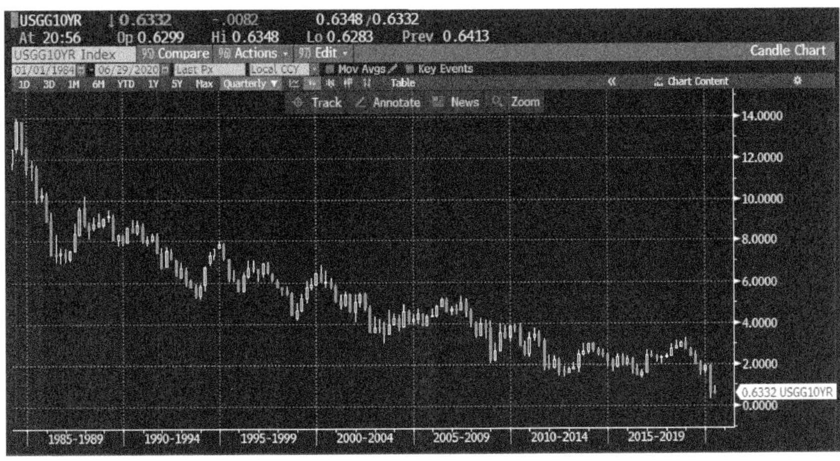

Source: Bloomberg

EXHIBIT A.19 Fed Funds Target Range Midpoint

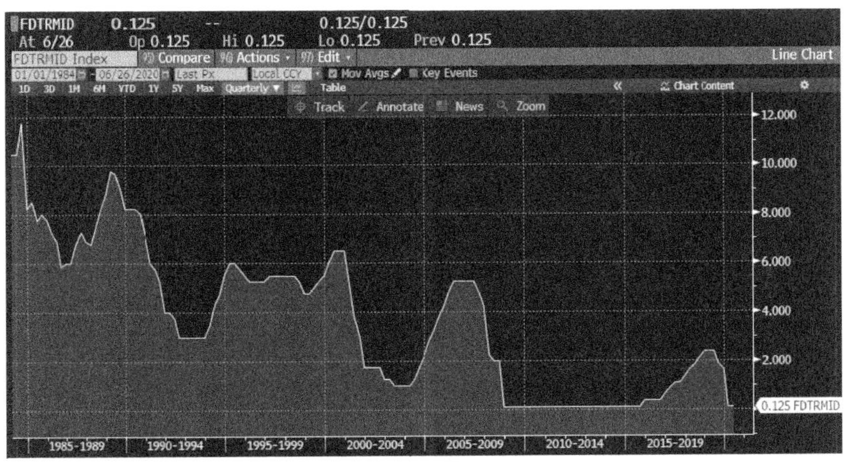

Source: Bloomberg

EXHIBIT A.20 Spread 10-Year vs. 2-Year

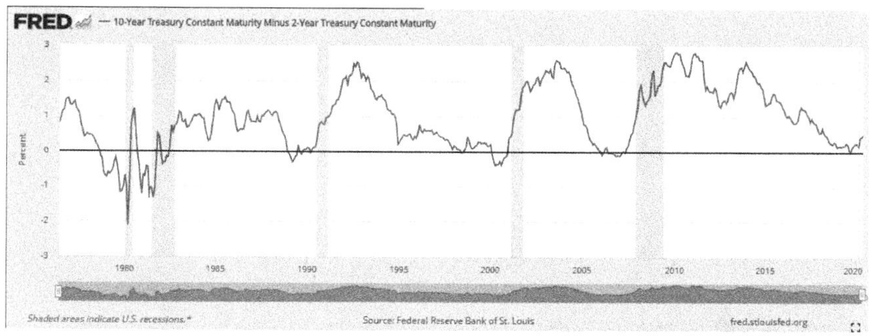

Source: St. Louis Fed

EXHIBIT A.21 NIM

Source: FDIC

EXHIBIT A.22 PPNR Ratio

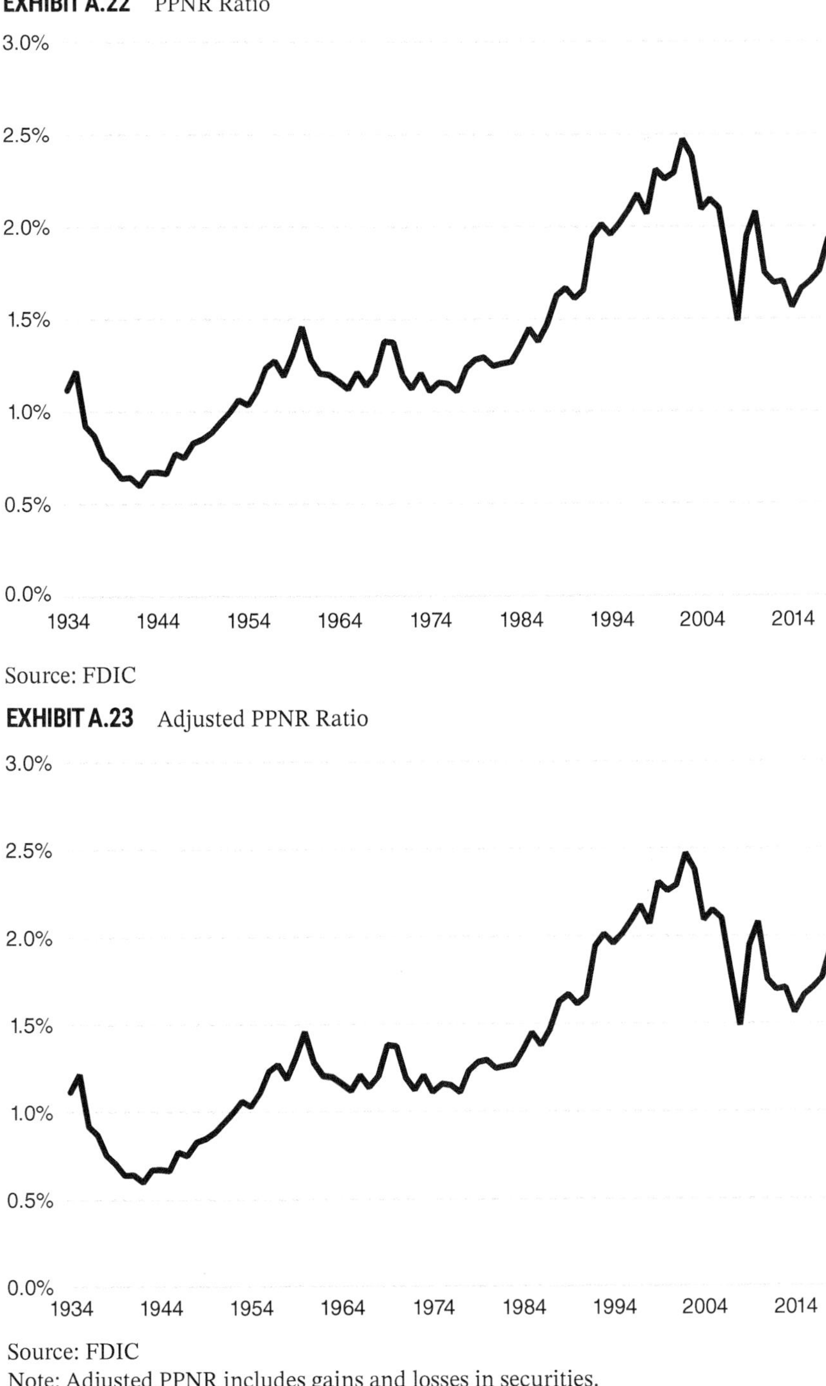

Source: FDIC

EXHIBIT A.23 Adjusted PPNR Ratio

Source: FDIC

Note: Adjusted PPNR includes gains and losses in securities.

EXHIBIT A.24 Gain and Loss of Securities Ratio

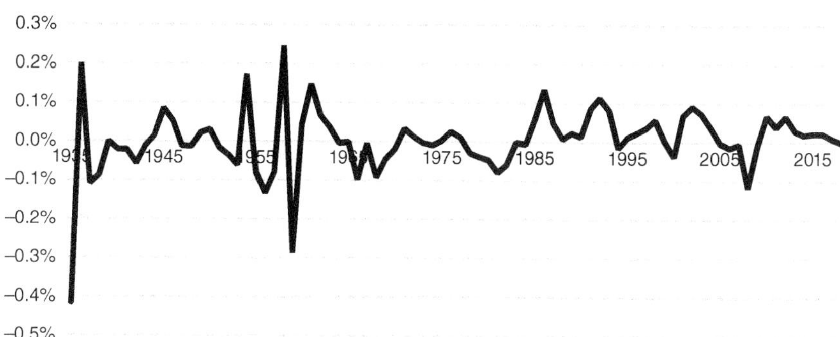

Source: FDIC

EXHIBIT A.25 Non Interest Income as a % of Operating Revenue

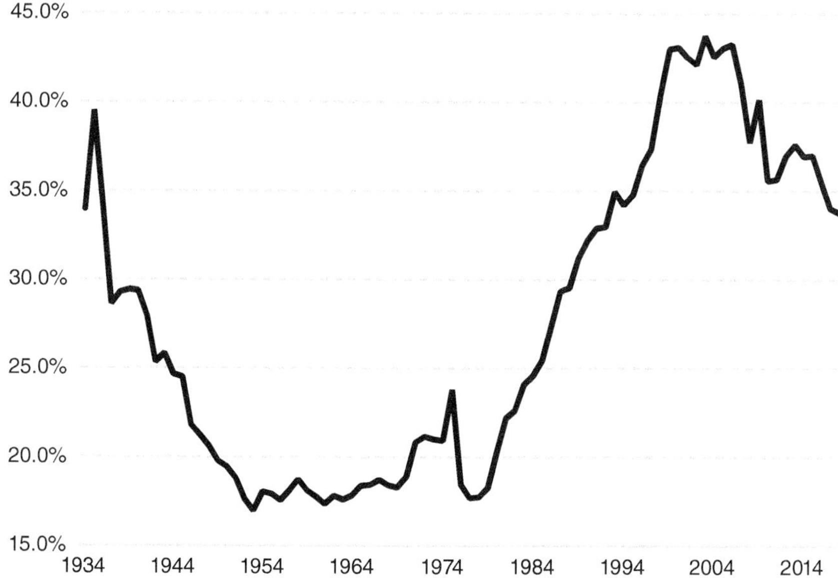

Source: FDIC

EXHIBIT A.26 Efficiency Ratio

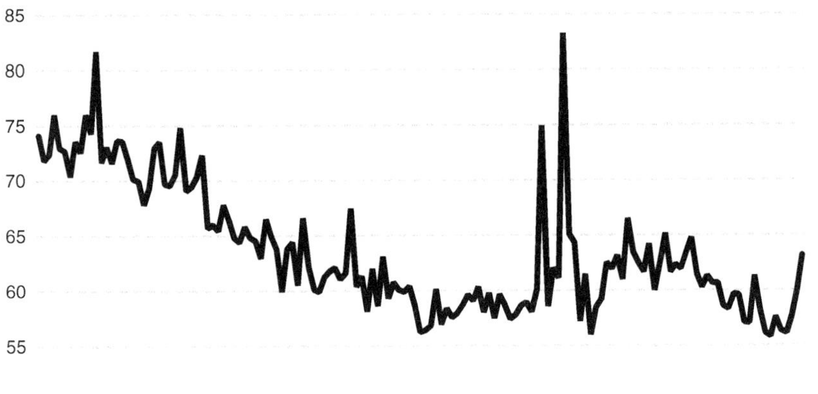

Source: FDIC

EXHIBIT A.27 Non Interest Expense as % of Asset

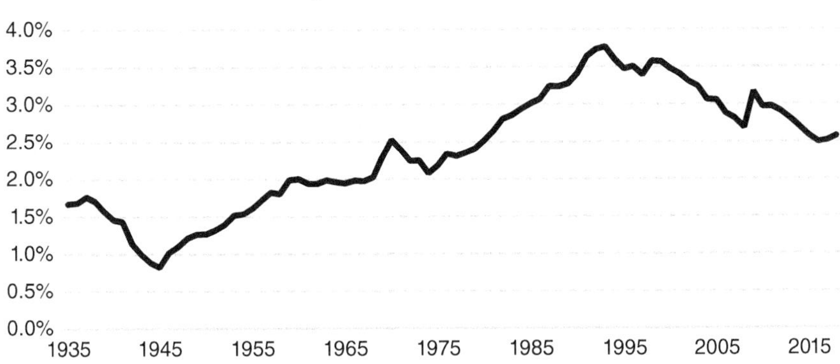

Source: FDIC

EXHIBIT A.28 Assets/Employees

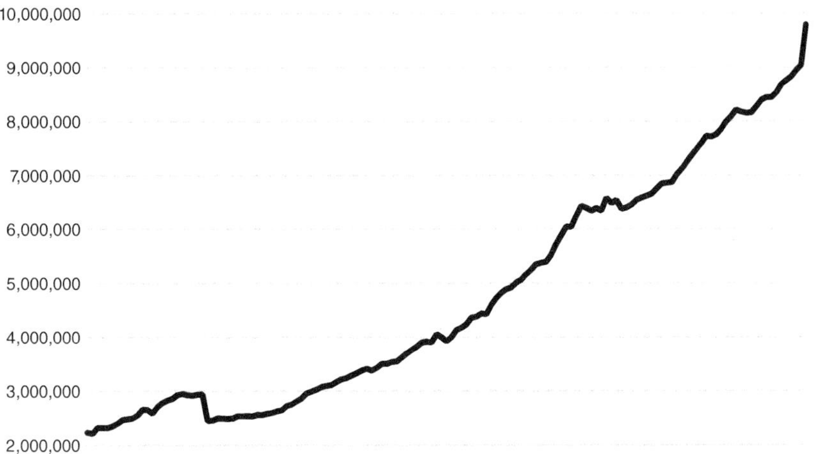

Source: FDIC

EXHIBIT A.29 L/D

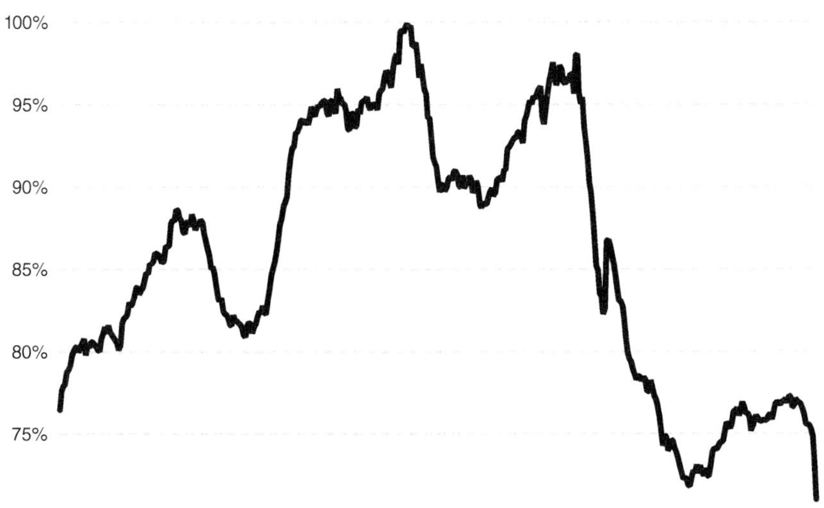

Source: Federal Reserve H.8 Data

EXHIBIT A.30 LLR/Gross Loans

Source: FDIC

EXHIBIT A.31 Reserves/NCOs

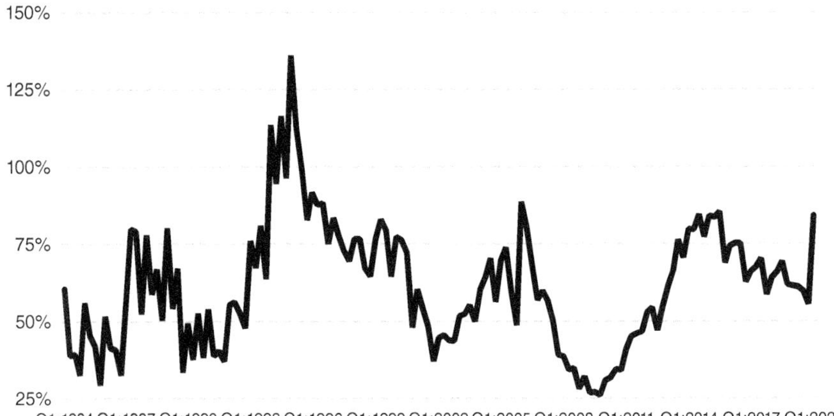

Source: FDIC

EXHIBIT A.32 NCOs/Loans (Not Annualized)

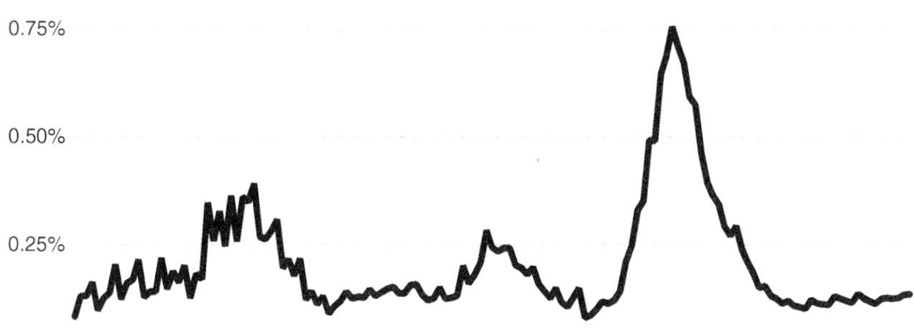

Source: FDIC

EXHIBIT A.33 NPA/Assets

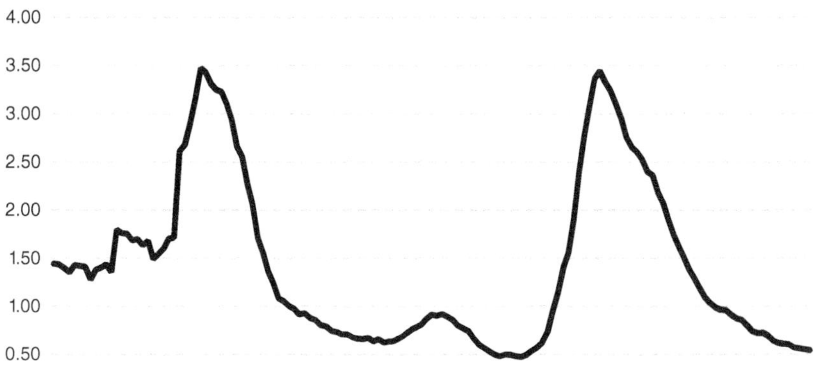

Source: FDIC

EXHIBIT A.34 NPL/Loans

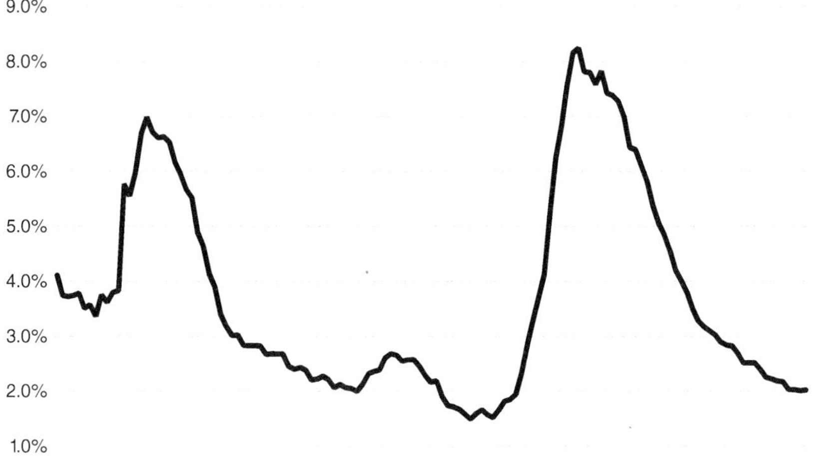

Source: FDIC

EXHIBIT A.35 NCOs – Total Loans and Leases

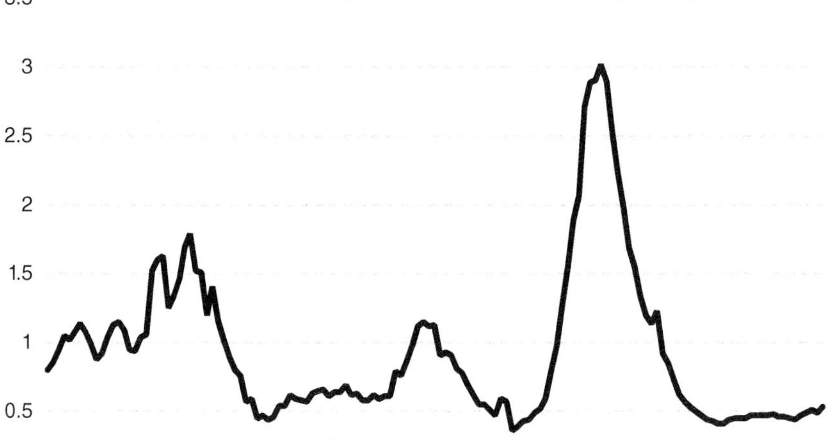

Source: Federal Reserve

EXHIBIT A.36 NCOs – Agriculture Loans

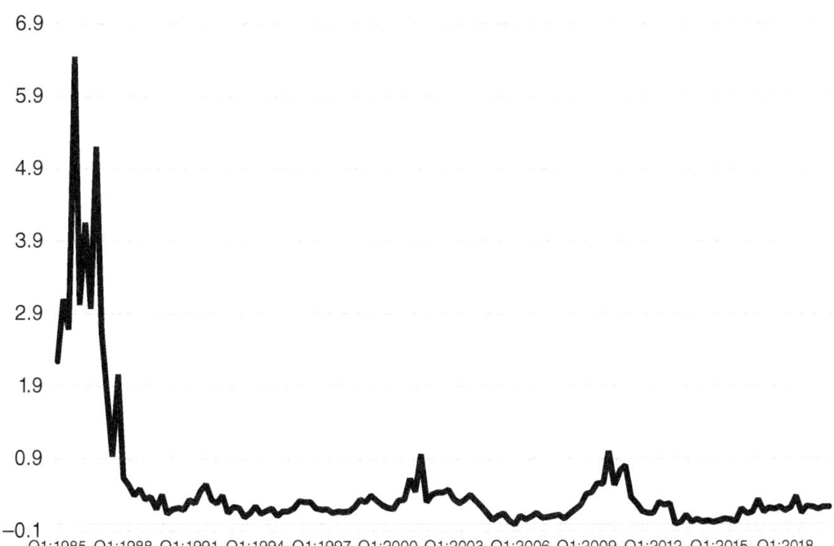

Source: Federal Reserve

EXHIBIT A.37 NCOs – C&I Loans

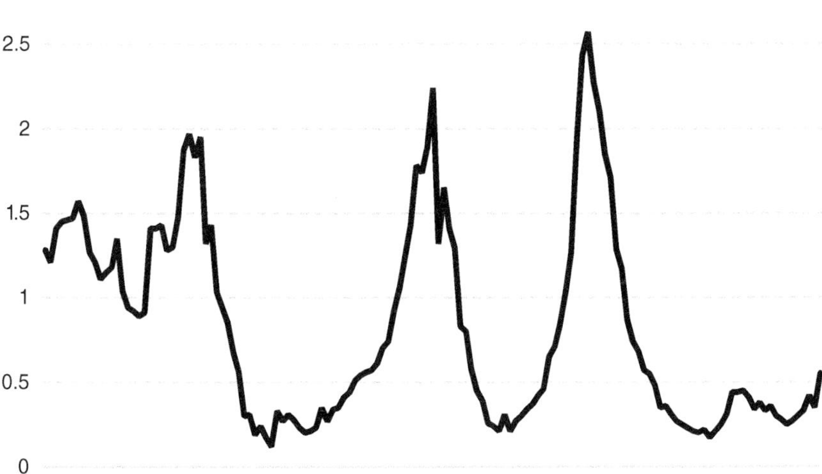

Source: Federal Reserve

EXHIBIT A.38 NCOs – All RE Loans

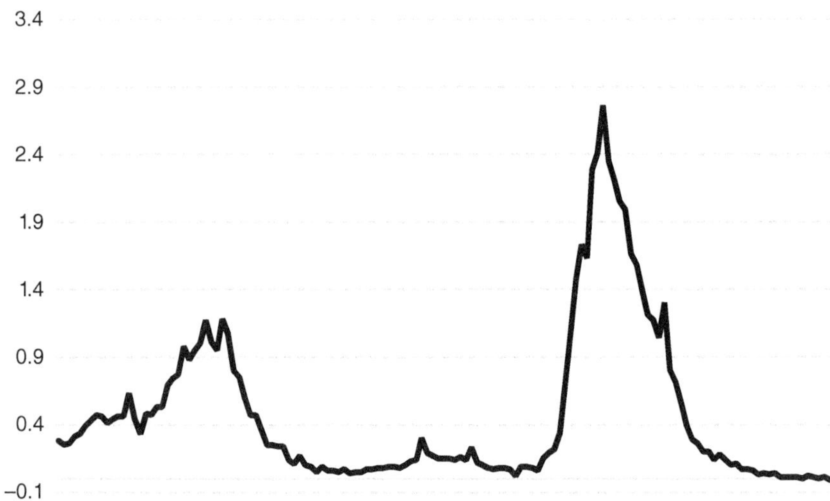

Source: Federal Reserve

EXHIBIT A.39 NCOs – All Consumer Loans

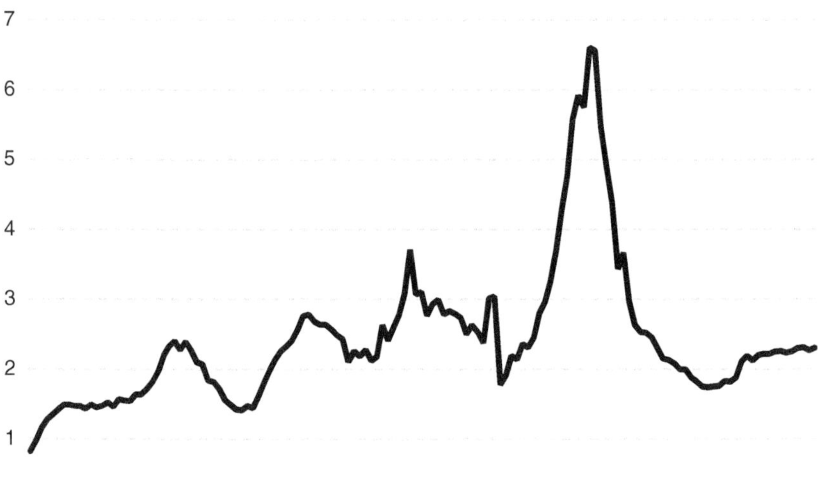

Source: Federal Reserve

EXHIBIT A.40 NCOs – 1-4 Residential Loans

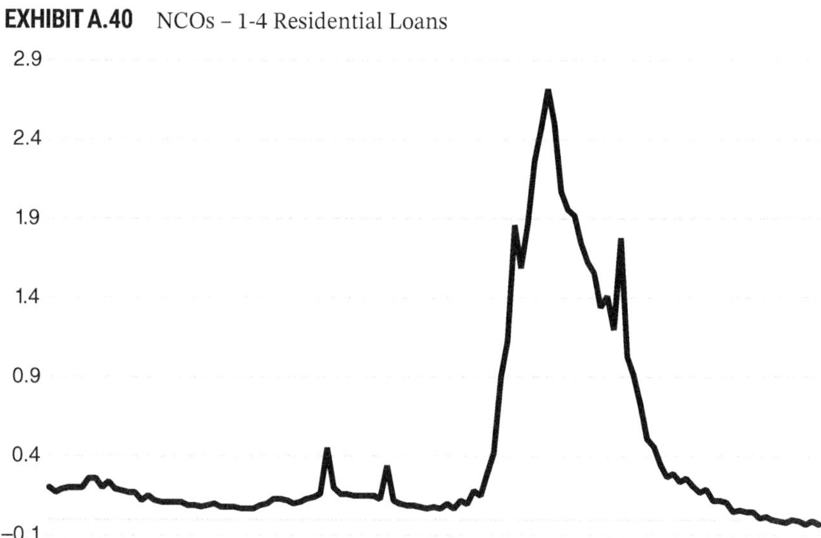

Source: Federal Reserve

EXHIBIT A.41 NCOs – Leasing Finance

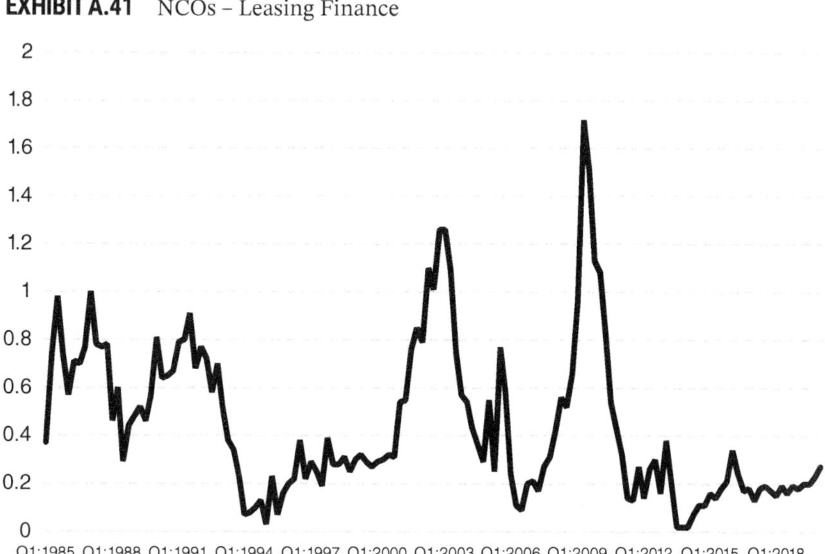

Source: Federal Reserve

EXHIBIT A.42 NCOs – Credit Card

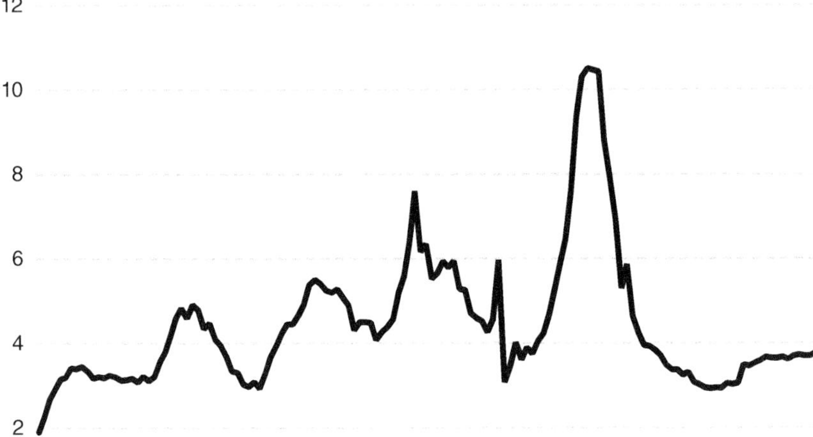

Source: Federal Reserve

EXHIBIT A.43 NCOs – Other Consumer

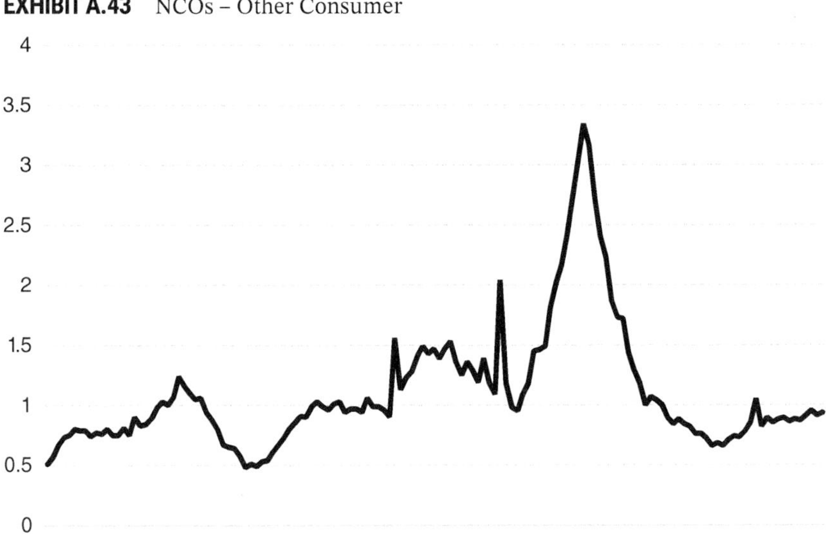

Source: Federal Reserve

EXHIBIT A.44 NCOs – CRE

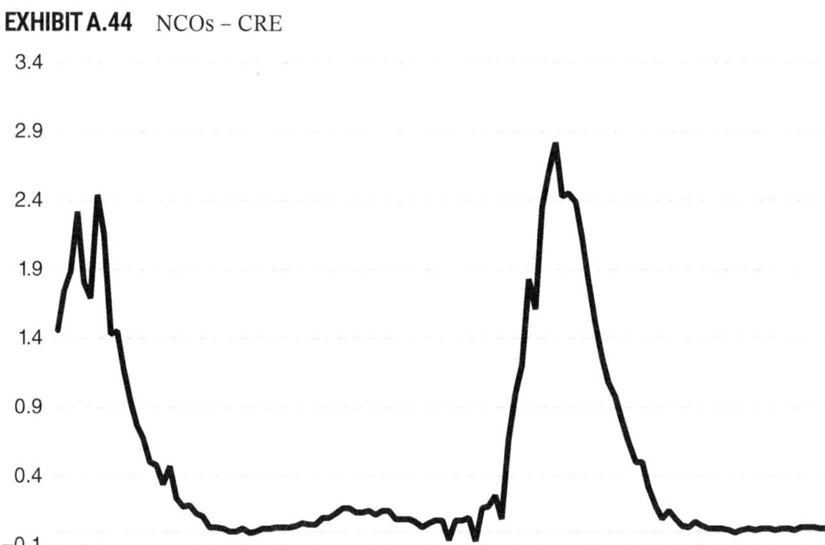

Source: Federal Reserve

EXHIBIT A.45 NCOs – Farmland Loans

Source: Federal Reserve

EXHIBIT A.46 Delinquency Rate – All

Source: Federal Reserve
Note: Past 30-day delinquent loans

EXHIBIT A.47 Delinquency Rate – Agriculture Loans

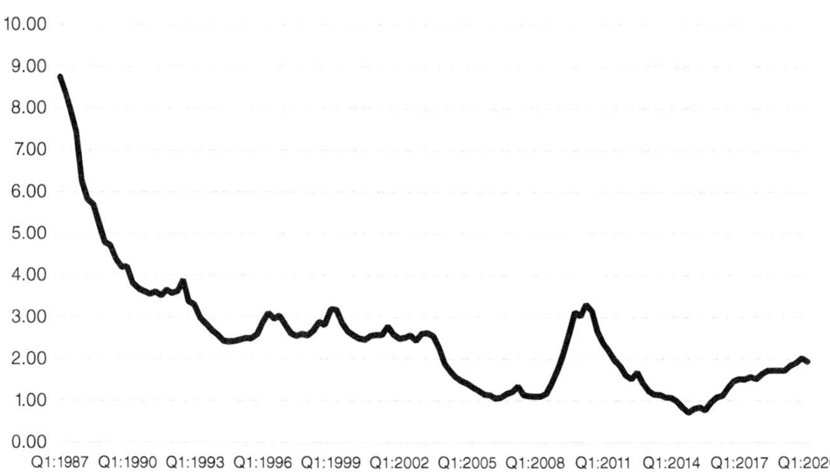

Source: Federal Reserve
Note: Past 30-day delinquent loans

EXHIBIT A.48 Delinquency Rate – C&I Loans

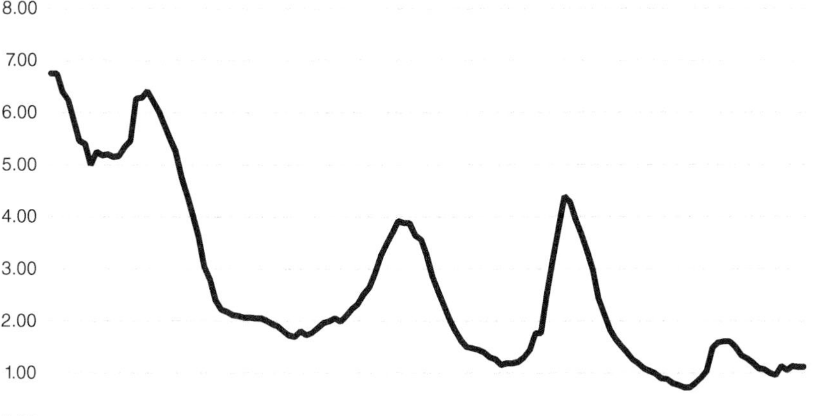

Source: Federal Reserve
Note: Past 30-day delinquent loans

EXHIBIT A.49 Delinquency Rate – All RE

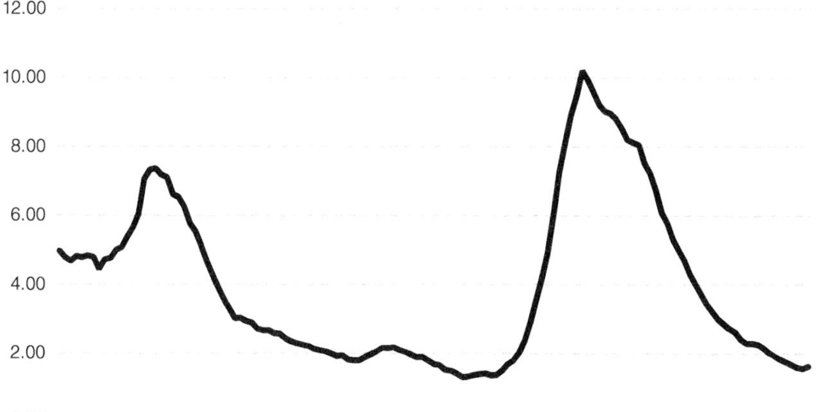

Source: Federal Reserve
Note: Past 30-day delinquent loans

EXHIBIT A.50 Delinquency Rate – All Consumer

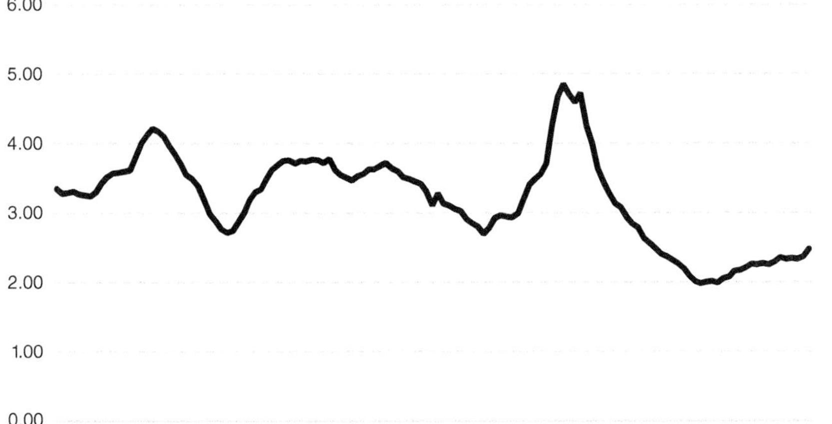

Source: Federal Reserve
Note: Past 30-day delinquent loans

EXHIBIT A.51 Delinquency Rate – 1-4 Resi

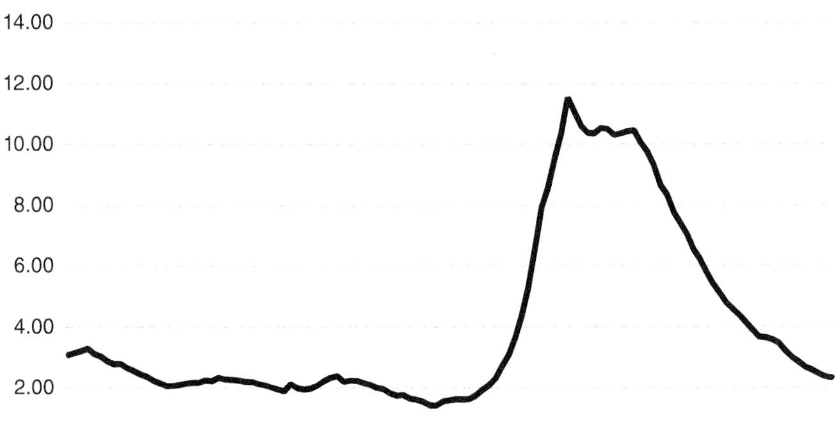

Source: Federal Reserve
Note: Past 30-day delinquent loans

EXHIBIT A.52 Delinquency Rate – Lease Financing

Source: Federal Reserve
Note: Past 30-day delinquent loans

EXHIBIT A.53 Delinquency Rate – Credit Card

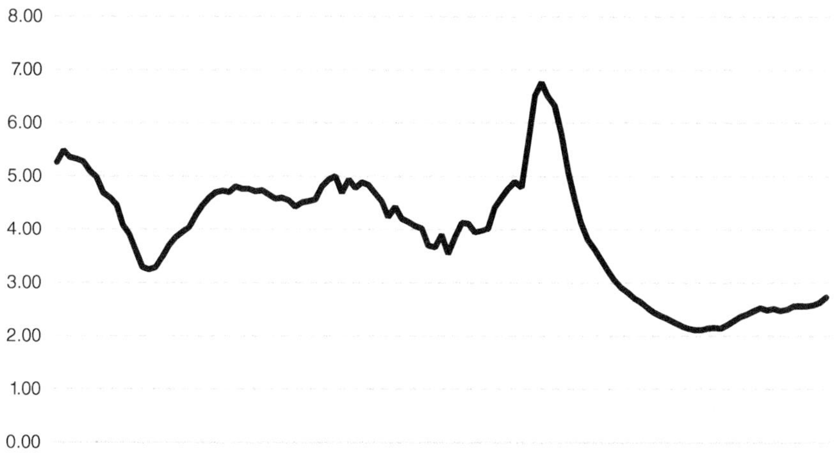

Source: Federal Reserve
Note: Past 30-day delinquent loans

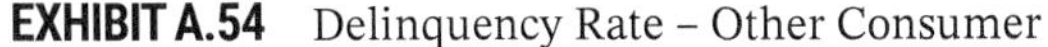

EXHIBIT A.54 Delinquency Rate – Other Consumer

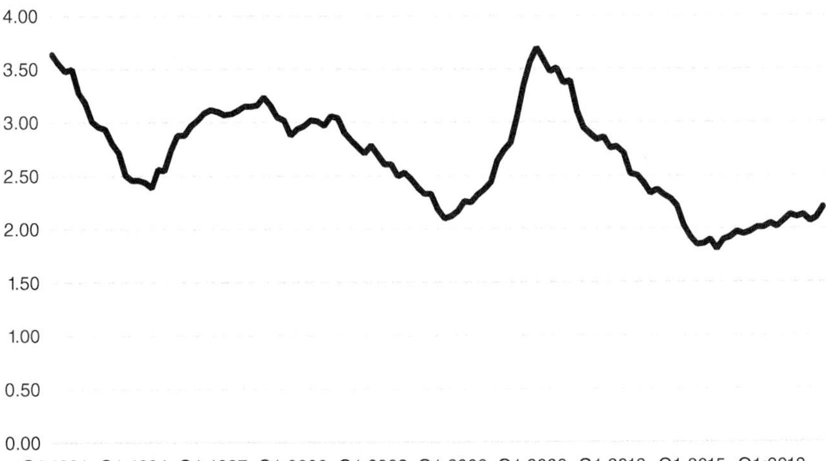

Source: Federal Reserve
Note: Past 30-day delinquent loans

EXHIBIT A.55 Delinquency Rate – CRE

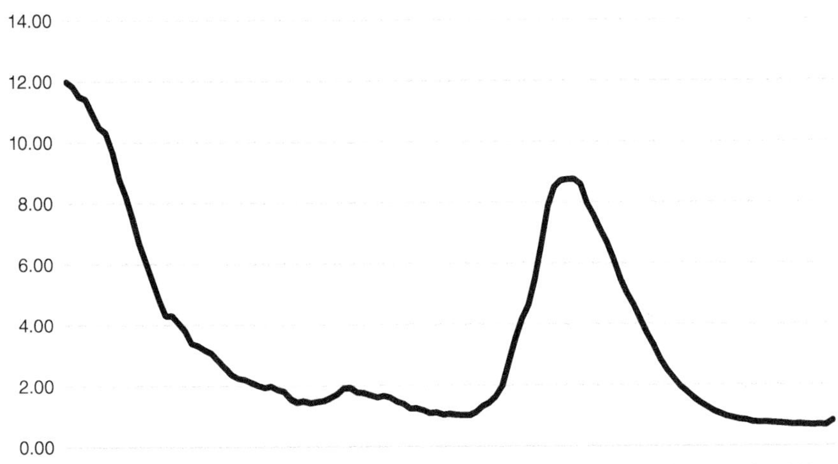

Source: Federal Reserve
Note: Past 30-day delinquent loans

EXHIBIT A.56 Delinquency Rate – Farmland

Source: Federal Reserve
Note: Past 30-day delinquent loans

EXHIBIT A.57 Net Percent Tightening Standards for C&I Loans to Large and Mid-Market Firms

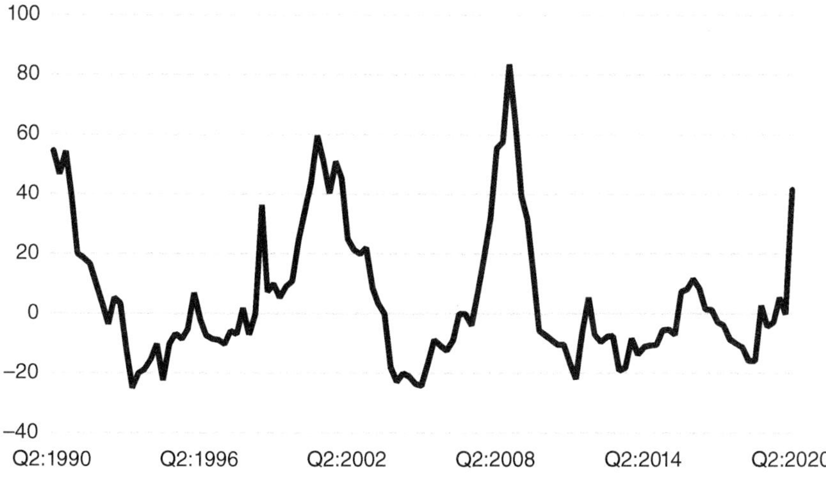

Source: Federal Reserve

EXHIBIT A.58 Net Percent Tightening Standards for C&I Loans to Small Firms

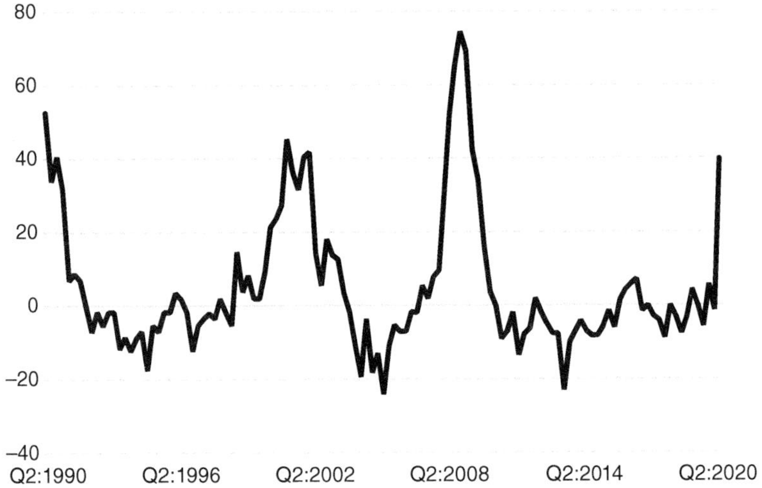

80
60
40
20
0
–20
–40
Q2:1990
Q2:1996
Q2:2002
Q2:2008
Q2:2014
Q2:2020

Source: Federal Reserve

EXHIBIT A.59 Number of Consumers with New Foreclosures (000s)

600
500
400
300
200
100
0
Q1:03
Q1:05
Q1:07
Q1:09
Q1:11
Q1:13
Q1:15
Q1:17
Q1:19

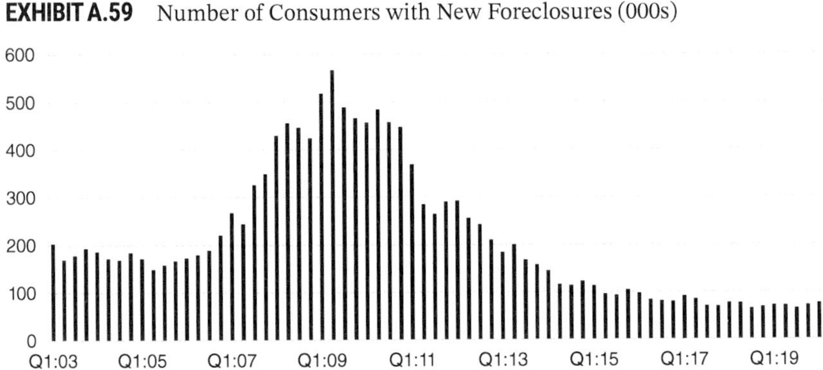

Source: NY Fed Consumer Credit Panel/Equifax

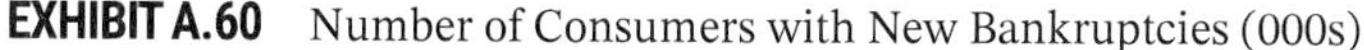

EXHIBIT A.60 Number of Consumers with New Bankruptcies (000s)

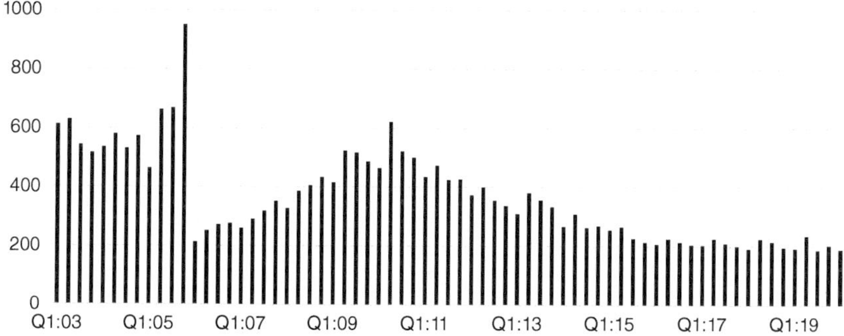

Source: NY Fed Consumer Credit Panel/Equifax

EXHIBIT A.61 90+ Day Delinquency Rate – All Consumer

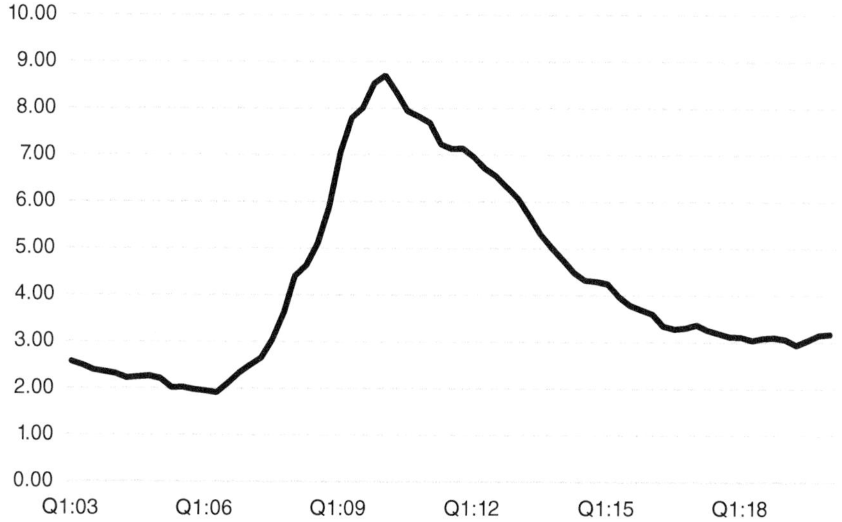

Source: NY Fed Consumer Credit Panel/Equifax

EXHIBIT A.62 90+ Day Delinquency Rate – Mortgage

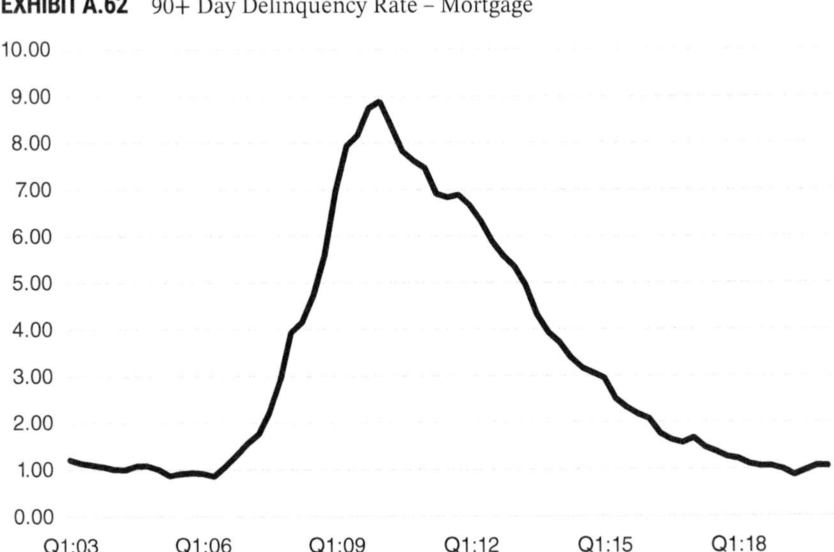

Source: NY Fed Consumer Credit Panel/Equifax

EXHIBIT A.63 90+ Day Delinquency Rate – HELOC

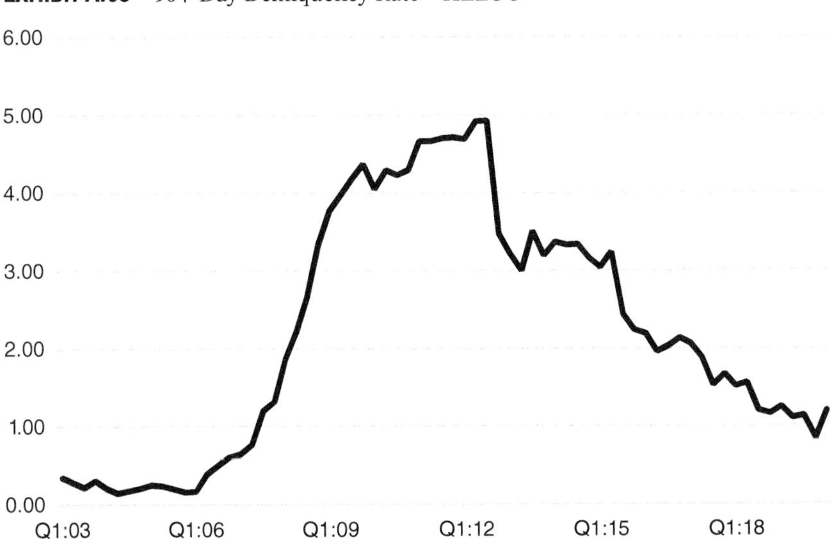

Source: NY Fed Consumer Credit Panel/Equifax

EXHIBIT A.64 90+ Day Delinquency Rate – Auto Loans

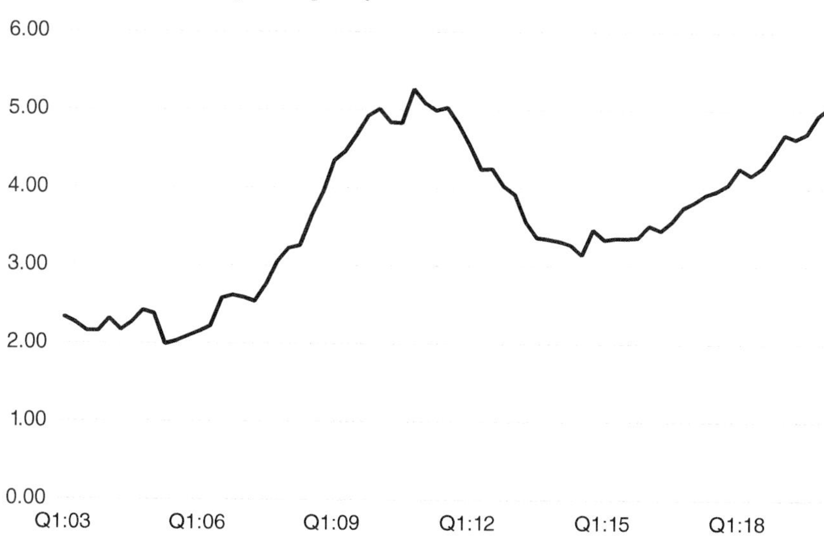

Source: NY Fed Consumer Credit Panel/Equifax

EXHIBIT A.65 90+ Day Delinquency Rate – Credit Card

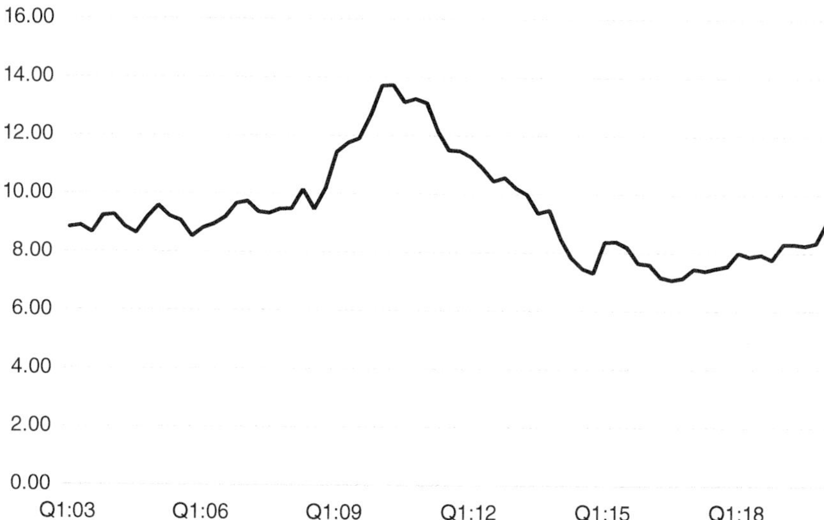

Source: NY Fed Consumer Credit Panel/Equifax

EXHIBIT A.66 90+ Day Delinquency Rate – Student Loans

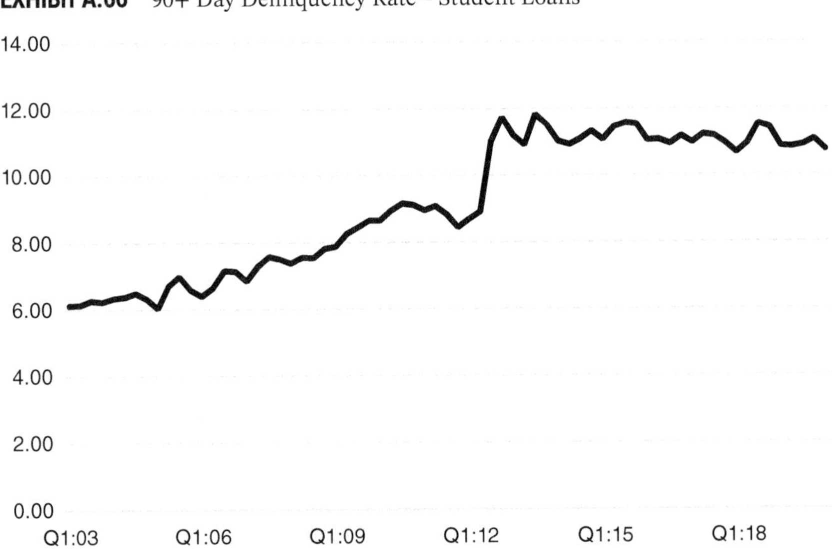

Source: NY Fed Consumer Credit Panel/Equifax

EXHIBIT A.67 Debt Balance $ Trillions – All Consumer

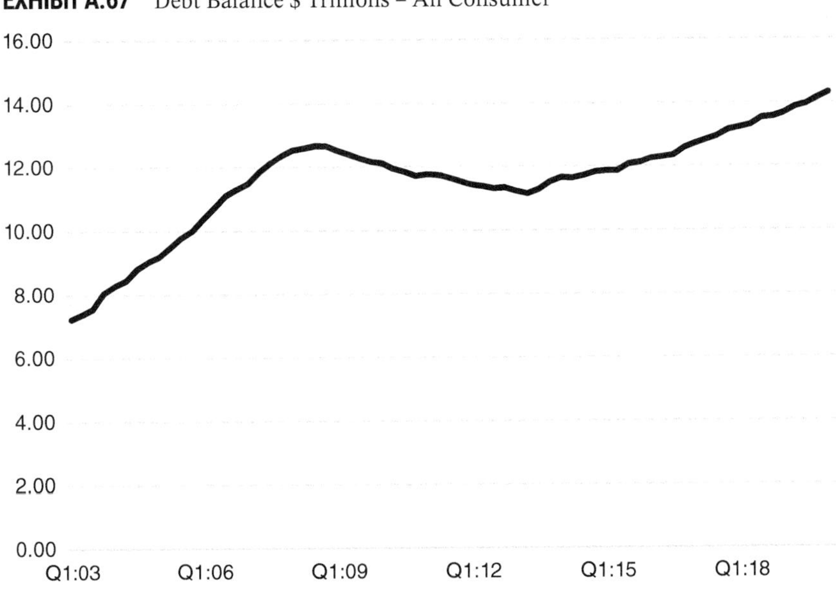

Source: NY Fed Consumer Credit Panel/Equifax

EXHIBIT A.68 Debt Balance $ Trillions – Mortgage

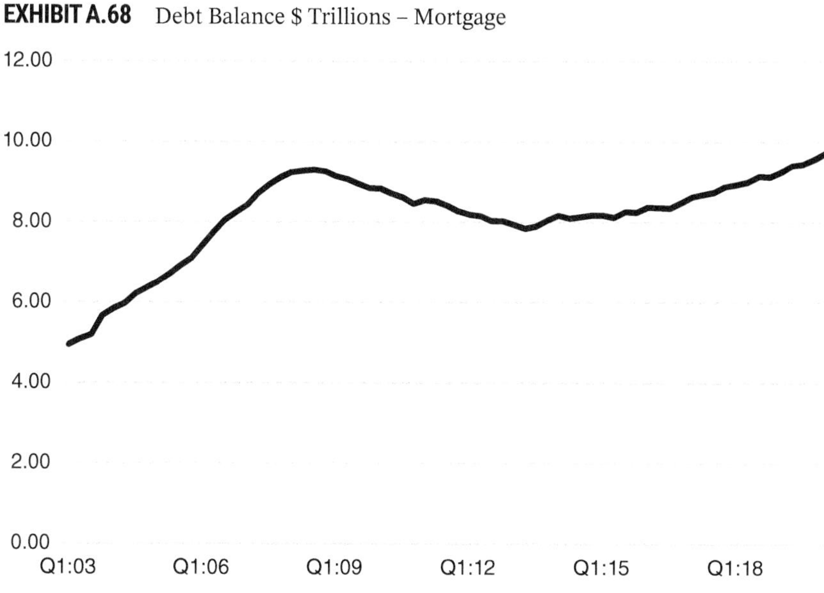

Source: NY Fed Consumer Credit Panel/Equifax

EXHIBIT A.69 Debt Balance $ Trillions – Home Equity Revolving

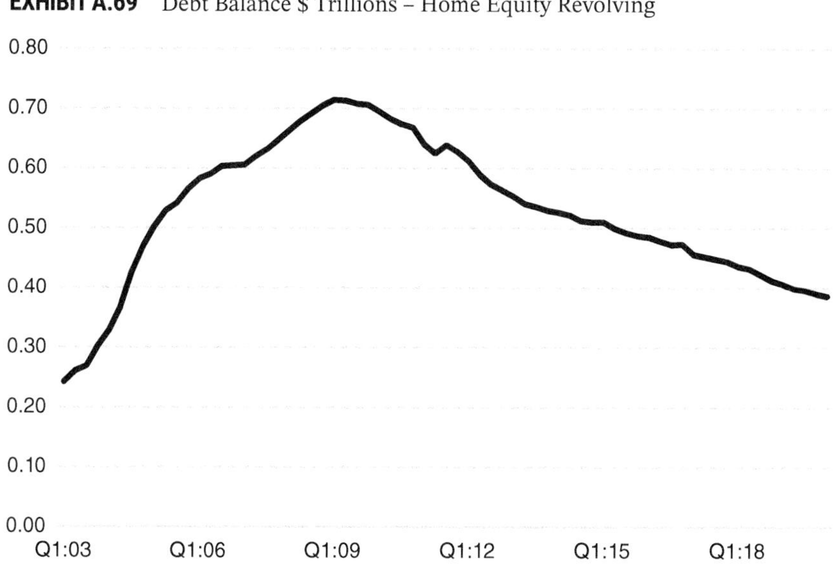

Source: NY Fed Consumer Credit Panel/Equifax

EXHIBIT A.70 Debt Balance $ Trillions – Auto Loans

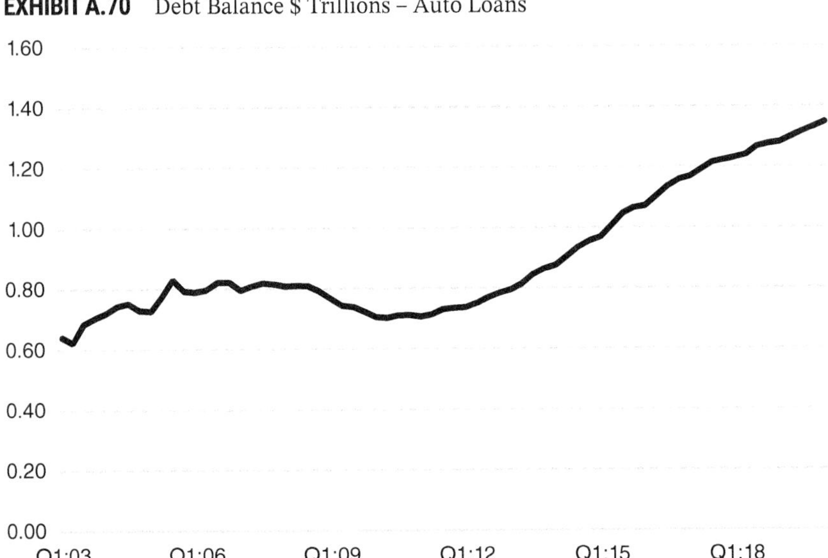

Source: NY Fed Consumer Credit Panel/Equifax

EXHIBIT A.71 Debt Balance $ Trillions – Credit Card

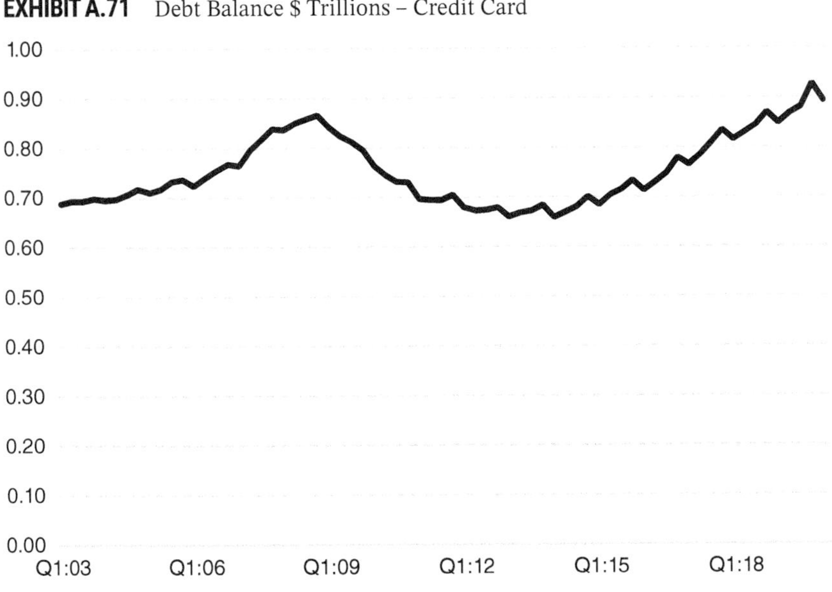

Source: NY Fed Consumer Credit Panel/Equifax

EXHIBIT A.72 Debt Balance $ Trillions – Student Loans

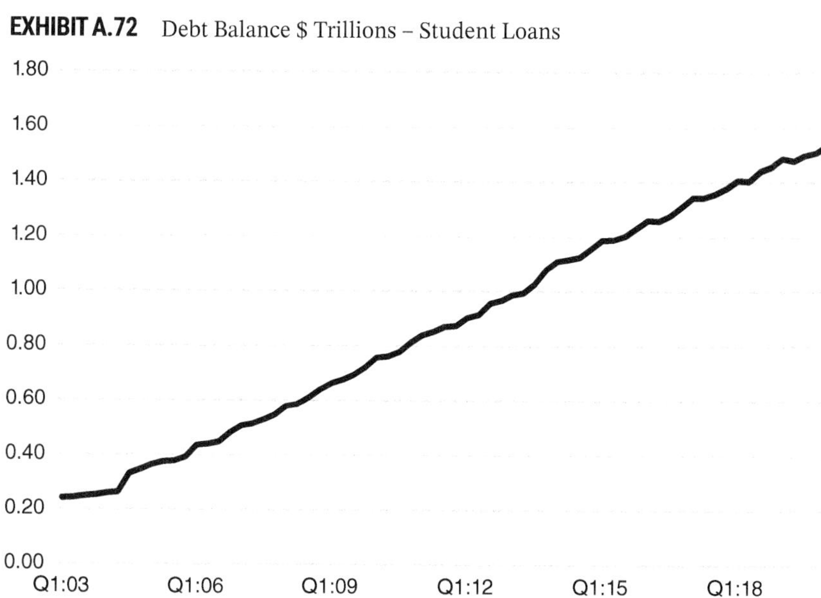

Source: NY Fed Consumer Credit Panel/Equifax

EXHIBIT A.73 Debt Balance $ Millions – Loans Secured by Real Estate

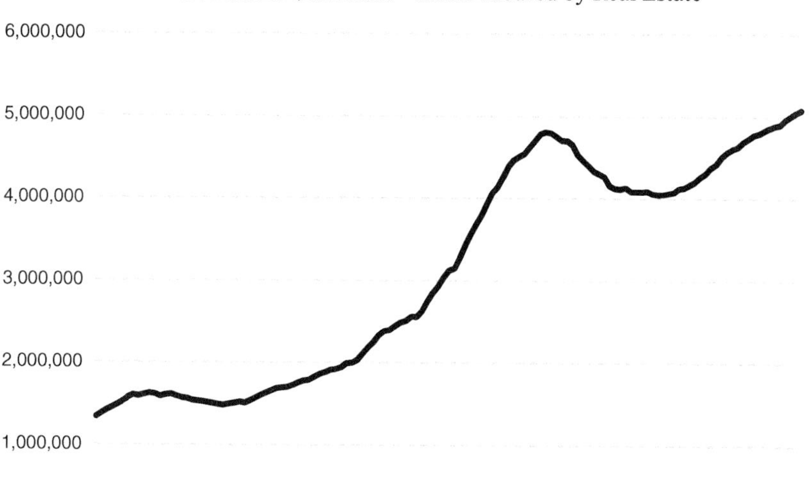

Source: FDIC

EXHIBIT A.74 Debt Balance $ Millions – 1-4 Residential

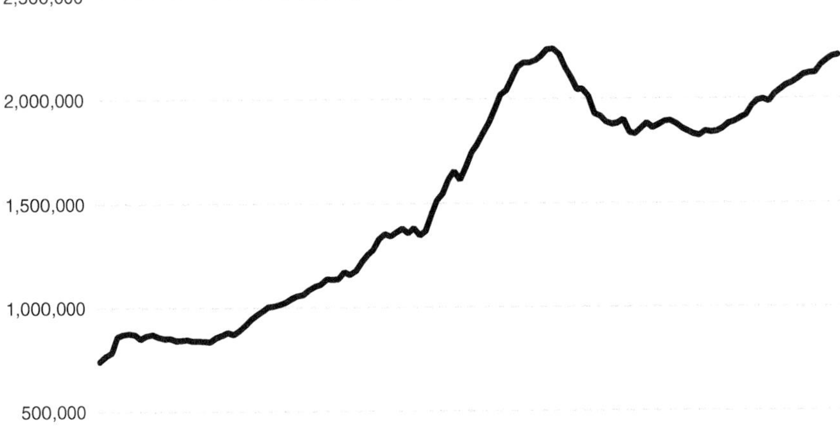

Source: FDIC

EXHIBIT A.75 Debt Balance $ Millions – Construction and Development

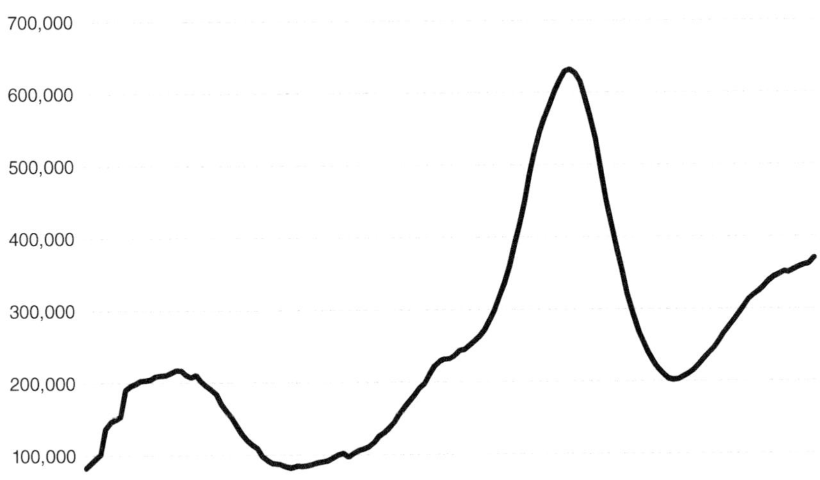

Source: FDIC

EXHIBIT A.76 Debt Balance $ Millions – Multifamily

Source: FDIC

EXHIBIT A.77 Debt Balance $ Millions – C&I Loans

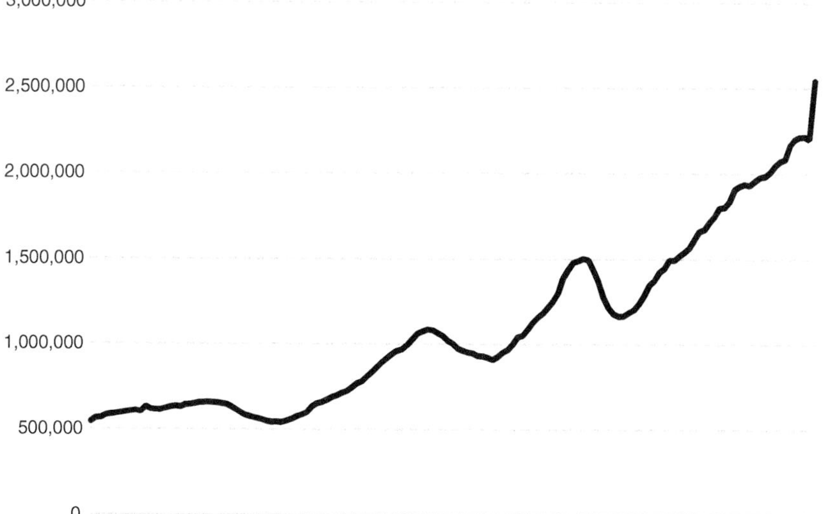

Source: FDIC

EXHIBIT A.78 Securities/Assets

Source: FDIC

EXHIBIT A.79 Equity Capital/Assets

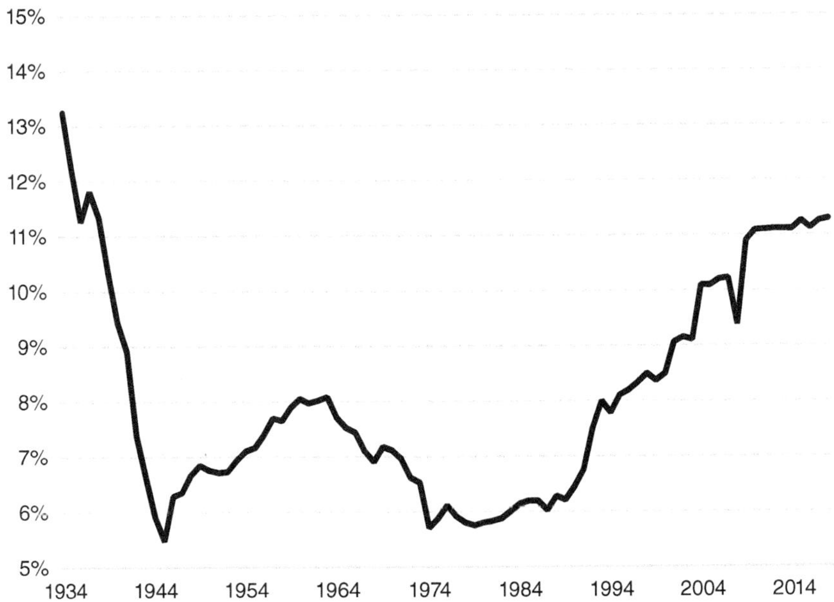

Source: FDIC

EXHIBIT A.80 Tier 1 RBC

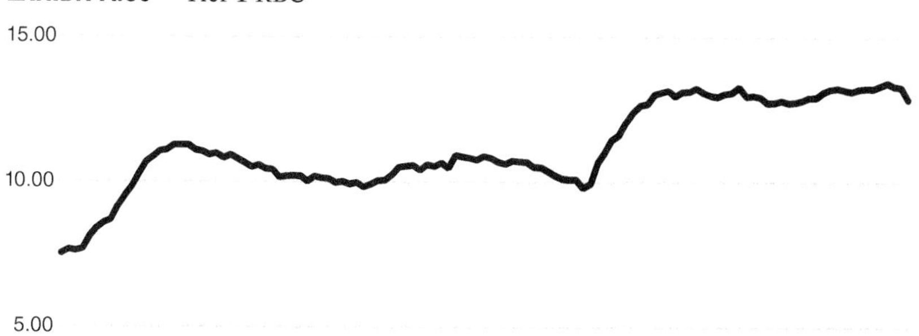

Source: FDIC

Source: Library Company of Philadelphia
Bank of the United States, 1799

Index